The
Trad Climber's
Bible

John Long & Peter Croft

FALCON GUIDES

GUILFORD, CONNECTICUT
HELENA, MONTANA
AN IMPRINT OF ROWMAN & LITTLEFIELD

FalconGuides is an imprint of Rowman & Littlefield
Falcon, FalconGuides, and Outfit Your Mind are registered trademarks of Rowman & Littlefield.

Distributed by NATIONAL BOOK NETWORK
Text and layout design: Casey Shain

Library of Congress Cataloging-in-Publication Data is available on file.

ISBN 978-0-7627-8372-4

Printed in the United States of America

metal used, and many other factors, these fixed protection pieces should always be considered suspect and should always be backed up by equipment that you place yourself. Never depend on a single piece of fixed protection for your safety, because you never can tell whether it will hold weight. In some cases, fixed protection may have been removed or is now missing. However, climbers should not always add new pieces of protection unless existing protection is faulty. Existing protection can be tested by an experienced climber and its strength determined. Climbers are strongly encouraged not to add bolts and drilled pitons to a route. They need to climb the route in the style of the first ascent party (or better) or choose a route within their ability—a route to which they do not have to add additional fixed anchors.

Your use of this book indicates your assumption of the risk that it may contain errors and is an acknowledgment of your own sole responsibility for your climbing safety.

Contents

Foreword:
The Long Silences

I was 15 years old—long before the terms "trad" and "sport climbing" were ever heard—when I cracked open the *American Alpine Journal* (American Alpine Club) at The Backpacker Shop in Claremont, California. There was a picture of a man standing in slings on a vertical wall that soared above him like a giant granite wave. I couldn't stop staring at that photo. Minutes passed before I realized I was holding my breath. The solitary figure dangling in that void looked lonelier and more fantastic than anything I had ever seen. I'd been reading Conrad and London by the truckload, so I wanted adventure but I didn't want to die.

I couldn't imagine what the climber was experiencing but for a dozen reasons I needed to find out. How could he handle being so high, so exposed, so

small? These questions terrified me. I had a hunch that the cliffside was a kind of philosopher's stone and that if you could negotiate those heights the universe would all make sense. You would no longer be afraid so you would know.

I wasn't worried about how the climber made his way up the rock, or how I might eventually do the same. That was a physical business and I could do physical things. The mental part I would learn on the job. I rifled the bookshelves of the library and The Backpacker Shop, trying to discover what the job required.

According to the journals and magazine articles, to scale a mountain of rock required a second mountain of gear, much of it steel and aluminum. And the big routes took a week or more to climb. That meant a week of rations you had to drag up the cliffside by means of spikes, pulleys, and elbow grease. At more than eight pounds per gallon, nobody could ever lug enough water. One report described hanging 1,500 feet up a rock wall and gazing down at a surreal land of ant people and miniature cars, where a river meandered through a lush meadow. The climbers were paralyzed by thirst as they watched tourists drifting in yellow rafts, splashing and occasionally falling into the river, one world and 2 days away.

All agreed that big wall climbing was sometimes terrifying and always exciting. Only one person climbed at a time, leaving the others marooned, often for hours, belaying in frightening locations with no getaway. Even veterans got stir crazy as the leader, out on the business end of the rope, was sweating the big drop.

Often there were no ledges and at night you had to squeeze into nylon hammocks lashed to the wall. Some spoke of being too tired to sleep, though anxiety was also poor medicine for insomnia.

Thin as a flagpole, cool as Debby's Waltz.
Nik Berry on Sysphus, Zeus, Canyonlands.

ANDREW BURR

Strangely, while most were awake most of the time, conversation usually died with the sunlight. The climbers would stare at the moon as they fell into the far reaches of themselves. I figured it was during these long silences that the universe gave up its secrets.

They took enchanting pictures, as if by accident, when they finally gained the top. The camera was often put on timer and set on a rock. Wobbly, but on level ground at last, the hollow-eyed men looked emptied out by the adventure, sheepishly glancing at each other or nothing at all, a mile beyond the camera. These shots were always more telling than the action sequences. They were the truth, and felt timeless.

I'd take the magazines to school and study them during class. Other students would sometimes skim an article and glance at the pictures. When they learned you could usually hike around the back and get to the top that way, they wondered why the climbers hadn't done so and avoided all the trouble. They didn't know about the long silences. Neither did I, though 3 years later I was scaling big walls myself.

At first I stuck with the easy walls and climbed with highly skilled partners so we could fly up the routes. There was a time when I had the peculiar record of having climbed El Capitan three times and bivouacking only once. My rendezvous with the long silences came a year later.

Most every climber felt honor bound to tough it out on a few big nail-ups, the kind of climbs that take 5 to 10 days to complete and where progress on a 1,000-meter wall is measured in inches and increments of fear. When I started putting up new wall climbs in Yosemite, in the High Sierras, Mexico, and South America, I started experiencing those long, silent nights.

Of course even the mightiest wall was no philosopher's stone, and none of them resolved the great mysteries. But they all made me forcibly present by the absence of distractions. Trapped on

Peter Vintoniv belaying on Desert Shield, Zion National Park, Utah.

ANDREW BURR

a small ledge half a mile up a rock face, I couldn't change channels or even change my mind. I had to stay put, slipping into the meditative stillness imposed by the circumstance, metabolizing things just as they were. Whenever I surrendered to the knobby ledge, the parched throat and the whole glimmering clusterfuck, I'd briefly wake up to my own life through being literally tied to a stake.

Some people find gentle means to wake up to themselves. Others scale big walls, where one can, for a while, make a clean break with the flat world. People discover strange and wonderful things in high places. But they also fashion delusions. If you are scared stiff, even the most miserable life below

will look like heaven. If you are simply there, staring at the moon, you might realize what you feel and want and need.

However you might consider the vertical life, many of the experiences just described are lost on those who stick strictly with sport climbing, where the accent is on difficulty and security, not on telling existential encounters. These encounters, universally found in the trad climbing milieu, are the "entire plot." And for good reason.

If we roll back to the early 1970s, say, to when modern free climbing came of age, we appreciate the evolution of climbing gear. SLCDs (spring-loaded camming devices), when they first arrived in 1978, revolutionized protecting the leader and anchoring. As the cams got more refined, so did harnesses, belay devices, biners, modern rope and sling materials, all of which transformed climbing into a high-tech enterprise. Boot technology in general and sticky rubber in particular radically changed physical movement. Cross training at gyms, yoga, CrossFit, and especially the fantastic fitness developed through sport climbing, have further steepened our learning curve.

But the experience on high places, the essence of trad climbing, has hardly changed in the last century, nor has the basic challenge: How do we securely and efficiently manage new encounters (read "on-sight") on the rock? Trad climbing will always be a physical and mental endeavor. This becomes clear the moment we get out on the sharp end of the rope and there's not a bolt in sight.

Some believe technology can eliminate the basic mental challenges, but this never works out as advertised. When the new trad leader jumps out on the steep open face, and is looking at a run-out on slick limestone, it matters little if he has a 50-year-old ring angle or a shiny new TCU buried in that bottoming crack. He will feel the same boulder in his throat that John Salathe and Al Steck experienced on the North Face of Sentinel, America's first big wall climb, in 1950. And also the same timeless questions: Where does the route go from here? What is the fall potential? What will I hit? How far to the next protection? How hard is it? How sound is the rock? Where's that water bottle? What the hell am I doing up here? Those questions won't change as time goes by.

All climbing is an ever-shifting adventure that answers old questions in fresh ways. We can never understand this as a function or a protocol—there's too many moving parts, so to speak. Rather than freeze-frame the subject and winnow it down to bits, we've attempted to evoke the whole damn thing, a kind of trad galaxy spanning both of our careers, believing the goods lay more in the arc of

ALEXANDRE
BUISSE

the whole rhubarb than in any of the many sub-plots. The photos, the stories, the sidebars, the historical ("retro trad") and curious artistic asides, are so many contours in the trad topography, in which partners, movement, environment, historical, and transcendent elements all find play. Trad climbing is a nomenclature and a culture, and there's no better way to "git jiggy" with it than through full immersion.

In a sense, we've tried to illuminate the trad universe in the same manner impresario Alfred Lyons tried to bottle jazz with his Blue Note

The legendary John Bachar soloing Hobbit Roof (5.10), Joshua Tree, California.

KARL "BABA" BRALICH

Records label, concerned as Lyons was "with identifying its essential impulse." This "essential impulse" is the glittering challenge of all trad climbing, which in sum and substance remains the greatest show on earth: Man against himself. *The Trad Climber's Bible* offers two perspectives about that adventure, as it unfolded for us, starting as green newbies and climbing our way toward the Long Silences—exactly where the rubber meets the rock.

JOHN LONG
Spring 2013

Pamela Shanti "Six" Pack chugging up Dark Passenger (5.12), Longs Canyon, Utah.

ANDREW BURR

Introduction

John Long

Every gym rat knows that sport climbs are protected by bolts permanently installed in the rock. Virtually all other forms of roped ascent are known as "trad" (from traditional) climbing.

Trad climbing is a do-it-yourself drill requiring the climber to negotiate a route and to carry, hand place, and remove most if not all components of the roped safety system: protection devices (nuts, cams, slings, etc.), belay and rappel anchors—the works. Well-traveled trad routes often feature fixed gear (typically, bolts; infrequently, old pitons), but just as many trad climbs are devoid of hardware. Even if the rock has seen 1,000 ascents, previous teams, influenced by the deep ecology movement, have not cluttered the face with trash and equipment, any more than a hiker on the Appalachian Trail pollutes the path with candy wrappers and cigarette butts. On a big trad climb, you'll likely have a detailed map (topographic map, or topo), but because the rock is somewhat pristine, you feel like the first person to ever tackle the wall.

Fair Means

Skilled trad climbers never conquer a face or a mountain, hoisting a flag and leaving their mark as a dog might squat on a fire hydrant; rather, they pass through like ghosts, leaving little to nothing behind,

Insha'allah! *Christine Balaz fiddling with pro in Barrah Canyon, Wadi Rum, Jordan.*

ANDREW BURR

taking only photos and memories. The nearly century-old trad doctrine holds that the face or the peak is a unique, nonrenewable resource, Nature's ancient sculpture—there to use and enjoy, but with respect for the rock itself and the other explorers certain to follow. Anything heavy-handed moves the venture out of the ghost climber's hands and into the conqueror's realm, where permanent gear, chipped holds, even glue are introduced for convenience and safety. Sport climbing areas often feature such tactics; by nature, sport climbs are "created." Conversely, trad routes are largely discovered.

In sport climbing, risk is managed through installing fixed gear in the rock and keeping a sound belay. Climbers thrive in the trad world through self-reliance, experience, judgment, skill, and moxie. We have no ownership granting us freedom to fashion a route to our desired level of commitment and security. We rise to the level of the climb, just as we find it.

The great rocks are the cathedrals of our persuasion. Not that we honor pagan temples; but when we approach trad climbing with reverence for the medium, rather than girding for a chance to exert the "rights" and good sense of the conqueror, our experience becomes richer for the effort. We are no longer bullies of the environment, or vigilantes for the safety of mankind, but equals. In this way we discover a sacred belonging lost on the man who would impose his will, his fears, and his answers onto the landscape. Trad climbing is the adventure version of cat burgling. We sneak in, steal an experience, then fade back into the shadows. There's no material evidence that we were ever "there."

The incomparable Alex Honnold with manky old bolts and homemade hangers striped off The Gran Giraffe (5.13), El Gran Trono Blanco, Baja, Mexico, following the first free ascent.

How To

Before the sport climbing revolution in the 1980s, virtually all ascent was trad climbing. With both the protection and belay anchors fixed on most sport climbing routes, rope management is typically straightforward and routefinding means following the chalked holds. Conversely, when a team must place protection and build anchors, a working understanding of the entire roped safety system is critical. In years past we learned the craft through climbing with experienced leaders, be they friends or members of an outing club or guide service. This

A distant wall where climbers, gently and hands-on, encounter rhythms old as the eventide.

KARL "BABA" BRALICH

is still the most effective method. No book can ever replace practical experience or initial professional instruction. For the opening stretch, get a guide and learn quickly and correctly. (One option is *Climbing Anchors,* 3rd edition [FalconGuides 2013], by John Long and Bob Gaines.)

What we provide here, by way of streamlined trip reports, is a hands-on "burn" through the vast trad climbing universe. Of the various styles to present the *Bible,* an anecdotal approach made the most sense. The key issues with trad climbing are the judgment calls starting the moment you rope up, all the way till your feet touch down on the last rappel. You have to get out there and make your own decisions. Most of us learn through mistakes. Later, "if I'd only known" is a common refrain, though there was rarely a way to have known beforehand those practical things that might have accelerated the learning curve. *The Trad Climber's Bible* attempts to present that very information beforehand, spelling out those things we wished to have known but

were left to learn the hard way. This won't make the hard way easy, but it might prevent an epic or two.

There are scads of technical issues, of course, and we might well understand the importance, in theory, of staying on route. But when I read Peter Croft's firsthand account of veering off the beaten path on the cushy Royal Arches (see Chapter 20, Royal Pains), battling through a Borneo of shrubs and oozing jungle, only to suffer a freak accident that nearly took him out of climbing forever—ever after will I strive to stay on route, at all costs.

Of course, reading a stack of climbing yarns is not especially instructive. The narratives must be presented and annotated with a progression in mind, so over the course of the adventure we might flesh out the whole miraculous shebang. That's what we have strived for here. Starting as complete novices, we climb our way through an increasingly ambitious repertoire of routes, from small to multiday. Described, analyzed, illustrated with a cornucopia of photos, we eventually tackle the most

Blue sky. White clouds. Gold granite. French Alps.

ALEXANDRE BUISSE

iconic rock walls on earth. As we encounter the real-world challenges of specific climbs, you will see our choices and solutions, effective and otherwise. This is the closest we can get to roping you into an actual trad climb. Sidebars and bullet points underscore key points and rules of thumb.

In a few cases, critical topics could not be adequately described without overwhelming the stories and trip reports. Rather than shorthand these topics, we mixed in sidebars throughout the text. Otherwise, *The Trad Climber's Bible* remains grounded in genuine routes found in actual climbing areas, the challenges we faced en route, and the decisions we made in the process.

Every expert trad climber relocates to, frequents, or spends long periods at established trad areas, where he or she teams up with local climbers. Only in this way can we see the standard techniques played out in practical settings, where we can apply them time and time again, refining the basic actions till our responses become intuitive. Often, in as little as one or two seasons, we will know what to do in most every situation. The rock is almost infinitely varied, so the specifics will change route to route, keeping the game ever interesting. But the system is basic, and no matter how strangely the rock forms up, the roped safety system can only work so many ways.

From Peru to Poland all trad climbing involves approaches and descents; the basics of routefinding and physically climbing; placing adequate pro and "good enough" anchors; staying hydrated, fed, and protected from the elements; accounting for the direction of pull (loading); and route, rope, risk, and time management. This is the game, even as technique and gear evolves forever.

Learning

How do we learn how to learn, on the spot and on fly? Put differently, how do we negotiate the unknown? What hopefully emerges here is a strategy on how to get the lowdown for yourself. Truth be told, trad climbing is much less a matter of applying pat methods than learning to navigate a feral, ever-changing world. The process is slippery as grunion to grasp and explain. But providing the process jumps to life in these pages, once you get some feel for the work, everything follows, just like it does "on high."

Orientation

Many climbers moving into the trad universe step straight out of the climbing gym or off the sport crag, are super fit, have belayed and lowered leaders countless times, and are experts at clipping protection on the lead. They enjoy excellent kinesthetic awareness and a developed sense for extreme effort. But it does not follow that a master sport climber will automatically crush the trad climbing world. This notion wrongly assumes that trad climbing is nothing more than physical movement. It is telling to note that this book is in excess of 100,000 words and focuses little on placing jams or crimping edges. Trad climbing, as covered here—and as you encounter it in the wilds—is largely about "the other stuff." Namely, those elusive judgment calls.

Nevertheless, the ace sport climber is widely expected to jump up on a world-class trad route in no time. But while many sport and gym climbers are solid at 5.12 or even the 5.13 standard, few

Gearing up.

MATT KUEHL

have scrambled over moderate but unprotected rock, know anything about cracks or chimneys, have ever established belays from hand-placed gear, and often are at a loss without face holds and bolts. Skilled face climbers can be pulling down thin cracks in no time—the technique is mostly a variant of face climbing. But why should we insist that the guy who flashed a grid-bolted face route at Riverside Quarry should seamlessly transition to a vastly run-out arête, with nebulous routefinding on chossy rock, 2,500 feet up a volcanic Apui in the Venezuelan rain forest? Who honestly believes that a person highly skilled at paintball can step straight into the crossfire in Afghanistan and be the next GI Joe in half an

JC Hunter getting after the sport climb Underdog (5.13), American Fork, Utah.

ANDREW BURR

hour? There are many other aspects to trad climbing beyond risk and potential dangers, but when you factor these alone into the equation, the game changes radically, regardless of physical abilities.

What is true, in our experience, is that about half of the sport climbing crew take up trad climbing like a fish takes to water, but that success probably has more to do with a native fascination with risk management than how well they crank on pockets. The other half could care less about taking silly chances and humping spine-bending loads far off the trail. Who can blame them? Like poetry, jazz, and the flying trapeze, trad climbing is not for everyone. And it's certainly not "better" than sport climbing. But it is a whole lot different—of that we are certain.

Trad is not some watered-down version of

Flint hard and flawless, Lost Arrow Spire, Yosemite, first climbed in 1947 by tossing a line over the rounded summit and praying it didn't twang off as Robin Hanson ascended the tossed cord some 120 feet, dangling on the outside face.

BEN HORTON

sport climbing, something duffers do who can no longer boulder hard or reef on overhanging face. Speed climbing and free climbing big walls are just as athletic and physical as the most arduous sport climbs—a fact verified by many who have transitioned from the gym and the crag, to the mega routes and legendary summits of the world. Either way, those first few outings are sure to be exciting.

At the lower levels, the trad experience quickly gets routine for athletic and motivated people. But crack climbing is tricky for most everyone. Without fail, every expert trad climber got proficient from putting in time on the rock. And almost to the person, the sketchiest days of all were those first few outings. We all have our memories.

But enough talking. Let's go climbing.

First Day: Joshua Tree

John Long

I had just gotten my driver's license when I saw the flyer for the Granite Mountain Guide Service on the bulletin board in The Backpacker Shop in Claremont, California. Technical climbing instruction went for twenty dollars. I had a job at a gas station and had saved up a few hundred bucks and was ready and willing to become a certified mountaineer. I had no idea what that meant but I liked the sound of it. I didn't fit the profile of climbers back then. At all.

Although I grew up in Upland, in the foothills beneath 10,000-foot-high Mount Baldy, I knew nothing worthwhile about backpacking, wasn't a Boy Scout, and had no interest in the Sierra Club. Or any club. I'd spent my entire life playing ball sports, fighting, and raising Cain. Deep ecology? The Ten Essentials? Huh?

But I'd seen the *National Geographic* article featuring Layton Kor and Huntley Ingalls scaling a terrible mud tower in the Southwest desert— The Titan, I think, but I wouldn't bet on it—and wanted to tie in straightaway. But what gave with all those crossing ropes and gizmos? No chance I'd ever survive winging it on mom's clothesline, or trying to learn the ropes on my own. So I started

rounding up a few friends from my high school baseball team, and we'd shag all over the local peaks, charging up and down scree fields and walls of tottering dirt that should have killed us ten times over. When one friend, a shortstop by position, pitched off a big mud buttress on the south face of Etiwanda Peak, took a mammoth toboggan slide, and essentially ground the ass right off his body, I knew professional help was indicated. And so I ripped that Granite Mountain Climbing School ad off the bulletin board, thumbtacks flying, and could already picture myself on the ice-plastered faces of the Matterhorn and the Eigerwand. And even Everest itself, while I was at it.

Instead, we rendezvoused at Joshua Tree National Monument, a recreational climbing area several hours from my home near Los Angeles. The rocks, strewn across several thousand acres of high desert, were not nearly so big as the Matterhorn. In fact, few were more than 100 feet high. I met instructor Jack Schnurr at a picnic table in Hidden Valley Campground, and we went over the basics he'd drilled into my head for several hours, a few evenings before, in the storeroom of The Backpacker Shop.

When Jack had been going over the Yosemite Decimal System (used to rate a climb's difficulty), and breaking down the several knots I'd need to know, and talking about remaining focused and not stepping on the damned rope and so forth, I wanted to skip this work-up and get to climbing my mountain right off. Now when I followed Jack over to the cliffside and we roped up, I was glad I'd gone over all the theory stuff and could even tie

The stark drive into Joshua Tree National Park.

ED BANNISTER

Hidden Valley Campground, Joshua Tree, California—"traditional hub of havoc and depravity."

ROBERT MIRAMONTES

the knots with one hand, in the shower, as Jack suggested. I had a qualified guide to double-check my system, but nevertheless my life depended on faithfully executing the basic safety techniques. Though some try to accomplish this all on their own, reading instructions out of a book, I intuitively knew the hazards of this method and was happy to spend the twenty dollars for Jack's expertise.

Jack said that while climbers were basically self-taught, there was plenty from a systems standpoint that one could bone up on while off the rocks, and that study would pay dividends in confidence and safety. The longer I would climb, the more that statement became true for me. For our purposes in this book, the key point is to understand that it is crucial that you get the basics worked out correctly from the get-go, and personal instruction, alone or in a group, is the only way.

Jack started up the crack and chimney system, while I belayed down below, anchored to a big block. Trad routes invariably followed either cracks or climbable features such as this chimney, a line of big knobs, say, or a featured arête. It was on these features, Jack explained, as he mounted higher, that one climbed and arranged the protection for the leader, just as he was doing now, before my eyes. Each route had a numerical difficulty grading, arrived at through consensus, ranging from 5.0 to 5.11. So far, so good. It all made sense.

For our first few climbs, said Jack, we'd keep things almost ridiculously simple till I had a feel for basic rope work and moving over the rock. Also— and this has always stuck with me—climbing is not for everyone. Some people get all the wrong internal signals the moment they step off the ground. A little nervousness and even fear is expected; but there are those, perhaps the sober majority, who are overwhelmed or put off by jumping up onto "the steep." Better to discover that early on, and head for the links or the beach.

I knew I loved everything to do with climbing from that first moment Jack looked over and asked, "On belay?" before he started up. Such a rush—that feeling of being engaged in difficult and tricky work, plus the intensely primitive medium of rock and dirt and sky and sweat. And that crick in my neck from staring up and dreaming of future walls looming, taller than my imagination. I would get there soon, if only in my dreams. I had just turned 16 years old.

Jack ratcheted up the chimney with measured moves, stopping here and there to place a piece of protection and to clip in the rope as I fumbled

Approaches at Joshua— sometimes thorny affairs.

GREG EPPERSON

Learning from an Expert Leader

For those stepping from the gym or sports crag onto trad terrain, the fastest way to rock star status is to hitch onto a skilled leader and follow him or her up trad routes till they pull you up to their level. You cannot vault up the trad climbing ladder nearly as fast as you can in sport climbing. Physically, yes. A fit sport climber can usually learn basic trad climbing technique much faster than a greenhorn, owing to vastly superior physical tools and the familiarity of moving over rock. Trad rope management is far more involved, however, and many crack climbing techniques are counterintuitive and require Massive Vertical Footage before you get the techniques "dialed."

Learn from the masters. Pass up no reasonable chance to get mentoring when and where you find it. When you see how it's done, the mystery and guesswork are largely removed. But expect to break in on numbers far lower than what you accomplish in the gym. Trad climbing is potentially dangerous, so it's not just a matter of physically climbing the rock, but keeping yourself secure till you know the game. And the beginning trad leader always faces one basic question: Am I doing this correctly? You'll always have to climb your own mountain (hence, we are all self-taught). But experts and worthy mentors are a beginner's best friends. So it goes in every field.

Basic instruction, though not covered in this manual, is the only way to start.

to feed out the line, standing on the rope half the time, hoping I was belaying correctly, but clueless withal. After about 40 feet, Jack vanished over the lip onto a ledge and in a flash yelled down for me to "Climb." I started up, slip sliding around before I caught the knack for counter pressuring between the two walls of the chimney. Then I started making fair progress up what was essentially a low-angled gully, but which felt like Yosemite's Leaning Tower.

It was hard to imagine how the roped safety system worked on paper, or when I was belaying Jack around the aisles in The Backpacker Shop and stumbling over ski poles and pup tents. But out here on the High Lonesome the system was the picture of simplicity. Full of nuances, it is true, but the basics were intuitive and obvious. Here and all around was that charmed bubble that over the following years would loft me to the wild places of the world, the moment I left the ground and "pulled for glory."

As the deck dropped away I detached more

and more from ground level, mundane life. Once I got up a ways above the desert floor, Jack taking in the rope smooth as choral music, the difficulty was secondary to the fact that I was climbing in the first place. I was a climber. It felt miraculous, and damn near holy.

It quickly came together for me, how the climbing game worked in the broadest sense: We met at a climbing area. We picked a route appropriate to my needs and novice abilities. Jack led up to a ledge, putting in protection. He anchored off and belayed me up and I took out the protection ("pro") as I climbed. Rather than simply clip the extracted gear onto any old loop, any which way, I would "rack" the gear on a sling (and later on harness gear loops), keeping things organized by size and specie. Then Jack and I repeated the process till we reached the top, and I had completed my first legitimate, technical rock climb, the Southwest Corner on Intersection Rock.

Cleaning a Route and Racking Gear

Just as you do with quickdraws, you have to unclip the pro from the rope in order to clean it, so you'll usually clip any cleaned gear right onto the gear loops on your harness. In some cases, some climbers prefer a shoulder gear sling featuring small loops sheathed with nylon tubing, loops much like those found on your harness. Whatever your choice, on easy to moderate routes it's easy to rack the gear keeping it somewhat organized. On difficult climbs, where you're hanging on for keeps, you'll have to clip gear off however you can.

The first order at the belay, after tying off, is to re-rack (reorganize) the gear for the next lead. Keeping ropes, protection devices, biners, slings, quickdraws, and all the rest neat and organized is an ongoing process, much as it is on a sailboat. (It's also a huge time suck, so organization is key, and the issue is covered many times in this book.) Clipping gear off any which way and all over the place will only waste time and eventually will stop you cold to unravel the cluster. Organize as you go, as you can. That's standard procedure.

Protection is generally racked big at the back, all the way to small at the front. The bigger stuff is heavier and wants to hang straight down, which naturally pushes the lighter gear to the front. This makes everything easier to see at a glance. Draws go behind the pro, as you can just grab those by feel. If one person is doing all the leading, a good tactic for the second is to clip, in order, the pieces directly onto the rope going to the leader's knot. That way there's no fumbling and the leader can grab them while the second restacks the rope or eats a sandwich.

Most everyone develops a personal preference and method of racking according to size and type of unit, big to small, and vice versa. Look around. Learn the options and develop what works for you.

Gear racked on a shoulder sling

BOB GAINES

Sidewinder, a Joshua Tree trad classic. ROBERT MIRAMONTES

Jack felt that since I was catching on and all, why not do another climb. And another. And another. At each belay—we basically climbed ledge to ledge up the rock, doing two or three short pitches to get the hang of things—we'd go over the anchor setup, reviewing in a general way how the system worked. I saw how Jack would set a solid anchor consisting of three or four bomber placements, then would tie off taut so he could belay at the edge so the rope didn't grate over any lip. He kept himself in the line of possible loading so should I fall off, he wouldn't be dragged into the fall line.

Securing a solid and convenient belay stance, and understanding fall vectors, and where a belayer might get dragged if his or her position was questionable, were things Jack repeatedly brought to my attention. We went over the act of belaying, of feeding rope out and taking it in. In 5 or 6 hours we'd climbed a dozen pitches and I had a working understanding of the basics.

The key to improving, or rounding into shape, said Jack, was the same with all the other sports I was playing at the time: repetition. Luckily I had nuclear kinetic energy so Jack's best efforts to burn me off were wasted. I was all elbows and

Joshua Tree nights. ROBERT MIRAMONTES

One Pitch, One Thing

Your first few months of trad climbing can pass in a confused daze since you must juggle so many new and crucial tasks at the same time, while also having to climb the rock. With all of this going on, it's hard to learn, and to improve at everything all at once. The process can be frustrating. A simple counter is to begin each pitch with the intention of paying special attention to one thing: footwork, say, or hand jams, or conserving strength, or placing nuts so they are easy to remove, or staying relaxed—whatever you can think of. This is a fun and creative drill that never gets old and is instructive every time. Your attention will be split between the immediate tasks at hand, with a special eye paid to your breathing, say, or how you place your jams. This one-pitch, one-thing approach helps foster a more conscious approach to climbing, which keeps the whole shebang rich and varied. You might even share the drill with your partner and at the belays, as you rack for the next lead, briefly discuss what you learned, and the one thing you'll be watching on the following pitch. In a subtle way, this increases your sense of command by shifting your impulse from trying to survive, to consciously observing one facet of the adventure. You might be surprised by the results.

was sketching all over in my Lowa Alspitz mountaineering boots, the same ones I used to tromp over the local mountains above my home in Upland. But my body was learning how to climb minute by minute, even though I didn't know the technical terms for the movements I was making and was only half aware of making them.

I was hooked. I had done proper technical rock climbing and had managed beginning level rope work and had gained several summits. I understood about basic wide crack technique and climbing on slabs, the idea of climbing a route, how to place and remove pro, to belay the leader, to build anchors, and saw firsthand basic rope management techniques. Then I rappelled off the summit of Old Woman and felt like Spencer Tracy in *The Mountain,* except younger. My understanding of much if not all of what I had experienced on that October day so many years ago was very incomplete. Only later would I learn that the single most important element was to gain familiarity with the vertical world, to learn to feel comfortable climbing a rock, and that the technical aspects would become clear slow and steady so long as I kept alert, was open to learning, and used common sense. The overall gestalt, the whole damn experience of that first day on the rocks, was so different and exciting that not much of it remained conscious or really known or understood. But one thing was for sure. I would come back for more.

Slot it! Arranging protection is often as hard as the climbing on a stiff trad route.

GREG EPPERSON

CHAPTER 2

First Day: Newcastle Island

Peter Croft

The moment I found climbing marked a clear transition from the sporting fields to a world of adventure. In hockey or baseball there were rules to obey and benches to warm, whereas the mountains appeared all guts and glory, life and death, 24 hours a day. After the schoolyard games, with far too little action, pulling off the ground was the first step in leaving civilization, and the schoolyard, behind.

My first stumbling block was location. I lived by the seashore in the far southwest corner of Canada, enjoying a virtual rain forest climate. I was 1,000 miles from the sunny nexus of California climbing, mired in a logging town where no one climbed.

In retrospect there was value in learning on my own, but I would've given the shirt off my back for a nuts and bolts lesson or bit of good beta from a real climber.

Although I was jonesing to get going, all the help I could get and the only help I could find was in books. There was little available on the subject, the best being an old instructional out of Great Britain. Though outdated, this little manual became

The faces change but the scene remains the same out at Joshua Tree, one of the world's leading winter climbing destinations.

BEN HORTON

9

Hands-on Instruction

Every climber is basically self-taught. But learning the trad climbing basics is best accomplished in a class or through private instruction. Focused, comprehensive instruction, whether casually or from a professional climbing guide, is a vital part of the road to competence. Although it is common to hear epic stories where someone, through no skill of their own, miraculously survives a novice epic, we should never count on luck. Fact is, trying to go it alone is too slow, too complicated, and often too dangerous. Plus we're all apt to learn bad habits that are tricky to unlearn. Once you've connected with a mentor, latch onto that person like a savior, take in the sound advice, and don't get freaked out by the scary stories (some of which might be true).

Fido might struggle to learn new tricks, but the rest of us can improve through repetition.

ANDREW BURR

One rule for all learning is basically chiseled in stone: Once you learn a particular technique, repeat the technique as soon and as often as possible. At the beginning, if you'll recall, the figure eight knot you learned on day one was best practiced when you got back home. Repeatedly. You got that short piece of rope, or the terrycloth towel belt from pop's bathrobe, or even the electric cord on your sister's hair dryer, which worked in a pinch. The same goes for *all things trad* that we will cover here.

Remember, we learn by rote, by doing things so many times they become instinctive.

my bedside bible, and I pored over it till the binding dissolved and left me with a shuffled stack of tattered pages. At a point where my eagerness could have easily landed me in trouble, I retained one key grain of novice wisdom: I knew I didn't know, so I kept reading.

My first climbing was on the scruffy basalt cliffs and boulders a mile from my house. Clad in high-top basketball boots, I used up a good portion of my beginners' luck making wobbly topouts onto tracks of wet moss and pitching off into ugly talus when holds broke. Surprisingly, I came away with little more than cuts, bruises, and the odd sprained ankle.

But I also knew that luck runs out and that, in light of higher aspirations, I would need to learn how to use the proper equipment. As the bigger cliffs and mountains held such importance to me, it made sense that when it came to gear, size had to matter. So I bought an alpenstock-size ice axe, an 11.5-millimeter rope, full steel-shanked leather

Reading and Research

In between sessions on actual rock with actual climbers, books, magazines, blogs, and climbing DVDs can provide valuable stopgaps in our progression. In fact, the combination of all media venues is likely the ideal scenario, allowing us to learn during any spare moments. Again, repetition is key to making critical info and experiences our own.

Seek out the most recent book editions, magazine volumes, and DVDs. Some of what is out there has become outdated, and other media, from obscure blogs to Facebook entries, for example, focus on confounding anchoring systems of little practical value though perfectly suited for knot aficionados and engineering duffers. Because there are so many dimensions in trad climbing, diversion into needless complexity wastes time better spent learning practical skills to keep us safe.

A dictum to follow in all climbing is a variant to Occam's Razor: All else being equal, the simplest technique tends to be the correct and safest one. Not always—there are few absolutes in trad climbing. But by and large, the many factors in the trad climbing game are most easily managed with a simple system.

Tape, harness, rope, pro. Simple.

MATT KUEHL

mountain boots—reminiscent of the old hob-nailers—and a Dumpster-size helmet (with a half brim) made by Mountain Safety Research (MSR). Though my logic appeared on firm ground at the mountain shop, it became clear during my first real rock climb that I might have goofed.

The tallest local cliff was on Newcastle Island a couple of miles from home. After I conned my high school pal, Bruce, into coming along and belaying, we rowed across the bay to what might have been my very last climb. There is no granite in this part of Canada and what towered over us as we stood on the beach was 100 feet of overhanging chossy conglomerate—basically assorted pebbles embedded in crusty grout. If not for the leaning chimney-size crack running up the center, I wouldn't have had a hope.

Inspired, psyched, I was setting myself up as the poster boy for *Accidents in North American Mountaineering.* In an analysis of what might go wrong, my list of errors was more or less complete.

Equipment and Expertise

The subject of gear requires research—and it will for so long as you climb. The competition for our money is so great that gear manufacturers are constantly turning out innovations that even other manufacturers struggle to keep up with. Be wary of Internet reviews, which might be written by people with little experience or who have a commercial or personal agenda.

If you can't get sound advice from a friend or at the cliffside, and are simply going to order online because that's where the best deals are, stop and reconsider. No deal is a good one if you order the wrong size rock shoe or melon-size camming devices for your face and finger crack adventure the next Saturday. Although you'll pay a little more, there are huge advantages in seeking out the specialty climbing shops. People working in shops tend to have solid information about the gear they sell. Oftentimes popular outfits are staffed with avid climbers who are keen to talk climbing till we stick a rag in their pie-holes. Nevertheless they provide a valuable service, not just in personalized gear selection, but in providing the beta, conditions, and access to local crags and boulders. Experts are a resource. Learning how to utilize this resource is a valuable skill. Once you know exactly what you need and have to replace a specific piece of gear, say, and have all the specs, that's when online buying makes sense.

The best climbing area in all of Canada lay just 60 miles away, as the crow flies. But I was clueless and I couldn't get there in a straight line, or anything close to it. Even when I got that commute dialed, much later, it ended up being a triathlon of beach walking, ferry riding, and hitchhiking.

Too excited about this first ascent to give my friend the belay lesson he richly deserved and I desperately needed, I looped the rope around his waist and told him to hold tight in the event of a fall. Amid assorted driftwood and the smell of low tide, I laced up clompy mountain boots, cinched up my harness, and arranged the carabiners and hexentrics on my gear loops. I then strapped on my outsize helmet, which was to play such a key part in what followed.

Quickly squirming up the first 50 feet, I slotted some nuts into the rotten crack in the back of the gloomy slot. From there the chimney overhung, and I stemmed out widely as the crack narrowed. I had reached the crux—Frankenstein boots bridged out on crumbly acorns, the rope sweeping down to some rattly hex as my keg-size helmet kept jamming in the head-size crack. Then, as I struggled, I must have keyed that helmet brim between some cobbles, because it lodged tight.

Claustrophobic and panicking, I thrashed to free my head . . . which was when both footholds broke and I was left swinging from my chinstrap. Trapeze-ing off that strangling strip of nylon with what felt like lead boots, bicycling at the wall trying to regain some purchase, I had no to time to reflect on how many things I had done wrong to get there—from a belayer who couldn't belay, to gear that wouldn't hold a mouse, to a rotten cliff that shouldn't have been climbed in the first place.

Just before I choked to death, I stemmed my feet to the last remaining footholds and quickly undid the strap. Free at last, I tunneled up through the depths of the crack, kicking my helmet down onto the beach, eventually digging and dry-heaving my way through a final dirt clod overhang. To an observer standing on top, I would have appeared like a zombie clawing its way out of a festering grave. Clearly, if I were going to get any good at this climbing game I would have to learn a thing or two about staying alive.

Visit Established Climbing Areas

Visit established climbing areas whenever possible, especially when first starting out. Breaking in on a rock or outcrop where no one climbs is improbable these days, but possible—and perilous. Even on solid rock, new routes frequently have loose flakes, crumbly lichen, and a host of unknowns, and there is little clue as to the difficulty or available protection/belay anchor options. If you are stuck with uncharted territory, stick to toproping, preferably off the fattest giant sequoia you can find.

Another perk of climbing at a well-traveled venue is the opportunity to glean key beta (info) from watching and listening to other climbers. Strike up a conversation but, being a beginner, don't let insecurities lead you to act like an expert, something most of us have done. This never works, and puts a stop to learning, which is the point. Comments like "You bet! Back in Tennessee I free handed a stack of rock walls" will single you out as a geek—and you'll eat your baloney sandwich alone. If you are honest about your inexperience, you'll likely receive plenty of useful info and camaraderie from all but the self-absorbed dork gushing about 5.14—and you don't want to hang with him anyway.

Grand Tetons, the destination climbing area in North America through the early 1960s.

JODY LANGFORD

CHAPTER 3

Tahquitz: First Lead on the Big Stone

John Long

It wasn't till the summer following my first taste of climbing at Joshua Tree that I took my second lesson from the Granite Mountain Guide Service. This was just after my sophomore year in high school. I was still a very dedicated jock, with hopes of someday playing professional baseball, a dream that had sustained me since playing Pee Wee ball at age 6. But once all the summer league ball was over and I found myself with a few spare weeks before school started, my mind went right back to rock climbing.

A few phone calls and I arranged to meet guide Bob Dominick at the Humber Park parking lot in Idyllwild, California, a mountain hamlet roughly 2 hours' drive from my home in Upland, California. It was time to get my steep on once again. Little did I know that this time, it would be for good.

Sun setting on west-facing Tahquitz, one of America's historical crags, where Yankee trad climbing was virtually invented in the 1930s.

KEVIN POWELL

14

I listened to Jimi Hendrix 8-track tapes all the way out to Banning, and when I pulled off I-10 and started up the 26-mile, twisty mountain road to Idyllwild, the thrill was on. When I pulled into Strawberry Valley, and Tahquitz Rock reared into view—a 1,000-foot-high white granite fist rearing up off the woody hillside—I wondered what I was getting into. In terms of sheer magnitude, Tahquitz is to Joshua Tree what a blowtorch is to a candle. My balls were up in my throat as I drove up the last few miles to Humber Park.

Bob Dominick was one of those unique characters fashioned by the conflagration of the late 1960s and early 1970s: part Eagle Scout, part Beat poet,

Old partnerships never die. UK's Ron Fawcett (left) and John Long, who first climbed El Capitan together as teenagers.
JOHN LONG

The spectacular Traitor Horn (5.8), Tahquitz, first led in 1938 by the great Jim Smith on manila boating rope prone to snapping during moderate falls.

BEN HORTON

and another of the self-directed, hippie athletes that have always gravitated to outdoor adventures. For one of the longest hours of my life, I followed Bob up the steep and shifting trail leading up to Lunch Rock at the base of Tahquitz.

Like many trad climbing areas, Tahquitz (rising off the rear escarpment of Mount San Jacinto) is situated in a wilderness area, which adds wildness and existential voltage to the experience. Even the greatest baseball diamond or football field totally paled before this granite monolith, for no game is played on a more impressive stage than traditional rock climbing. And Tahquitz Rock was no "gimme." Over the next 15 years I would slog up that trail hundreds of times, and it always kicked my butt.

I would later come to know most every crack and handhold on Tahquitz. But to this day I'm not certain what route I climbed with Bob, who likely just wandered from one crack to the next, following no route in particular. Bob's method of instruction was "show and tell." Sometimes a little easy on the tell.

We briefly reviewed the belay procedures and rope commands, then Bob started up a wide chimney and ran the cord out to a big ledge. I followed, removing a few small nuts, marveling how much easier climbing felt when shod in the smooth-soled Varappe shoes Bob had lent me. After a second pitch, also ending at a big ledge, we were gaining some good exposure, and I felt that addictive, full body rush of finding myself pasted in the sky against all reason, thwarting gravity with courage and skill—and a toprope. Much like Jack Schnurr, Bob, although not overly talkative, was patient in explaining how the anchor was constructed, the basics per rope management—how to cut down on rope crag, and keeping the gear well stacked and sorted and so forth.

Just as they do in sailing, the rule of keeping the gear organized is a vital protocol, especially appreciated if and when an emergency should ever arise and you have to move quickly. And you can't move

Approaches—Getting to the Cliff

Strenuous approaches are common for long, serious trad routes. You have to earn your summit, in many cases. None of this fu-fu pocket pulling for three moves, then high-fiving all your homies. Some areas feature trad climbs up the cracks, and sport climbs up the faces between the cracks. Just as many areas are dedicated trad or sport climbing areas. Perhaps a geologist might know why trad areas often require longer approaches—challenges that most gym climbers initially hate though many come to enjoy, or at least tolerate. Either way, few trad venues have such short approaches as the Shawangunks in upstate New York, or Eldorado Canyon above Boulder, where public roads run nearby. More often you'll be left to trudge in, often uphill, getting to Tahquitz Rock, say, or the Hulk, in the northeastern Sierras. Use your $100 sneakers for approaches only if you want to destroy them in 2 miles. Dirt, gravel, scree, and slabs ravish the best approach shoes. But you'll need a pair anyway.

Make sure your pack is big and comfortable enough to hump in a day's load of gear, grub, and water, as well as spare clothes and rain gear as needed. The most dreaded approaches are those where you have to descend for miles to get to the wall, then muster for a death march getting up and out after a day's pulling down, when you're thirsty, starving, and fagged. You won't be the first to complain about the Long March in and out. You almost get used to it after 10 or 15 years. The reward is getting out there past all the crowds and the rhubarb. It's always a blessing—once you're there, and even along the way given manageable loads.

BEN HORTON

*Kay Yamamoto on the classic lieback pitch,
El Camino Real, Tahquitz Rock.*

GREG EPPERSON

fast if your gear is a jumble of knotted slings and
mismatched widgets clipped off willy-nilly. So keep
that gear straight. Make it a habit. It might save you
more than time.

Bob surprised me after the third pitch and said
that it was my turn to lead. But I didn't know what
I was doing, I said. Then I should get up there and
find out, said Bob. And then we had a remarkable
conversation.

Bob was no guide, he said. He was a climber,
who occasionally took people out, mostly as a favor
to his friend, Jack Schnurr, who owned the guide
service. Bob was there to climb. He was glad to have
me along—my twenty dollars wasn't enough to
make demands on the man, but if I could pull my
weight—fantastic. I was not accustomed to hearing a
person talk so frankly, which felt almost illegal.

This was my first lesson in self-reliance, one of
the fundamental aspects of all traditional climbing.
Bob was a great teacher in that regard. And I would
later learn that the crux of trad climbing is self-
reliance and teamwork, usually with one other partner. Because you are so often isolated from others
during a trad climb, the seeds of self-reliance have
to be sewn from the beginning. Self-trust follows
naturally when you repeatedly make decisions that
might be life sustaining—or life ending.

And so I took off up the wall on my first lead.
I vividly recall climbing up the steep face on good
edges, and Bob not paying out any more rope till
I walloped in a piton. I wondered out loud how I
might know if the pin was good or not, and Bob
yelled up that if it rang loud and true, like striking
a key on a xylophone, it likely was "good enough."
"But how can you know for sure?" I asked. "You
can't," said Bob. That's why they call it an adventure. The concept sounded heroic. And illegal. I
pushed on.

I ran out of runners and clipped six biners in
a long strand, into the eye of one piton. I repeatedly got off route and had to downclimb. I used
my knees all over the place. But I made it to the
next ledge and tied off to a big pine tree, and felt
like Columbus discovering the New World. Bob
was handy at keeping things organized, keeping
the rope nicely stacked, the gear separated, the
slings and biners neatly racked. And I marveled at
how he would spot a friend a few routes over, and
how they'd maintain a running conversation about
Yosemite or the Tetons, about future routes and
past girlfriends. Here was my initiation to a kind

Descents—Getting Off the Cliff

Most sport routes are one-pitch affairs and you merely lower off the anchors to descend. But you'll rarely rappel a trad route, especially on multipitch climbs. The exceptions are small pinnacles and towers at the base of much larger walls, like the one- to three-pitch crack climbs at the base of El Capitan, in Yosemite, or the cracks in Indian Creek, Utah. Otherwise, the rule of thumb is to walk down off the "top," rather than rappel. If the walk off is 2 miles long, involving treacherous slabs and hanging gardens, and you can make a couple quick raps off stout trees to regain the base in 5 minutes, you do so. But once you start having to rig multiple rappels off self-placed gear or even fixed anchors, the chance of ropes getting stuck and the inevitability of leaving expensive sling material make walking off more attractive.

What's more, popular trad routes are climbed all day long, and descending past a team on their way up is not only bad form (the chance of hitting people with tossed ropes is high), but can cause crisscrossing lines, people-jostling on hanging stances, and the danger of falling equipment or debris. Granted, there are a select few routes in places like the Red Rocks and Yosemite where popular climbs ascend only four or five pitches up 1,000-foot walls, so on weekends you have a conga line marching up and down the route. But as mentioned, when a walk-off is possible, it's often the safer and better method of descent, where you have direct control over your situation and are not dependent on gear, anchors, and the graces of others to see you through.

While we will take this up in greater detail later on, find out beforehand where the descent goes. No credible guidebook is without this information, though local climbers may be a better source since they know the common practices, arrived at through consensus. More on this, and the business of sketchy descents, once we venture back out to the land of Oz: Joshua Tree.

Heather Hayes rappels from the summit of Castleton Spire in high winds (North Face route).

LARRY COATS

Self-Reliance and Self-Rescue Techniques

Trad climbing is a do-it-yourself endeavor so self-reliance remains a crucial aspect of the game. Expect no one else to bail you out of trouble, to help you complete your climb or assist you on your descent. Your ropemate helps as she can, but as difficulty and commitment ramp up toward your limits, each climber ultimately has to meet the challenge and look after himself. Having to "carry" another climber on a difficult trad route is a crapshoot; if the stronger climber gets hurt (not unheard of), the team is "hosed." On easy to moderate trad routes, climbing with understudies is common. On harder terrain, recruit someone of your own ability, to stack the deck in your favor. Because teams sometimes need to extricate themselves from dangerous situations, acquire a working understanding of basic self-rescue techniques. Climbers bred on gym climbing—where the route, the protection, the anchors, and even the rock itself have been engineered to perfection—are often shocked by trad routes in the wilds, which are not the domestic article by a long shot, but feral beasts requiring skill and courage to wrangle.

of Magical Mystery Tour, held on a vertical theater, and I couldn't get enough of it.

At the end of each lead we would briefly discuss how things went, what we did right and how we might have done things differently or better or more efficiently. These mini reviews rarely took more than a minute, and were normally done while we were racking for the next lead and getting a sip of water, so they never stalled the onslaught. These reviews, I would learn, where full disclosure is the rule, are very instructive and keep a fluid line of communication open between partners. The value of doing these on the spot is that crucial issues are fresh in your minds; waiting until later is a good way to forget. I'm not talking about yammering on and on here. You just hit the strategic points hard and fast, get on the same page with your partner, and decide how to best proceed. Once you get in the hang of doing this, decisions usually come quickly.

We topped out a few pitches later and I experienced the excitement of having scaled a legitimate stone mountain, with a true summit. Back then, it

even had a register, a notebook inside an ammo can, which old hands like Bob didn't bother with. In fact, the summit meant little to Bob. It was all about the climbing.

Typical with longer traditional routes, there was a technical descent off the back side of the rock, which passed a climbing route called Fitschen's Folly, where pioneering American climber Joe Fitschen (I would later write the foreword for his book) had misjudged the descent one winter and had plunged down the wall some 80 feet into a snowbank. Descents, said Bob, can be as tricky as the climb. Truer words were rarely spoken.

We made several more laps up Tahquitz that day. While I started getting a feel for the vertical environment and the basic roped safety system, I never felt ready to move out from under Bob's wing. In fact, the more we climbed, the more awesome and overwhelming the experience felt. How would I ever manage the routefinding, keeping the gear straight, rigging anchors, keeping my lid on? I couldn't see the way ahead, how to ever get out there on the big stone and start calling my own shots. It felt like a quick way to die.

"Go to Rubidoux," said Bob.

Forget the guide service, he added. I had enough knowledge to go to a practice area like Mount Rubidoux, just 20 minutes from my pad, and start toproping and bouldering and getting the basics dialed. Rubidoux had been a popular practice climbing area with the Sierra Club classes for going on 3 decades. At an area like Rubidoux, Bob promised, the basics of rope management, placing protection, belaying and rappelling, not to mention actual climbing techniques, could be broken down to easily manageable bits, to a scale sometimes no bigger than 10 feet high.

Little did I know how prominently Mount Rubidoux would figure into my life and my climbing career, and how my dreams of playing professional baseball would quickly morph into visions of El Capitan, Half Dome, and a host of other giant rock walls rising on the far side of imagination.

Communication

Develop the habit of openly communicating all pertinent observations and hunches about the route—as you climb it. Not to encourage babble, clowning, or small talk—trad routes require sobriety and concentration. But the more valuable data you can relate in real time, the better your chances for success—and the greater your enjoyment. If you see obvious belay stations, or hidden protection opportunities, or dark clouds rolling in, and feel raindrops, or feel scared, or have questions, or you want your partner's advice about the next wide crack, or whatever—speak up. Usually, a 30-second exchange at the belays can make known everyone's thoughts and feelings and in this way you can keep the air clear of issues and have your faculties for the climbing itself. Periodic review of the topo is standard practice. Stay aware. Stay current. Stay on the same wavelength. Two heads are better than one, but only when both communicate.

Brittany Griffith and Kate Rutherford perusing the topo on the Venturi Effect (5.12), Incredible Hulk, eastern Sierras.

ANDREW BURR

CHAPTER 4

Mount Rubidoux

John Long

Mount Rubidoux is a 400-foot-high mound, roughly a mile long and half a mile wide, rising out of the old California city of Riverside. A winding road, long ago shut down after flood damage, leads to a towering cross on top, and a bridge and monument to peace, erected in the early 20th century by a local dreamer. Hundreds of diorite boulders, including steep faces, several split by cracks, spangle the hillside. As I understood from instructor Bob Dominick and others, Rubidoux had for years been a practice and training area, principally for the Rock Climbing Section (RCS) of the Sierra Club. So the Rubidoux rocks were home to countless beginner and intermediate routes.

I first visited Rubidoux with fellow climbing novice and high school buddy, Ricky Accomazzo. We drove out one weekday afternoon after class and were amazed to discover a Disneyland for climbers,

Katie Jo Myers ready to hike up and bust a move at Rubidoux, a popular So Cal bouldering and toprope venue since the early 1940s.

KEVIN POWELL

with countless little slabs and overhangs and cracks and arêtes, ranging from 10 to 40 feet high. Unlike the far larger cliffs at Joshua Tree and Tahquitz, these practice rocks were relatively small, and right there for the climbing. Some were literally on the winding access road. We immediately jumped on a few of the slabs and started traversing up and around.

After my second guided day out at Tahquitz, I loved the climbing but felt overwhelmed by the prospect of dialing in the whole system on my own, even though I had a little experience with the basics. Here on the boulders of Mount Rubidoux, Ricky and I enjoyed the immediate gratification of lacing up the boots and getting on the rock. It was

**Boulder competition,
Mount Rubidoux, 1982.**

RENE ARDESCH

Matt Stanich. Practice, practice, practice.

MATT STANICH

Develop a Practice Area

Practice makes perfect. You can practice trad climbing at an actual crag, or at a practice area where the scope (size) of the routes is small and the accent is on developing and honing technique and fitness, rather than slaying dragons (climbing routes). Practice routes are shorter, are climbed with a toprope, or no rope at all—meaning most of the learning is done in a controlled environment. The difficulties are condensed, the routes centrally located, so an enterprising climber can log high mileage and learn quickly. The little nuances and strategies for milking a practice area are covered in detail later on. Just know that you need to find a practice area, just as a golf pro practices his long ball at the driving range and his putting on the greens. Practice areas are the most efficient way to improve. Many times on each outing you will set anchors and topropes and climb cracks. The basics rapidly become routine. For the days you can't go cragging, even a half an hour at a practice area is enough to keep a hand in the game.

clear after just a few minutes that learning the ropes at a practice area, where we could chew off 10- or 15-foot bites, was perfect schooling for young boys anxious to get to climbing but unsure about everything from basic technique to toproping.

Late that afternoon, several other groups showed up and strung a few topropes over the larger formations, and we watched to see how things were done. We had many questions about belaying, and anchors, and rigging the toprope, and placing the protection, and most of all, about how to climb this face or that crack. As we were quickly learning, keeping a close eye on more experienced climbers was a useful way to answer many of our questions, for we literally saw things done firsthand. Anything we didn't understand, we asked about, and most everyone took the time to explain the finer points of that anchor setup or that bit about hand

jamming. If someone was simply winging it, they had to say as much, whereas a person who understood what he or she was doing could explain what they were doing, and why. In this way we quickly got the basics dialed, and learned to separate the gold from the pyrite.

We starting going to Rubidoux every day after school, stringing topropes and climbing ourselves to failure. As with most trad areas, to engage part of the game is to engage the whole thing. For instance, to rig a toprope, we had to set a series of primary anchors, which made us practice our nut placements. We needed to rig the placements to a Master Point for the toprope, so we learned rigging basics in the bargain. Since we were already on top of a formation, with a doubled rope strung and running to the ground, it was easy money to zip down the line on rappel; and it doesn't take many "raps"

The Great Divide

The rich history of Mount Rubidoux makes mention of a man who likely was the mountain's first true "rock scrambler"—The Right Reverend, Henry van Dyke, who presided over the legendary Easter sunrise services that were nearly invented on the mount, circa 1905, and which drew over 50,000 souls, well into the 1920s.

According to parish minutes and other archival documents, as well as anecdotal evidence from the Right Reverend's many descendants in the Riverside area (the reverend had nineteen children), Henry Solomon Leviticus van Dyke spent many weekday afternoons "wandering about the majestic heights of the verdant knoll, communing with Our Father, seeking inspiration for his forthcoming homily."

This was the conviction of the flock, anyhow, till a few parishioners were one day "upon the mountain, taking our exercise," when they witnessed the reverend "moving up the great boulders by mysterious means, rather like a gargoyle, so clearly pushed by unseen hands for the terrible sheerness of the stone faces and the dearth of ready purchase for man or beast." The deacons believed they were witnessing an enchantment, quite possibly a miracle, "so precipitous were the heights to which the Right Reverend scaled, rather closing the Great Divide between mankind and the Golden City."

Amen.

Watch and Learn

We will cover this point fifty ways to Sunday: When you're just starting out in the trad world, watch and learn and ask questions with the intention of making things clear to yourself. Most people are glad to explain and sound off like experts. Some actually are. When a party or individual has what you want, or seems especially skilled and efficient—which are usually the same things— watch closely and keep asking questions. Some climbers expertly spout the lingo and crank hard but are dicey posers. If some daddio does something that looks or seems dangerous, don't disregard this and assume everything is cool. Ask questions till you understand.

Watch how they build anchors and set up belays, extend the rope over the edge, clip off the toprope with doubled locking biners, how they organize their gear and what they take for a day at the crags or practice area.

It cannot be overstated: Most all of us learned at a practice area—and from watching others.

Pulling over the roof, Peak District, UK. ALEXANDRE BUISSE

to get the setup and the feel of the work dialed in. Now we had to take turns belaying each other up and lowering each other back to the deck. And as always happens, the belaying and lowering became second nature after a few visits, since one or the other of us was belaying most of the time. Without even knowing it, a few weeks into our Rubidoux experience we were executing many of the primary maneuvers—rather poorly, it is true, but we were making progress, and what once took 10 or 15 baffling minutes—finding that anchor setup or stringing this rope—was now getting done in seconds. As kids who grew up playing sports (Rick was an All-American water polo player), we were dying to climb all of the standard beginners' routes, then move onto more ambitious lines.

We diligently began working on the fringes of the fabled Joe Brown Boulder, a 40-foot-high undercut face, thinking we were making rather quick work of Mount Rubidoux, when around the corner strode two climbers who changed our universe: Paul Gleason and Phil Haney. While we were turned out in knickers, knee socks, and mountaineering boots, this duo was shirtless, and wore cutoff jeans and skintight Varappe boots specially imported from France. They looked like Olympic gymnasts who hadn't shaved or cut their hair in years. They passed between them a block of gymnastic chalk, dusting their mitts with the white stuff between ropeless laps on Joe Brown Boulder, which they climbed repeatedly all kinds of ways. It was a little like watching monkeys swinging around trees. Rick and I were astonished.

What Haney and Gleason were doing—modern gymnastic free climbing at the very top grade—was so far beyond our expectations, following several weeks watching duffers at Rubidoux, that we weren't exactly sure what we were seeing. Gleason's dynamic style, lunging past bulges and overhangs like Clark Kent, was as amazing to watch as Haney's gruesomely strenuous static moves, inchworming up the bulge on fingertip divots and wrinkles in the diorite.

Only later would we appreciate our fortune in meeting Paul Gleason and Phil Haney within weeks of first roping up. Both had climbed extensively with legendary bouldering pioneer John Gill. They understood the technical human limit (as it was back then) and were happy to prove it at Rubidoux and elsewhere. So basically, we lucked out and got a sneak peak at "rock gymnastics," an orientation largely unknown at a time when rock climbing was in large part the stepson of mountaineering.

Many of America's leading climbers had seen Gill and had spent their time bouldering, especially at Stoney Point, a famous San Fernando Valley training ground for the Yosemite pioneers in the late 1950s and early 1960s. But we got the full exposure from day one, and went from there. In 15 minutes on the Joe Brown Boulder, Gleason and Haney showed us the way, and the image was burned into memory like a brand.

After the pair left Joe Brown for more bouldering, I ran to one of the "problems," touched the initial holds, and sighed. I couldn't pull my boots off the ground. But we were determined. We returned home, mothballed the knickers and mountaineering boots, drove an hour to West LA and West Ridge Sports, bought the skintight Varappe boots, stole a couple blocks of chalk from the gym team at school, lost the shirts, grabbed the shorts, and drove back out to Rubidoux looking exactly like punk kid versions of Phil Haney and Paul Gleason. The game was *ON*.

CHAPTER 5

The Circuit

John Long

Our first month at Rubidoux passed in a kind of hallucination. On the weekends, the rocks swarmed like an ant farm, with all the parties "roping down" and clambering up the easy slabs, and the handful of boulderers pulling on holds we couldn't yet comprehend. We usually climbed till dark—even beyond, by the light of headlights, if we felt especially jacked. Quite naturally, and because we were just learning the basic physical movements, we never strayed far from the beginner slabs and chimneys, toproping them endlessly, till we knew every hand and foothold.

Less from design than from accident, or because it always just happens that way, we soon developed

Kevin Powell on the Bridge Traverse, 1978.

KEVIN POWELL

The Bridge Traverse today.

a hacker's circuit consisting of our favorite beginner routes, maybe a dozen boulder and toprope "problems" scattered about the sprawling knoll. The Joe Brown Slab, Smooth Soul Wall, Borson's Wall, and a host of others became our standard fare, the anvils on which we forged our basic technique.

We quickly appreciated the fruits of accidental circuit training. Through rote, cracks and faces we barely could manage on day one were becoming simple after only a few weeks, as we became increasingly efficient on familiar moves. Slowly, imperceptibly, we started uncoiling in the middle and relaxing, getting our weight over our feet, trusting our feet and instinctively grabbing the holds just so. Basic face climbing became automatic, requiring little to no thought. Our fingertips, rasped raw from our first efforts clasping the gritty diorite, were callousing over like rawhides. And our finger pads,

digits, and knuckles were getting used to the strain and pain of yarding on sharp and rounded holds.

Another practice we began, basically from day one, was to climb ourselves to failure. This is standard these days and has been for 3 decades; but when we were first starting, for many, climbing at Rubidoux was as much about donning the clammy lederhosen, the felt hats, and all the rope gadgets—as well as constant grazing from the picnic basket, a la Yogi Bear—as it was about "pulling down." Running laps on climbs was similar to the repetitive drills we had grown up with in ball sports, and it was this approach, drawn from traditional athletic training, that stoked our appetite for Massive Footage on the stone.

Early on in my baseball career, an enlightened coach explained to me that you needed four components to excel at anything. First, you needed

Road to Excellence: Circuit Training

Circuit training is to rock climbing what practicing scales is to a musician. Except trad climbing is rarely boring so there's great fun in developing a circuit of routes or toprope/boulder problems at your crags and practice area. While you always strive to try new things, which vitalizes the trad game, running laps on a "circuit" is a peerless way to hone efficiency, master technique, and gauge progress. It's very true: Practice makes perfect. And when you can practice climbing something perfectly, the feeling carries over to your on-sight efforts. Every outing is a chance to broaden your circuit.

Oftentimes you will do a few short familiar things to get warmed up, then get to work on the day's "project," which is generally something new (for you). Later you can jump on your circuit and milk it for mileage. Keeping things fresh and intriguing means mixing in the old with the new, and in the process, making the new part of your personal circuit. Granted, many routes are "one and done," for various reasons. It's only the worthy stuff you add to your circuit. Coming to know a climb in an intimate way is another way of meeting yourself, and in some wordless way, the features of a rock wall become totems for the vast reaches of ourselves. They call it adventure for good reason.

aptitude, or raw ability. Climbing wasn't for everyone. But it seemed like it was invented just for us, and we were learning quickly. Second, you had to have convenient, world-class venues on which to practice. You can't get great at surfing while living in Omaha or Terre Haute. But we could get good at rock climbing in So Cal because there were rocks everywhere. Third, you had to have skilled mentors who understood the game. While we lacked a principal guru, most everyone was more experienced, and as typically happens in the climbing world, most eagerly pointed out our foibles. Some of this coaching actually helped. Finally, you had to have

massive desire and drive and the head to keep trying. The rest was all about practice.

We were barely climbing a month when it dawned on us that we were legitimately onto something. We were edging into intermediate terrain and starting to do a few hard bouldering problems, including overhangs and some basic cracks. I couldn't keep my mind from shooting off into the future, into legendary adventures. Rock climbing was not so much of a sport or activity as it was a magic carpet we would ride right onto the great rock walls of the world. We never once questioned that this and this alone was what we were made to do.

CHAPTER 6

Giant Step

Peter Croft

After my first brush with near disaster at the choss cliff, it became obvious I needed to climb at a real climbing area with real climbers. The first issue was easy to sort out. Squamish was the biggest and best climbing center in all of Canada and a 2-hour ferry ride and 40-minute drive to reach. Sometimes referred to as simply "The Chief,"

Squamish is a granite dome towering 2,297 feet above the town of Squamish, British Columbia, and the cool waters of nearby Howe Sound. Some claim The Chief is "the second-largest granite monolith in the world." Either way, it's huge.

The best I could do for a partner was Richard Suddaby, an old childhood friend who had moved to the mainland. He wasn't actually a climber but his dad was, and that made Richard the next best

Jasmin Caton stretching for the wooden handhold on Tantalus Wall, Squamish.

ANDREW BURR

ANDREW BURR

thing. He was keen to try, plus he owned a blood-red Ford Mustang which, then as now, is as sporty a transport as a budding climber could ever wish for.

The following Saturday I boarded the ferry and spent the couple hours of the voyage wondering how I would acquit myself, daydreaming about my reserves of bravery, strength, and skill. Climbing requires more than athletic ability. It was clearly just as important to have style, a tricky thing for a youngster to wrap his mind around, but I hoped to know it when I saw it. Style, I would learn, is what gave climbing character and gravity beyond mere sport, and in turn spoke volumes about the practitioner. What I couldn't know was that style is formed over time and that life events and person-ality quirks would play a major hand in defining what that word meant for me and for everyone else.

Richard fetched me at the dock and we roared off on the 35-mile voyage to greatness. The high-way to Squamish is an infamous gauntlet, hair-pinning its way along a deep fjord lined by cliffs overhead and gulping drop-offs below. It is a road notorious for causing car sickness and is all dizzying terror when your driver is an impatient teenager who drives a red Mustang at speed. We skidded into the gravel parking lot near the base of what climb-ers know as the Squamish Chief (technically called the Stawamus Chief), the granite wall rising off the head of the inlet. We knew our place, however, and headed for the meeker and lower-angled Apron, a 700-foot slab that our fearful novice eyes tilted ver-tical. Scooping the tangle of gear out of the trunk, we straightaway bushwhacked up through scraggly cedars and spongy green moss before breaking out into the sunshine and clean wide-open rock.

Our first route was a 5.8 called Sickle that followed an arching corner system up to a large tree ledge. For the first time I got to tie into real anchors and to place my sweaty hands where expe-rienced climbers had placed theirs. Most of our gear was the latest, but our footwear was not. Richard wore cheap sneakers which smeared pretty well but edged like butter. I still sported my steel-shanked mountain boots—just the ticket for ferrying loads on Everest, but they had no smearing capacity at all. Also for the first time, I got to clean the gear as I followed that first pitch, finding that fear had a taste when I re-racked to swing into the lead.

After about 2 hours we arrived at the third and crux pitch. I went first, underclinging and trying to smear precisely with clodhoppers that felt like blocks of petrified wood on my feet. I placed nuts whenever I could, lengthening them with long slings so I wouldn't suffer rope drag as I wandered back and forth on the vast slab. Things progressed just like in the book—then I came to the crux. It wasn't like hitting a blank wall. It was a blank wall. Who could ever climb it? A body length below me drooped a slung Stopper I hoped to God was good; above me loomed 15 feet of impossible glass. There were no cracks and no holds, not even a meager crystal to wrap a digit around. This was impossible. This was 5.8!

Knowing that strength and technique were of no use I tried to bluff my way up, to use the power of positive thinking. Since I couldn't see any foot-holds I just placed my feet wherever they landed and forged on with pure will and poor judgment.

Then I came off!

As I rocketed down I glimpsed my last piece of pro and made a grab at it. My speed exceeded my grip strength by a mile and the sling burned through my flesh. The gear held but I was too freaked to have another go so I swapped ends with Richard. Anyone who has experience with big whippers and piss-your-pants terror knows the warm comfort of being back at the belay, trading off the sharp end and sending someone else up to finish what you started.

Richard did perhaps even better than me because when he pitched off his bendy plimsoles skidded to a halt before he even weighted the nut. He even tried running up the bulge but it was no good. He still came sliding down. From the safety of the belay I came up with the answer: We carried a second rope for rappelling and Richard could use this to lasso a small tree 20 feet above. Tying a number of our heaviest hexes onto the rope end, Richard made a number of tosses before he got

the length right. Then, he made an almost perfect toss—I say "almost" because although he hit the tree, the hexes jammed in a rotten branch on the side of the trunk. The idea was that the cluster would go clear around the tree so the weighted end could slide back down to him. Richard wanted no part of Batmaning off a twig. I told him it looked great from where I stood. So up he went and unbelievably, the twig held.

With the help of the rope, I made it up too. From there the climbing eased to easy 5th class so we decided to rap off. Although I grew up peak bagging, where summits meant everything, I was a rock climber now and could care less about some 5.2 fluff. I was only interested in 5.7 and the rarified air beyond.

Back at the base we turned our attention to the classic 5.7 corner crack, Diedre. Though already late afternoon, we launched up it. After all, it was a grade easier than Sickle. Never mind we hadn't free

Squamish Chief, British Columbia, Canada.

ANDREW BURR

Early days at Squamish.

PAT MORROW

climbed that route. If fact we hadn't even properly aid climbed it.

The hours on the rock made themselves felt, however, and our plan of swinging leads never panned out. Every time I followed a pitch I was too exhausted to think of leading through. All I can remember is rope length after rope length of fingertip laybacking interspersed with hip-chafing sling belays. Our progress was miserably slow and

even the long summer day was too short for us. A hundred feet short of the top a moonless night enveloped the gray wall. We couldn't see to climb and had no idea of the descent. Beginners' luck is a real thing, though, and suddenly we heard voices and saw headlamps.

In retrospect there were a number of points where retreating was the wiser course of action. The what-ifs—if that dead branch had cleaved off, if

Style

Anyone who has read about the history of modern rock climbing appreciates how style determines what we do on the rock, and more importantly, how we do it. How closely we adhere to a given style, and how much we come to identify with it, goes a long ways in defining who we are. Style is subtler and runs deeper than providing fodder for bragging rights. True style is an inner compass that helps us determine whether we are ready for a given challenge or whether it is wiser and more satisfying to retreat and come back when truly ready. In simple terms, the underlying conviction with all matters of style is that success at any cost is no success at all. But again, this is subtle terrain, and much depends on our point of view.

Although some may use the term as a shallow form of one-upmanship, the core concept is that style allows a climber to personalize what climbing means for him or her. Think of it—all of those rules in organized sports, those positions you were made to play inside the narrow lines; in short, all of those things that restricted what you did, imposed by people you didn't know or by rule books you never read. Now fathom the opposite. A wide-open playing field. With rules of your own making. In a very real sense, the trad world is where we fashion our own reality, informed and inspired by the past, but free to discover our own nuances.

None of this comes in a flash while you are learning to tie a figure eight knot. Personal style evolves from a multitude of successes and failures. Some of those successes will ring hollow even while pals are slapping you on the back; but there will also be the near-misses that finely exhibit and give a glimpse, however brief, of the best you might hope to be. And you will be the only person on the cliffside to know or care.

Ultimately, style becomes a tool for self-expression and a way to clarify and make real the best you have to give. Self-imposed rules make far more sense than those spelled out in some dusty book from an irrelevant past. "Be all that you can be!"—that's what the army says and it might just work—so long as you can follow orders. But for those who run truant from such a framework, climbing can be remade for our liking.

Peter Croft soloing Bearded Cabbage, Joshua Tree.

BOB GAINES

Laurel Burr rapping off The Devil's Golf Ball, Kane Creek Valley, Utah.

ANDREW BURR

Retreat

Early on, when faced with the choice between fight and flight, mistakes are unavoidable. You might bail on account of threatening clouds that evaporate as soon as you step to the deck. The next day with a clear sky above (but no clue as to the actual forecast) you decide to press on only to get deluged two pitches from the top. What is important is to identify mistakes—regardless of success or failure. Sure, you might survive that downpour with no more than chattering teeth, but only a mistake (not always avoidable) put you there in the first place.

Identify those times when you made a poor choice gambling on available daylight or bad weather, and you simply got lucky and squeaked by unscathed. Climbing mags, watering holes, and campfires are full of summiteers wahoo-ing about close shaves when a more sage tactic would be to admit stupidity. Let it be true, because it is: Luck eventually runs out. Stack the odds in your favor.

In time you can approximate the time needed for a given route, will have a better sense as to what the weather might do (as well as the common sense to check the forecast), and will develop more realistic beliefs about your abilities. In the meantime, err on the side of caution by doing Three Crucial Things.

1. Start earlier than everyone else (yes, even eating Sugar Frosted Flakes and drinking a Starbucks Double Shot in the dark) to give yourself the extra time that, eventually, you will surely need.

2. Carry a rain jacket. Most reputable gear companies have a low-cost, lightweight—less than a pound—model that functions 98 percent as well as the $600 article. Buy one, jam it into a stuff sack the size of a baseball, and leave it in your pack.

3. Carry a headlamp. Modern headlamps with ultralight LEDs and tiny, AAA batteries have become standard tackle for every climber on every full-day climb. Ounce for ounce they go further than any other piece of equipment in eliminating unplanned bivis on the hill. Whether it is by lighting the way for a predawn start, descending in pitch black, or even finishing off the last few rope lengths to avoid spending the night in slings, a headlamp can be as crucial to the climb as the rope.

Make sure the batteries are fresh, and never fudge or cheat this issue. Even with new batteries, many headlamps nearly require a jeweler's loop to replace them—or at least a second headlamp to fuss with the fiddly open/close gizmo, not to mention aligning the positive/negative into the case. Again, get your batteries sorted at the house, before you rope up, so you don't have to sweat it in the dark.

Buy the stronger rather than the very lightest lamp. An extra ounce or two on your head will hardly be noticed, but a missed turn on an approach could send you in the wrong direction for miles. It's happened to us all. It's best to get a lamp with a couple of settings—full brightness for commando approaches and technical climbing, and a half-bright setting to conserve juice while walking on a sidewalk or a trail.

These Three Crucial Things have prevented more epics and retreats than all the fingertip pullups ever done in the history of the world.

A teenaged Tami Knight belays Peter Croft at Squamish.

PAT MORROW

our beginners' nutcraft had led to gear pulling and resultant whoppers, if we hadn't received help, etc. In short, if guardian angels hadn't showed up from nowhere, things could have turned ugly.

Three climbers who had just finished a different route were waiting for us on the summit, shining their torches down on the last few handholds. Once on top they asked about our day and especially our ascent of Sickle's burnished crux, their headlamps swiveling between our funk footwear and our faces. Richard claimed to have simply climbed fast and let momentum carry him to glory. I gamely nodded,

probably a little over enthusiastically, but perhaps they bought it. They said they were impressed, but it was dark and I couldn't see their eyes. In fact we cheated our way up one route and got rescued off the other—then lied to the people who saved our lives.

In spite of the long list of my physical weaknesses and character flaws, I still felt exhilarated. I now knew what I wanted to do and I reckoned I wanted it as much as anyone who had ever put a hand on stone. That, I thought, had to be worth something. As it turns out, it's worth just about everything.

CHAPTER 7

Projects, Cracks, and Faces

John Long

Have you seen the Turtle Dome Crack?" Greg asked, and I said, "The who?"

Greg Bender was about my age (16) but had been climbing for several years. I followed him down the west flank of Rubidoux to a 15-foot-high boulder called Turtle Dome. A perfect, thin hand crack—widening to fists at the top—bisected the flawless, egg-shaped sphere, which like the best of Rubidoux rock, was glass smooth and slick to the touch. The bottom few feet were undercut and the initial body length passed over a slight bulge, meaning one had to jam up an overhanging crack, which seemed a wonderful thing at the time. I watched amazed as Greg stuffed his mitts and twisted the tips of his red and black PAs into the thin gash and tomahawked his way to the top in about 30 seconds flat. Looked hard, but doable.

By this time I'd climbed the easier cracks at Rubidoux; but these were well off vertical and I could basically thieve my way up them by keeping my weight over my jammed feet. But on Turtle Dome, I had to pull most of my bulk up on thin hand jams, with my feet pasted on crappy face edges at the bottom, where the crack was too thin to toe jam. At first, and for two agonizing visits, I couldn't get the hang of placing and flexing my hands, and couldn't muster enough torque to keep my paws from immediately ripping out soon as I got my feet off the deck.

Turtle Dome became my first real "project," something I could not manage at the outset and which required me to learn something entirely

John Long still sparring with Turtle Dome Crack, 40 years later.

KEVIN POWELL

new to succeed. Turtle Dome was not only a boulder blocking my future, it was the gateway to crack climbing the world over, and the technique I learned in the process of finally bagging that blasted crack would serve me on some of the finest rock climbs on earth. But those first few days of trying

First Cracks

Some gyms have faux cracks, but by and large, crack climbing is learned at trad crags or outdoor practice areas. The basic jamming techniques will at first feel bizarre and unstable, like they could never hold your weight. They soon become so routine that a practiced crack climber often prefers a bomber hand jam to a jug. But not at first. When a technique is brand new, it's best to work on it one move at a time. Jumping on a steep, 150-foot hand crack for your first experience in hand jamming will be a miserable error—and can rip your hands to shreds.

For most of us, we found a 10-foot crack at the home scrap heap and kept floundering around on it till the hand and foot jams started to make sense. That first practice crack, once mastered, will be with you forever, burned into memory as the place you learned how to jam. It most likely will happen suddenly, as that first hand jam, say, feels solid and you move right on up. It's an amazing experience, like learning how to breathe underwater. Work the nuances out your own way—we all do.

By setting your sights low at first, you move up the ladder with less pain and quicker progress. And believe it: Whatever the first crack you mastered, you will have a hard time walking past it so long as you live. It's where the broad doors of trad climbing first fly open, and from the threshold, we can see the throne. With any luck, your practice area will have cracks running from finger size to wide flares. More likely you'll have to learn these techniques on the beginning crack routes found at most every trad cliff. Pick a route tame enough that fitness isn't the deciding issue. You want to work on technique without flaming out. Take it slow till the various techniques start to feel natural. Again, work one particular route till it all comes together. Then fly.

Pleasure to meet you, I'm sure . . .

MATT KUEHL

Keeping It Fresh

Most of these sidebars are not so much strategies as they are breakdowns of how things are performed in the real trad world. For instance, California climbers started frequenting Stoney Point, in the San Fernando Valley, in the 1930s. By the early 1950s, a cadre of teenagers—all future Yosemite pioneers—were gathering at Stoney many weekday afternoons. They faced similar challenges that modern climbers face when frequenting the same spot day after week after year: how to keep the game fresh and challenging. The solution is simple: Keep trying new things. Not merely hard. But new.

There are photos of Royal Robbins climbing Rock Two at Stoney with no hands. Eliminating holds on old favorites, contriving traverses on the same old rocks, downclimbing, link-ups, circuits, projects, repeated burns of toprope problems—all are standard means of squeezing another drop of nectar out of the old crag. Things as simple as joining others on their circuits are certain to steer you off your own beaten path. Here, the home turf becomes strangely new. Visiting new areas is a certain way to enliven the game. Working the home crag and practice area is bound to take some ingenuity. The ways are many, and all needed.

were frustrating and painful. Unwilling to rest or evaluate the situation, I kept hurling myself at the crack, staunching the weeping abrasions on my hands with gymnastic chalk. Each jam was like a crucifixion.

Finally, after many tries, my hands started staying lodged for a move, for two moves. Then three. I was getting some little feel for the work, one dastardly jam at a time.

On my second day I drove to Rubidoux and marched straight to the crack and didn't leave till finally clawing my way to the top. I would climb the Turtle Dome hundreds of times over the following years, every which way, including liebacking the thing from both sides, nearly blowing a gasket in the process.

Gleason's Chimney, the S Crack, and several others became successive projects and with each small victory (few of these routes were longer than 20 feet) I learned the basics of finger, hand, fist and off-width climbing. This is the way it works

for many of us: Learn the basic movements on a given route, quickly develop a medley of practice routes—all of which were one-time projects—and through brute repetition, the once impossible becomes routine.

Rubidoux crack boulder problems were basically the equivalent of crux bits I would encounter out at Joshua Tree and up in Idyllwild, on proper roped climbs. Whenever a hand crack pinched down I'd naturally recall Turtle Dome, and so forth. Getting the technique wired under manageable conditions, on the boulders, removed most of the fear and doubt and let me concentrate on the actual technique.

What's more, as we ranged around, rubbing elbows with the few other boulderers frequenting Rubidoux back then, we started making our way up legitimate face climbing problems that felt impossible just a few months before. You're never quite sure when you cross the divide and suddenly you are climbing for real. It just happens.

Projecting

Projecting means picking a particular "impossible" face or crack and making a project out of trying to climb it. When an Olympic gymnast and their coach determine a given routine, down to the last move, they make a project out of perfecting said routine, knowing it is too hard to "clean" all the way through just now, or even in the foreseeable future. But with a systematic approach, working patiently, the moves start coming together. Of course, there's no timetable or criteria for how long a project will or should take. The important thing is to have one, and to consciously work on it as a project. Because this has little to do with how hard you pursue climbing, the casual climber has no excuse not to have projects.

In actual practice, projecting is the basic strategy for the entire trad game. Most everyone is aiming for something. Some projects we can do first try, providing we'd done the work on the run-up. We climb easier versions of our project, and jump up on it once primed. Without a project, however soft or hard, our climbing often lacks a certain direction. The payoff is skunking a problem or a climb that's thwarted us for weeks or, in some cases, years.

ANDREW BURR

For now, know that most of us are energized by having a few goals and projects—the difficulty being our own business. These projects need not dominate our climbing. They're just polestars. More on projecting later.

After perhaps 6 months of nearly daily visits to Mount Rubidoux, we had developed an extensive circuit of problems running the gamut of steep faces, roofs, mantles, cracks, chimneys, and slabs. The great and exciting thing about this process is that never would our learning curve be so steep, and hardly a visit went by that we didn't add a few more climbs to our curriculum. The basic rope management skills of placing protection, building anchors, rappelling, and belaying had all become routine from our countless toprope sessions on the larger formations.

Through convenience and instinct, we'd left the proper climbing areas and consolidated our technique at Rubidoux, becoming addicted to bouldering and running our circuit, climbing thousands of feet of rock and returning home so gassed we couldn't make a fist. And while for many years we'd continue frequenting Rubidoux and other practice areas, as summer approached and the weather heated up, so did our ambition to get back to Tahquitz and Suicide, and the rest of the historical venues. It was high time to see where we stood in the "real" game.

CHAPTER 8

The Very Next One

Peter Croft

After that first memorable visit, Squamish became my second home. Every weekend, every holiday, every chance I got, I trudged the beach from my parents' home, hopped the fence into the ferry terminal, and took the next sailing to flesh out my new world.

Richard and I soon met others who like us had recently declared themselves climbers. As it played out, nearly all the old hardcore had moved on— some to other interests (which I couldn't understand), and a few on their one-way migration south to sunnier rock. What that meant was that each of us only had fellow knuckleheads as partners and teachers—always a sketchy business. Case in point was my getting a finger crack tutorial from Carl Austrom, who had 8 months of climbing experience on me and who I listened to as I would a seasoned technician.

For this, my first pure crack pitch, I followed Carl over to the area's most classic finger crack, Exasperator, at the base of the Grand Wall. The first bit passed brilliantly—then I stuttered to a halt when the big footholds ran out. With nothing for my feet and only a ¾-inch crack splitting the wall above, all my previous experience couldn't move me up an inch. This is where Carl chimed in, both hands cutting through the air. What it boiled down to was to take the middle finger and poke it down into the crack while drawing the thumb upwards till the two digits met, an action similar to what one might use to pluck a hair from an omelet. Apart from being stupid, this would be an inefficient

Peter Croft leading Sentry Box (5.12) at Squamish.

PAT MORROW

means of getting anywhere. But Carl's seniority spurred me to try, till my arms were pumped silly and my fingers were bleeding and I concluded I didn't have what it took to climb cracks.

Peter Croft leading Exasperator (5.10) at Squamish.

PAT MORROW

Later I learned there were other ways to twist digits into cracks. Carl's bizarre method was one of many techniques I tried on for size and discarded—things that might work in a few quirky situations, but which amounted to the climbing version of flipping sizzling burgers on the barbecue with your bare hands. You might get away with it now and then, but a spatula was indicated.

Many bad ideas came and went, but some were solid and stayed with me, becoming valuable tools for stacking the odds. Like the time Richard and I set out to do a "first ascent" of a route that had never been climbed. In those days Squamish had continents of virgin rock and we spotted what looked like a prime candidate on the right side of the main wall, a 300-foot buttress of flawless clean rock. Things went swimmingly for the first couple pitches—a clean 5.8 dihedral, a 5.5 face climbing pitch—it felt almost too good to be true. It was. And it almost killed me. The third pitch wound up the right side of a steep prow followed by a bottoming thin crack. Amid the crumbling rugosities I finally squeezed in a tiny Stopper strung on a fuzzy strand of 5mm perlon cord. The nut was most likely worthless, but I hadn't placed anything for a long ways and couldn't see any good gear coming up. So I clipped the fuzzy cord and pushed on.

Twenty-five feet higher I stemmed out wide to avoid a fat

Trad climbing in the Flatirons, high above Boulder, Colorado.

DAVE VAUGHN

Advice

Along the way to refining technique we all encounter poor advice from a variety of promising sources. Climbers with more stone under their harness or a more confident swagger will often share with you some detailed recipe, if not for disaster, then at least good for bloody knuckles and knees. This rarely is an attempt to sabotage your progress (although it could be a good joke). Far more likely they have fallen victim to getting it "almost right," a hazardous position in bomb squads and on rock climbs. Good technique is full of subtlety and feel.. Accept advice, but toss it if it feels all wrong after some experimentation. This is especially true for the intricacies of jamming, which initially will feel awkward, even when perfectly performed.

ANDREW BURR

Double Up on the Pro

Whenever the ground ahead turns "heady" or uncertain as to where the next pro might show up, place something as high as you can before casting off. Sounds self-evident, but having something in just a few feet higher might eliminate that dreadful ledge fall. If you simply cannot see good gear on the horizon, double (or even triple) up on your pro. As well, even if the piece looks like little more than a gesture, clip it if nothing else is available. The climbing world is full of stories of near catastrophes averted by a measly widget jammed in some flaring slot. In love and pro, most anything is better than nothing.

If the way ahead is dangerous, reserve the right to bail. Looking up into a big unknown, lacking in gear placements and topped with visibly wet, black slimy rock, the price of retreat to wallet and ego is a bargain no matter how much gear you leave behind. No climber enjoys a 100 percent success ratio, or anything like it, often for good reason—like no decent pro. The majority of injuries reported in the annual *Accidents in North American Mountaineering* involve leader falls and pro ripping out. When in doubt, double up—or bail.

black water streak. Both boots instantly got slimed and I could feel them slipping. I glanced down at that skinny yellow cord clipped in leagues below. It would never hold—the nut would rip or the tatty sling would bust. Either way I was toast, and no last minute promises to quit climbing or aid orphans and widows could possibly save me now. But I was so close. A fat cedar swept from the lush groove just above my head, and if I could just latch onto that trunk I'd be saved and could then decide if I meant to honor my vows to those orphans.

Planting and replanting my sliding feet, I reached up, got both hands on the underbelly of the cedar, and slowly groped my way around its waist, stretching, almost there, hands curving over into its barky lap. Only inches now. Noooo! Both feet blew at the same time and I flew.

Richard later reported that I let out a strangled "Help!" and vanished behind the corner. Fifty feet lower I marveled at the wonderfulness of being alive, wondering how such a terrible nut with such a terrible bight of fuzzy 5-mill could do such a miraculous thing.

The golden lesson here was that I'd almost removed that nut and had clipped it off as little more than an afterthought. Just before I pitched, I stole a glance at that furry cord so far below, swaying like a straw in the wind. In my mind's eye it was only this blade of grass, or strange and hidden hands, that kept me in this world.

This is one of several incidents from my early years that makes me shake my head and bite my lip. The what-ifs are horrific, and it came down to a single piece of pro that should have ripped in a situation where I should have stopped climbing and rapped off.

CHAPTER 9

Tahquitz Redux

John Long

I hadn't been back to Tahquitz Rock since my second guided outing with Bob Dominick, the previous summer. But I'd climbed most every afternoon since, out at Mount Rubidoux. Hiking up to Lilly Rock, as they called it in the old days, was an interesting drill since I had no idea how I'd perform. And what's more, that hike up to Tahquitz is an ass-kicker. As mentioned, approach marches are an integral part of the trad climbing experience, and if you want to go far in this realm, you'll end

Mike Lechlinski and Randy Leavitt racking up for El Capitan, 1980.

KEVIN POWELL

Leader's rack circa 2013: flexible-stemmed cams, wired nuts, and sewn slings.

BEN HORTON

up throwing down some serious miles, often with crushing, off-balance loads crammed with spikes and turnbuckles jabbing your vitals. No one said it was easy.

I hadn't given much thought as to likely routes to climb nor had I studied enough about Tahquitz to know a classic from a gully. So we headed up The Trough—the standard rookie ditch, first bagged in the 1930s, that ran from bottom to top. We wanted to tick an easy one and find our sea legs, then sail for Tahiti.

The first pitch headed up a low-angled ramp, and it felt like the fluff I often downclimbed, sans rope, while getting off toprope problems at

Tahquitz aka Lilly Rock.

KEVIN POWELL

Rubidoux. The second pitch, a simple crack in a gully, was also easy money, and landed us on Pine Tree Ledge, where a striking variation soared up and left.

Now here was some real climbing—steep, with good holds and a decent fingertip lieback crack bisecting a diamond-hard wall. Fixed pitons festooned from strategic spots in the crack, leading to another ledge, visible maybe 100 feet higher.

This was the historic Piton Pooper, one of the original aid routes (1937) at Tahquitz, and so comparatively long that early ascents exhausted their store of pins en route. In 1949, which sounded like a date from the Bronze Age, seminal climber Chuck Wilts made the "First Free Ascent" of the route, basically inventing the practice of trying to free climb existing aid routes. Standing on Pine Tree Ledge, I was all about the Piton Pooper.

Nuts were just becoming popular and I spent hours at my gas station job hack-sawing and drilling aluminum stock and fashioning "artificial chock stones." I had maybe fifteen of these hack jobs, as well as some Clog and funky Euro units on my rack, along with enough biners to clip off the fixed pegs. I spit for effect and started up.

Used to cranking on small holds out at Rubidoux, the sharp edge of the lieback crack on Piton Pooper (rated 5.7 but all of 5.8) felt solid as a rain gutter. But as I clipped and pulled past that first rusty peg, the crack thinned, the wall jacked up to near vert, and my knees started getting a little loose. I clipped the next fixed peg and my teeth started chattering out loud. The holds were okay but I wasn't used to the big air or climbing above protection, and what if I popped and the old ring-angle pitons yanked out? I was done for.

The long second pitch (5.8) of the Open Book, Tahquitz.

KEVIN POWELL

Twenty feet off the ledge and I was frozen in a wide stem, yanking off the edge of the crack, trying to wiggle in a gas station wedge and unable to commit to one more move. Finally my arms gave out and I lowered to the ledge.

I felt confused and ashamed. I hadn't come close to falling off. But being up there, bridging past the pro felt harrowing. And hanging on fingertips for minutes at a time with my legs all splayed out—this was a new sensation, a confidence game that felt vaguely like do-or-die, even though the protection was stout and plentiful. But that vertical wall and the 300-plus feet of mountain air beneath my boots—I was scared.

Nonetheless, I couldn't accept that I was getting hosed by this thing after our spectacular success on the 20-footers at Rubidoux. After a short rest, I swarmed back up, got 20 feet higher to where the crack arched over left, and once more nearly shit myself, frozen stiff by the exposure and the wild adventure of free climbing up a vertical wall. After maybe 15 minutes hanging on for dear life, I slumped back onto a pin and lowered back to the ledge.

I wasn't embarrassed or confused any more. My arms were thick as blue fin tuna but I was thrilled by the experience and knew I was heading back up there soon as my limbs and my sac recovered. It was impossible to explain to my partners that while I might look solid on the lieback, my insides were flying apart. But it was a wonderful destruction. And a fantastic high.

I swarmed back to the high point and felt every one of those million volts coursing through me once more. I backed up a fixed ring angle with another homemade chock and surveyed the situation. Without trying, and by no conscious choice of my own, my body had relaxed and I was able to get past the paralyzing fear and appreciate my station with some little objectivity. The protection was stout and all over the place; my body felt fine and understood just how to go about things. In a few minutes I pulled onto the next ledge and belayed the others up.

A long, wandering pitch led over much easier ground. A final short pitch and we were on the summit, having bagged our first multipitch trad route beyond the beginners' gullies. This 5.7 had felt downright horrific.

On our way down we passed a team just clearing the roof at the start of pitch 3 on Open Book, touted as America's first multipitch 5.9 (first free climbed by Royal Robbins in 1950) and to our rookie eyes, a remarkable and frightening, 90-degree dihedral, soaring up off the talus for many hundreds of feet. The leader was fist jamming

Kay Okamoto on Open Book at Tahquitz.

GREG EPPERSON

On-Sight

On-sight climbing, aka on-sighting, flashing, and any number of other terms, simply means that the first time we ever try a given route, we climb it straight through with no falls and no resting on the gear. Flashing hard trad routes becomes difficult for reasons other than just the technical challenges of climbing the rock. The protection may be lacking or hard to arrange. The runouts may be frightening. The climbing might be unrelenting, or loose, or strangely awkward.

Either way the goal for all trad climbers on every trad route we ever attempt is to on-sight the bad boy first try. We can't do better than that. As we approach our limits, on-sighting becomes improbable and eventually impossible. We cannot process that much data under such strenuous conditions and still perform. So we "work" the pitch, and with each lap the lower bits get more familiar and we climb them more efficiently.

Eventually, we aim to lead the whole shebang with no falls, bottom to top. This might take three tries or 3 months of trying. We will be astonished with how much more manageable some sections feel after climbing them several times, as the moves become more familiar. Case in point is the speed record for the Nose of El Capitan, which is under 2 hours (after dozens of rehearsal ascents), but is closer to 7 hours for the on-sight. More on this later.

Heather Hayes balances on the summit of Ancient Art.

LARRY COATS

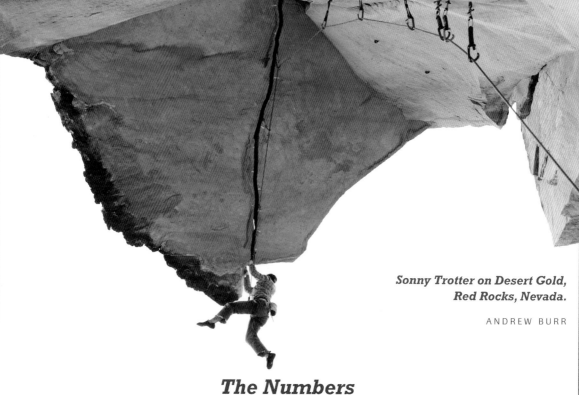

The Numbers

Chasing big numbers (5.11, 5.12, 5.13, etc.) is a central if not essential part of gym and sport climbing. In a venue where technical difficulty is the larger part of the game, numbers quite naturally become the Holy Grail. But in the trad arena, where many factors come into play beyond simply climbing the rock, chasing numbers is a complex game. And even the merely technical side of things presents formidable challenges because trad climbing is so varied, calling on many dissimilar techniques.

Since as far back as the mid 1970s, a true 5.11 leader is a rare bird in the climbing world. This sounds almost laughable. After all, 5.11 is only borderline expert terrain nowadays. But in fact, there are very few climbers who can go to Yosemite and on-sight lead Twilight Zone (run-out off-size crack), Tightrope (run-out slab), Edge of Night (difficult flare) Center Route on Independence Pinnacle (thin hands), Final Exam (fist crack), Spooky Tooth (steep and scary face), 1096 (squeeze chimney), and Waverly Wafer (wide to lieback)—and none of these routes are harder than 5.10. People might argue correctly that such a list is Yosemite-centric, and that other lists for gritstone, limestone, etc. are more telling. But the point stands: Rare is the climber who has mastered all of the techniques at the 5.11 level, and those climbing wide to thin to face, all at the 5.12 standard, number a few handful in any country.

Nevertheless, always striving to improve and reach the next level of difficulty—be it 5.8 or 5.13—is a fun and enduring part of the trad game, and helps keep up motivation and excitement. Goals, set at one's own level and pace, tend to give structure and direction to an activity that can become aimless or boring through rote. So pick a number, just as you would a compass point before a long voyage. And either ardently or casually—or anything in between—get after it. Most of us find that the actual number is immaterial. What animates the game is that we've set our sights on a goal, a route at a particular level of difficulty; and during the dog days of midweek, we always have that route to go back to, fluttering in our minds like a flying carpet.

out the small ceiling above the second belay and he stopped in the middle and said to his partner, "No worries. It's only about 5.7 here." I stopped in my tracks.

I was learning that when just starting out, it is not so much the physical moves as the mind-boggling mental challenges that stun and humble a would-be rock god. Our minds toughen up in their own time—or not at all. And that is always the big question on many trad adventures: Do I have the head to do this? The tricky part is the difficulty in seeing past our immediate level of expertise.

When the man up there on Open Book yelled over that it was "only 5.7," I wondered if I would ever feel that way. I couldn't imagine that a few seasons later I would be up at the same place with two other friends, all of us without a rope, thinking nothing of the roof, the exposure, or the difficulty.

Classic for a Reason

Visit the Getty Museum or the Louvre and you'll bolt straight to the classics because they represent the best of what mankind has achieved in the arts. Same goes with rock climbs at the cliffside. Most every crag has its classics, and that's where many of us start. In fact, most weekend warriors have limited time so staying close to the classics remains the yellow brick road to the goods. There are classics at every level but for unknown reasons they often cluster in the 5.8 to 5.10 range. Since the 5.10 grade is open to just about any enthusiastic climber, a majority of the world's storied free climbs are within reach for most of us.

Classic is a subjective word, it is true, but routes universally given classic status usually bear spectacular vertical relief and positioning (read, big air), interesting features, superb rock, engaging movement—the list is endless. Oftentimes a classic will be a quintessential statement about a specific technique, like the All Time Hand Crack in Indian Creek. The point is that classics have usually earned their status for good reason—the highest peer review. They take the guesswork out of route selection.

Most climbers want to range out and do a few obscure and even junk routes on occasion to keep themselves honest. But the bread and butter of most climbers' dockets are the classics. Most guidebooks have an introductory page or two and a short list of recommended routes. If nothing else, these are a great place to start. And remember, reminiscing is a part of the climbing experience. Bagging a classic is in essence roping in with every hero and yahoo that has ever climbed the route, and these experiences will forever be yours to share and to remember.

Retro trad, 1952, Wyoming.

JODY LANGFORD

CHAPTER 10

Down South in Leavenworth

Peter Croft

Squamish was the best in all of Canada but the weather posed a massive obstacle. Most of the year it rained, and when it didn't, the clouds hung low over the forested mountains, always threatening to dump. I was rabid enough to go anyway, virtually any time, and needing someone on the other end of the rope, I resorted to various Jedi mind tricks to convince people I knew things about the weather that no one else did. Occasionally I conned someone to venture out under spitting skies but in those days, since most free climbing ascended slabs, we'd slip and slide to a halt on the damp green rock.

In the summer of my second year of climbing, a particularly dismal stretch of weather found a few of us bivied in the gravel parking lot under a van. Come daylight, the downpour continued, and we decided to hightail it down to Leavenworth, Washington. This, I was assured, was the one place we could count on blue skies and bone-dry rock. On the 5-hour drive we were pounded by a torrent, but just after Stevens Pass and 30 miles short of our destination I saw a glorious triangle of blue nestled between two distant ridges. Traveling, whether by thumb, car, or plane, would turn our backwater activities into a wide world of opportunity. All we were looking for was a chunk of dry stone; what we often found was a whole lot more.

Leavenworth, as promised, was the Promised Land. Safe in a buttressed rain shadow, the area smelled of dry pine forest, and steep granite crags sprouted from the hillsides. And it was here, in the antithesis of Squamish dankness, that I received my first ego crushing. One of my initial climbs at Leavenworth was following my friend Don on Flame, a 5.8 hand crack. Back home I was leading low-end 5.11 slabs so this piddling crack, I was sure, would be a mellow intro to Washington cragging. The cruisey warm-up, however, turned out to be the cruelest smackdown.

From the start the climb made no sense—I cupped my hands, trying to make progress through skin friction and finger strength. Neither was sufficient and I ground my way up, more or less falling skywards. I could never have led Flame, and when I staggered onto the belay ledge, blood pumped from both hands, hanging like bunches of bananas, and my flamed forearms throbbed.

I climbed the pitch, sure, but was depressed at my poor showing. I aspired to do the long routes down in Yosemite and all across the great ranges of the world. All of them entailed miles of crack climbing and here, on a measly 5.8, was clear and present proof that I had no place in the Valley or in the great ranges.

It didn't yet occur to me that I lacked an acquirable technique. Working on your weaknesses is a truism in all of sports training, but this particular beat-down felt more like an utter defect, pointing out the fact that I would never climb cracks. More to the point, Flame exposed me as a Noob and I would always be a Noob. We camped in Icicle Creeks' Eight Mile Campground, dining on cottage cheese ladled home with corn chips while sparks from monstrous campfires burned holes in our down jackets.

After dinner I was shown Classic Crack, a 5.9 splitter at the west end of the campground. Here

**Ridge Traverse,
Superstition Mountains.**

LARRY COATS

I was told stories of how staggering drunk heroes soloed the 50-foot gash in the dead of night, stuffing empty beer cans in between jams. On toprope and stone sober, I couldn't imagine it. My legs got in the way of each other and my hands never found the right jams. Fighting my body as much as the climb, I never found my balance, couldn't trust my hands or feet, and couldn't dream of how some staggering Viking could pillage his way up this crack in the dark. But Classic Crack was close to our tents

Heel hook.

ANDREW BURR

Randy Atkinson on Zombie Roof, Squamish.

PAT MORROW

so we'd lap out on it after every day's cragging, and slowly my awkward gimping evolved into basic struggling and the barest bones of crack technique.

On that same trip I got my first taste of over-hanging face climbing, on Castle Rock's Jello Tower. Graded a casual 5.7, the route loomed over me like a tottering Tower of Pisa. The climb would later be upgraded to 5.9, a fact that mattered little in the flurried context of my thrashing. My 2 years spent climbing faces were no help on Jello Tower. Halfway up, with elbows winging out sideways with the pump, I tried a new technique I'd seen in *Mountain Magazine,* the celebrated heel hook. I kicked my foot at what had to be the perfect heel hook-able flake, latched it and—I was stuck. Ten

feet above a hastily placed nut, I freaked. Instead of holding me in balance, my body locked up in the utterly foreign, sideways position, terror choking me per my imminent upside-down whipper. Franti-cally untangling and righting myself, I resumed an upright posture and raced my torched forearms to the summit.

That 5-day trip to Leavenworth was exactly what I needed. In Squamish I had risen to the upper grades and was starting to feel confident about my abilities, a confidence founded on the specialized techniques found on slabs, a meager base to launch from while aiming for the walls of Yosemite. This early trip away from Squamish was the first step in becoming an all-around climber. I

Road Tripping

As we progress through the grades, we will often go only so far and then plateau. The solution is to mix it up. Add more crack climbing, for example, or schedule in more bouldering. Always focus on our weaknesses, which are often the very things that we avoid. This will surely help, but the best way to break out of a pattern of sameness is to travel.

For some, like most of my fellow Canucks, visiting other areas is a way to escape foul weather by sneaking away to rain-shadowed desert locales like Joshua Tree. Seeking out mild climes means more cragging but in the larger context, traveling is arguably the single most important factor in becoming a better and more complete trad climber.

Encountering different rock types is a big part of it. Even visiting crags with the same basic rock type will reveal a wide variety of formations. For example, the climbing is vastly different on Glacier Point than on Higher Cathedral Spire, though both are granite formations located in Yosemite Valley.

Some areas enjoy incredible friction while some have virtually none (usually limestone cliffs buffed by climbers' hands and feet—or granite polished by the last ice age). There are areas with splitter cracks that are easy to protect while others feature flaring grooves requiring extensive fiddling to arrange any pro remotely "good enough." Places like the Gunks, in upstate New York, are famous for their baffling sequences of twisty turny moves, even on easy routes. Same goes for Australia's Mount Arapiles.

Regardless of how much of a slap down we receive, every schooling can yield real benefits. Because unfamiliar rock types and foreign techniques test and bully our weaknesses, fitness and technical skills improve exponentially. In Yosemite Valley the bulk of countless jamming classics are primarily endurance problems, so over time, endurance always improves. Upon returning from my first trip to Australia, I assumed my crack climbing might have suffered. After all, I had done very few cracks Down Under, focusing mainly on the steep face climbing for which the area is renowned. What I found, however, was that my crack climbing had vastly improved, partly due to a more all-around fitness, partly from acquiring a wider repertoire of moves. This is perhaps the biggest benefit to traveling—returning home with more tricks in your bag.

Road tripping!

BEN HORTON

rattled and bled on the easy routes, thrashed up the hand cracks, and stood gaping up at gruesome off-widths I would avoid, at all costs, for the next half dozen years. Climbing had just turned a whole lot gnarlier, and I left Leavenworth humbled, but took away more than weeping scabs on the backs of my hands. It would take weeks for my skin to heal, but my eyes had seen a bigger world.

Mileage on the Rock

No matter the lessons learned or epiphanies experienced, there is no substitute for mileage on the rock. This remains a basic tenet of this book and of all trad climbing. Even once you understand the mechanics of technique and appreciate subtle movement, repetition can take you from halting, herky-jerky thrutching to gliding ever more fluidly up difficult ground.

Crack climbing, in particular, initially feels unnatural to most people. To Fred the greenhorn, hand jamming feels insecure so he keeps both hands and feet deep inside the fissure. Any upward movement is by pulling up with both hands and pushing with both feet—which finds him barndooring side to side, which in turn burns up much of what strength he has left. When Freddy moves his feet he finds that, because he has punted them so deeply in the gash, they invariably get stuck and a wriggling whimper-fest ensues—again devouring more energy. With repetition, subtleties are revealed and over time, the hand jam feels more secure than a jug.

After some practice, Fred finds that when a good jam is found for, say, the right hand, the left can be palmed out for balance. Of course, that same familiarity is also found with the intricacies of the foot jam, allowing him to place his foot just deep enough to stick, and not so deep as to despair of extracting it. The new Fred is now in almost constant motion between gear placements, pulling up off a single jam instead of two, palming out and flagging to reduce the barndoor effect and easily placing and removing his feet from the crack as he styles his way up the wall.

This is just one example—there are loads of others. Back stepping, heel hooking, wide cracks, etc. require plenty of practice just to thrash past the "spaz" stage, no matter how much pulling down we've done in the sport climbing arena.

Beyond that, the ever-retreating ideal of mastery could be a lifelong pursuit. For now, pick on your weaknesses like the bullies picked on the ninety-pound weakling—hazing, smacking, kicking sand in his grill, turning him into Charles Atlas!

"Ahhh, Brad, did you mean what you said last night . . ."

ANDREW BURR

CHAPTER 11

Crossing the Threshold

Peter Croft

Whenever we could, our small gang of long-haired scruffs gathered on an old abandoned road at the base of The Chief. Overgrown with salmonberry bushes and scabbed over with rotting asphalt, this wrinkled road was the one clearing in the rain forest where we could throw down our

sleeping bags. We called it Psyche Ledge and there never was a truer place name.

We slept under the stars when the weather was good, gazing up at the wall until it got dark and then into the fire till we fell asleep, dreaming of what we would try next day. All of us skipped through the grades fairly quickly: quickly, that is, until we ran into 5.10. All of us could climb 5.9,

History

To some people climbing is just a sport, a pastime among a slew of hobbies. History, for them, will be of little value. For those who hurl themselves into adventure climbing, however, the historical heart and soul of the enterprise takes on personal and practical importance. Reading about landmark climbs, techniques, and inventions helps to put our new world into context. Understanding how one event or way of doing things led to the next breakthrough gives us insight not only to what has happened, but what might happen next. It shows us that no matter how advanced we are presently, new advances are right around the buttress. In other words, there will always be more to learn and new events to thrill and amaze us.

It is instructive to go to the beginning, or close to it. The early heroes of climbing provide grounding into what we do as well as goose-bumping inspiration. Continuing up to the present day illustrates how each leap builds on the one before and how each generation benefits from the previous one.

The various gadgets and gear have helped facilitate many changes, but it is the people, the techniques, and the seminal climbs that are most worthy of our attention. Understanding Royal Robbins's moxie in his breakthrough solo climb of El Capitan can help us with our own breakthroughs. Putting history's noteworthy routes onto our agenda leads on a logical path to finding our own limits—and maybe pushing past them.

Visiting the seminal areas makes climbing history come alive. Whether we're standing at the base of Cenotaph Corner in North Wales, the Naked Edge in Eldorado Canyon, or The Nose of El Cap in Yosemite, we are gazing back into the past as well as up into the air.

Zac Robinson on Pipeline, a classic 5.10 Squamish crack.

ANDREW BURR

Peter Croft on Crying Time at Tuolomne Meadows.

but our bodies and minds stuttered to a halt when we neared the force field aura of the 5.10 grade— and it wasn't just the double digit that did it. None of us claimed to know anyone who could climb 5.10. The only climbers we had read about who'd mastered that grade were living in other countries, under sunnier skies, were pictured in magazines, and were rock-star famous. To us they felt every bit as foreign and distant as Greek gods living in the sky. Down on earth in our climbing backwater, we crept toward the 5.10 threshold like the Cowardly Lion approaching Oz.

One summer morning Richard and I launched off Psyche Ledge, determined to break through the mythical 5.10 barrier. Throughout the season we had consolidated our abilities,

Goals

There are many ways to consider goals, and we will investigate more than a few. It is good for the soul to have something to stir our embers—a level of difficulty, a classic long route, or a road trip full of fun and discovery. There are those, of course, who insist on maintaining concrete ambitions and slavish timetables. Motivational speakers and coaches preach the virtues of charting weekly, even daily, goals along with the steps and timelines for success. There are mounds of literature on the subject supporting this theory—and much of it is bunk.

Not to say you should never set a schedule. Time is a commodity that requires managing, especially for those with heavy work schedules. But in the trad world, where we have skin and bones in the game, and many factors out of our control, goals should be acted on only when they feel right and in a way that makes sense. Writing down a list and trying to maintain a timeline can lead to unrealistic expectations and, worse, premature actions.

Goals are experiences with the sound turned up.

MATT STANICH

climbing every 5.9 around until there was nowhere to go but up.

Since it always rained in coastal Canada, I stuffed my camping gear and extra climbing gear in a nearby cave. Grabbing Richard's rope, we chose the four-pitch White Lightning, a line streaking up the steep slab between Sickle and Diedre—the first two routes we ever climbed. This time, however, we were set on sterner stuff. After an easy pitch we polished off the runout 5.8 fluff on the second lead. Now the route steepened up—a high step surmounting an overlap and then thin edges and friction scoops to the belay. Guidebook said 5.9, so not too bad. Years later the new guide raised the grade to 5.10—good thing we didn't know that then or we would have pitched all over it.

Now it was my turn for the 5.10c crux. I'm not sure how I got the lead; I was probably just the alpha male that day.

I set off, pleased with the edging and smearing capacity of my new EBs. These shoes were it back then. There was no shoe in second place. Imagine a world with only one type of cell phone or one

**Peter Croft, pulling
for the clouds.**

CHRIS FALKENSTEIN

flavor of ice cream—or only one type of rock shoe. Like many others, I wore my EBs super tight, the thick-lipped inside seams crushing my toe knuckles. And this day on White Lightning, I cinched them till the grommets sighed.

I led out left from a belay at a scrawny pine, clipping bolts up the steepening bulge. The holds slimmed to pencil-lead creases and baby barnacles. Then I clipped the last bolt and everything stopped—the edges, the crystals, and me. Fall after

Breakthroughs

Breakthroughs often come from achieving goals but just as likely are birthed from the unforeseen or from epic circumstances. Obviously the likelihood increases if there is a conscious effort to thrust the boat out into deep waters, but it always is difficult to manage or orchestrate a genuine breakthrough. Known variously as "boundary experiences," such moments have the selfsame thunder as honest-to-God miracles.

Breakthroughs happen when a new view of the world opens up, along with our place in it.

DAVE N. CAMPBELL

Plainly put, exploring new territory, on the inside and out, is the key to nurturing breakthroughs. When they happen, a new view of the world opens up, along with our place in it. What was once ominous or threatening is now simply tricky or difficult. As they say, the merely difficult we can do right now, but the impossible might take a little time. Once through the next threshold, we've taken one more step toward feeling like we were born for this wild place. This is an experience we cannot fake and is one of those rare things we can truly call our own. Can I get a witness . . .?

grinding fall ensued, interspersed with hanging on the bolts to remove my painful new shoes. The EBs were nutcracker-ing my toes. I pulled them off fully expecting to see blood. I don't know how many times I fell, thousands, I suspect, till finally I tumbled my way over the crux and hove to on the belay ledge, blinking like an owl, shocked at what I had pulled off.

Richard followed and we sat on the ledge, delirious. No sound barrier or 4-minute mile could have been a sweeter success. Never mind that I'd hung on the bolts—I didn't know the rules. And never mind that Richard's lead was really our first 5.10, for that upgrade came later. For the time being I had gone somewhere I never thought I

could go, and become someone I didn't think I could be.

Transcending yourself is a heady business—one that transformed the way I viewed and experienced my life. When I got back to my cave, I found all of my stash had been stolen—my sleeping bag, pack, rope, money, food—all gone. The empty can of plums I had for breakfast sat on a rock—they even filched my spoon. In one swoop about 80 percent of my net worth had vanished—and I couldn't stop grinning!

The psychological breakthroughs always have a larger effect than the physical ones, but that first big one, crossing the 5.10 barrier, was the game changer. After that I was set to try just about anything.

CHAPTER 12

Big Rock

John Long

Big Rock was a longtime practice climbing area frequented by the local military base, the Sierra Club, and the Riverside Mountain Rescue Team, comprised of a few big-ass Jeeps and several dozen mountaineers dispatched to find lost hikers and cars that had driven "off the edge." Legend has it that Big Rock saw its first climbing activity in the late 1940s, when Army Rangers sieged the water trough running up the middle of the 150-foot-high face. In the ensuing years, several generations of Los Angeles– and San Diego–based climbers filled the gaps, mostly via bolt-protected face climbs on the smooth diorite slab. When we finally showed up, the innovative work had been done. The place was largely abandoned and felt like a lost wing of the Smithsonian, the forty-something routes so many relics of the pioneers who used Big Rock as a testing ground for evolving face climbing techniques.

We were still in high school, anxious to follow the chalk marks of the cast of knights who had dominated Southern California climbing for over a decade—then largely and suddenly vanished. We'd heard all about these guys and yet rarely saw or had met one. Naturally they became mythical figures in our young minds.

Their numbers included Paul and Phil Gleason; Pat Callis and Charlie Raymond, who developed Suicide Rock when both were grad students at CalTech; the preternatural Phil Haney, who cranked V10 boulder problems in the late 1960s; and Keith Leaman, John Gosling, the ebullient, chain-smoking Don O'Kelly, and a few others (many were members of an ambitious Eagle Scout group, we later learned). On the gritty Big Rock slabs this gang had established a score of difficult, and in a few cases, desperate face climbs, right into the 5.12a grade, including the improbable English Hanging Gardens. Then they moved on and apparently never returned or looked back. Where were they now? What had gone on here?

Problem was, by the time my generation started climbing, the public was locked out of Big Rock while county workers built the Perris Lake Recreation Area. That never stopped us. We'd park out on the road and sneak in. We were well out of the way of the derricks and skip loaders so by the time a foreman was bothered to chase us off, we usually had ticked a handful of routes and were good to go. When the same cranky boss kept catching us, we worked out an arrangement of leaving a half pint of Old Forrester (in a brown paper bag, of course) on the boulder near the base of the slab. Then we were free to climb all day—no questions asked. These were simpler times.

Several of the more notorious formations, such as the Trapease, had been destroyed, the rock used for dam ballast. But the majority of the routes were still intact. Giant Step and Let it Bleed felt like stiff 5.11 in the lug-soled Kronhoffers and Robbins boots fashionable in the 1960s, but were a touch easier in the smooth-soled Varappe boots that appeared around 1970, got easier still with the EBs of the mid-1970s, and ultimately were moderate 5.10 in the sticky rubber shoes of today. It was always an ego boost to return to Big Rock once every couple seasons with the stylish new slippers,

Big Rock in profile.

JONATHAN BECK

Flexing at The Gallery, Red Rocks. LAURIE NORMANDEAU

sticky as a chameleon's tongue, and waltz up routes that spanked us silly in the hard-soled articles. Man, we sure were getting better . . .

But the glorious days out at Big Rock were when we first visited the place and seemed to have it all to ourselves, knowing we were using the very footholds of the climbers who established the spectacular climbs at Suicide and Tahquitz, where we came of age as adults and as climbers. We might have known next to nothing of these shadow figures, but we came to know their handiwork. Their names were lavishly strewn across the guidebook pages of all the local venues, but they were gone

now and there was nothing but rusty ¼-inch Rawl Drive contraction bolts, widely spaced, to suggest that here at Big Rock they had smoked their Marlboros and told lies and took huge skidding falls, if the rumors are true, taking pictures of each other with Keith Leaman's Kodak Brownie stuffed in a gym sock inside a Folgers Coffee can as they mastered small hold and friction climbing and learned how to engineer face climbs.

I had visited Big Rock perhaps a dozen times over several years before I was made aware (by former Big Rock regular Don O'Kelly) of another formation called The Nose, a 120-foot-high, glass

Haunted House

At an old abandoned crag, the anxious silence reaches back to the long lost who worked out a way before them on the rock. Decades later at the juncture of back then and not yet, we rope up for a route and climb it right now. Riding old routes into the future. Following the line of phantoms whose bones might well be dust. We are the same ghosts following the same holds. Made real at the short span between our fingertips and a razor edge. We dangle side by side at the belay, paying out the memories. The collected astonishment, engrained in the rock, murmurs to those still on their way. Every route is an enchantment. Every crag is a haunted house.

ANDREW BURR

smooth arête with several extreme lines including the supposed "last great prize"—the Roman Nose, which followed the very arête—left over from the previous generation. Located about a quarter mile from the main slab, the lake nearly lapped the lower wall. Of course we had gazed across at this impressive prow many times while belaying from slings on the main face. I was unsure we could ever get onto the rock without a rowboat. Turns out we could, and Tim Powell and I snuck over to The Nose one afternoon and managed the first free ascent of the Roman article—by the skin of our teeth.

Such was our crowning achievement at Big Rock, and it knitted us into the continuum with the heroes we had silently grown up with. Climbing their routes at Big Rock was a rite of passage and by finishing the work they had started on the Roman Nose, we finally connected with those whose shadows we'd chased, up all those slabs, for all those years.

Of course Big Rock was but a brief aside of the larger drama we all eventually found in Yosemite and beyond. Its charms are mostly lost on outsiders but were dear to us owing to its regional legacy, which read like the college diary of the home team. One's early history always exerts a special hold on us; and to every successive generation, Big Rock will feel like a wall of phantoms, when the past meets the present where the rubber meets the rock. It's an unremarkable place but still feels enchanted, as for a moment in time we had it to ourselves, when the dam was rising and the entrance fee was a short dog of cheap bourbon.

CHAPTER 13

For Real

John Long

As largely unproven and wannabe rock stars, the crux of the biscuit was to develop our comfort zone on the rock. Without the confidence of feeling like we belonged up there, all the strength and technique in Tarnation was of no use because we couldn't let it rip. Fear would freeze us stiff. Like on Piton Pooper.

We had to get the hang of being out there on the "sharp end," on the lead, so early on, to accelerate the process, we started leading the few climbs we could out at Rubidoux. This was a ridiculous plan in actual practice, since the climbs—none over 40 feet long—were either easy cracks that we could scale up and down with no rope, or steep faces that had no protection anyway.

Richard was the first of us to start soloing these faces, busting out on the 5.8 route on the right side of Joe Brown boulder. I thought police copters might swoop in and arrest him for criminal endangerment. How could he be up there with no cord?

Suicide Rock, Idyllwild.
KEVIN POWELL

It looked outrageous. Ricky and I were soon up there as well. I felt like a jewel thief, getting away with a secret fortune—and as good as shot dead if we were ever found out. I would chase that feeling for the next 15 years.

Free soloing is not advisable. A fall means hitting the ground from bone-crushing heights, and it's a wonder that none of us did. Probably the only thing that saved us were the countless laps we had already logged on these climbs. Foolish—absolutely, but the exercise helped get our heads prepared for the transition to climbing routes at established areas. And that's what we'd been angling toward since we first hit Mount Rubidoux in our mountaineering boots all those months before. So after a few

weeks soloing the walls out at Rubidoux, following our victory on Piton Pooper, Rick, Richard, and I drove up to Suicide Rock, in Idyllwild, to jump back on the real deal.

Suicide had only been developed for about half a dozen years. The established routes had few ascents; it felt new and almost undiscovered. Following a half-hour, vertical trudge up to the base of the rock, we jumped on the first climb we ran into, a steep lieback leading to a short hand crack and a vertical "bombay," or bottomless, chimney above. The little guidebook called it Frustration, and it had a 5.10 rating. The crux is the first 25 feet, and over that span I came to understand the meaning of the route name, having to hang on the hardest

Embracing the wide "is like dancing with a greased hog."

ANDREW BURR

Free Soloing: Where's the Rope?

Climbing without a rope is inevitable in the trad world. Because the practice covers a range of difficulties, few blanket statements apply across the slab, and there is no objective evaluation that satisfies everyone as to what is dangerous and what is, or should be, routine. While we take up the subject in greater detail later on, know that scrambling unroped on easy ground, on both approaches and descents, can hardly be avoided in many cases. Wherever you feel uncomfortable, whenever you approach that line that if crossed, you fear bad things might happen, break out the rope, or back off. A surprising number of big-name climbers have died on "easy" approaches for reasons ranging from loose rock, to grabbing brittle tree limbs, to being pulled over backward by towering loads, to nothing at all. Often if they are burdened with a "pig" (haul bag), even moderately steep terrain is enough to set a falling climber tumbling rag doll style. That never ends well.

Soloing is always a matter of degrees. Most of us feel okay walking up low-angle slabs, and over time, as we get our legs underneath us and the trad world grows familiar, moderate (3rd and 4th class) soloing comes to feel reasonable, even pleasurable. Mountaineers have been soloing such ground for centuries, so the practice is nothing new. But the potential dangers cannot be overstated.

A young Peter Croft free soloing on Hobbit Book.

CHRIS FALKENSTEIN

Few of us ever solo actual routes, and instead limit our soloing to approaches and descents. After some years of experience, it is only the rare climber who doesn't occasionally solo, over short stretches, into the low 5th-class level. This is not an endorsement or directive to start soloing, especially not at first. It is simply a statement of fact about real-world practices in a majority of cases worldwide. But we must always be our own judge in this regard, knowing the penalties for erring on the high side can bring the curtain down. The climbing community itself is good at self-regulating this practice, and once you get knitted into the crowd, standard practices are soon made known and understood in practical terms. Since soloing is an applied practice, the theory will always seem vague and lacking. More on this later.

Modern camming devices usually provide welcome security for wide cracks previously scaled with little protection—or none at all.

ANDREW BURR

bit and bang in a big bong piton. The crack above felt simple at 5.9, and the chimney was over in a second. Ten minutes later I belayed Ricky up to the ledge and Richard followed in no time. I remember standing up there on that big ledge with my two hometown partners and looking across Strawberry Valley at Tahquitz and thinking, Man, we have arrived.

We returned to the base of the wall, called the Buttress of Cracks, started on one end and ticked off the routes one after the other, all short, one-pitch affairs, mostly low-angle cracks requiring more face climbing than pure jamming. Then I cast off on a deep and nasty-looking gash called the Sword of Damocles, rated 5.9.

We'd been plucking off 5.9s and lower-end

First Hard Routes

As we've seen—and this holds for most trad climbers—breaking into the 5.10 realm is the first big step. Each additional decimal point requires more skill and commitment—often lots of it. Unlike sport climbing, nobody broaches 5.12 trad routes without native athleticism, and serious effort and time invested. But whoever you are, those first few "hard" routes are unforgettable.

I remember my first week in Yosemite and hearing how Rixon's Pinnacle was one of the Valley's first 5.10s. The crux lower pitch felt terribly hard, but the squeeze chimney on the second pitch destroyed us, and I wondered if I had the stuff to ever be a climber. A few days later down at Arch Rock, I led Midterm, a middling 5.10 crack that goes from fingers at the bottom to a polished flare up high. I wasn't used to climbing above protection that I wasn't sure would hold. I wasn't used to such slick rock—it felt like ice. I wasn't used to running the rope on flared chimneys. As you'll learn, busting a hard route is often not so much climbing the beast as dealing with the doubts plaguing any inexperienced but ambitious leader. You're likely going on feel and youth and exuberance. With a meager stockpile of routes under your harness, there's little you know for sure. But this is not entirely correct, either. It just feels like it is.

In fact, by the time I was starting to climb 5.10 cracks I had been active for over a year and had climbed hundreds of routes. 5.10 was not a different animal. It was simply harder—but more of the same. Accept that the first hard routes will be intimidating. This will pass, so soak up the excitement while it lasts. If the doubts are huge, slot an extra cam or two at a convenient place, so if you whip, you're covered. This has been key for me many times. When confidence and momentum start wavering between fight or flight, plugging in an extra piece, right beside the one already clipped, often provides the go-for-it motivation to complete the lead.

Give yourself a fighting chance to succeed: Recruit a belayer you trust entirely so that is not a concern whatsoever; pick a route within a hold or two of your best effort to date; don't rush or get frantic—a failure means nothing at this stage; don't stop in the middle of crux sections to place pro; let yourself put out your best effort; have enough calories and water on board; let your natural desire catch fire—and go.

Expect some air time for those first hard climbs.

MATT KUEHL

Spanked, with the scars to prove it.

MATT KUEHL

Getting Spanked

Expect that as you work up the ladder, some routes are going to spank you hard—and you've just got to like it. During my first few months of climbing, I tried to lead Dogleg at Joshua Tree, a steep 5.8 crack, and totally flamed out at the halfway point, barely 40 feet off the ground. My first 5.9 found me hanging on the nuts. One of my first 5.10s out at Suicide saw me lowering off several times before I finally swarmed up the steep gash.

Failures are often more instructive than when we waltz over a route. We rarely fail owing to a lack of power. More likely our approach is off, our technique a little lacking—it can be a dozen or more things that beat us back to the ground. Not to worry. There's usually some way to retrieve your protection and not leave expensive gear behind. Rather than throw yourself at the climb once more, ponder your last effort and learn something. Develop a strategy and consider options for the next time. If there's a technique that is especially troublesome and which sent you down, find an easier route and practice on that. Trying routes unrealistically above your limit is a sure way to practice poor technique and develop bad habits. A constructive spanking is often where you learn something. A destructive spanking happens on routes so far beyond you that you can only get worked and discouraged. In fact, corporal punishment is almost always counterproductive and can slow the learning process. That much understood, accept that failing is part of the learning process; no climber enjoys a 100 percent success rate, or anything close to it.

5.10s for going on 5 or 6 hours and were feeling invincible. But the moment I wiggled into that greasy flare, maybe 40 feet up, I had absolutely no idea what to do or how to do it.

With limited experience on the real crags and established routes, we were vastly ignorant about wide cracks, and the laundry list of mottos and tricks for climbing them: always counterpressure; arm bar whenever possible; heel and toe jam to unweight the arms; bridge to rest; go slow and husband your strength; resist the urge to burrow deep for security, rather stay on the outside where you can move; and never, ever thrash.

I started right side in and got nowhere, then switched to left side in, but couldn't manage to swim up the short flare. I ground both knees raw, trying to chimney the damn thing and couldn't. I nearly pulled my fingers off, yarding on tiny face edges, attempting to face climb a chimney. I ended up in an all-out, no-holds-barred wrestling match, slipping and ratcheting and flopping my way up, making twenty moves for each foot gained and totally wasting myself, using no technique and thrashing like a gaffed tarpon. Here was a straight technique problem and I was trying to muscle it— and I was losing badly.

Sword of Damocles was named after a perilously loose chopper flake the size of a longboard, and which the guidebook said to avoid at all costs. A protection bolt had been placed on the face so one could climb around said "sword" of this man Damocles, a purported Greek who could kiss my ass. Since I could not manage this flare by any means, and had ruined myself trying, and was too proud and stupid to back off, I mounted the fatal sword directly, heaving up the thing like a Hawaiian Kanak scaling a palm tree, the floating blade shifting horribly, dirt and pebbles raining out the bottom as Rick and Richard dashed down into the forest for cover, basically abandoning the belay. Eventually Richard, for fear of getting guillotined, belayed me roughly 50 feet back from the wall, where he was lost from sight, just the line snaking out of the pine trees. God knows how that sword didn't rip off the wall.

Anyhow, by toeing off the very quick of the blade, so to speak, I reached some holds above and finished off. My partners followed and had just as hard a time, but managed without having to bear hug the sword.

I'd been shut down hard and I knew it, knew that I'd thieved my way past the difficulties through recklessness. I needed to bone up on my flares. Anything featuring steep faces and thin edges—replicating the climbing at Rubidoux—we could usually dick straight off. But as we quickly learned, when other techniques were required, we didn't know what we were doing.

Next time I walked past the Sword of Damocles a few months later, I looked up and the sword was gone.

CHAPTER 14

Woes of the Wide Cracks

Peter Croft

One spot on the globe had become the center of the climbing universe: Yosemite Valley. Like a black hole, it produced an all-powerful and overriding gravity that sucked all climbers into its orbit, into this Eden of sunny white granite, green meadows, and all the ice cream you could eat. It had become more than just a place to come test yourself. It was where all the new techniques were being invented even as the new ethics took form. Not just Mecca, Yosemite Valley was the future. We had to go.

In a crusty Toyota Corolla, rusted around the edges by a dozen winters of salted Canadian highways, we piled in four teenagers' worth of crazy and headed south of the border. We made the thousand

Yosemite had the biggest walls we had ever seen . . .

WALTER FLINT

miles in a valiant push, fueled by Doritos, candy, and all kinds of sugared sodas, never stopping longer than what it took to take a leak and fuel up. After 24 hours we settled in under the biggest walls we had ever seen.

Strangely, we went to bed in California and seemingly woke up in coastal Canada. Being April, storms were not all that unusual, but this time they crushed our spirits. For 2 days it rained on the Valley floor and snowed up high. Finally it dawned

clear and we rushed to the rock. For some reason we thought it was a good idea to first tick a number of the short routes at the base of El Cap. Arriving at the cliff under crystal-blue skies, we were surprised to find the place vacant. The wall was stunning—the lower 2,000 feet of water-streaked orange stone melding into the upper 1,000 feet encased in gleaming ice.

It rapidly warmed and soon large sheets of ice were separating from the headwall half a mile above,

The Valley of Light.

ROBERT MIRAMONTES

alternately spiraling, glinting, and Frisbeeing at shocking speeds—like window panes from a 3,000-foot skyscraper. The ice sheets were beautiful to watch, till they hit the lower-angled section of the wall below. We were still uncoiling ropes when the first of us got hit. Then it was all dodging ricochets while belaying, and taking it like a man if you were leading. After all, we thought, this was probably one of those things you had to deal with if you wanted to climb in the Valley. All of us got nailed with ice chunks the size of plums and tangerines, and one of us caught a nasty glancing blow from a cantaloupe. Yosemite was more than living up to the hype—like a cross between rock climbing and the Himalayas.

We were (luckily) living proof that a little bit of knowledge is a dangerous thing. We assumed "The

World-Class Venues

There are many reasons to visit world-class areas. Foremost it is to sample, test, and thrill yourself on routes that are the embodiment of that rock type and skill set. There's also the wonder of traveling, connecting with foreign climbers, and the feeling of entering into a charmed nexus somewhat like a battlefield and to experience what is going down. Yosemite has all of those qualities in spades. What's more, photographer Ansel Adams has burned the timeless Valley vistas into world consciousness with his many images. In a milieu of such brilliant reliefs, the Valley, more than any other place, has come to exemplify rock climbing to the world. From boulders to big walls, Yosemite remains the planet's showpiece of stone. Certainly there are other locales with galaxies of exposed rock, but difficult access and poor weather have made them far less attractive. California sunshine, cheap living, and granite gigantism have combined to make Yosemite the point of convergence for every trad rock climber from Toronto to Timbuktu.

For the tradster especially, it is important to make the pilgrimage. The Valley has played key roles in every part of trad climbing's development. From a historical point of view, it helps to understand where climbing came from. From an instructional point of view, few places will school you like Yosemite. And from a fun-hog's point of view, you will get more bang-for-buck thrills than anywhere else on earth. Like they've said for going on 50 years: "You gotta go."

Peter Croft stemming out on Coarse and Buggy, Joshua Tree.

GREG EPPERSON

Yosemite . . . like a cross between rock climbing and the Himalayas.

BEN HORTON

Captain" was simply a bigger Squamish, and since we had that place dialed we had no need of embarrassing ourselves by asking local advice. That same mindset would've seen us traveling to Sumatra, say, drinking ditch water and eating fruit bats raw.

Of course we were stupid. That's what first-timers do in Yosemite—stupid stuff. We also received our first spankings on smooth Valley cracks. El Cap is especially glassy granite and nowhere more so than on the glacier- and Noob-polished stone along the base of the southeast face. Moby Dick Center

was the route I most remember. First knuckle led to second knuckle finger jams, feet paddling on the smoothest surface I had experienced. Pleased as punch on firing the greasy 5.10a finger crack at the start, I forged on, certain that the upper 5.8 fist-to-off-width jams were a mere formality. The progress I'd made up to that point, however, stuttered to a halt in the face of this supposedly moderate terrain. I clenched my fists and stuffed my toes and still felt like I was falling out backwards. Most of the jams I'd pulled before were on crystalline or sandpaper-rough

Wide Crack Smackdown

There is no technique that can deflate an ego as quickly as off-widths and chimneys. Don't take this personally—wide cracks hate everyone. It is not enough to drop your standard a number grade. Try two or three. Much of what you have learned, especially in sport climbing, flies out the window when climbing wide cracks—or trying to. Admonitions like "Don't use your knees!" or "Always maintain three points of contact!" quickly become obsolete in the no-holds-barred world of wideness. Where most rockwork could reasonably be compared to climbing a ladder, off-widths and squeezes are accurately described as the awkward fusion of spelunking and "Lucha Libre"–style wrestling. Every part of your body comes into play, including parts you were unaware of even having, particularly in the beginning as you struggle to make something, anything, stick. It is not that uncommon to see climbers' noses and ears raspberried with scrapes following their first attempts at some wide testpiece.

If at all possible, wrangle an off-size crack ace to join you on your first forays into the wide—and get him or her to go first. Watch and learn. See how the heel-toe jams, knees, and chicken wings work. More than anything, pay attention to how Off-Width Man, after every move, is able, unbelievably, to rest. Food for thought for when you go up next and get spanked. And you'd better believe it—you will.

Perry Beckham
on Hypertension.

PAT MORROW

Local Lore

When visiting any new area, the first order of business is to check out the scene. Stop by the local mountain shop for weather updates and info on closures due to raptor nesting and so forth. Locate the climbers' campground and check the notice board for pertinent beta. Your best source for the inside scoop is always the locals. They will be the ones with more than just the basics. They'll have the best clue as to which routes dry out first after a storm, which ones get the most sun or shade, which climbs or descents might have been affected by rockfall, and which place has the best french fries and the cheapest beer.

Remember to act like a visitor. Arrogance is unattractive and will set you up for sandbagging. Politeness and humility will net you all the information you need to safely get out on the rock.

cliffs in Canada or Washington—quite fake-able if poor technique is all you have. This El Cap granite was of another magnitude, and I quickly realized I had neither the skills nor the courage to go for it.

Luckily there was a jammed chockstone with some old rappel slings drooped over it. For now, this would be my summit. I clipped in and lowered off. Over the next few weeks I would climb dozens of polished Yosemite cracks, cracks that start as thin fingers and slowly widen to the dreaded off-width. And every time, as luck would have it, a jammed chockstone would appear at the base of the widening, wreathed with colorful runners marking the end of the climb—for me and many others. Of course not all of these Thank God natural anchors were entirely natural—many before me had failed

to measure up to the much-feared off-size cracks for which Yosemite is infamous.

We all flailed on the wide, and in fact, most visitors steered clear of the heinous-size fissures. The few climbers who took to the wideness as a matter of course were the case-hardened Valley denizens schooled long ago. To see these Chosen Ones chug up a world-class flare or off-size crack was like watching a magic show. They looked to all the world like they had been sashaying these monstrosities all their lives. What I was to learn was that nobody looks good the first time. Or the first twenty times. In fact, as a climbing destination, Yosemite brutally exposes your weaknesses. And, man alive, had I been exposed.

Starting the second pitch of Valhalla.

GREG EPPERSON

CHAPTER 15

Valhalla and the Birth of "The Stonemasters"

John Long

Ricky, Richard, and I met Mike Graham up at Suicide one Sunday afternoon. We were fast friends immediately. Mike was also a wannabe rock star still in his mid-teens. Known in later years as Gramicci, Mike worked at Ski Mart, a big outdoor recreation retailer in his hometown of Newport Beach, and he kept us all dialed in with the finest gear. Mike also thought it essential that our growing little band should have our own logo, in the form of a sizzling lightning bolt (forever chalked beneath Yosemite's famous boulder problem, Midnight Lightning). It was through Mike that we met Gib Lewis and Bill Antel and the other dozen or so "members" of our informal group of So Cal punk

BEN HORTON

climbers who called themselves "The Stonemasters." It was never much of a club, but we were fanatics nonetheless.

We had a name and a lightning bolt and marching orders to peaks unknown, but as a group we'd done little more than repeat Suicide's standard hardman routes and shoot off our mouths. We desperately needed some dramatic victory to assert

our arrival and establish ourselves as the shizat. But nobody was quite sure how.

The king of Suicide Rock was Bud Couch, the last, and perhaps the best, of the traditional line of Idyllwild masters that ran back 40 years, to John Mendenhall, the father of California rock climbing. Bud had his circle of partners, whose names and photos were peppered throughout the guidebooks

Fear of Failure

The aspiring rock star never wants to fail. But we can't start skirting routes where failure seems possible, even likely. Better to accept failures as part of the learning process and forget the value judgments. Try to imagine the effort you might muster if you never feared failure. You'd approach each climb entirely open and willing to succeed. This is not some Pollyanna-on-a-cord strategy, but a conscious effort to avoid submarining our efforts before even tying into the line. Imagine the shy dude trying to get a dance at the club. He's so gripped about getting dissed that he might never ask anyone, and when he does, he's so dialed off and rattled that Sheila takes one gander at the sad sack and says he must be kidding.

There are many ways of dealing with fear, and what works for one may not work for another. Some days you'll want to "ride" topropes—on others you'll shoot for the stars. Whatever method you choose, know that fear of failure is a common challenge for every climber of every ability and each of us will have to deal with it at some time.

Wide crack. Big Bro. Raw fear.

MATT KUEHL

*Pulling for glory on the
Sunshine Face.*

KEVIN POWELL

*Darrell Hensel running the rope on the sparsely protected **Obscured by Clouds**, Suicide Rock.*

KEVIN POWELL

and on the walls of local restaurants and bars. We were awestruck by these guys and secretly wanted their blessing. But they'd have no part of us. We were too loud and obnoxious. We had to find our own way.

The hottest climb on the planet was the new Couch route, Valhalla. Bud had done all the hard work of placing the bolts and leading each individual pitch. But Couch and his two partners, Larry Reynolds and Mike Dent, had yet to put the whole thing together in a continuous ascent, bottom to top.

Enter Robs Muir and Jim Hoagland, two UC Riverside students, both standouts at Mount

Climbing with No Pressure

Taking pressure off yourself to succeed is a simple concept to grasp but not so easy to implement. The case of Valhalla shows how two ignorant kid climbers can accidentally approach a seminal climb with virtually no pressure. Looking back I realize the trick was the elimination of all expectations. We went up merely curious to see what happened, what the route looked and felt like. Consciously eliminating expectations is a magical process that's almost impossible to do. Expectations, if we look closely, are attempts to determine the outcome and avoid an equivocal process where anything can, and often does, happen.

So perhaps the trick here is not so much trying to dump expectations, as developing a tolerance for the process, for not knowing what might happen. The true definition of an adventure is an endeavor in which the ending is not known beforehand. To what extent can we come to thrive on this, as opposed to trying to eliminate it through expectations? Approaching a climb with a "Let's see" attitude fosters curiosity as opposed to believing we must succeed or all is lost.

In a word, we often achieve our best results by forgetting about results. Case in point was a route called Hades, at Suicide Rock. While the climb was likely low end 5.13, the very last move of a two-pitch climb stumped me for 2 days. The second day I ate New Age vittles in the morning followed by meditation, recited affirmations all the way to the base—and promptly fell off low down on the first pitch. On my third try, I drank five cups of joe, listened to acid rock on a boombox all the way up the trail, smoked a cigar at the base of the wall, and sent the climb first try because I didn't care what happened. Point being that by whatever means, once you dump expectations, your boots have wings—or so it seems.

Amy Jo Ness, High Priestess of the High Sierras.

AMY NESS

Rubidoux and Suicide. It took the pair several tries, but while Bud and the others were coiling ropes, Robs and Jim managed the first continuous ascent of Valhalla. This was the initial statement from climbers of my generation and we were anxious to ride Robs and Jim's slipstream. But Valhalla had become such a monolith in my mind it seemed out of reach for now, and possibly forever. Robs and Jim seemed like gods to us.

It must have been a weekday. There was no one at the rock at all. Rick Accomazzo and I had been climbing all day around the corner and were stumbling by when, on a whim, we went over to the base of Valhalla to take our first close look. We'd done most of the other routes on the Sunshine Wall, so we were not strangers to the work.

The first pitch started with a mantle and just above we could see two bolts closely spaced, so I said, "What do you say we fiddle around on this first bit?" Fine by Ricky. We had no intention of doing the whole route. I tied in and cast off and kept thinking I was going to run into some upside-down backwards move requiring three arms, but aside from a thin step-down by the second bolt, the first pitch felt routine. Like the stuff we did out at Rubidoux most every day. No big.

We found ourselves on a good ledge looking out right at the steep, burnished wall. The climbing looked straightforward to the first bolt—just a traverse right on big scallops. I said there was no harm in going out and eyeballing the thing, just for future reference. Ricky said, sure, have a look. We had no plan or even desire to climb this pitch, but

Kevin Powell reefing on meager carbuncles during an early assault on Paisano Pinnacle. The only problem was there were no good holds, the only protection was the rope flipped over a rounded knob, and the route didn't go at all.

KEVIN POWELL

we both were very curious to see genuine 5.11 up close. I traversed out and clipped the first bolt and stood there on a big black foothold looking up at the crux bit just above.

Surprisingly, I could see what looked like good, sharp edges, and the second bolt was only a few body lengths overhead as well. Rick said it didn't look all that far to the next bolt and anyhow, the rock below was smooth as a window so any fall would surely be a harmless skidder. This was all true, so I agreed to go up a few moves and check out the holds. Just a probe. A look-see.

What was happening here, I later realized, was that by placing no pressure on ourselves to succeed, we were avoiding the fear of failure and were totally free to pony up our best possible effort. This is a point worth understanding, since fear of failure is such a limiting factor for many climbers. And when a route has a big reputation, as Valhalla did at that time, self-generated intimidation can freeze a climber on the holds. Beginning a lead plagued by doubts is a poor starting point—it's easy to see why. A more fruitful approach is to suspend judgment about your prospects and find out through doing or trying what you can and cannot do. In some strange, paradoxical way, going into a difficult lead with a kind of curious indifference, to the point of not caring, might eliminate the pressure and free you up to throw down your best effort.

Anyway, moving out onto the second pitch of Valhalla, I experienced one of those odd times when I was aware of watching myself, almost as a spectator, as I climbed. I didn't feel any pressure because I still was in "discovery" mode, not at all going for it. Just scoping the holds, thinking I'd jump off after a body length or so. This was, after all, supposed to be the hardest high-angle slab climb in America, if not the entire world.

I started up, climbing slowly, working off good edges. A couple moves and the bolt's at my feet. I still felt solid and Ricky said the edges were looking pretty cherry and that the crux was just above me.

I cranked up another move and paused, clinging hard but still in control. Then I spotted a bomber slanting edge up and left. I latched it and my body automatically yarded up and I stretched out my right hand and latched a good shelf. Then the world came rushing back and I was no longer watching myself. I was in my body on the crux of Valhalla.

Ricky's voice got pinched and he said, "Man, you mantle that thing and we got it!" No way to reverse it now. And if there was anything I was doing a lot of in those days, it was mantles. I pressed it out, clipped the bolt and Ricky started laughing. I wondered out loud if that was really the crux and Ricky said he was sure of it—he'd been studying the description in the guidebook for weeks. I felt more confused than excited. I'd just climbed the crux of Valhalla on my first try and had no idea how to process the experience because in my mind the thing was some otherworldly climb, miles beyond what us kids could manage.

Then Ricky says, "Hurry up, I want to try," and a little while later, Ricky hiked it as well, something we attributed to having found the "hidden hold," that big edge out and left at the crux. But the fact is, we had been doing far harder thin-hold climbing out at Rubidoux for going on a year. Now our climbing was starting to catch up to our bouldering, and things were heating up quickly.

Aside from removing the pressure, our bouldering background had taught us that any climb, no matter how long or short, must be climbed a hold at a time. Most bouldering is so difficult that if you start the climb by worrying about the summit, your mind cannot be present for the climbing in front of you. Better to forget the summit, develop tunnel vision, and take things in small increments: I'm getting to that knob, then I'll reassess and try for the next bolt, or the shelf, etc. That way, one long climb becomes a series of small ones.

Valhalla, en toto, was too big a bite for me. But I discovered I could climb the thing, one small hold at a time. Even when you are totally intimidated by a climb, you can often give yourself permission to go another 10 feet to the next protection, and maybe another 10 feet after that. No one has to, or can, climb an entire route right this second. It's always a process.

Next weekend we climbed Valhalla once again, making the third continuous ascent, with Richard leading the first pitch. This was a huge step for us because we were still so unproven—especially to ourselves. Over the next few years I must have climbed Valhalla a dozen times, but it was never the same as that first time with Ricky. That's when we first got the idea that the climbing world would hear from us.

CHAPTER 16

The Bird and Reed's Left

John Long

I was 17 and had 3 weeks before starting my senior year in high school, so I took the Greyhound bus up to Yosemite. I had read every stitch ever written on Yosemite climbing—and none of it prepared me for the magnitude of the place.

The big blue Greyhound bus dropped into the Valley and we chugged along the loop road, roughly a mile across from El Capitan. The window, about the size of a garage door, cut off the crown of the granite monolith no matter how low I squatted in my seat. It looked . . . huge.

The bus dumped us out at Yosemite Lodge and

I headed for Camp 4 which, since the 1930s, had remained the traditional hang for climbers, and where I hoped to meet that legion of heroes and maniacs I had read about in *Ascent, Mountain,* and the *American Alpine Journal.* I had shot my mouth off to anyone who would listen, weaving preposterous narratives about my plans to get up on those big-ass Valley walls and pull for glory, cha cha cha. One of the guys I had yelled at down at Tahquitz was Jim Donini, who later would help rewrite Patagonia

climbing history and who had several Valley seasons under his harness. Our secret hero and nemesis from Suicide Rock, the flinty Bud Couch, had recently failed on a Valley testpiece called Left Side of Reed's Pinnacle, and I was dead set on getting that climb out of the way before I set up my tent.

I ran into Donini within minutes of stumbling into Camp 4 and he introduced me to another guy who looked like a recently paroled bank robber who'd spent a few decades on the rock pile—the

The Valley.

KARL "BABA" BRALICH

rippling muscles, the shoulder-length hair, and a handlebar moustache besides. "His name is Long and he wants to go climbing," is all Donini said. The bank robber presented his hand and said, "Jim. What do you want to climb?" I said, "The Left Side of Reed's Pinnacle." Mustachioed Jim said, "Grab your stuff."

I got my gear and left my backpack in Donini's tent and a few minutes later we were smoking cigarettes and hitchhiking down to Reed's. My new friend was gracious and mostly listened while I blindsided him with all my crazy ambitions to climb "everything" in no time. I was unsure about Jim's credentials as a rock climber—looking like a guy off a chain gang and all—but figured I'd lead

Continued on page 101

The Bird and Reed's Left   **97**

Off-Width Climbing: Treading Treacle

Dave Rose once said, "Cracks are fine—till they get out of hand." Dave was talking about off-width cracks—wider-than-fists, smaller-than-chimney-size fissures on which the word "thrutch" was first coined. They typically are strenuous, desperate, repetitive, and difficult to protect. *Trad Climber's Bible* is not a tome on climbing technique, but we'll broach the subject here, again, for several reasons.

Most of us approach an off-width route like that hideous aunt who makes you kiss her on the lips and do yard work in the beating sun with no water, no pay, and no thanks. Naturally you avoid her. Problem is, you can't. Not if you want to climb the big, legendary routes. So you learn to cajole your Aunty, using finesse, not power or raw effort. Slowly, as you come to fear her less and less, you find she is not without her charms. Eventually you might even come to enjoy her company. But never straight off. Never. Everyone's first impression runs the gamut from revulsion to terror, frustration, fear and loathing. You try and force the issue and she plays you like a cheap guitar, slashing at your knees, your elbows, and your pride. She'll have you know you are a pretender, a chump, a silly little Nancy boy with no sac and no chance. Until you take her on her own terms, you'll never move past her. And you'll have to, because she's the gatekeeper to some of the finest rock climbs in the world, where Aunt Hagatha always seems to pay a guest appearance for a pitch or a short stretch—just that section where you have to romance her straight up and cannot thieve your way past with charm and bullshit. You kiss her on the lips—or you bail.

Sounds horrible, and it is. The trick is to keep the learning curve as steep as you can so your time in mortal combat is short. Most areas have some manner of off-width crack on which to practice. You suck it up and put in the time to get fluent on this the most difficult technique of them all. Again, it's never fun at first.

Off-width covers a wide range of sizes, roughly from 4 to 10 inches, beyond which we can usually slip inside the beast. Mastering the various chicken wing and arm-barring configurations, as well as foot stacking, is a matter of seeing the techniques done and then practicing same. Everyone has to figure these out for himself—there's no other way. But here's a few rules of thumb that hold for every off-width you will ever do.

First is the "ceremony" (coined by Vedauwoo, Wyoming, climbers steeped in the wide), whereby you choose one side or the other to jam in the crack—meaning you're going "left-side-in" or "right-side-in." Considerations include which edge has the better lip to grasp, and whether or not the crack leans left or right. If it leans right, you go left side in, and vice versa.

Next, resist the impulse to burrow deep. This might seem more secure but it makes upward progress gruesome by constricting movement. Stay mobile by staying on the outside, finessing the beast with counter pressure and magic. The inside leg is usually in a leg lock while the outside foot is heel-toe jamming. Try never to thrash—you'll only lose a pound of flesh and fag yourself. "Chicken wings" only work one way; arm bars work best. In a good arm bar, the arm and hand are placed diagonally down and away from the shoulder, elbow higher than the hand, so you're not so much torqueing as sort of mantling off the "bar."

Off-width technique is largely feel and resembles a centipede movement where the upper body is momentarily locked off while the legs are ratcheted up and locked, allowing the torso to move up in turn, ad nauseum. Seeing a true off-width master is a miraculous experience, and assures us the thing can be done after all. But till you get some practice, it's likely to feel like treading treacle.

Treading treacle.

MATT KUEHL

Jay Anderson on Off-Widths Are Beautiful (5.10), Potash Road, Moab, Utah.
ANDREW BURR

Continued from page 97

Reed's Pinnacle all kinds of ways if need be. And Bud Couch could watch and weep.

We scrambled off the Tioga Road and up to the base of Reed's Pinnacle. When I peered up at that yawning cleft soaring about 250 feet directly overhead, smooth as an urn, dead vertical, pitch black and laser cut, I almost shit myself. I think Jim was also feeling a little spooked, since he suggested I take the first lead, a 120-foot-long cavernous knee chimney with a few crap pins for protection. After the lead I found myself at a chilling belay off slung flakes. Above me a flawless squeeze chimney ran for 30 or so feet and abruptly pinched down to 5 to 7 inches. The pitch looked impossibly steep and unprotectable. Jim's lead.

Jim put a couple small wired nuts on his rack and started up the heinous slash, running it out about 20 feet straight off the belay before slotting a #1 wired Stopper behind a flake. Apparently, the climbing was considerably easier than it looked because Jim was ratcheting up that crack with the greatest of ease. Then, just as he wormed into the crux, slotting his left knee deep into the narrowing crack, the wired nut fell out and slid down the rope. He had no protection in at all. Easy or not, I yelled up to Jimbo that if he whipped, we'd surely perish. He casually looked down and said, "I could call this 5.7 if I wanted to," and proceeded to motor up the crack without pause. A few minutes later he yelled down for me to start climbing.

These Yosemite climbs looked horrific, it was true, but judging by Jim's performance they were actually rather moderate—or so I thought. I learned differently once I had thrashed to about 10 feet

Levitation—Hand Stacking

Advanced off-width technique is not required for anything but off-width testpieces. Godzilla arm bars, chicken wings, foot stacking, and so forth will get you up most anything else. However if you develop aspirations for the notorious "wide," you'll have to make levitation (hand stacking) a special study. There are a wealth of articles and videos that go into exhaustive detail about the whole business, which at this level is a combination of Greco-Roman wrestling and an Olympic high bar routine, with a little Jungle Gym thrown in for flavah. Like most everything else pertaining to climbing off-widths, hand stacking, roof shuffling, and jamback techniques all require lots of practice to even understand. Mastery can take several years, and puts you in elite company.

Hand stacking, Veduvoo.

GREG EPPERSON

Protecting Off-Widths, Flares, and Chimneys

Off-width cracks were first protected with wooden wedges slugged into the crack. Then came steel and finally aluminum "bong-bong" pitons (or simply, bongs)—name derived from the sound when hammered. Next came tube chocks, then Big Bros (still very useful), and finally big cams custom made for wide work. All these protection devices are nearly as huge and unwieldy as the climbs themselves.

Because friction and grating are problems, go with a low profile harness, a thin rope, and get that knot as tight and flat as you possibly can. Anything that can get hung up surely will. Rack all gear on a shoulder sling, never on the harness gear loops, and arrange the sling so the rack hangs on the "outside," opposite the arm bar. If you are a harness-gear-loop guy and don't have a gear sling, make certain to rack the cams, etc. on the outside. Because the gear is so bulky, take no more than what you intend to use.

Big Bros are notoriously finicky and require practice to place well, or at all; but once you get the knack, they allow you to keep the heavy and bulky cams to a minimum. Brainchild of late climber and engineer, Craig Luebben, Big Bros involve two aluminum tubes, one sliding within the other, plus a stout inner spring that expands the tubes. Once the device is spun into place, its beveled edges flush against the walls of the crack, and a twisting collar locks the tubes in place. Clip and go. Big Bros can be placed with one hand, but not nearly with the ease of a cam. And a poor placement is often no good at all. They require parallel-sided cracks without radical flaring and irregularities. Many off-width cracks tapper in the deeper you reach inside and traditional pro can be placed therein. Otherwise it's Big Bros and big cams all the way. Per placing Big Bros, get a tutorial from an expert, or look at videos online. Practice will make clear

below the belay. I had climbed a handful of off-width cracks out at Josh, but none with such perfect symmetry and on such smooth rock. I wasn't so much climbing as swimming up the thing. And Joshua Tree grit is forgiving. If you muff a move, something is bound to stick on the gnarled surface. But a sloppy foot stack or heel and toe jam on the Valley's smooth granite would leave me hanging off an arm bar, buttering out by the second. Reed's Left felt like oiled teak. If delicate face climbing is some fancy, top-shelf cocktail, this was Polish vodka—neat.

Maybe a dozen feet shy of the belay, after what felt like miles of battling and slipping out backwards, trying every foot stack, arm bar, and funky limb configuration I could imagine, I ran out of ways to make my body conform to the hateful dimensions of that flared and burnished crack. I was nearly out of gas. But I gathered myself enough to listen to Jim's move by move instructions, flashing a hand out right to a feature to prevent an embarrassing ripper at the very end, then belly crawling onto the belay ledge more dead than alive. It was nothing what twenty pages of yammering never can.

A popular technique on especially hard off-widths is to attach a cam to a long sling and slide it up the pitch as you go, creating a "perma-toprope." Of course the crack has to maintain a fairly uniform size for this to work. Also know that big cams are prone to walking as rope drag is applied.

Flares and chimneys present special problems because the crack is either too flared or too wide for most protection devices. There is often some pro to be gotten in cracks nearby. Sometimes bolts are added. Otherwise, there's nothing. Don't fall.

Queen of the off-widths, Pamela Shanti "Six" Pack, with the tools of her cruel trade.

ANDREW BURR

but stubbornness and fluke—and Jim's advice—that carried me to the belay.

This was my first of many trials by fire with the dreaded off-width climbing. Over the following decade I would get the technique squared away rather nicely, but those initial efforts, probably totaling thirty or more routes, and stretching well into that first summer, were hateful. Many climbers become proficient or even world-class at other techniques while avoiding "the wide" with a vengeance because it is so counterintuitive. However,

that really limits your possibilities since many long climbs, from Yosemite to Zion and beyond, entail a little or a lot of wide crack climbing.

Jim let me lead the next and last pitch to the top, just more 5.8 scampering, and my first Yosemite climb was a done thing. Bud Couch could weep in his beer—again. But my days of shooting off my pie-hole about climbing "everything" were destroyed by that brutal off-width fracture. Slowly, over time, I caught on and the technique became familiar—but never easy.

It wasn't till we rapped back to the base of Reed's that I saw the name scribbled on the flap of his pack with a felt pen: Jim Bridwell. I hadn't been played, exactly, but that convict on the other end of my rope, who had just free-soloed the crux of Reed's Left and coaxed me up by a whisker, was at that moment the finest all-around rock climber on earth. And we were just getting started . . .

Pamela Pack in the belly of the wide.

ANDREW BURR

CHAPTER 17

Arrowhead Arête

John Long

Our Rubidoux mentor, Paul Gleason, had a brother named Phil who was younger than Paul but half a dozen years older than us, and who fooled away most summers climbing rocks in Yosemite. When I once more found myself in the Valley during a short break from school, minus my Upland partners, Rick and Richard, I searched out Phil and glommed onto him like a chigger on a dog. I had big plans, of course, but Phil was content to try our partnership on for size before heading onto the mighty big stuff I kept yakking about. He suggested the Arrowhead Arête, a storied route that when first climbed by Mark Powell in 1956, was likely the most continuously difficult free climb in America—according to historical sources.

Powell was another Tahquitz pioneer and the first acknowledged American climbing bum, so I was happy to follow familiar footsteps. Whatever was good enough for Mark, was good enough for me, I said. I was all about the Arrowhead Arête, la-d-da. When Phil asked what I knew about the climb, I said, "Loads," and he laughed. I didn't know the Arrowhead Arête from Tuba City, and we both knew it.

Phil had culled some notes from several guidebooks and an old copy of *Ascent*. We quickly reviewed the material, committing the route to memory: 750 feet long; normally climbed in eight pitches in 4 to 7 hours. The approach was a humdinger said to take 2 to 3 hours. Likewise for the descent. The route, according to the guidebook, was obligatory for hardmen throughout the 1960s, was

"committing with incredible exposure, finishing on a striking knifeblade ridge. Though rated 5.8, this route is only appropriate for confident and fast 5.9 leaders." On a subsequent ascent, Phil added, Powell had fallen high on the route and suffered a compound fracture to his ankle. So the venture was no gimme.

Next morning Phil and I trudged from Camp 4 a couple miles over to the Church Bowl and found the switchbacks leading up Indian Canyon. We hit the trail at speed and pulled up beneath the Arête in less than an hour. All that slogging to Tahquitz and other Sierra peaks and we could march like Sherpas. When we busted out of the trees, Arrowhead Arête, a thin, angular buttress, fired overhead like the edge of a colossal tomahawk. Holds looked ample, the angle steep. We tied in and shot up the butte, narrowing as it mounted higher, passing bulges and roofs on a wall that availed itself to every lover of vertical life.

Unlike many Yosemite climbs that are tucked into cracks and chimneys, the Arête zagged from this feature to that, in order for the climber to arrange protection, while the climbing was mostly on divine edges peppering the naked wall. As it usually goes on big face climbs, regardless of location or difficulty, routefinding and rope management—keeping the lines nicely lap-coiled, watching for potential snags, and sagely engineering pro and slings to reduce rope drag—were the keys to efficient ascent.

Arrowhead Arête was well traveled, with boot marks in the lichen and patina, and occasional fixed gear vaguely pointed the way. Following the line

Amy Harris in tree pose on Arrowhead Arête.

DAVE N. CAMPBELL

Lower slabs, Arrowhead Arête.

MIKE MORLEY

Jeff Crow on Arrowhead Arête.

MIKE MORLEY

of least resistance was key. As with most face routes, there are fifty ways to go. Choosing the "best" line is a matter of priorities, and involves decisions per rock quality (avoiding or tackling choss), purity of line (whether you traverse around, or take a direct and more difficult line), protection (veering to features with obvious nut and cam placements), and rope management (taking a clean line to avoid drag). A great physical climber might be a clueless liability on the lead, oblivious to all nuance, wasting time on poor choices, needlessly adding danger and difficulty. The Arrowhead Arête was a quintessential

trad route because it called on all these basic skills and more.

But my first trip up the Arrowhead Arête made one thing clear, or rather, Phil made it clear: There are two approaches to routefinding, and I was leaning too heavily on the wrong one, and wasn't getting far. Sure, there were some scuff marks in the lichen, but there were no bolts. So trying to find signs of the last party, like a Navajo tracker following an outlaw, I saw little and wondered what the hell. Phil said true routefinding was what the first ascent party did, which is to look up, put a mental line together connecting the most obvious features, and take it from there.

For someone with so little experience, this is a daunting task. Unlike most Yosemite climbs, which follow spectacular crack and corner systems obvious as Vernal Falls, Arrowhead Arête was half the time out on the open face. The guidebook mentioned the big features, but which ones? There was every reason to want more info, and to have some solid criteria or protocol that would settle exactly where to go. Neither existed, and I had to like it, then and now. You look for signs. You follow the probable line. Initially, you guess at both. You find a way somehow, less from science than from trying things on for size, one body length at a time.

We all too soon found ourselves on the grainy "Great White Flake," a short ways below the summit. It was easy to appreciate why Arrowhead Arête was an all-time classic. The convex aspect of the adventure, sticking right out there on the cutting edge, was so stimulating we barely noticed the darkening clouds till the first drops nearly drilled us off the face at a short 4th-class stretch one pitch below the top. Phil said storms in Yosemite were no joke and that we had to get off the wall—fast.

Phil started paddling up a blackened 5.7 face, and in seconds a thick sheet of water was splashing over his hands and feet. I wasn't sure what was keeping him on the wall. He somehow swam to the top of the arête and lashed off on a pulpit so slender and exposed it looked like he was perched atop a chimney stack. I was glad to have a toprope, dunking hands underwater and clawing around for an edge or rill—somewhat like panning for holds—and pulling for the next one as the torrent sloshed over.

Weather Reports

Modern weather forecasting, combined with the Internet, mean that we can basically get an immediate take on what the weather is and what it likely will do over the next few days—for any place in the world. Because many trad areas are near or in the mountains, even summer months are prone to flash showers. So read the weather reports. It takes 30 seconds. Heading up on an all-day or multiday route without consulting the weather report is lazy and reckless. Just know that forecasting beyond 48 hours becomes increasingly dodgy. One of the biggest concerns is afternoon thunderstorms—one more reason to go for the early, even predawn, start to avoid getting hosed.

Chain lightning storm south of Joshua Tree.

ROBERT MIRAMONTES

Routefinding on Open Faces

The primary concern on big open faces is finding and remaining "on route." Expect tense moments when you find yourself off route, well above crappy protection, basically lost on moves that look doubtful if not impossible. Big routefinding errors can cost us valuable hours, and can prompt unplanned bivouacs, to say nothing of the expensive gear left behind if retreat becomes the only option. As mentioned, guides, topos, anecdotal reports, etc. are all valuable resources per your trip plan, but they should never replace personal navigational skills.

To review: As you approach a big climb, study the wall closely, taking mental notes on prominent ledges, cracks, chimneys, trees, roofs, and so forth, plus any nebulous or broken areas. Correlate this data with what you have read and heard. Revise your plan if need be. Most big face routes connect lines of weakness, usually cracks, or stretches of well-featured rock. Rarely does a face route track an entirely blank wall. Normally you will link cracks and corners and ramps by way of brief forays onto the bald face. Older routes tend toward prominent cracks, ledge systems, chimneys, arêtes, and buttresses. Modern routes came to attack the

KEVIN POWELL

naked face, sometimes never leaving it, though routefinding on these climbs is often a matter of following a line of bolts, sometimes widely spaced.

Many routes bear traces of previous climbers in the form of old pin scars or even fixed pins and bolts, boot marks, or areas where lichen and other surface textures are scuffed clean. However, on a majority of big face climbs, the signs are few and subtle. When all else fails, when topos and beta don't jibe, look around and ask yourself where you would go if you were making the first ascent. This has led people out of no-man's-land more often than not. The route has gone before, so go and find it. Many suggest that we leave our topos in the pack lest we never develop our routefinding skills, where instinct and observation guide us home—or to hell in a handbasket. We always have the topo to fall back on. Either way, developing our on-sight routefinding skills is a vital step on the route to becoming a viable trad climber.

Scouring the topo for something to dream on.

MATT KUEHL

Reviewing the Route

The more challenging the route, the more you benefit by reviewing whatever documentation you can find, from guidebook descriptions to the ubiquitous trip reports now found all over the web. Routes can change, especially the status of fixed anchors, so downloading info from someone who just climbed the route is a fairly reliable way to get pertinent info. Things morph strangely in the telling, however, and people forget things. But by canvassing all data on a given route, you can generally get a fairly accurate idea of what to expect, including the recommended rack. And if there is a significant approach and descent, copy down pertinent info on a cheat sheet and, along with a hand-drawn or photo copy of the route topo, take it along. Again—know where you are going (approach) and how to get off (descent). A trip plan is not complete without this information. People have had all manner of horrendous epics by failing to find out what gully to descend, say, plunging into the wrong chute and groveling out a day later with rattlesnake bites and a shiner. Researching a route is literally a click away. Often you can simply photocopy a topo from a guidebook and go from there.

I finally breast-stroked onto the tiny summit and squinted out at the knife-edge that cut across 50 or so feet to the north rim. On both sides the wall dropped away terrifically, for what felt like miles. Rain poured off the rim. Then the air crackled with static electricity.

"Run for it!" said Phil, shoving the rack into my hands.

I unclipped from the anchor and waded out across that sawblade, tormented by firehoses, hoping I didn't pitch off and take the King Swing from Hell and dash my brains out. I hit the rim and kept running till I reached a towering pine, lashed myself off, yanked up the slack and yelled for Phil to gas it. About halfway across, the sky snarled and Phil lit across the streaming blade, and if he came off it was going to be an ugly body slam into the north wall. I must have yelled something: Phil fairly long-jumped over the last 20 or so feet and I swear to God the moment he hit solid ground a sizzling bolt of forked lightning dashed the summit we'd been hunkering on only seconds before.

Straight off we untied and left all the gear where it fell and ran a few hundred yards back into the forest and away from what was essentially a weather-vane. The clouds had nearly cleared by the time we returned back to the ample pine and organized our gear. Phil said we had to get moving; the descent was involved and he didn't want to get benighted.

The descent followed a vertical ditch described by the arête and the wall just left, and required numerous rappels off duplex-size chockstones lodged questionably in the shadowed maw. The thunderstorm had lasted nearly an hour and a regular Euphrates of runoff, mud, and flotsam was pouring down our descent shaft like a merciless sluice. When one or the other of us would bail off and start a long free-hanging rappel, we might have been rappelling down Bridalveil Falls. But somewhere down toward the bottom, when the sun broke out and we warmed up a bit and the ground came into sight, we started laughing, gasping in the gusher, soaked to the bone, filthy, exhausted, famished—and having the time of our lives.

Half hour later, after jogging back down to the Valley floor and a perfect bluebird afternoon, I wondered if we'd nearly gotten blown into the next world by chain lightning, then ridden a riptide back to the deck. Phil looked like a rock cod, so shriveled, puckered, and filthy—cotton cloths still soaking wet and covered with leaves and soot. I've never gotten so much out of a 5.8 route. And never would again.

Many years later I visited Mark Powell (who did the first ascent) in his home in Woodland Hills. He was 84 years old. When I mentioned the Arrowhead Arête, his eyes glimmered like sapphires.

CHAPTER 18

Yosemite Pilgrimage
(Sad Saga of the Sodden Screamer)

Peter Croft

That first road trip to the Valley was an eye opener, a clobbering and full dressing down all at once. El Cap, in particular, looked like the universe—not only bigger than we had imagined but bigger than we were capable of imagining. On rainy days we'd hike up to the right of The Nose, up under what we called the "Crazy Wall" and stare up and space out. The walls back in Squamish were half as tall and were lined here and there with tree ledges which gave them scale and some little perspective. Looking up at the overhanging Crazy Wall I couldn't sort out whether it was 1,000 feet or a mile high.

Although we were among the top dogs back home it was a very small group of dogs—hardly a pack, really. Now, faced with the enormity of Valley walls, we resolutely turned our attention to the

Fingerlocking: Difficult when dry; perilous when wet.   ANDREW BURR

Fight or Flight

Before launching out on a sketchy runout, or any all-or-nothing effort, carefully appraise the situation. If it's a go, fully commit to the venture. Hesitation will rob you of your chances. Often backing up one good piece of pro with another exerts enough calming influence to empty your mind and kick you into overdrive.

Sometimes, partway through a big burst, unforeseen difficulties or a sudden pump (the dreaded "flash pump") warns that this time, success is unlikely. For many reasons, no climber ever born licks every crux on the first try. If you're done for, immediately try and climb back to the last piece. Be decisive and make it happen—now! If a fall is imminent, make doubly sure that the rope is pushed safely to one side or the other so if and when you whip, you won't trip or get flipped as the cord twangs tight. If necessary, push out at the last instant to try to clear any ledges during the plunge.

We'll discuss this often: Some climbs require a sporty go-for-it quotient you should try and evoke only when conditions are good if not ideal. In any potentially hazardous situation it is important to recognize the ideal moment, and to have the smarts to walk away or rap off until the time is right. World-class performances in any field reveal that timing plays a pivotal role. Again, whenever hazards are part of the equation, sense into how the whole thing feels, if it makes sense or seems probable right then and there. Any doubts and you'll struggle to muster the total effort and commitment to forge new worlds. While these situations run the spectrum from moderate to extreme, the psychological dynamic is the same if you climb 5.9 or 5.14.

smallest cliffs we could find. Even that was tricky in that we were always trying to avoid even the shortest sections of off-width climbing. We were hardly alone in this. It's an old message. Even a tired message. But it's worth repeating: OWs are the most soul-crushing lessons available in Yosemite. Or anywhere else. Square-jawed badasses are regularly brought to tears on their first visits to the Valley. Being skinny, pale Canadians, we opted for slabs and thin finger cracks whenever we could.

Part of our reluctance to branch out was because we seldom, if ever, climbed with hardened locals, those who might have turned us on to the technical peculiarities of the Valley. Although Squamish was considered the Canadian Yosemite, it was in many ways quite different. Back home there were just two off-widths, both burly 5.10s,

and no easier ones to learn on. Plus both routes were isolated one-pitch affairs, making them hard to approach and easy to avoid. At that time there was also precious little in the way of hand and fist or even steep face climbs, so although we were heading south to more granite—basically our main course back home—we nevertheless were entering a different world.

Sunnyside Bench, close to Yosemite Falls, was unintimidating, and we spent a number of days building our confidence on the 5.9 and 5.10 finger-jamming pitches on that short cliff. Although I didn't know it at the time, the trick to getting used to a new area was to go for mileage in a casual state of mind.

The classic hard pitch at "The Bench" was a 5.10d thin finger crack called Lazy Bum. What

ANDREW BURR

makes the Bum harder than the others is the sneaky way it gets too thin for fingers, then too thin for gear, and then dies out entirely a full sobbing body length below the belay ledge. That's right where you find the "heartbreaker move."

That spring season had been a wet one for California and a number of routes had long dark wet streaks drooling down out of them—some a mere film of water, others thick with black and green slime and layers of grit washed down from recent runoff. Lazy Bum looked fine, and I felt like this was my day to lead it.

Halfway up, my fingers started coming out of the crack and I saw they were damp and dirty. By

Awareness of Conditions

Always be aware, not just of the present forecast, but of the general conditions over the previous days or weeks. If, for instance, there were thunderstorms the day before, know that sections of today's route are sure to have a few or a lot of wet sections. Place more gear than normal, even though it's dry "so far." If new in town, ask around for what the weather's been doing, as well as the forecast.

Even during stretches of perfect weather, springtime often means drainage from snowmelt, damp forested areas above, or seasonal creeks bleeding onto your route of the day. Once, while climbing on my own, I (Peter Croft) made it halfway up the East Buttress of El Cap before running into a waterfall and having to carefully reverse, all the way to the ground. A little research around the campground would have informed me about the danger of that adventure.

Ask around. Keep your nose to the ground about conditions, weather, forecasts, recent rockfall—all the stuff that locals know and share as it becomes known. No one's climbing career is long enough to find out everything firsthand. What's more, no one needs to.

JODY LANGFORD

Embracing the Weird

We naturally want to ease into a new area by playing toward our strengths, sticking with our pet skill sets. It's even advisable to do so while we get used to the local rock, the way things generally feel. We must take care, though, not to turn a whole trip to some new area into a version of what we would normally do back home. We've traveled some great distance to see new places and do different things, including the deviant "wide," or even rattly finger cracks.

Obviously, we drop the grade some, or a lot, dropping the ego as well in our quest to embrace the weird, the brand new and the shockingly unfamiliar. This is a bitter pill for stalwart sport climbers accustomed to reefing down big numbers, and who suddenly find themselves thrutching around on 5.9s. For perhaps half of the population who are cut out for trad climbing, the learning curve is generally quite steep, the Noob phase being far shorter than for Joe Citizen with no time on the clip-and-go or plastic circuit. But those expecting instant mastery are sure to cry a river.

Again, dropping the difficulty is the key to understanding, appreciating, and coming to honest and intimate terms with any new area. Virtually all "destination areas" have a slew of must-do's that should be on your list but perhaps are not owing to some deficiency (normally wide cracks) in your repertoire. This is a standard quagmire encountered for many climbers first exploring Yosemite. Most of the Valley's celebrated mega routes possess totally unavoidable stretches of stark wideness that might strike all-world classics like the Rostrum, say, or the Steck-Salathe, off an otherwise ambitious visitor's itinerary. For some this reluctance will extend to hand and fist cracks as well, or runout face climbing, or flares. The list is long enough to pretty much keep visiting climbers in the kiddie pool for the duration.

Taking the time and putting in the effort to make the weird become familiar will eventually pay huge dividends. Although at first it will feel a little like asking someone for a whooping (and having them comply), before long the blinders will come off and what was once a narrow horizon will open into a glorious panorama.

Embracing the weird.

ANDREW BURR

the time I got to the base of the crux I was more pumped than I should have been and saw right away that the one good but rounded foothold was soaking wet. So much for a rest. I had to place gear while hanging off my arms, fiddling in small wires, ever resetting my sliding feet and trying to deflate my forearms. I placed four tiny wired stoppers that looked funky to so-so. With fingers buttering out and a draining reservoir of courage, I wangled in one last backup piece below the others, an old, puny Chouinard stopper, tucked in sideways—along with a prayer. As soon as I placed it I knew it was crap. I gave it a few tugs to take it out but it was stuck, so almost as an afterthought, I clipped it and pushed on.

That last crux section is well etched, most notably for that launching out feeling, knowing that there's no more gear till the belay. It's just a seam at this point with an offset edge that allows you to layback off of the very quick of the crack, fingers wrapped over that edge and toes smearing way up high on the near side of the crease. The higher the feet, the more solid they feel, but the more pumped you got in a hurry. At the top, where the crack petered out, I was decidedly flamed. Lazy Bum shares the stance with a couple of easier routes on the flanks and someone was on the belay ledge just above, newly arrived to witness the fear.

I doubted I could make it—probably couldn't downclimb either. The witness yelled down to dyno for the jug that was tantalizingly out of reach. But I had neither the gumption nor the guns to see that maneuver through. I glanced down at those thread-like wires poking out of the crack a couple of body lengths below. I looked back up and locked my eyes on my slowly uncurling fingers. Lacking the instincts to try and scuttle down a bit to lessen the fall, I simply watched and waited as one finger at a time pianoed off.

Then I was airborne, whistling down for about 25 feet. I felt the first stopper rip out, then the next, the next, and the next. Finally I bounced to a halt hanging off that worthless stopper, a nut I would never have grabbed or expected to even hold body weight.

I cursed myself for being a coward, for not going for the hold or, failing that, for not mustering a braver effort. But I also damned myself for going for it in the first place, in wet conditions with sketchy gear. I had sneaked my way past a bad situation, but such fortune could never hold for long, not hanging off a manky old stopper.

The next piece below the stopper was decent but so far down that I wasn't sure it would have stopped me before punching into the talus. I had blown it on this one. The relatively moderate climbing low down tricked me into running it without pro, while the obvious dampness should have warned me to sew it up. The saving grace was clipping that one dinky Stopper, seemingly hinging between two crystals. Only the strangest physics might unravel how such a lousy piece had saved me. Perhaps as my hurtling mass shock-loaded onto the top piece and blew it out, it absorbed some of the force, the next one a bit more, and so on till I bounced to a midair stop suspended by an aluminum fingernail.

Don't try this at home . . .

CHAPTER 19

1096

John Long

The climb was called 1096 Crack—or simply, 1096—so coined after my friend Phil Gleason took a gallant shot at leading this 50-foot-long, wildly leaning slot, and had his picture immortalized in *Ascent* magazine just before logging a Homeric whipper that nearly splattered him on the boulders below. There were supposedly other attempts to free climb the route—all failures—and some of the stories were worth hearing.

I had only been in the Valley for a couple days and got no more warning for our adventure than the Bird's (Jim Bridwell) direct order to fetch water, a pack of Camel straights (cost: $1.60) from the Lodge store, and my gear. Apparently I was joining Jim and his longtime partner, Mark Klemens, for a go at 1096. Klemens was one of the original off-width gurus who regularly free soloed (no rope) 5.10 flares and chimneys that only the best climbers could manage with a cord.

Jim, Mark, and I took the shuttle bus to the Arches Terrace area and trudged along the base over to the route. Many chuckled at the strangeness of Bridwell's dreams, but were cowered by their size. 1096 was merely strange. Most climbs I could look up at and get some idea about how to scale them—or at least get the impression that

Right side in.

there was a route there. But with my first glance at 1096, I thought I had it all wrong, that I was missing something—like what we came to do. I only saw a big, ominous flake cutting out right at a grisly, 40-degree lean, opening up at the lip to full-body width. Maybe a lunatic might wriggle up into the thing, like a bat tucking under an awning. But how would one move from there? You'd be shuffling out upside down, or horizontally—I couldn't tell which. I walked back from the wall and the climb still looked as screwy as an M. C. Escher painting.

Mark had first-go at the lead. As with all wide cracks, he had to decide to stuff either his left side or his right side "in" (into) the flare. You normally rack your gear on the opposite side that is "in"— i.e., if you're right side in, you rack on your left side, which is not crammed inside the flare where the tackle might snag and be difficult or impossible to unclip off a harness or sling.

While all harnesses have gear loops at the waist, wide crack pro is bulky and often is slung on longish slings. Many find it unwieldy to have this gear hanging down about their lower thigh, so big cams, Big Bros, and tubes (very rare) are racked on a shoulder sling. What's more, you'll occasionally change sides while climbing the "wide"—inevitable in S-shaped cracks—and this presents problems not easily solved. For 1096, Mark decided to go right side in, and he racked a load of big nuts on his left side.

A couple body lengths of liebacking and Mark crawled into the flare, facing out, back pressed against the main wall, right hand reaching for wide jams in the shadowed back of the flare while his

Improbable Techniques

As we've seen, "embracing the weird" involves techniques we never imagined, or which we'd rather avoid. The next step concerns techniques or approaches that will never work "no how"—but do. Such cases are admittedly rare. Most climbing challenges call for obvious solutions. We don't use off-width skills on a knob climb because there's no way to make them work. But on a queer route such as 1096, climbers from China to New Mexico have led it facing the wall and facing out, basically chimneying horizontally. I've even heard of someone following by half liebacking, half underclinging the flake, which supposedly lowered the difficulty to moderate 5.10, but was a suicidal tactic on the lead since you'd never be able to slot pro hanging so far out of the crack. The point is that unconventional methods are occasionally possible, even essential. Climbing is a creative problem-solving game. Little can be ruled out.

Full inversions receive little mention in the service manual.

MATT KUEHL

left hand clasped the serrated edge of the flake. A grand master of these hellish slots, Mark arranged a foot-knee jam with his outside (left) leg, slowly ratcheting up the flake, moving almost horizontally, or upside down, or some way I couldn't quite reckon glancing up at him. This was some years before cams, and the reliability of the hexes, lodged with a prayer in the slanting crack, was suspect.

After powering up near the end of the flake, Mark set a good nut and lowered to the ground; only by watching him drop down the plumb line, as gravity dictated, could we appreciate how much this flake overhung.

With the rope already strung to nearly the top of the flake, Jim tied in and chugged it out to the high nut. He clearly had planned his strategy,

Alexy Zelditch wriggling toward the difficult exit move from the lower flare, 1096.

Protecting Liebacks

J im Bridwell once called liebacking "the technique of no technique." In fact, there are many
nuances to difficult liebacking. We've seen how it's usually more difficult to stop in a lieback than
it is to carry on, and how the standard strategy is to place bomber protection and pump it out to
the next foothold or suitable place to pause. Stopping in the middle might cost you any chance at
climbing the route. But pressing on when the pro is poor and there are ledges to hit below is asking
for trouble. Because we're pushing against the wall and pulling out with all our might, pinging out
of liebacks can send you catapulting into space. So whatever pro you arrange for that grim lieback,
make it solid or double it up.

If footholds are lacking, aim to place pro from hand or finger jams. Jamming uses your muscles
differently than liebacking, yielding a semi rest in many cases. This allows you to juke around and
look straight into the crack, helpful to achieve precise placements. If stopping feels doubtful, and the
cam is good and there's nothing below, pump through the hard bit and be done with it. If stopping
is required, get your gear arranged so you can unclip and slot the right piece quickly, and bust on.
Fumbling for gear on a lieback is poor planning.

**Karine Croft on Ten Years After,
Yosemite Falls.**

PETER NOEBELS

**Hesitating on hard liebacks drives up the
difficulty faster than you can say, "Falling!"**

MATT KUEHL

That'll leave a mark!
Woes of the wide fetish.

MATT KUEHL

because he no sooner gained the nut then he did a half twist and flipped over and faced the wall, left side in. He reached up behind him, grabbed the lip of the flake, and swung out into a chancy lieback that looked spectacular and dangerous as hell, like a circus trick or something. I remember thinking that if he makes this, I'll never follow in a million years.

Jim paddled his feet directly off the wall and powered up to a good ledge on top of a flake, not pausing in the lieback to try and place pro, which might have flamed his arms and sent him flying. This is a strategy often employed on liebacks. You want that pro badly, but stopping to try and place it with your hands up by your grill might be the shortest way to failure. Ironically, pushing on sans pro is sometimes the safest strategy. It's always a judgment call. For sure, I'd never seen the likes of Jim's performance, so gymnastic and innovative, scampering up that cleaver like a ring-tailed lemur. And all executed on-sight, with no falls.

I went next. Luckily, I had climbed a few extreme, leaning flares at Mount Rubidoux (none

longer than 15 feet), and so this queer route felt vaguely familiar—but super strenuous. Arranging the heel-toe jams, kneelocking with the outside leg, worm-driving up in fluid little fits and starts as opposed to wholesale thrashing, were elements I managed imperfectly. When finally I groped up to the top nut, I was climbing on fumes.

"Grab the edge!" Jim yelled down. I fumbled to unclip the nut, leaving Mark to clean it. I grabbed the jagged quick of that flake and corkscrewed out into a layaway. The torque was severe and I nearly hinged off. I was scared of letting Mark and Jim down, and I nearly pulled that flake off the wall as I slap-dashed the last dozen feet up to Jim on the ledge.

"Man, that's got to be 5.11," I gasped.

"It's close," said Jim.

I would do dozens of other first ascents in Yosemite, many with Jim, but few as memorable as that early day on Royal Arches. I had no business making that climb, but a strong partner can inspire you to exceed yourself on occasion.

Effort

They called him Big Game James—that is, former Laker basketball standout, James Worthy. James could rise to the level of the competition, seemingly at will, and has five championship rings to prove it. A vital part of climbing hard routes is the ability to summon your best effort on cue, like James. This is largely a developed skill. Tobin Sorenson used to commit himself to such horrendous situations that he had to rise up, or die. He died. Most of us find softer, saner methods. But we need to learn this skill. This dynamic can play out just as surely for the 5.9 climber as it can for the North Face athlete. It has nothing to do with the level at which we climb, rather the willingness to climb past ourselves. That's when they'll say, "She's got game."

Got game?

ROBERT MIRAMONTES

CHAPTER 20

Royal Pains

Peter Croft

After a month I was getting accustomed to the grandeur of Yosemite Valley. I didn't yet have the backbone to throw down with the big walls or introduce myself to Camp 4 royalty like John Bachar or Ron Kauk. Their force field was simply too great.

My time spent on Valley classics was beginning to pay dividends, though, and if there was no swagger in my step when I approached a hardman's crag like the Cookie or Arch Rock, there was much less cowering than before.

Experience gained on the short burly liebacks and jam cracks got me looking up at the impossible-to-ignore granite waves sweeping up to the rim. A measure of my rather subdued confidence was that I chose the Royal Arches route to stretch my legs. Of all the must-do long climbs, "The Arches" has the much deserved rep as the fluffiest and most

Painted stereograph. Washington Column, Yosemite, 1890.

Royal Arches and North Dome on the left, Half Dome, right, soaring in the mist, 1896.

popular—by a long shot. The slight buttress-y archi-tecture and panoramic views make for a vertical scenic tour while the reliable sunny aspect and cush ledges describe the ideal date climb. Cat-scratched by flared groovy cracks and rampy corners, the scores of options on many pitches make it easy to pass slower parties—and just as easy to get lost.

I teamed up with my Canadian friend Jock for our Arches junket. We were fit, the days were long, and the route was well within our abilities. At a mere 5.9, a full two grades below what we were managing on the short walls, there was almost nothing that could go wrong. We started early, that is to say somewhat early, had a leisurely breakfast, and wandered over to the base. Right off we spot-ted a party some 500 feet above, which triggered a surge of competitive adrenalin. No one is fond of climbers overhead, who can boot missiles onto your head, so we charged up the initial chimney and easy ramps, bent on making the pass as soon as possible.

In a little over an hour we caught the lead party and, using a different crack system on the right, quickly blew by. We continued on at our accelerated pace, letting the hot air of youth loft us up and out of sight of the others. Pleased with our speed, we didn't notice when we made the mistake common to everyone in a mad rush: When we should have gone right, we took the "other right." Namely, left.

Getting Back on Route

The moment you realize you are lost and off-route—stop. Set a solid piece or two and take stock of the situation. If it looks simple or feasible to angle back on course without retreating, then go for it. If, however, it appears a traverse or other maneuver will introduce even greater danger and uncertainty, back off directly, either by downclimbing or by lowering off. You've already had one thing go wrong—don't compound the mistake by counting on heroics to drum up a happy ending.

There usually are good reasons why the first ascensionists went the way they did—and everyone else since. Most likely they found the easiest way with the biggest holds and most protectable cracks. Once you stray off the standard line, you'll likely encounter lousier pro on looser and dirtier terrain. Bottom line: Off-route variations rarely if ever go as easily as the established route—so beware.

To limit the damage, course correct sooner than later, rather than climbing into dire straits because you can't be bothered or are too proud and stubborn to reverse direction. Don't make the situation worse and have to get rescued or worse, risk a perilous fall by trying to grope up some rubbishy jungle pitch.

There are such routes where a blind man could never stray. But we're not talking about those.

ANDREW BURR

Soon we were thrutching past vegetated ledges and up scaly, mossy corners. Of course we should have retraced our footsteps, should have at least made the effort to get back on track. Instead we forged on, trusting that things couldn't possibly get worse. The corner we were following arched over, and after groveling through an acre of snarly shrubs, the crack in the back filled with weeds and oozing slime. The water-streaked slab out to the left looked unclimbable.

Over what probably took an hour, I pieced together one of my hairiest leads. I might have gotten some gear in low down, then ran the rest of a full rope length out over smeary edging on crackly micro-flakes and crusty black lichen. Every now and again I had to cross broad water streaks, pleading with my shoes not to skid off.

I glanced back down the way we had come, knowing we should have retreated and climbed back on track. I kept on hoping for clean cracks,

Passing Parties

Once we basically know what we're doing up high on multipitch routes, on occasion we'll likely have to pass slower parties. One option, which should never be discounted, is to choose a different route. Getting up early and marching to the base counts for something, too—namely, you've won dibs on the route.

Put simply, the first people on a given route have the right of way and are in no way obliged to let others pass, climbing into a position of raining rock and debris onto them—a surprisingly common occurrence between parties stacked one on top of the other.

If a team is demonstrably slower, consider a more relaxed approach to the outing—every climb needs not be a race to the top. Then what? We march down, coil the line, pack up, and we're right back to wrestling down some grub, begging Daphne's favor, or not, and ferreting out whatever serenity we might find in heaven and earth. Why not, strictly for fun, toggle off the pressure and allow some little grace on the climb before us,

just this one time. If daylight is long, and getting beaned by rockfall unlikely—though, again, it's always possible when climbing below others—consider tooling along at your leisure and acquiring charisma points with those up above. An occasional Daddio route, executed at half-speed, can work wonders on a tightly wrapped soul.

If, however, the decision is made to pass, it is standard etiquette to pass efficiently and at a convenient time—that is, convenient for the upper party. Polite communication, starting with asking permission to pass (remembering that they have the right of way), usually smooths out the transition and avoids a cluster. The first party may want to finish leading or following the next pitch before leap-frogging. That's only reasonable.

The easiest way to pass on easier routes, where a number of variations are available on the flanks, is to simply keep up a head of steam and, momentarily veering off the beaten path, book by without inconveniencing anybody. Be mindful not to drop anything and that your rope does for good pro and dry rock—but wishing changed nothing and I kept climbing myself into deeper and deeper trouble.

Dry throated, I finally (and luckily) pulled up onto a good ledge just as the rope went tight, threw a long sling around a lone pine tree, and yanked up enough stretch in the line to clove hitch in. Safe! From my stance an easy ramp led up left and spilled over the top into the forest. We were home free.

Then I heard a loud jangling and glanced up. There, maybe 25 feet overhead, was a figure in midair, in the crazy aspect of a plunging rag doll, trailing great loops of slack and heading straight toward me. I glanced at my clove-hitched short leash—there was nowhere to go and nothing to do but cringe. Then it came, that horrible punched-in-the-nose feeling, but this one was a terrific full-body blow.

not dislodge rubble as you sweep past. If at all possible, avoid climbing directly over the head of others, even if this means taking a harder variation in order to flare off left or right.

If you're all battling up a single wide crack, say, and no variations are available, wait until it is convenient for the other team, then try to wriggle by without stopping and log-jamming their belay. Either link two pitches or belay short and skirt past, avoiding the awkward chumminess that occurs at a crowded anchor—especially key if the party is arrayed at a hanging stance. Hitching onto stranger's anchors is the cragging version of crashing someone's wedding. No matter how gentile, you're still a nuisance and an embarrassment because you don't belong there and weren't invited. You're the rube with the clown suit traipsing through their home movie. Far better that each group should have their own belay—safer, less confusing, and far less intrusive.

Climb quickly but not frantically. This is the way to pass safely and to make sure that, once by,

The descent, Yosemite.

ALEXANDRE BUISSE

you don't miss that crucial traverse, get lost, and scamper up some vegetated crack. Apart from the sketch factor, it is lame to surge past a party only to hold up the parade while freaking and futzing about off-route. Situations vary, but so long as you are gracious, things can usually be worked out with no ill feelings.

Analyzing Mistakes

Whenever epics or accidents happen—from cave diving to skydiving—official analysis is usually conducted within days if not hours to determine what went wrong. Freak accidents and acts of God are rare. Random factors may contribute, but decades of accident reports suggest there usually is something you could have done to reduce the likelihood of trouble.

Not all accidents are fatal, thank Earthmaker, but without rigorous honesty about our actions, we can never determine the real cause(s) of any untoward incident. And without grasping root causes, we will remain a dicey ropemate doomed to repeat our fiascos. In other words, we cannot learn from mistakes unless we see and own what they actually were in real time.

Some accidents are caused by poor execution of standard protocols or momentary lapses of attention that trigger the error in the first instance. But very often problems issue from an unsound method or approach to our climbing—not so much our physical moves or even our specific execution of standard maneuvers, but rather, a more fundamental and global problem about our general orientation to the work.

A "tight ship" is not the result of doing a few things perfectly; instead it comes from avoiding half measures and doing all the little habitual things consciously and intentionally. You "do what you mean and mean what you do," as opposed to pulling on the peace pipe, neglecting the boring details, and counting on strong forearms to save the day. How do you approach climbing in its entirety? It is an elusive question, but we need to answer it to know where we stand.

For instance, habitually getting a slow start—essentially being late for work—is a certain way to

The tightest ships know when it's time to drop anchor.

BEN HORTON

get marooned behind other (slower) parties, or to get caught in a storm and possibly get benighted. On the other end of long routes, failing to pack a headlamp and a waterproof shell are two ways to sign up for no fun at all. And both of these oversights point out a reckless indifference to what demands our full attention and commitment. Trad climbing is not sport climbing. It is only as secure as we consciously make it.

When we look at most world-class climbers, they got to that level not from preternatural gifts, but because from very early on, they took the whole thing seriously, and meant every move of it. They do what they mean and mean what they do.

I blacked out, and when I woke up my white T-shirt was bright red.

I could see out of only one eye, and when I raised my hand to wipe blood off my face all I felt was tattered flesh where my right eye should have been. I wiped away more blood, horrified that I'd lost my eyeball. Using the edge of my T-shirt, I mopped up some more and finally saw a glimmer of light from the bleeding side. With huge relief I relaxed—and passed out again.

Our self-rescue took hours. The fallen climber's partner rapped in and brought Jock up, and the three of them scrambled as I staggered up the ramp to the summit forest. The descent down the North Dome Gully passed in a fog as the others babied me down, wobbling and bleeding. At the Yosemite Clinic, the fallen climber was diagnosed with a banged elbow—modest damage for a 50-plus-foot whipper. And for the human crash pad—dozens of stitches sewn into my grill, broken ribs, and a medley of cuts and bruises. I stumbled out of there like the Mummy.

That was the end of my Valley adventures—possibly for good, I feared—and was topped with a dreary 36-hour bus ride back to Canada. The more lasting effects showed up later. My neck and shoulders were bashed so far out of alignment that for several years afterward any attempt at steep climbing made both shoulders throb and sent my neck into spasms. I had seen my future, looming on the mighty granite walls, and now I was sentenced to hard labor on the slabs for the next 4 years.

For a long time I viewed this as a freak occurrence—two parties on a climb of that length, and the only place humanly possible for Falling Man to orchestrate a head-on collision was the very place he pitched off. What were the odds? This was nothing but lousy luck. Or was it?

If we had gotten a proper, predawn start, crashing bodies would never have happened. If we had been less anxious to pass and more focused on routefinding, it would not have happened. And if, once we knew we were off-route, we had backtracked till we found the way, again, it would not have happened, and I wouldn't have spent thousands on therapy, herbs, Indian poultices, witch doctors—and years on slabs.

There is little like the black hole of injury to suck us into endless rounds of "Why me?" mulling that confounding conflagration of Fate, Karma, and Chance. This frequently degenerates into "I'm not a bad person" rants and "I didn't deserve this." Per Royal Arches, perhaps I didn't. But for the rash and foolish there are few endeavors less forgiving than rock climbing. Since there's no value in bitterly circling the drain, I somehow had to discover and stick with some sane protocols that could reduce the likelihood of Royal Pains.

I had plenty of time to pore over *Accidents in North American Mountaineering,* and *Close Calls,* which showed that virtually every mistake I could ever make on the cliffside, someone else has also made. And if I was still alive to talk about it, then the fates had been easy on me, and it was my job to change up my way of doing business. Some of us learn the hardest lessons this way, but I couldn't tell you why.

CHAPTER 21

Steck-Salathe

John Long

By my freshman year in college I had visited Yosemite a half dozen times, spending up to a month at a go, slowly getting the measure of the sweeping, glacier-polished cracks. I hadn't thrown all my energy at rock climbing yet, because my dreams still lay with professional baseball. I rarely scaled anything longer than a few pitches, tending toward short, technical routes. Occasionally I'd climb one of the storied lines at the base of El Capitan, which shot overhead like a blinding granite nightmare. No one had actually climbed the whole thing, it seemed. It was done with trick photography, dummies, and shenanigans.

The first time I saw a team dangling a few thousand feet up the Big Stone—a rare occurrence back then—the picture looked insane. Freaky. And fatal. Like most climbers new to the Valley, I had to live among the big walls for a while before I didn't cringe and go dumb from the magnitude. But someday I hoped to go high. The opportunity came during Easter break during my freshman year at college. I was 18 years old.

That year I had spent most every winter weekend out at Joshua Tree, regularly climbing a dozen or more crack routes a day. I felt ready for the big time, knowing I could physically last. The moment I pulled above the pines, my brain might melt down and pour out my ears. Or maybe I'd thrive up there. One way or the other, I was going to find out.

My mentor Paul Gleason said to carefully vet whoever I chose to head up with me on a big route. I didn't want surprises half a mile off the ground. With such stakes in the game, most climbers went with proven friends. But Ricky and Richard were back in Upland. I was on my own.

Jim Bridwell introduced me to Jim Orey, also staying in Camp 4, and we decided to immediately climb the Steck-Salathe, on Sentinel, one of the "Fifty Classic Climbs in North America." Jim had already climbed The Nose on El Capitan—the most sought after rock climb on earth—and had just finished a 10-day stint in a Northern California jailhouse for tossing an apple core out the window of his Pontiac. The sheriff didn't care for Jim's attitude. I was fine with it, and the hard time Jim just put in was all the cred I needed to rope up with the convict, also 18, for my first Grade 5.

The Steck-Salathe was an obvious choice since we were always staring up at 1,600-foot Sentinel, rising off the far escarpment directly across the Valley from Camp 4. It arguably was the first true big wall climbed in Yosemite (I had read Alan Steck's 1950 epic, *Ordeal by Piton,* about the first ascent, at least twenty times). My first climbing hero, fellow Tahquitz climber Royal Robbins, had made the second ascent when he was my age, so I felt obliged to get on the same page as Royal and "ink" this landmark route, towering in the distance "like a somber gray tombstone," according to one author. I had read some about Royal's ascent and knew he'd climbed the wall with two other So Cal boys, and they were all wearing tennis shoes.

There are many critical decisions to make before going on a big route. Being teenagers, Jim

1885 Collodion print of Sentinel. The upper wall is more than 1,600 feet high.

and I were bothered by few of them. We had one good lead rope between us, so that was settled—one rope. We took a daypack for the second to carry and filled it with peanut butter and jelly sandwiches and two quarts of water, having read about Steck and Salathe, during the first ascent around 1,000 years before, and how they huddled in the shade of the upper chimneys, whimpering and dying of thirst and gazing down at tourists frolicking in the river, falling out of rafts into the lucent mountain stream—and forget that. We knew the route started up the right side of the Flying Buttress, the most prominent feature on the entire wall. I hand-copied a crude topo on a napkin in the cafeteria but didn't waste time researching the approach or descent. It looked dead obvious.

We got up early—what time I couldn't say since neither of us had a watch or alarm clock—hoofed it across to Sentinel, slogged up the "Four Mile Trail" to a talus field and a series of ramps cutting across

the foot of the wall, arriving at the base of the first crack pitch an hour or so after leaving Camp 4. We were more lucky than skilled to have on-sighted the approach so quickly, never losing our way on the confusing grass and shale ramps.

I glanced up at the fractured crack system just above, licked my chops, and shot off. Jim was also climbing at the 5.10 grade, and we felt solid and made good time. Cramming my way through the shoulder-wide Wilson Overhang (rated 5.9, later upgraded to 5.10b), with that damn daypack grinding off the back wall, was awful duty. A couple of pitches higher we gained a big flat ledge atop the Flying Buttress, not quite halfway up the wall.

Bridwell and Gleason both told us that one of the challenges of doing long routes in one day was that you had to take food and water to sustain your energy, as well as sweaters for the cool early and late hours—plus lightweight shoes for the descent. Because we would return to where we started, we left our sneakers and some other stuff on the trail at the base of the ramps. We'd suffer the descent in tight climbing shoes and save weight. But we had those peanut butter sandwiches, two lightweight sweaters, plus those two quarts of water, so color us golden.

But two quarts of water is slim rations, even in mild conditions, when you're thrashing up wide cracks and chimneys. And even going super light on the other articles, we still had around a dozen pounds of crap stuffed into that daypack, which the second had to mule up the climb. Of course we couldn't always fit through the chimneys with a pack on, and it made the climbing horrendous besides. So after the Flying Buttress we started attaching the daypack to our waist with a long sling and dragging it behind, where it entangled in our feet and jammed itself into constrictions and was mostly hateful. Modern packs have streamlined—but not eliminated—the hunchback that every team must bear when the second follows with the cargo. Hauling the pack would have been better in some cases, but we only had one rope. Such is the trade-off.

We slouched back on top of the Flying Buttress, tore into those sandwiches, and the peanut butter stuck in our throats like quickset cement. Even in cool temps, you need a flume straight from Yosemite Falls to gut down PB&Js. Working out the food for a long climb is as essential as staying hydrated—and back then we didn't know the fine points. Now we had no grub but were on a roll and figured to dust the last seven or eight pitches in no time.

We sipped the water, which vanished quickly, and smoked the Marlboro cigarettes I'd brought along because the British gritstone climbers always

Rope Options on Long Climbs

It seems an obvious thing—ropes are used to get up a given route, and also to get down, to retreat off a climb when untoward circumstances force us down. Retreat must never be ruled out since—as mentioned—no climber and no partnership enjoys 100 percent success on rock climbs. I once had my partner stir up a hornet's nest a few pitches up, and by the time I got to the belay his face was swollen like a fright mask. My friend Billy Westbay got beaned by a small rock on Middle Cathedral—nothing life threatening, but he saw stars for 2 days and couldn't continue. It rains, it snows. People get sick. One time on the regular South Face route on Mount Watkins, it got so hot on the white, convex face that climbing was inconceivable and just escaping without heat stroke was a concern. So we safeguard the option to "bail."

With a route featuring long pitches, retreat with one 50- or 60-meter rope is problematic. A doubled rope will often not reach belay to belay, and if you're having to stop wherever the rope runs out and place rap anchors, you'll likely run out of gear in no time. The old-school solution was to take two ropes—a full-size lead line and an 8mm "rat tail"—just enough for emergency rappelling. The leader could trail the rat tail, but the spindly line seemed to always snag or hang up or clump and twist into a Gordian knot. The second could twine the thing around him or carry it over his shoulder or lash it around him in "mountaineer's coil," or even cram it in his pack. But all of these options made climbing awkward or worse. Some climbers just threw the dice and went with one rope and hoped for the best. Then manufacturers began making 70-meter lines (230 feet), and this nearly solved the problem since few pitches, on average, are much longer than 115 feet. In the real world, the 70-meter cords have proved themselves in getting climbers off most every big climb from Yosemite and beyond.

The other rope options were mentioned because two ropes are still required under certain circumstances. For example, when the second wants to follow-free every lead, but the climbing is too hard to carry a pack and an extra line, the leader trails the rat tail and hand-hauls (usually) the other gear. Or when you are heading up onto a climb where the pitches are mostly "strung" to full rope lengths, typical for sweeping, single-feature lines (a continuous hand crack, say) found in wilderness areas like Baffin Islands, Patagonia, or the big Andean walls in Peru. There are many such examples. The 70-meter ropes have solved the problem by and large, but not entirely. More on ropes later on.

Goldline rope, first available in 120-foot lengths, 1953.

JODY LANGFORD

ANDREW BURR

smoked. From the brink of our ledge, the Valley spilled below us for an age, the flat tableau looking like a movie from another land. Separated by a vertical mile and the long arm of Old Man Gravity, we'd joined a small brotherhood that had also experienced adventures that felt out of this world. We'd soon return to level ground, having only been gone one day. Somehow it all felt different. Smaller. I imagined myself, decades later, gazing up at myself, high on the great gray tombstone, my boots now too heavy to ever leave the meadow. But I would always have that ledge, far above the pinyon pines, to go back to.

Then my heart jumped knowing that with one rope we probably couldn't get down from much higher. As is we'd have to make ten half rappels to retreat, and unless we wanted to bail off one-piece anchors, which is shit-your-pants scary, we'd quickly run out of gear. Yet deep down I felt solid, even pleased that the only way off was up. All those grainy cracks I'd thrown down out in the high desert were paying off handsomely.

Every big adventure has a texture, and the basecoat of this one was once again self-reliance, the belief that I could call on myself and that I was good to go. I could thrive in high places. I had

Climbing with a Pack

Much like harnesses, pack technology has come so far that a newish crag pack rides one's back like a cloud. You might even forget you have one on. There are several ways to climb long free routes. Most teams swing leads. Either way, the second is likely to carry a pack unless the route is short or you want to starve and be thirsty—the purest misery for anything beyond a few hours. Even for an all-day outing, the pack rarely needs to weigh more than fifteen pounds, though this is significant. It will lighten appreciably as the hours pass and the water is polished off. Food and a pile sweatshirt or two weigh almost nothing. As we've just seen, the advent of 70mm and 80mm ropes mean the old days of schlepping two ropes for an emergency descent are largely past. That also means we can't haul the pack, and on chimneys that presents a problem with basically only one solution—clipping the pack on a sling connected to our waist loop and dragging the bugger behind us. You will hate the pack and all creation when you do this. But it's all part of the game.

One option is for each climber to wear a small hydration pack—discussed further in the next sidebar. The liquid stays close to your back and moves along with you. Pick the smallest one that will serve you, and you'll forget it's even on after 50 feet.

Short off-width stories, like Dolphin (5.8), right, at Joshua Tree, are required training for the full-length dramas found on the mega cliffs of the world.

GREG EPPERSON

worked my ass off for months, and somewhere in there, as we powered up the final 800 feet of wide cracks and bombay gashes—including the infamous "Narrows," the most famous squeeze chimney in American climbing—my aspirations for professional baseball calved away, into the void. Climbing was my game, and had been since the first day I roped up with Jack Schnurr, three years before out at Josh. Accepting this felt like taking my place in the natural order of things.

The last part of the Steck-Salathe battles up cracks that have retired people from the sport and almost killed a few outright. Of the dreadful squeeze chimneys, one climber said: "Get four friends to lay a garage door on top of you, each sitting on a corner of the door as you try and wiggle out from the center to escape. That's the Steck-Salathe."

But I was fine in "the wide," thanks to my Joshua Tree curriculum and repeated months of polishing up on Valley fare. So following a few

Food and Water and Sunscreen

If you read the accounts of speed climbers, they often only pack a quart of water between them—and blast off. Of course this is sustainable only for a few hours, for climbers who have tanked up beforehand and have a ready canteen to quaff the moment they summit. For the vast majority of trad climbers heading off for a day climb, food and water are essentials. Sports medicine has determined that remaining hydrated is the single biggest factor in maintaining performance, so if you're going to skimp on weight, go easy on the cashews and Mars bars and schlepp the fluids. Yosemite big wall pioneers knew back in the 1960s that every man required a gallon of water a day, and even this felt insufficient during summer months. Abandon the idea that you will ever be able to lug enough water on a rock climb. A standard strategy is to rise early, eat some high-calorie food, drink as much water as possible, and carry the minimum for the route. This is especially effective if you camel up on liquids 24 to 48 hours prior to liftoff—an essential drill

if you've been traveling, which dehydrates you like a piece of rawhide.

Since lugging more water is realistic only to a degree, try to limit the effects of the sun. Wind and sun can sap energy just as quickly as dehydration. Go easy on the booze, caffeine (both are diuretics), and sugar leading up to the climb. Sunscreen is a must, and on any long climb, most leaders stuff a tube of lip balm in their pockets. The nervous lip-licking before hard pitches, along with putting rope in your mouth when clipping, dries out the kissers ferociously. Likewise, a well-ventilated hat is handy tackle. So are loose, light-colored tech garments that wick sweat and shield you from direct sunlight. Seek shade whenever possible. Even a dog knows to do so.

Everyone has their preferences for food, running from bars and gels to gorp to fruit (nice for the liquid) to hauling burritos and even sandwiches and vegan burgers (wrapped in tinfoil). There's one group of climbers from Alabama who only eat items that have a face. Tastes

tight squeezes, we found ourselves on a ledge at the base of the final, 5.9 pitch. Jim was fading fast, so I grabbed the last lead and tomahawked up a steep hand and fist crack, placing one big nut and running the rope to a tree at the end of the roped climbing. I knew the descent went down the left-hand gully, and from the summit, we seemed guided by ghosts as we traversed over to big chossy chute and wended down a quarter mile to the Four Mile Train cutting across the base of the wall. Since we'd drained the last of the water at the base of the Narrows, we were desperately thirsty and spent some minutes at a stream drinking and gazing up at the wall we had just climbed, a ritual I would repeat countless times over the following 15 years. Having climbed ourselves out of civilization, briefly, but entirely, we had that momentary feeling of being strangers on the flats. Brothers from another planet. Then we huffed down the last of our cigarettes and blasted for the Valley and some grub.

differ, and no two teams do things the same way. But for all-day routes, especially when it is hot, trying to get by with less than three quarts of water can feel murderous. One of the leading makers of hydration packs recommends drinking a liter of water for every hour of outdoor activity, but again, few climbers carry anything near that amount, however much they might need it.

Many teams store fluids in "poly bottles" (polyurethane), while just as many wear hydration packs such as Camelbaks. Still others blend a dash of sports powders (electrolyte replacements) in with the water, or lug separate containers of Gatorade. If you are prone to cramps, use a more expensive—and better—sports drink, like Cytomax, a longtime standby for all endurance sports. Experiment and discover what works for you. And remember, always keep drinking, even if you don't feel thirsty. If you wait till you are, you're already dehydrated and you'll never catch back up.

ANDREW BURR

Linh Nguyen, smooth and cordless on Big Mo (5.11a).

KEVIN POWELL

CHAPTER 22

Josh:
Full Trad Value

Peter Croft

Back before the rock climbing universe expanded to its present size, the undisputed place to be was in California. And the undisputed winter hot spot was Joshua Tree National Monument (now a national park). No other place was even in the conversation. The high desert moonscape, splitter So Cal sunshine, and exotic Joshua trees themselves combined to produce the utopian escape from the gray slushy streets of Vancouver, British Columbia. What's more, once the word got out in the early 1980s, thanks to countless magazine articles and photo spreads, climbers from all across Europe, and Asia as well, began flocking to Josh to flee the sad and dour Euro and Oriental winters.

We waited until after Christmas (to cash in on presents and stocking stuffers), then loaded up for the 1,500-mile drive south for the Promised Land. There were three of us—girlfriend Tami, best friend Greg, and me, sardined into Greg's red beater VW bug. There was room for two sitting and one lying nose-to-ceiling on top of a junk show of ropes, carabiners, and cereal boxes. That's 36 hours of nonstop cramped quarters for less than a week of sunshine. Seemed like a great deal for us.

Driving those last few miles at three in the morning was the perfect intro. Bathed in full-moon milky light, our sleep-deprived senses hallucinated the granitic domes into Frankenstein skulls, while the twisted limbs of the Joshua trees morphed into giant tarantula legs. We pulled in to Hidden Valley Campground, threw down our sleeping bags, and fell face first into the sand.

Tia Stark crossing the popular Rubicon, Joshua Tree.

ROBERT MIRAMONTES

Always the early riser, I woke at first light and charged off for a run. Throughout those early years I never paced myself and never warmed up. Why waste energy and risk fatigue doing anything sub-maximal? One of the wonderful and terrible things

141

Planet X, one of the countless all-time highball boulder problems at Josh.

ROBERT MIRAMONTES

about being a climber: no experienced coach to tell us things like the absolute importance of a proper warm-up.

I didn't know Josh at all, had no maps, and simply charged at the nearest hill, quickly finding myself in open terrain, hurdling prickly pears and yuccas in a steep beeline for the summit. In no time I was red-lining it, choking on that familiar acid taste surging up my throat. Near the top a cramp clawed at my side, which quickly spread to both sides and then, just as fast, head to toe. I collapsed into a ball, my whole body a clenched fist.

Unable to even sit up, I imagined the vultures circling, the bleached bones, a final resting place amid lonesome boulders and yucca palms. What felt like hours was probably only about 20 minutes but every second passed in a crushing paralysis totally new to me, and it felt like the end of the world. Eventually the seizure eased off and the vultures flew away. I wobbled to my feet and made my way back to the campground just as my friends were getting up.

This was classic youth having no clue as to holding anything back. It's one of the wonders of being a kid, that clumsy pup ignorance of running full tilt into trouble. Although I eventually grew out of this, I often experienced a psyched-out kind of freeze while staring up at a mega route, and the

Pace:
Modulate the Pump

On the trail to the cliff and on the rock itself, we must find our own pace. Too much early red-lining results in a lactic acid bath and the dreaded "flash pump," which fries the muscles and tanks performance. We need to gently climb through the first warm-up phase, feeling like we're holding back, like we could go faster—but we don't. Then we find a natural cruising speed and settle in, sticking with easy to moderate terrain, taking care to modulate the pump, pausing to take rests on the stiffer ground. This is the standard warm-up drill preceding all serious physical adventures. But a general approach is not enough. We need to personalize the ritual to our own specs. And this requires that we know ourselves, which can only happen from a long, conscious process of self-observation, exactly the thing youth is geared to preclude. Nevertheless, until we've calibrated our personal tachometer we should err on the side of slowing down and resting. Once we're good and warm, and only then, should we put the hammer down.

Janet Q. modulating the pump.

GREG EPPERSON

Air climbing at a secret Josh campfire.

ANDREW BURR

rabbit-scared twitchiness on a crux pitch. Most every time I'd bolt mindlessly forward to try and power through the fear. Had someone mentioned slowing down and hanging with the process, I would have laughed.

I could always recognize scary moments but struggled to devise ways to avoid them in the future. For instance, warming up is something well known to all athletes, but somehow I felt climbers were different. Our oddball vocation was so divergent from stadium sports, I reasoned, the rules of human physiology probably didn't truly apply to us. And when our exploits turned into punch lines we dusted ourselves off and tried harder. And we could always try harder.

Josh provided fine schooling. What appeared at first as a kind of high desert cartoon became a serious place after the first route. In fact the brief nature of many of the climbs was the larger part of their danger. The problem was the dreaded ground fall, crashing into the deck from low down, but plenty high to leave bones showing. In Yosemite, the cruxes usually involved long enduro sections of repetitive moves, but the J Tree goods featured much more techy weirdness and wildly different types of moves, typically packed into a much shorter pitch. Often I'd find myself battling some flaring finger-lock while dicking about trying to set a stopper or anything else that might fit the crack, all while looking at a 30-foot grounder if I blew out.

Every morning we'd wake to frozen water bottles, but quickly the desert sun warmed the air and made climbing feel inviting all over again.

Continued on page 149

Transition to Trad

There are a host of difficult rungs on the long ascent to trad competence—for everyone. But for the dedicated bouldering and sport climbing crowd, there quietly lurks the potential for an additional challenge—namely, the reckless notion that whatever skill level you have managed in the sport milieu is quickly achievable on the crack and mega free climbing circuit. For the rank beginner there is no such assumption and they immediately get down to the ABCs. The sport climber, conversely, is commonly buffaloed by his own skill and fitness, especially how he routinely outclimbs if not demolishes trad climbers in the gym and on the boulders. There are few leading trad climbers who do not sport climb as well, usually at a stout level; but the ace sport climber—so long as he sticks to his specialty—will routinely out-shine the tradsters. With their expectations bound up in their experience, why wouldn't an accomplished sport climber assume he could leap right in and do well?

As we've touched on earlier, the problem is often the danger—that these steel-fingered climbers usually have little or no experience with anchoring, loose rock, rope shenanigans, and screwy-feeling techniques like arm-barring and finger stacks. These techniques and the adventurous environment is as different from the well-managed sport area as Oslo is from the middle of Borneo. lunging in at a high level and expecting to do well is like traveling the world and expecting English to work perfectly wherever we drop anchor. Yes, kind of like that—except far more dangerous.

The key, as it goes in most new activities, is to ramp down the difficulty and up the mileage. Tackle too difficult a long route and we spend so many hours bumbling with gear and other weirdness that our main focus becomes escape—up or down, whichever comes first. Tackle a particularly fearsome off-width, say, without the requisite training and we transform much of our epidermis into festering lesions. When so many variables come into immediate play we need to pursue the game through manageable doses. Otherwise we can tank a person's taste for the work—plus we're asking for trouble in more ways than we can mention.

Some will progress more quickly than others owing in part to fitness and innate talent. All told, climbers who usually thrive in the trad world are those with the right attitude, those willing to jump the grade down and get busy on some moderate classics. The aim at the outset is to be stoked on the whole trad climbing adventure in the first place, that you're out there routefinding, placing your own protection, running out the rope, building your own anchors, feeling you're traveling "where no man has gone before." Finding the thrill in that experience eliminates any shame in slapping down an "easy" climb, drawing inspiration from the challenge instead of feeling humiliated by the modest numbers. It's also the fastest way to improve because the learning environment is thrilling rather than terrifying.

Continued on next page

The Incredible Hulk.

GREG EPPERSON

Continued from previous page

The great American boulderer and soloist, Lisa Rands, is a prime example of a boulderer who rose to the trad occasion. Lisa is freakishly powerful on the boulders, whether plastic or real rock, as demonstrated on countless videos and photo spreads. She already had vast experience on everything from Buttermilks granite to English gritstone, as well as a string of victories at World Cup competitions, when she confided to me that she wanted to try the trad game, especially alpine rock climbing and big wall free climbing. Lucky for me she lived just down the street, so we began plotting her path from boulders to big walls.

Since her explosive power was strictly world class, I put her on a strict boulder-free diet. Although I suspect she cheated here and there, she was determined when we hit the local sport climbs at Owen's Gorge. She was just clipping bolts, but scaling full-length pitches one after the other was a handy and enjoyable means to boost her endurance. We also sought out pitches featuring extensive crack climbing sections.

Initially it was a study in contrasts. Where I sunk a hand jam, shook out and chalked up, Lisa man handled the crack as if she were ripping a phone book in half. Where I would lever out off thumbs up fingerlocks, making long reaches to the haven of the next jam, Lisa would pimp and campus up ¼-inch edges. Because of her atomic bouldering power, this strategy worked—for a while. In the long run, though, my ability to husband strength and rest, exactly where Lisa "cruxed," meant that I could go farther and faster.

Jamming in particular involves coordination, rhythm and timing, plus a visceral feel achieved only through mileage. Slowly one achieves efficient movement and flow, and in this manner the gap between Lisa's jamming and face climbing skills began to close. We started hitting other areas nearby, particularly those granite crags featuring styles in keeping with much of the big wall free climbing in California. When we switched over to gear routes, we dropped the grade; when we ventured onto the techy face climbs, which were closer to Lisa's forte, we upped it a bit. We tasted the splitter cracks at the Needles and Yosemite, adjusting and choosing our itinerary so the climbs were hard enough to test and challenge, but easy enough for learning to continue.

As incentive to stay on the fast track, we agreed to be filmed on one of the classic big wall free climbs of the High Sierra: the Incredible Hulk. The route we chose, the 1,200-foot Venturi Effect, follows a line of thin cracks—fingertip laybacks, stemming corners, and straight-in finger and hand cracks—up the tallest part of the wall. This climb would be a perfect measuring stick as well as a milestone in Lisa's progression. Half the pitches are 5.12, with the burliest crux lying on the sustained ninth pitch. Lisa's challenge would involve the wide variety of crack climbing, her fluency with the gear and overall system, managing her economy of motion, the considerable endurance required, plus the mental challenges of keeping a tight head a thousand feet off the ground.

We stomped across 5 miles of backcountry to the base of the wall. Ropes were already rigged and cameramen poised to make us look courageous or ridiculous. We readied ourselves for the pimpy moves right off the deck. It was July, well into summer, but the temps were freezing so Lisa threw a few chemical hand warmers into her chalk bag.

Lisa was on fire over the first half of the wall, on-sighting a handful of 5.12 pitches. Following the eighth, though, a series of weird flaring hand jams seemed to short-circuit her poise and her technique. Her delicately placed shoes skipped

out of the shallow scoops and her methodical jamming reverted to the phonebook-tearing tomahawking. She made it up to my belay, but the effort had taken a lot out of her.

I pleaded with her to rest longer, to relax and recover, but she quickly started out on the crux pitch. Now, though, her earlier fire had waned to a flicker and even straightforward climbing was a challenge. Launching out on the steepest section,

Continued on next page

Thumbs-up jamming on pitch 8 on Airstream, Incredible Hulk.

GREG EPPERSON

Continued from previous page

she blew a fuse, attempting to gaston (pull outward on the edges of a crack) a hand jam while spazzing out with the gear. How she hung on for so long baffled me and the photographer as well. Finally she lobbed off onto a very sketchy cam. Following the pitch, I noticed that she had missed a perfect hand jam as well as an easy cam placement.

We topped out but Lisa was running on fumes, having dug so deep there was nothing left. That's the measure of a great climber like Lisa Rands. With the sun riding low we ripped down the rappel lines so Lisa (and the rest of us) could get warm and fed. Exhaustion that deep is a risky thing when an icy nightfall is an hour away.

Our Incredible Hulk adventure is a clear example of what happens when we stress test techniques that aren't deeply engrained. When pushed hard enough and we inch out past the red line, we revert to what we know best. For Lisa, this meant abandoning good jamming technique and essentially trying to face climb a crack. In doing so she missed a good jam, couldn't rest, and couldn't manage a good and available piece of pro. Then the whole shebang went downhill to a point where even her superior strength couldn't save her.

In some ways the next day was the true test. As I guzzled strong coffee and Lisa sipped her herbal tea, we examined her swollen and scabby hands. Was this the end of her quest? She had, after all, given it everything and taken a thumping. But instead of excuses or resentments, her eyes lit up in inspiration. She had just spent a fantastic day in a wild setting, climbing one of the finest mega routes in the High Sierras. She quickly sketched out a plan for the next leg of her trad voyage.

Lisa—first pitch, first moves, freezing cold.

PETER MORTIMER

Trad climbing is a world of wild diversity.

ROBERT MIRAMONTES

Continued from page 144

Over that first week our climbing improved but our aspirations sobered up in the face of stout grades and full trad value on the obscure domes.

The Josh experience was never merely climbing Fisticuffs or Intelligent Gas from Uranus (Josh is infamous for kooky route names), rather the entire enterprise of getting lost in boulder-strewn canyons, finding the cliff and the route, climbing same then scrumming around extravagantly on chossy tilted slabs to find an anchor or the way off. Squamish or Yosemite, say, usually sported moderate walk-offs or convenient anchors for rapping and belaying. But here in Josh we'd pull onto another euphoric summit only to wander about for 10 minutes searching for any hint of an anchor, often tossing loops of rope over impossibly situated boulders. Or maybe scrambling off the far side to stuff cams in a hidden gash and then backtrack, trailing enormous lengths of cord for a requisite leash to belay at the climbs' distant topout. Where the rubber met the grain, Joshua Tree much more resembled an alpine adventure than what's currently found at larger and populous cragging venues, with their ubiquitous fixed anchors and well-worn rappel routes.

After 7 straight days of coarse quartz monzonite, the backs of our hands had scabbed over like lepers, our fingerpads were so raw it hurt to hold a spoon, and our muscles were so worked it was a relief to squeeze back into the Bug and motor north. Long before we hit the Canadian border, though, I was already plotting ways to get back to Josh.

DNB

John Long

When Will Tyree asked me to join him for an ascent of the 2,200-foot-long DNB (Direct North Buttress of Middle Cathedral), I was the new hotshot in Camp 4. I climbed with Bridwell. I could boulder with the best of them. I came from Tahquitz and Suicide, with all that dire face climbing, and the DNB was mostly open face. I was perfect for the route—a total lie, and never would it be made more obvious than the day Will and I started up the Direct North Buttress.

The DNB had the reputation as being the hardest long face climb in Yosemite; to our knowledge it had only been free climbed three times. The night before the climb we slept in the woods below Middle Cathedral, ostensibly to get an early start, though I suspect Will wanted to keep me under tight reins so I couldn't duck out. This was his fourth attempt on the route. I slept well because I didn't know what I was getting into.

Will roused me before daybreak. Ten years my senior and vastly more experienced, he was not named Will Tyree at all; that was a moniker he'd poached from astrology and white magic. As we ate a spare breakfast of gorp and Rye Crisps, Will gazed up at the last visible stars and said everything looked right. I never learned his real name.

Longtime Yosemite climber and photographer Karl Baba high on the East Buttress of El Cap. The DNB follows the prominent half-shaded buttress streaking up Middle Cathedral in the background.

A short steep march through the pines gained us the base, with the great gray and orange bulk of Middle Cathedral rearing high into the dawn. We stopped at a left-facing chimney system on the narrow prow of the North Buttress, and as Will uncoiled the ropes, I gaped up at the sun blushing the top of the monolith, seemingly in the stratosphere.

"It's . . . it's a . . . pretty big cliff, Will," I said. "Very big."

Will was to lead the odd pitches. The topo showed a mantle on the third pitch as the hardest technical bit, and since this climb was Will's idea and all, we both felt he might as well lead the crux.

I followed the first lead with a gallon plastic water jug hanging around my neck that made chimneying a real bastard. So I was glad to start leading the second pitch, glad until I ran into the oily off-width slot about 40 feet above. Thrashing and cursing, I cared little for the fixed ring-angle peg 25 feet below and was certain the 5.7 rating on the topo was a cruel joke.

"Just layback it," Will yelled up. I did, and got the spins as I groped to the belay stance 50 feet above. As Will followed I gazed up and couldn't reckon where the route went at all. There wasn't a chimney or a crack or anything but a dinky layback flake. And that ended after 30 feet. I had by this time climbed several long Valley routes but these were all crack climbs, bottom to top, and being out there on the open face like this felt terrifying.

Will arrived and gave me the water jug, a white Clorox bleach bottle with a sling threaded through the small handle. Hauling water is a crucial aspect

Mixed Climbing

Mixed Climbing" is a term borrowed from alpine climbing, referring to a route featuring a mixture of rock and ice. In the trad world, mixed climbing means a route sporting a mixture of features and techniques. The term is apt for most long routes. Short crag climbs are often known for this hand crack or that chimney, for a flare, a steep face, a dike—meaning the route ascends a single feature for one or more pitches and generally involves that feature and a given technique. On big climbs like the DNB, you're certain to encounter varied features requiring a medley of techniques.

As with off-width climbing, we don't have to love every technique; but we have to know them all or many classic routes will remain out of reach. So it is the varied natures of long routes that encourage if not force us to develop skills we might otherwise avoid. This pressures us to work on our weaknesses, as opposed to indulging our strengths. Most people struggle to do this with any aspect of their lives, and even more so with snarky climbing techniques like unprotected flares. Strangely cruel how it works out that whatever our weakness, we are sure to encounter that very technique at the worst possible times—when we're thirsty and starving and exhausted and fighting to make the top before sundown. And there's Aunt Hagatha herself, glaring at us. Or maybe that fist crack or lieback we've been avoiding all these years.

High in the trad zone, Zion.

ANDREW BURR

Point is, big routes are the place to exercise technique, not learn it. A useful drill is to take a little time each outing or every couple of outings to do a climb or practice a technique we'd rather not touch or see or even hear about. The practice will pay dividends—of that we may be sure.

*The crux mantle on
pitch 3, DNB.*

CLINT CUMMINS

of every long climb. Few options are ideal; fewer still are as awful as what Will had brought along—a Clorox bleach bottle. After we took our first sips, which burned all the way down, Will admitted he should have rinsed the bottle out a few more times after finding it in the Camp 4 Dumpster.

He surveyed the wall above and said, "This is where Arnold backed off, that little chicken shit." Then he laughed so loud I swear it echoed off El Capitan, a mile across the valley. I thought Will

had been gazing at the moon too long and, look-ing up, knew that whoever Arnold was, he was no fool. Will had tried this climb three times in the last month and each partner had backed off at this very stance. But just now Will scared me more than the climb and anyhow he was already halfway up the flake.

When the flake ended, Will fulfilled my worst fears by traversing dead left, directly onto the bald face. He got to the crux mantle, fell a few times, and

Climbing Anchor to Anchor

On any long climb that sees much traffic, standard belay positions have long been established, rarely through the installation of belay bolts, but rather certain ledges, stances, blocks, trees, etc. have become the common and often obvious belay stations used by all. The topo will list these, yet we still find ourselves searching for the next belay. "Stance" or "ledge" often refers to features so ubiquitous on a route like the DNB that the question becomes: Which one? Remember that a pitch longer than 150 feet is rare on any rock climb. So what to do when the options are various and none seem better than the others?

As a general rule, we never pass up a natural place to belay, providing we're near—or greater than—half a rope length out. We can't start belaying every 50 feet no matter how good the stances. But once we have pushed the rope out a ways, rarely should we pass an obvious ledge or convenient crack. And we never do when the next 100 feet look devoid of options. Remember that all belay anchors are built around at least one bombproof placement, which we then shore up with back-ups. If we are out 100 or so feet, and we can find a decent stance and a handy crack for bombproof stoppers and cams, the smart move is usually to stop and belay. The station can be built quickly and securely and broken down just as fast. That's what we want.

**Bomber belay ledge,
Cloud Tower, Red Rocks.**

MATT KUEHL

Beyond this, the criteria begins and ends with finding that place affording the most secure individual placements. That might be an awkward stance—or no stance at all. But we don't move to a higher or lower locale and anchor off bunk placements because it's easier on our feet and back.

Our first priority is our security, which sometimes results in us belaying in unnatural places, wherever we can get good anchors. Beyond that, if the options are mostly the same in terms of security, decisions will hinge on time. If you're hurrying, run the rope and take what you can get in terms of stances and ledges, as long pitches cut down on belay setups and transitions, and generally are more time effective. If time is not pressing, get the rope out there a decent ways and stop at any good stance or ledge. Seventy-meter ropes give us flexibility in this regard. We often can run two pitches together, not so much to save time as to bypass wanting belay stations and press on to the good ledge and the crack overhead. Climbing "belay anchor to belay anchor" should always mean moving from one good anchoring array to another, comfort coming second to security.

finally pulled up on the bolt to a wee belay stance right out there in open space. I could look straight up and across at him and see gray sky between his chest and the building-like wall, which just steepened and soared out of sight above. The sight of him dangling out there in no-man's-land scared the shit out of me. He slugged in a piton and the rope came tight almost immediately.

"On belay, John."

Meanwhile, hanging at my belay with 1,900 feet of uncertainty overhead, I'd gained that threshold every wannabe rock star confronts, when he or she determines once and for all if they're really cut out for this work. I could bail off and go back home. Or I could press through the door and into the beyond, where the game is not simply fun, but for keeps.

Even terrified as I was, I couldn't face going back home. I'd worn my bright blue Robbins boots to school just so I could field questions about them and admit I was a rock climber. I'd studied guidebooks tucked into my schoolbooks and while camped on the toilet. I'd climbed with Jim Bridwell. Unless I unclipped from that anchor and started liebacking I knew it had all been charades—but I couldn't unclip. Then stubborn conviction kicked in. I was a rock climber. Maybe not a bold one. Certainly not an experienced one. But I wanted to be one, worse than anything else in the world, and though my knees were clacking like wood blocks I unclipped and started up the flake.

I was learning one of the basic truths about all big climbs: Without the head to handle the fear and the trouser-filling exposure, the greatest technique in the world was utterly worthless. Put differently, there was no substitute for experience and confidence, which mostly amounted to the same things.

When I got to the stance and saw its one anchor pin—a baby angle driven straight up—I grabbed the rack and raced for a good crack about 30 feet above. After blasting home three pitons, I told Will he'd better lead this pitch, lowered back down to the belay, and stared at the baby angle. I was flying apart inside.

"Are you with me, John?" Will asked.

This was probably the closest I had ever gotten to a moment of truth. I could tell how much doing the route meant to Will, but to his credit, it didn't mean so much that he'd drag me along against my will. I took a sip of bleach and told him yes, I was with him. But I totally lacked experience. It was my fault that I didn't admit as much before, but on a route as steep and scary as the DNB, I simply felt overmatched. But if he'd lead, I'd do my best to follow, even if I had to hand-walk the rope.

We still had what seemed like 10 miles to go, and the only way we'd succeed was if a real climber took over, a climber like I wanted to become, a climber like Will Tyree. I told Will he was on belay. He cast off.

I cleaned the baby angle with two blows and my knees set to knocking again. But once I got moving, and felt the gentle tug of the toprope, I settled in and understood why the DNB is one of the world's great rock climbs. Steep and amply fitted with holds that, if not terrific, are good enough, the route follows an almost invisible string of grooves, flakes, and thin corners, all connected with steep face climbing on rock ranging from flint gray to flame orange. Stray 10 feet off route and the way is insuperable; stay right on line and the climbing rarely lags under 5.8, with the odd 5.9 and 5.10 section to remind you that you're on the real McCoy.

Like many climbs that track the open face, the adventure is made exciting because the features are mostly flakes and shallow, discontinuous cracks that make you work for good jams and adequate protection. Because the rock forces you out there on the naked skin of the thing, you never feel good and plugged in, rather you're working the wrinkles and divots, sometimes wishing for a deep crack to crawl into and never getting same. Here is the quintessence of "exposed." And vexing are the routefinding duties. Perhaps more than any other skill, routefinding on a climb as steep and nebulous as the DNB is never an exact art, but the experienced climber works at a significant advantage. And to be sure, the nuances of routefinding are part intuitive and part objective surveying, and just then I had little of either skill. On the first ascent, Yvon Chouinard and Steve Roper said that had they not "moved as smartly as coyotes on the hunt," they never would have succeeded.

In an hour we gained the notorious undercling pitch, where Eric Beck had broken his arm during an early free climbing attempt. When I pawed

Notes on Trad Anchoring

Anchoring and protection are separate studies requiring ongoing attention. Both issues are well covered in other manuals in the How to Rock Climb series. However, there are special considerations for trad anchoring. These considerations start with the guiding principle issuing from the Yosemite System, in which every aspect of climbing should strive toward "safety and simplicity."

It is worth repeating: Along with tying in and belaying, anchoring ourselves to the cliff is possibly the most important procedure we execute every time out. On mega trad climbs—which remain the gold standard of the varied trad opus—time is a commodity that needs constant managing. This along with several other factors underscores our guiding principle: Everything else being equal, the simplest solution is always the best. The more links and complexity we put into the anchoring system the greater chance for something going wrong or being overlooked—not to mention wasting time we may need for the climb, descent, etc.

The most common belay anchor found on both sport and popular trad climbs consists of two bolts placed side by side. Biners are clipped into the hangers and rotated so the gate opening is down and each biner is facing away from the other. Here, once the knot is attached and tension applied, the gates rotate away from the hanger, so they cannot come unclipped.

There are countless ways to tie off or "rig" such an anchor. Consider going simple and secure, using a figure eight on a bight clipped directly into biners clipped into the bolts. Although not equalized, the eight on a bight does the job nicely off solid bolts in solid rock—and nothing less will do. If the bolts are widely spaced (rare), or some other troubling factor, and equalization seems a good thing, we tie a double figure eight and equalize this way. This is an underutilized technique commonly seen with world-class climbers. Another option is the bowline on a bight, also known as the Atomic Clip. For lovers of clean, simple rigging, the Atomic Clip is a work of art. But the cordelette and the equalette (although more gear- and time-intensive) are good options too (see FalconGuides' *Climbing Anchors* for details on how to rig various equalizing systems).

A side note on equalization: Comprehensive drop tests have shown that true equalization, or anything where the load sharing is spread equally between the pieces, is virtually impossible to achieve in real world climbing. It can best be approximated with two good bolts closely spaced, but in most other circumstances we're left with partial equalization. Noting the remarkable

up to the actual undercling—a thin, razor-sharp flake leading dead left to Will's sling belay—he warned me not to fall because his anchors were "questionable."

Since he had called the baby-angle belay "fine," I reckoned he had no anchor at all. But I was feeling more and more like a real climber, so I shuffled straight across, feet up by my hands. When my foot popped near the end, Will gasped. But I made it okay. His anchor: a thin, "horizontal" piton waffled into a flaky seam down by his feet. Several pitches of superb face climbing led to a nasty flare

rarity of total anchor failures seen over the last decade—of the many millions of belay anchors built and disassembled worldwide—we can fairly conclude that whatever degree of equalization we are getting must be "good enough." The subject, and the countless rigging options, is one of the biggest time sucks in all of climbing; beyond what has been mentioned, it's not instructive for us to go there in this book.

Always remember: It's important to get our tie-in length just right so we can relax, get comfortable, and recover at each belay. If we're left hanging at awkward attitudes and fighting the rope and gravity just to get a load off, we are no longer climbing efficiently, and we'll pay on the next pitch or the one after that. Belays are our only chance to decelerate out of action mode, if only briefly, and the experienced climber knows the value of copping a rest when she can get one.

On most well-traveled trad routes, belay anchors are readily found and arranged. If no fixed anchors are available, and normally they are not in the wilds, then cams are most commonly used. Cams are especially effective because they are multi-directional and can often be moved up and down a crack, making partial equalization easy by clipping into the sling on the upper cam, then the stem on the lower unit (though not all camming devices have this option). Because stoppers are not so easily maneuvered, it is often best to use a double figure eight to clip into them. And always bear in mind that we need something for an upward pull as well. This is where equalizing with just the rope gets tricky, and why many climbers still carry a cordelette.

Although we use many types of anchors for belays, the basic principles remain the same. Make it bomber, keep it simple, and never trust one piece of gear unless it's the rope. Of all the mottos and strategies relating to anchors, redundancy is probably the most important. Simply put: Double, even triple up whenever necessary. Of course there are exceptions. The giant sequoia is a good example—we only need one of these for our belay. A bad example would be the locking biner used by some as the sole attachment to a belay anchor. The problem with this (over the more conventional two biner clip-in) is that, although a locking biner rarely if ever breaks, they routinely come unlocked, whether from the vibration of belaying, jostling at the station, or from the spring-loaded locking unit failing to engage because of grit in the sleeve—or more likely, from forgetting to lock it in the first place. Though a single locker seems to fulfill our keep-it-simple recipe, the "locking" aspect introduces more complexity than a simple two-biner clip-in, which is much easier to check at a glance.

in which even Will struggled. That tenth pitch took us to a big ledge system forming the lower right side of a U-shaped bowl, a prominent horseshoe-shaped scoop running the length of the north face. We were over 1,200 feet up and relished the first opportunity in 5 hours to kick back and relax. The sun beat down and we polished off the last of the Clorox water.

One of the principal challenges of these pitches, and perhaps even more so above, was trying to find adequate belay anchors. Straight-in cracks were basically nonexistent on the lower face, leaving us to piece together short flake and ramp systems, often settling for anchors fashioned from thin pins beaten into seams or behind flexing flakes. This is perhaps one instance where modern wired nuts and cams are inferior to thin chrome molly pitons that you can wallop into those incipient cracks. Advanced rigging systems using sliding knots and various equalization strategies can also add a little security nowadays; but for us, way back when, the main challenge was to find a stance where we could sink at least two bomber pieces, which typically were horizontal or baby angle pitons. Even if we had to cut a pitch short, like 80 feet, whenever we gained a good stance affording reasonable anchors, we always stopped, and with the one exception low down, managed to avoid some pretty sketchy belays.

Will pulled out a crumpled photo of Middle Cathedral and we both smiled to see how far we'd come, though nearly half again as much rock lay overhead. But the way was clear now: straight up a huge crack system formed by the left side of Thirsty Spire, a colossal tangerine pinnacle towering 1,000 feet above and right. We talked about Frank Sacherer and Beck, who had made the remarkable first free ascent of the DNB 5 years prior. Still, we figured that during the first ascent in 1962, Chouinard and Roper must have been free climbing for the most part, since the hardest climbing was out on the open face, in linking the nebulous corners and flakes. There was little if anything to nail out there.

The two had probably just used the bolt for the mantle, as we had, and maybe tensioned across the undercling. Either way, they'd bagged a plum.

We looked around and across at El Capitan, which someday I hoped to climb. Will had, and he assured me that I would too. He knew the right things to say, and his invitation to lead the next pitch was just what I needed to regain confidence.

A long 5.7 pitch led to a cruxy 5.9 traverse into a bombay shaft that rifled straight to the top, and in which I set up my sling belay. Will set off, jamming a grueling 5.9 hand crack deep in the corner above. Suddenly he yelled, "ROCK!" From my belay in an alcove, I glanced up to see a medicine ball of granite ricocheting down between the corner's walls. I hunkered into the alcove and felt the concussion as the rock blasted off the wall. Slowly withdrawing my head, I saw a huge powder mark on the rock about 3 feet higher. Will seemed almost more scared than I, and after checking the rope for chops at the next belay, we started climbing really fast. But the route never let up.

While we were now in a huge crack and chimney, visible from nearly anywhere in the Valley, the cracks were if anything even more flaky and incipient. Arranging bomber anchors was virtually impossible with the gear we had. We could usually get one, but rarely two good anchor pins. And the lead protection was often worse. There was not a whole lot that was holding us on that wall, and Will made it plain that we couldn't make a big mistake up there—and he let it go at that. Twenty years later, a leader fell out of one of these upper chimney pitches, ripped the belay anchor clean out, and the team plunged an estimated 1,800 feet to their makers. Like on the lower section, whenever we reached a spot where we could get a couple truly stout pins or big hexes, we'd stop and belay, even if it was only 80 feet above the last stance.

Nearing the top at last, even the 5.6 chimney pitch was a polecat, and the 5.8 slot on pitch 17 felt like 5.10—and in fact was later upgraded to 5.10a.

These dastardly exit chimneys didn't let up till the exit slab, where Middle finally lay back and we frictioned higher, searching for the true summit. The heat and bleach-water scorched our throats, and our hands were cramping. We'd been going for 10 hours straight.

A 4th-class shoulder provided an escape off left, but despite our blinding dehydration we scrambled another couple of hundred feet to the top. Somehow Will found the summit cairn and a log book inside an old can. "Our best climb," he wrote. "My only climb," I told Will. If I wasn't a real climber then, at least I knew I could have a chance at it.

When we finally stumbled back down into the valley, I was so fried I crawled into the Merced River and damn near drank it dry. I would do that at least a dozen times after long climbs.

Three years later, Will Tyree figured prominently during the planning of the first 1-day ascent of El Capitan. He took down mine and my partners' Jim Bridwell and Billy Westbay's birthdates, and figured out the day when our zodiac signs lined up in a power configuration. That same year I climbed another big route on Middle Cathedral with Will. Then he quit coming to the Valley and I never saw him again.

Approaching the undercling on pitch 6, DNB. CLINT CUMMINS

Northeast Buttress of Mount Slesse

Peter Croft

The southwest corner of British Columbia is crumpled into a nexus of mountain ranges, as choked with peaks as it is with Douglas fir and slide alder. The Squamish Chief is a single monolith nestled into one of the many deep green dividing rifts fingering out toward the sea. Soon enough I wanted to try my hand at something wilder than The Chief, to apply my crag learning to the larger alpine world.

The 2,500-foot Northeast Buttress of Mount Slesse sits atop the throne of must-do alpine rock climbs in southwestern Canada. Although taller

Mt. Slesse, rising in the background.

JOHN LONG

Reading the Rock

Learning to assess the route ahead or the cliff in general is a critical skill for the adventure climber. Reading the rock helps keep us out of trouble—or simply turns us away from a bad route. Once we are fluent at reading the rock we usually find the best stone and the primo lines. Sometimes it is obvious. A dark black swath often means a wet streak—greenery, probably bushes, etc. Other times the signs are subtler—different shades of gray denote clean granite or rock carpeted with corn flake lichen. Buff yellow and fiery orange granite cliffs tend to overhang in terrific clean sweeps, while the same colors in conglomerate rock may presage flaky or crumbly passage.

Our knack to read the rock draws from our past experience, including the knowledge that each new cliff will sport unique characteristics. Time spent in different parts of Yosemite Valley, for instance, will pay dividends when we tackle the varying granite encountered on, say, Sentinel, as opposed to Middle Cathedral, with its versicolored face and discontinuous cracks, and Elephant Rock, which features laser cut splitters running bottom to top.

Especially on the prolonged efforts found on new routes, awareness of conditions and the subtleties of the wall aid us handsomely in navigating the drier, better quality stone, as well as finding protection along the way. Sometimes a cliff will perfectly resemble a climb from our past so we naturally assume conditions will remain the same. This often proves the case—but we need always to stand ready to adapt and learn. Trad climbing has been described as an adventure in creative problem solving. This is not only correct, but tells us there is never a final answer. We keep learning till we coil the rope that last time—so help us God.

peaks are nearby, Slesse rears up like a black fang. Spectacular from a distance, it is monstrous from below and has a morbid history to match. The story of its first ascent (1963) is benign—another Fred Beckey route in a continent riddled with them. But 7 years earlier, one of the worst air disasters on record occurred when TransCanada Flight 810 slammed into the mountain's east face and sixty-two people were lost.

I knew little of this tragedy when approaching the climb with fellow Squamishite Mike Down. In the predawn gloom we picked through boulders and twisted aluminum and tried hard not to get spooked, feeling like truants sneaking through a graveyard on our way to attempt something already at the limits of our courage. Even the normally friendly sunrise did little to stay the creep factor as we reached the base, where 2,000-foot walls of gray diorite and dark granite spun crazily above our heads. I clenched my jaw and stared at the ground.

Although understandable, my unwillingness to gaze into the heart of the beast meant I forfeited all rights to spy out the route ahead. On big backcountry climbs like Mount Slesse, routefinding, I would sadly come to realize, is half of the game.

At the rope-up spot Mike fished out his cord—a hefty 11mm, though a measly 130 feet long. Even I could foresee the problems. Climbing a 2,500-foot route with such a puny line meant that many more pitches, that many more anchors to build and

Another Look at Rope Length

Picking the right tools for a particular climb helps us to climb faster and safer. The choice of what length of rope to use can be the most important of all. Too short and we'll never reach the belay ledges and anchors on long pitches. In case of retreat, we'll use up our rack long before we're halfway down. Too long and we'll spend ages stacking and untangling heaps of superfluous cord. As well, any amount of simul-climbing will likely be hateful when hauling, for instance, an 80-meter lunker of a rope. Unless you're right at the cutting edge doing FAs or early repeats, the appropriate length cord has usually been established by the third or fourth ascent. Ask around. When in doubt, go longer.

Nylon rope: hallmark of technical climbing.

BEN HORTON

changeover and break down, plus the unspoken horror of fifty rappels if we had to bail from high on the buttress.

In no time we ran into time-consuming nastiness. Hard climbing, vegetated cracks, and lousy pro slowed us to a pathetic pace. Time and time again we would thrutch and gimp around on dicey terrain, only to look down at the end of a pitch to see moderate cracks and ramps to our immediate left or right, seemingly obvious lines of weakness that would have saved chunks of valuable daylight.

Both of our packs bulged with food, drink, and bivi gear. The sheer bulk of these loads ensured we would have to bivi. Every time we leaned back and peered up to scope the route our packs would shift horribly and we'd totter wildly out of balance, clutching for holds and closing our line of sight. Our technical climbing ability (which I thought was everything) was easily up to the challenge. Everything else was not. Darkness caught us halfway up.

We slept a ways apart, on small mossy ledges. Mike had done things like this before, so presumably he relaxed and slumbered comfortably. I lay wide awake, at once thrilled and terrified. I kept thinking how fantastic it all would be if I only lived through the whole adventure. I couldn't foresee any lethal obstacles, it is true, but if it was possible to simply expire from the sheer magnitude of the experience I felt I might not have much time left.

The orange dawn changed everything. It warmed us up long before the pocket glacier was

Scoping the Route

Always eyeball the line, long and hard, when approaching a big route. Any mega cliff is subject to foreshortening, but the farther we are from the base, the less distortion. Try and take a clear mental picture of the overall line—especially halfway points and dominant landmarks like large trees, ledges, or exit gullies. Cross check with the topo and watch for telltale features that might mark, say, the beginning of a crucial traverse. Though there will be a lot more detail to scrutinize close up, much of the upper wall will be obscured by the bulges and ledges lower down, possibly masking features to a surprising degree.

Often the approach march switchbacks or angles enough to give a broad scope of vision. Left-facing corners, for instance, may be all but invisible when viewed from the right, where the features appear to merge with the face, but appear in bold relief as we traverse to the left and below them.

It's common to scan a guidebook and believe the real world will prove as simple and direct as our line-drawn topo. Where the page tells us to start up the obvious corner, we look up and see three separate corners, all looking pretty obvious—or totally nebulous. There is no single trick to spare us the teeth-gnashing frustration of sketchy info and a sketchier route, but much can be sorted out by periodically scanning the line during the hike in. When all existing beta makes no sense at all, think like a first ascensionist: What would I do and where would I go if I was doing the first ascent of this climb? This will often re-boot the decision-making apparatus, removing the clutter and opening our eyes to the obvious or the probable.

illuminated, thousands of feet below. Breakfasting on chocolate and cheese, I lay back and watched first light trace a line on the wall above. The buttress on the upper half narrowed and steepened, limiting options and making the route much more straightforward for a crag rat like myself. Although this was the routes' crux, we could make time. Having consumed the better part of our baggage, our lumbering pace picked up and we started enjoying ourselves.

The route ended abruptly on the summit and we basked in glory as the sun slowly sank.

Eventually we started poking around for the descent. Late afternoon slid into evening. Finishing the rappels, we realized we didn't have time to descend to cars, hamburgers, and milk shakes.

We were well off the peak but the entire, sprawling flank of the mountain was tilted about 30 degrees. The only spots secure against a terminal roll-down loomed by some old dead trees. Once again we settled into separate bivi spots, this time at tree line, a lonesome nowhere between worlds, spooning the splintery stumps of storm-battered pines instead of our soft girlfriends.

Jungle Bivouac. Venezuela. ANDREW BURR

Summit Glory

Hitting the top of some mega classic climb is worthy of proper celebration. It is the culmination, perhaps, of months of dreaming in technicolor and training till our fingertips bleed. Take care, however, not to pop the cork until the appropriate moment. The summit is no place to linger when the sun dives over the horizon and a gnarly descent beckons. Take a breather and behold the panorama—but keep the psyche adrenalized until the whole adventure is a done thing.

"Nice work . . . if you can find it."

ANDREW BURR

CHAPTER 25

The Vampire

John Long

To get to Tahquitz Rock from LA, you drive a dismal freeway a couple hours due east, passing town after town rammed together ass to cheek, till the housing tracks and strip malls and the whole shambling heap gradually thins out past Riverside. Soon you enter a low valley between the San Gregornio Mountains on the left (11,503 feet high), and the San Jacinto massif (10,834 feet) on the right. The biggest face is the north wall of Mount San Jacinto itself, known as San Jack, which gains nearly 10,000 feet in less than 7 miles, and is the largest vertical rise, or "prominence," in North America. The great face seems to sweep straight up off the dry flats of Banning, a nowhere town infamous for meth labs, alcoholism, and wife beaters. It is here that all through high school we'd start zigzagging up San Jack's shambling right shoulder, chugging along the old two-lane mountain road, heading for Tahquitz Rock.

After 20 steep miles, a clear view opens up through the pines, and from a striking high vantage, marble-white Tahquitz rears off the escarpment 10 miles across Strawberry Valley. The striking feature is a bulging shield-like wall on the west face. When we first learned that The Vampire bisected that bulge, it became our ultimate goal. The guidebook told us this spectacular route was first climbed by

Tamara Hastie at the start of the Bat Crack, The Vampire. JEFF JOHNSON

Royal Robbins and Dave Rearick in 1959, which sounded like a thousand years ago. During that time, way back when, the history of American rock climbing was largely written on the steep cracks and soaring buttresses of Tahquitz.

"To climb in Idyllwild is to tread the footsteps of legends that pushed new limits, and helped invent technical climbing in the process," wrote guidebook writer Bob Gaines. "Arguably, the first climbs in America to be rated 5.8, 5.9, 5.10, 5.11, 5.12, and 5.13 were done here."

Yosemite pioneer Yvon Chouinard wrote about the influence Tahquitz had on Valley climbing, in his influential article, "Modern Yosemite Climbing," published 50 years ago in the *American Alpine Journal*.

"All the techniques for free climbing were established not in Yosemite Valley, but at Tahquitz Rock in Southern California. From the 1930s to the present day, it has been a teaching ground for nearly every prominent Valley climber. Because of its accessibility, compactness, and solid cracks, Tahquitz offers ideal conditions for pushing free climbing to its limits. Most of the routes were first done with direct aid, but over a period of time nearly everyone has been done free."

That is, almost every one but The Vampire—by a country mile the best and scariest looking of the old Tahquitz routes. When Robbins and Dave Rearick bagged the first ascent (5.9, A4) in 1959, nailing pitons in The Vampire's thin and expanding flakes, it was a breakthrough and a precursor for 1961, when Royal teamed up with another

Tahquitz vet, Tom Frost, and Chuck Pratt for the first ascent of El Capitan's Salathe Wall, widely considered one of the greatest rock climbs of all time. Royal would go on to become one of Yosemite's preeminent big wall climbers and most talented free climbers of his generation. It all began at Tahquitz—just like it began for us, decades later.

Anyhow, we were progressing nicely and starting to pick off the last of the big aid routes from the Robbins era, each one getting progressively bigger and more difficult till The Vampire was the only one left. Somewhere in there our bouldering mentor at Joshua Tree, Paul Gleason, mentioned that The Vampire's first hard pitch, called The Bat Crack, just might go all free. I went up to look, and remember little besides the hand crack that pinched to fingers, and that the hanging stance came none too soon. At 5.11a, The Bat Crack was an instant classic. But a

Photos

Before the digital revolution in the late 1990s, photography was cumbersome and expensive. Most older climbing history involves the written word; though most climbers had cameras or access to a camera, comparatively few shots were ever taken. Nowadays, $200 buys us a tiny digital camera with a gazillion megapixels that can yield photos suitable for a magazine cover. The

Arrested moments, otherwise lost in time.

MATT KUEHL

great thing about the new technology is how we can share with others by way of trip reports and so forth, chucked up there on the Internet. Not everyone brings a camera on every route, and only a few pics are ever great ones. But we all love to see photos of routes we've done and places on high where we've cussed and cried and laughed and thrown things and lost skin and one of our nine lives. In a sense, our personal photos come to comprise a community photo album available worldwide. Take a pic or two when you can and post them for everyone's enjoyment. It allows all of us to climb a route two times—the first time, with a rope, and the next time, with our eyes.

Near the top of the Bat Crack. JEFF JOHNSON

Personal Milestones

As we are starting to appreciate, most of the strategies put forth here have little to do with how hard we pursue the game. This is especially true for the milestones that we all experience on the cliffside. To be sure, Roxanne's little pond is Danny's Rubicon, but this hardly detracts from his experience. The man with the casual approach might sound too demure to have milestones, but he is mistaken if he believes as much. He too will have remarkable memories, routes he climbed that stand out in his mind in the sharpest possible relief. Most all climbing is an intense experience evoking full presence from all who tie into the line. And anytime we are fully present for our lives, even if only long enough to scale a short rock wall, that memory will be one we will often return to, the time when the world momentarily caught fire, and 2 or 20 years later, still glows at the edges. These are the milestones accenting all of our climbing careers. Surprisingly, many such experiences have only a passing relevance to technical difficulty.

For instance, some of my most memorable moments came early on, while slogging up through the grades. My first grand tours up classics such as Mechanics Route (5.8) and Open Book (5.9), at Tahquitz Rock, were life-altering experiences. The great Dick Jones, with tennis shoes on his feet and a manila yachting rope lashed round his waist, first led the Mechanics in October 1937, running the old whiteline out over vertical face climbing that still sees some modern climbers calling for their mothers. And the notorious Open Book, first climbed in 1947 by John Mendenhall, who fashioned custom wooden wedges in his garage for the wide crack on the second and third pitch. Then 17-year-old Royal Robbins came along and free climbed the route in 1952, quite possibly accomplishing the first multi-pitch 5.9 in America.

This is history. When we make it our own, we climb ourselves into the pantheon of the "steep" and rub elbows and exchange silent moments, out there on the sharp end, with the Dick Joneses and Royal Robbinses of the world. In fact everyone who ever climbed that route is your partner, across time and forever. These are the moments we remember. These are the moments that make a life, be it 5.7 or 5.13.

Racking for work.

MATT KUEHL

glance out left where the next pitch traversed onto the bald and terrifying shield told us this first crack pitch was tame stuff after all.

A month later, Mike Graham, Rick Accomazzo, and I were hanging from slings atop The Bat Crack, eyeing a thin series of holds leading left to The Vampire's flake system. The holds were about 10 feet above the A4 seam Robbins had followed to gain the flake. The tremendous exposure terrified us, particularly Mike Graham who scratched part-way out these holds and cranked a mantle he could not reverse. The flake was still some ways left, and Mike said the moves looked impossible. He would have to sink a bolt or risk a bone-crushing fall back into the dihedral. The wall was so steep he could hardly drill, but somehow he managed.

Ricky launched off, gained the bolt, and said he thought he could jump left to the flake. Say what?

Classic Repeats

We reviewed the strategy of keeping an eye open for the established classics found at most every crag. It's worth knowing that there are some cases where the route itself will be less than a five-star masterpiece and what in fact is "classic" are the experiences people have had over time on a given route. A photograph, an anecdote, an outright lie can become something we have to check out firsthand. Most of us grew up with pictures of the "old guys" on El Capitan, Half Dome, etc., and when I finally found myself yanking my way through the Zig Zags, clipping the bolts off Texas Flake, or pulling the Tyrolean traverse off Lost Arrow Spire, I was stepping right into those old photos and stories and I felt like a time traveler and a hero. None of these feats represented any notable technical achievement. Not even. Rather I was revisiting moments in time, as classic right then as they once were and will be for so long as we tie into the rope.

Diary entry July 1952, Summit, Middle Teton.

JODY LANGFORD

Remarkably, he tried just that. However, his hands only brushed the flake and he took a sensational, arching fall. He tried several more times, each time blowing Mike and me away with his outrageous falls. But not so much as when he latched onto the flake and began to layback up the vertical wall, saying it was only "easy" 5.10.

Over the following years, boot technology so improved that this traverse, nearly impossible in the old hard-soled shoes, became low-end 5.11 in the sticky rubber models. Likewise, Robbins and Rearick had to drive pitons into that wildly expanding flake—subtle work and probably dangerous as hell. But now, Ricky could slot Stoppers at will into the ready pods and constrictions, and with this extra security, hinge up the frightening feature with impunity.

An even harder thin crack began directly off the hanging belay at the end of the flake pitch. But that required no dramatic leaps. Thin locks—which once accepted tied-off pegs, and now finger-tips—led to dicey smearing on glossy lesions, all positioned on what felt like The Shield headwall. Then the wall eased to 5.8 below the summit.

The Vampire was the most pivotal climb I ever did, more than El Capitan, Astroman, or any of the others, since we knew by then what we could do. After The Vampire, gazing way down Strawberry Valley from the summit, we could not believe we had free climbed Tahquitz's greatest prize, which along with the Nabisco Wall in Yosemite, and the Naked Edge in Boulder's El Dorado Canyon, became one of the most sought after and well-traveled free climbs in America.

For most trad climbers, there are a few routes, or maybe just one route, that are total game changers, where once you climb them, the possibilities open up exponentially. For us, that route was The Vampire. What followed is something I could never have foreseen. Most of our little group of "Stonemasters" would gain success through experience, technique, savvy, and wild gumption. A few would push this gumption to extremes, the following year, most notably out at Joshua Tree National Monument.

Mia and Guy Kesse on the spectacular second pitch of The Vampire, 5.11

KEVIN POWELL

CHAPTER 26

The Weight of the Rope

Peter Croft

I had lucked into a key epoch in Squamish climbing. Although The Chief was punished by abysmal weather much of the year, new routes were everywhere for the taking. With the plum tree so heavy with fruit, our small band racked up dozens of first ascents and first free ascents. Others had steelier fingers and more innate talent, but no one chomped so rabidly at the bit as me. I saw my eagerness as simply a quirk I could not shake. Some of my friends made fun of me and sometimes I felt embarrassed. But there was nothing I could do. I

had to go. The slightest easing in the low pressure troughs rolling in off the Pacific had me hustling to the crags and booting up.

A break in the storm occurred one winter afternoon, leaving us a few hours before nightfall. I sped out to The Chief with Tami Knight, a former gymnast and acrobat who was as game as any to invest in my optimism. With most of the main wall running with dark wet streaks, we headed for the Malemute, a more exposed seaside bluff with just enough gravel along its base to support a railway. These train tracks were our path to the rock.

I set my sights on Overly Hanging Out, an

Hunger for Stone

Of all the many talents beneficial to the climber, none provide the base, the potential to improve, or the staying power like raw desire. Tempered steel finger tendons and double-jointed flexibility will speed the journey through the higher grades, but without the enduring fire in our belly the trip will be cut short by burnout, boredom, or both. This is true, to a certain extent, in many endeavors; but in climbing, self-motivation is usually the driving factor. From injuries and plateaus in performance to a dearth of rock and crap weather, the rock climber deals with it alone—or he takes up golf.

ANDREW BURR

Tami Knight styling the crux of Exasperator in Squamish.

PAT MORROW

Managing Rope Drag

A leader is not merely trailing a rope behind him. She is dragging it through every point of protection and over every corner, roof, rim, shelf, lip, bollard, bulge, and buttress. So any change of direction on a climb must be addressed (usually by using slings) or heinousness will occur. It's simple geometry: Rope drag is reduced to the extent that we straighten the path that the rope runs between belayer and leader.

When the line runs through pro to the left and to the right, we extend the lead rope off the pro so it runs more toward the middle, to that imaginary plumb (direct) line. The straighter, more unencumbered (less friction) that the line runs, the less rope drag. It only takes one cantankerous bend in the flow of the line and that groovy feeling of gliding up the wall is gone and Old Man Gravity is pulling at our harness like grim death. Climbers commonly extend every piece with full-length runners, an unnecessary waste of time, effort, and equipment, as well as exposing the leader to a bit longer fall—potentially critical if you're just above a ledge. Shorter slings—often just a quickdraw—usually do the job. Extend with long slings only when the rope takes a sharp bend, at the beginning and end of traverses, under overhangs, and so forth.

Sometimes after clipping a higher piece we might downclimb to unclip a problem piece lower down. Sometimes it is difficult to predict what clip is going to contribute to the drag higher up. If in doubt, sling it!

Sling it!

ANDREW BURR

old aid route angling up and right, following huge arches and finishing up through a medley of stepped roofs. The first part had already gone free at 5.10 but the last lead had rebuffed all attempts. With only a few hours of daylight remaining, we opted out of the first two pitches and instead found a direct start to the business.

Having just spent weeks staring at the rain, I pounced on the overhangs, underclinging, and laybacking like mad. Much of the climbing was sandwiched between the overlaps and entailed undercuts with feet up so high my knees were knocking my elbows. Wangling in gear was desperate and the fear level sky high; I saved strength and calmed my nerves by not fiddling with slings and just clipping the rope directly into the pieces. The aid line had led in a B-line through several roofs, but I snaked my way through following meager holds out right, back left, and finally up and over, placing nests of two or three pieces of pro wherever I could arrange them.

A desperate stab for a lousy layback hold finished off the crux. I skedaddled my feet up and over the last overhang. Flush with success, I hardly noticed the sun dropping behind the mountains or that the rope drag had doubled after surmounting that last lip. I was on easy ground and on my way to splendor when the shallow, low-angled groove I was following abruptly ended 15 feet from the top.

A last slab, crinkly with lichen, was all that separated me from the summit, from victory, from being better than I was at the beginning of the day.

I placed the only nut that would fit at the top of the groove, stemmed out and crimped up on crystals on the lichen-flecked slab. Sixty feet below and now out of sight, the line zigged and zagged between pieces of pro, each hard angle compounding the rope drag on what should have been cake.

With just some mossy friction to go, I

A wonderland of funky descents.

ROBERT MIRAMONTES

Funky Descents

Every so often, descending is anything but straightforward and in some cases is more challenging than the ascent. No anchors on top and technical, unprotected ground to negotiate will test the inexperienced and the old pro as well, particularly if the light is fading fast. What to do?

As soon as you realize this scenario (for instance, as soon as the leader tops out and finds no anchor), immediately start to visualize your options. For instance, if on one side you can arrange a full-length, single-rope rappel to easy ground, have the less-experienced climber rappel the single cord to safety. Once down, the stronger climber needs to evaluate whether she's good to downclimb or whether a rappel or two is necessary—possibly off a different committed—and the one nut popped out, rattled down the rope and disappeared under the roofs. Now 50 feet out from my last piece and facing a move I didn't think I could make, my mind slowly unhinged. Never mind that Tami couldn't hear or see me, or that she must be freezing by now. And never mind that dusk was on me. Standing there on that slab, I crumbled—a heroic winner, pulling through those roofs, now a shameless loser, a sniveling bottom feeder. The weight of the rope felt like all the bad things I had ever done in my life were chained to my swami belt and were dragging me down to hell. My high ideals and strict ethics were gone. I would have chopped steps with a jackhammer if I'd had one.

With no one to throw down a rope or call for a helicopter, I somehow pressed on. I've heard that extreme duress can void the mind so that memory doesn't traumatize us after the fact. Sounds about right. Those last moves are a blank, so I assume my sobbing and begging actually worked.

side. If rappelling is clearly unnecessary, coil the rope and toss it off so it doesn't get in your way. If you suspect that an emergency rap might be needed somewhere, keep the cord or risk getting stranded. In most every case, downclimbing ability is an invaluable skill.

If rappels are necessary and require makeshift anchors, make certain the gear is good. Anything merely okay should always be backed up. The loss of a few pieces of pro is less painful to the pocketbook and self than a visit to the emergency room or funeral parlor. And always make sure the rope will pull through easily from below, especially if the anchor is set in the back of a flaring crack or well back from the edge, where friction can strand a rope as thoroughly as a line twist or kink snagged in a crack, tight as a fly in amber. Always try and pull the rope from below before the last person bails off. Lengthening an anchor with sling material is good insurance for retrieving the rope, as is running the rope through a biner, instead of the sling itself. Whatever configuration you end up with—barring an outright emergency, which might necessitate leaving the cord behind—the last person never raps off till the climber on the deck demonstrates that the rope can be pulled through.

While this seems like common sense, accident reports cite many examples of this very scenario—climbers stranded on top of a small formation with no fixed anchors, tired, dehydrated, failing light, and half-measures with provisional anchors resulting in stuck lines or accidents. Point is, extreme vigilance is required in all aspects of trad climbing, especially so with anchors, when we are tired, and when we have to move quickly and make snap decisions as darkness falls. Just make sure it doesn't get dark forever. Stay sharp. Back up your systems. Test before you commit.

Nicky Dial on
Coarse and Buggy,
Joshua Tree.

GREG EPPERSON

One Hundred Pitches in a Day: The Century Club

John Long

Charles Cole, future owner of 5.10 climbing shoes, always loved physical tests, the bigger the better. When establishing new routes on El Capitan did not measure up to his expectations, he switched to Half Dome and began climbing without a partner. Then he got caught high on the wall, solo, on a new route, in a daylong thunder and lightning storm that far exceeded his expectations. After that, Charles Cole sought other challenges. One of them was joining me on a sea kayaking marathon, when we started up by Oxnard, California, and paddled all the way to Malibu, a distance of 50 miles, measured with my odometer. Charles hadn't been in a kayak much and when we got caught off Point Dume in 15-foot storm surf, he questioned his decision and our friendship. But we made it. Somehow, we always made it. That influenced our thinking when we decided to try and climb one hundred pitches in a day at Joshua Tree, becoming the first members of the illustrious (in our minds) and currently nonexistent "Century Club."

The Century Club was a natural outgrowth of many lesser practices that incrementally led to the Big One—as often happens in climbing and everything else. Most of us have a home crag, and most home crags sport a traditional campground or meeting area. The surrounding routes become most frequented because they're right by the jalopy or the fire pit. We do these climbs fifty or a hundred times and never ask why. We learn every move by heart. If we eventually forgo the rope, we

do so when it feels right—or we don't. The point is that eventually we stockpile a few dozen routes that are no-brainers, that we can climb in our sleep. There are probably another two dozen that are either local favorites or roadside standards that we have also climbed repeatedly. That gives us fifty routes right there. We'll probably know another twenty-five that are likely candidates for the Century Club, and maybe another twenty-five that sound good or are conveniently located. But we'll have to on-sight these last ones, just to keep things honest. So it went as we plotted a likely strategy for the not-too-distant day that we'd go for the Century Club.

The advantage of having experience is that you often can foresee the main issues and plan accordingly. Charles and I had both done fifty climbs in a day and realized we could physically do fifty more, but the logistics were formidable. We couldn't wander and pick off routes at our leisure. We needed to focus on areas with a high concentration of centrally located routes that we could climb quickly and which had easy descents—and in the labyrinthine jumble that often is Joshua Tree, descents often take as much time and effort as the climb.

We struck on a workable plan based on a dozen or so areas that we'd hit in sequence. We started with the on-sight routes, thinking these were safer to tackle fresh. We climbed solo, mostly, 5.10a being the minimum cutoff range, just to keep us honest. Soon as we got to an area we'd lead the hardest route on the tick list and would string a rope off the nearest available anchor. Then we'd dash off and

" . . . The lone and level sands stretch far away."

ROBERT MIRAMONTES

Shoat Tremble on White Mamba, Joshua Tree.

GREG EPPERSON

solo the routes in turn, zipping down the fixed rap line in no time and were on the next route before the dust settled. We ate and drank as we drove from one area to the next, lathering on the sunscreen and making certain we stayed fueled up. In later afternoon we ended back at Hidden Valley Campground, host to the routes we knew best, figuring to tackle these when we were already tired. By this time we no longer were limiting ourselves to routes 5.10a and above, concerned as we were with just ticking the one hundred mark, which we hit with half an hour of daylight to spare.

I felt reasonably solid considering we'd climbed 8,000–9,000 feet of rock and had descended the same. The palms of my hands were rubbed raw as flank steaks from so much downclimbing, and my toes were on fire. But the Century Club was now official and Charles and I had checked another excellent adventure. Within a year, half a dozen of our friends had joined the Century Club and shortly after that the practice caught on at other crags worldwide, areas that had enough routes to facilitate the blitzkrieg.

But we were just getting started with this idea, and as often happens, the original notion morphed into something else we came to call the "Grand Sweep." Fun and exciting as it was establishing the Century Club, we limited the routes to middling

Plotting Logistics

Dropping down the difficulty late in the day and executing all the other protocols so far mentioned—staying hydrated, fed, shaded, relaxed, etc.—remains the overall strategy for anyone breaking into Massive Footage. We're not splitting the atom here or writing sonnets, so any enterprising climber can sort out the details once they dive off the deep end. Everyone approaches "lap work" or "mega burns" with their biases and proclivities, and adds a little of their own shizzle to the community opus. Like so much else in the trad milieu, we can't tell you how to do it, nor should we want to. We point out a few holds and you motate yonder in your own manner, at your own pace. It can work no other way.

Once you plug into the work and aspire toward high numbers, toward really pulling down mega pitches in one day, you'll have to dial in your strategy with increasing precision and detail. In short, once you've decided on climbing twenty-five pitches in a day, say, you'll need to draft a detailed itinerary and timetable based on many factors, the most important being density of routes at a given area, combined with ease of approach and descent. I'm basically talking about doing Massive Footage at small crags like Josh or the Gunks in upstate New York, where the climbs are usually one pitch long. If you're at a big cliff area the process is simplified—and different—because you can log many pitches climbing fewer routes. This process will be taken up later ("enchainments").

"Density" means there is a cluster of appropriate routes in one area. You can't be chasing around the place to do one or two routes at this area and two more over there. You'll run out of time. You want five or six manageable one-pitch climbs in a small area, with short approaches and quick descents. You ace that batch then bolt to another area—preferably a short drive or walk away—featuring five or six more. Four or five of these areas and you've got your twenty-five routes.

The level of technical difficulty matters little in this drill. That is, mega footage is a game for everyone at every level. The strategy does not change much if you're climbing 5.7s or 5.12s. To do a stack of pitches, you must get the logistics dialed. Period. Expect this all to be a work in progress. You need to course correct in mid-stream as you discover your capacities and preferences. No one can tell you what those are—even you can't know beforehand. Expect to go through the Massive Footage drill a few times to work out the minutiae. Eventually the procedure will define itself and drafting up war plans with Massive Footage sorties will become an intriguing part of your trad experience. Massive Footage is a game within a game, available to anyone at any level, and it can electrify your experience by framing another cragging weekend as a mission of sorts. Pulling off this mission carries its own rewards and is yet another wrinkle that keeps the experience fresh and innovative.

***Bebop Tango
at Joshua Tree.***

GREG EPPERSON

fare because we were on the solo much of the time. As said, we tried to keep the fare at 5.10a or above to keep things sporting, but we climbed several dozen easier routes that were right there for the jamming. But considering how much and how well we were climbing back then, this was really a kind of crag version of jogging. We needed to step it up.

The next incarnation of this practice was to tackle more difficult terrain, stuff too hard to do without a rope. The practice happened spontaneously when my friend Dayson and I first visited a small practice cliff called Hueco Wall at Echo Cliffs,

Big Numbers

From business to meditation and most all things in between, we often put a premium on volume: how much we can do and how long we can do it. Very few players get into the Baseball Hall of Fame, for instance, without performing at a high level over 15 or so years. In rock climbing, more is not necessarily better, but it sure can be fun and memorable, especially when throwing down Massive Footage.

We all naturally pass through several stages en route toward climbing dozens of routes in one go. At first the limiting factor is efficiency. In college I had a job in a racquetball gym and for that first few months I'd be blasted after a couple matches. I was wasting too much energy chasing after that bouncing rubber ball while flubbing the shots. Over time I got more efficient, working half as hard for twice the results. Same goes in climbing. At first we can't do more than a dozen or so pitches in a day owing to a high thrash factor. After our technique starts evening out and we take on some little of "the smooth," we start gliding over moderate ground with little effort and even those grim bits start to feel within our control envelope.

Not surprisingly, the straightest line to Massive Footage is Massive Footage— but far below our TL (team leader). For instance, at the end of the day, drop the difficulty down to almost playpen routes and start climbing and keep climbing. When cranking routes well within your ability you start to experience mastery, when everything feels simple and routine; this experience carries over when incrementally you begin inching the difficulty up till without ever knowing when or how, you're smoking twenty or twenty-five pitches in a day.

Pulling down, Joshua.

BEN HORTON

a popular local LA crag. We started at one end of the wall and climbed every route there, better than fifteen sport climbs up the slightly overhanging wall. By the time we were finished my hands were like claws. A few months later we exported the Grand Sweep to Josh and Idyllwild and beyond.

Then world-class climbers began teaming up with novices and trying to do as many 5.7 routes, say, as they possibly could in a day. Over the winter we came up with dozens of variations on a theme. As always, variety was the ticket to ride and the possibilities were, and are, endless.

Pacing

Most people are surprised that speed climbing is not jamming fast as a speeding bullet, rather eliminating down-time and needless procedures—basically streamlining the drill till the bulk of the time and effort go into the climbing itself. In the Massive Footage game, however, especially once you edge toward the twenty-five pitch mark—which given approaches and descents, is about one climb every 15 minutes over an 8-hour period—there's no way to get through those numbers without climbing quickly.

The trick to physically climbing fast, and to retain some modicum of security, is to learn to recognize the easier sections straight off and to dispatch those fast and without pause. A typical 5.9 route will only have a section or two at that grade. Even if the difficulty is continuous it will likely be straightforward. So strive to move quickly over easier sections and take whatever time is needed to work through the cruxes. This is particularly crucial if you're soloing or running the rope. Limit barreling to the easier stretches and never hurry or race through the cruxes. Extreme vigilance must also be given to any and all rappels and tricky bits of descending such as grainy slabs and chasm jumps, common in places like Lumpy Ridge, Joshua Tree, Smith Rocks, etc. Don't be in such a hurry that you bungle your basic procedures, which frequently happens even to guides and world-class climbers.

Keep the accent on security and Massive Footage delivers exhilarating, even unforgettable days. Botch a rappel or a solo and Massive Footage is a fatal liability. Know your limitations. If you don't, go easy on the Massive Footage game till you better understand your true capacities.

Lastly, you will eventually tire, and the only sane and proven strategy is to slow and place more pro. There is no trick to climbing tired, no secret—save to be extra careful.

Tim Alexander racing up
Stem Master (5.10a), Lover's Leap.

ANDREW BURR

CHAPTER 28

East Buttress, El Capitan

John Long

I'd had some solid success on Yosemite climbs and was full of myself and my ability. I figured I could do nearly everything with little or no problem. I was heading for doom, and didn't know it.

I'd bagged a handful of long free routes but not the Nose or Salathe or any of the other trade routes up the 3,000-foot El Capitan, home to the most celebrated big-wall climbs on earth. Like many climbers before and after, I considered El Cap's East Buttress a stepping-stone to the big time.

While an ascent of the East Buttress, located on the far right margin of the monolith, cannot earn you the same bragging rights as having climbed El Cap proper, you nevertheless mount some 1,500 feet of the Big Stone, top out, and descend via the fabled East Ledges. So in a kind of flanking maneuver, you really do sort of climb The Captain. Sort of.

One of the boons of trad routes is learning how your ascent fits into the continuum. Once you've scaled a legendary climb, you do a virtual lap every time you remember or read your notes afterward—and the notes of others as well. In this regard the history of the East Buttress is rich and worth mentioning.

In the early 1950s, with their canvas tennis shoes, white-line ropes, and ring-angle pegs, climbers took one look at the terrible face out left of the East Buttress and said forget it. But the way the Valley historian Steve Roper tells it, "The beautiful black-and-gold buttress on the far eastern flank showed distinct cracks and chimneys on its lower section. Higher, the prospective route blended smoothly into the wall, but here also the rock looked broken and perhaps climbable."

Enter Yosemite hardman Allen Steck, who'd already established the punishing Steck-Salathe on Sentinel (1950) as well as that towering junker, Yosemite Point Buttress (1952). Naturally, Al looked to El Cap, and he started up the East Buttress with

Bill Dunmire and Dick Long in August 1952. This adventure ended suddenly on the first pitch when Dunmire logged Yosemite's first-ever "zipper" fall and nearly decked out, sustaining a nasty knock to his brainpan that cost him several pints of red stuff and a night in the clinic.

Steck returned later that year with Willi Unsoeld, of future Everest fame. They battled halfway up the East Buttress before rain and waterfalls drove them off.

In September 1972, Willi lectured at my college and he had brought along his daughter, Nanda Devi, who was my age and looked like an angel, with blonde hair and a thousand-watt smile. Four years later, she died in her father's arms on the Nepalese peak for which she was named. When I read her obit in the *Alpine Journal,* I chucked an ashtray through my dorm room window. In 1979, an avalanche on Mount Rainier carried Willi away.

Steck returned to the East Buttress a third time, with Unsoeld, Bill Long, and Will Siri. Bivouacking twice on the route, and using lots of aid, they reached the summit on June 1, 1953. Eleven years later (the same year Unsoeld lost all his toes on Everest), wrote Roper, Frank Sacherer, father of modern free climbing, along with Wally Reed, "freed the entire route with hardly a pause." In the following years, if you thought yourself the shizzle, you jumped up on the East Buttress of El Capitan, Grade 4, 5.10, one of the finest long free climbs in the Valley.

I thought myself the shizzle, so I snagged my childhood friend Dean Fidelman (aka Bullwinkle)

ALEXANDRE BUISSE

The East Buttress follows the far right margin (black streak) of El Capitan, just left of the climber and a mile across the valley.

BEN HORTON

and told him to get his stuff; we were heading for the East Buttress. Dean was an art student and bohemian who would later develop the fantastic ability to inveigle languid climber girls out of their yoga tights to pose on boulders and flying buttresses for his legendary Stone Nudes calendars. Nice work, if you can get it.

We thumbed down to El Cap and marched up to the Nose and another 20 minutes out right along the base, quickly gaining altitude on a narrowing ramp ending at "The Edge of the World." From there, the East Buttress fires directly up a prominent, symmetrical bombay chimney. Go 20 feet past this start and you pitch off a 1,000-foot cliff.

In those days the Yosemite ethic was safety and efficacy, which some of us interpreted as, Use the least amount of gear humanly possible and climb just as fast as you can. We considered this the best strategy, and for a time some of us idiots tried to outdo each other. Dean and I brought one 9mm rope, several slings, around eight assorted nuts, and no pack, water, or food. Aside from swami belts and chalk bags, we had nothing else whatsoever. I didn't even wear a shirt, nor carry along sneakers for the long hike down.

I shot up the first pitch and stemmed right over the 5.10 crux at the start of pitch two, not bothering to place protection because back then we were

B-Lining for Disaster

Staying on route is the climbing version of staying on topic. When we drift and wander, we rarely cover much useful ground and invariably must return to where we veered off track. Peter's foray on Royal Arches and mine here on the East Buttress show the possible downside of taking your own line. Not to say that climbers never find tidy variations from the original. But these are the exceptions, and for the majority of us, on 99.9 percent of the routes we'll ever climb, the route has been reckoned to the last foothold. The moment we start straying off the standard line is usually when we start making things more difficult. This might be appropriate if we're on a moderate climb that traverses around difficulties. Sometimes we take a direct path to quicken things up, terrain obliging. But forging out onto blank rock for the thrill of it is almost always a losing proposition.

And on long routes, where time management is essential, fiddling with variations is usually pointless if not foolish. Established routes usually follow the line of least resistance and over time have been cleared of most loose rock—an important consideration for leader and follower, doubly so if there are others behind you. In controlled circumstances, tinker with variations. But once the game is for keeps, especially on longer routes in wilderness areas, follow the easiest line instead of inventing difficulty en route. If difficulty is your goal, climb a harder line.

You might be on the only chimney within 20 miles and still wonder if you're really on route.

LARRY COATS

Looking where the sun goes down from 1,500 feet up Lost Arrow Spire.

ALEXANDRE BUISSE

usually soloing our brains out at Joshua Tree, so never mind the gear. Plus this route was done two decades before, by a bunch of old guys who were like 40 now, so it couldn't be hard. Fortune's fool.

Above, the route soared up the mostly open face, wandering from crack to flake to shallow corner. I was counting on a load of fixed pins; there were none and the few nuts I brought along were mostly the wrong size so the pro was thin—two or three pieces for 150-foot pitches. It was August and hot as hell and I needed a lot more of that water Bullwinkle didn't bring along. My stomach sounded like the Ganges in flood. I should have

eaten something that morning. Instead, I got eaten alive by piss ants at the belay tree atop pitch 2, and never found those hoped-for fixed pins until pitch 6. I remember trying unsuccessfully to wiggle in a nut up there somewhere and finally yelling, "I don't need no stinking pro."

But this was great climbing for sure, way out there on that face and so high off the deck and pretty continuous. Several of the belays were from slings and less-than-ideal anchors and for brief moments we'd hang there, not drinking the water Bullwinkle failed to provide and wanting a burger badly but liking the breezy location. Of course, we

Confidence vs. Arrogance

When we mistake aggression for confidence, it might cost us dearly. Confidence that we can crank 5.12 in a thundershower is encouraging but not essential. Every climber phases in and out of shape. If our confidence rests entirely on our technical prowess, we will have little to go on but strong fingers. A more mature article issues from the self-assurance that we will go about our work judiciously, that above all, the security of ourselves and our partners remain a priority. This is the wider view, and it develops slowly for most of us. Certain experiences can hasten the process, sometimes terribly. I've been witness to various climbing accidents, some fatal.

Almost all of these were due to pilot error, but they nevertheless drive home the fact that Old Man Gravity tolerates us at best, and will smash us to pieces if we underestimate his real and present threat. Deep confidence is tinged with humility, based on real-world circumstances, not all of them about glorious summits and sublime views. Respect, safety, humility, and the capacity to know when we're going poorly and to go down, are all aspects of being an experienced and confident leader. Some of us are naturally more assured than others, but this curve eventually flattens out as we gain experience.

Arching cracks, scant footholds, big air—all prerequisites for a classic.

ALEXANDRE BUISSE

Minimum Required Gear

The early Yosemite pioneers arrived at their "safety and efficiency" approach through trial and error during the first ascent of Valley's granite big walls. Safety came first. Many wanted to climb El Capitan and Half Dome and Lost Arrow, but nobody wanted to die. The pioneers quickly learned that lugging more equipment did not necessarily make the climb any "safer," a fact many modern climbers never accept. Notice how in the business world, zealots throw money at a film or a high rise, hoping to improve the project—a strategy that rarely pans out as hoped.

In climbing, hauling too much gear can quickly result in systems that are overbuilt and even dangerous. Much better to use a minimum of the right equipment, keeping the process manageable, and concentrate on executing. What's more, because those first up Washington Column, Leaning Tower, etc. were inventing the techniques as they climbed, progress was often painfully slow, so every effort was made to become more efficient lest they never got up a climb.

Over the years, the basic "safety and efficiency" strategy proved useful, and largely remains the modern method. People transitioning from the gym and sport world are often taken by gear company claims that every trad climber needs flashy gadgets and do-dads, when in fact the bulk of the finest climbs on earth were accomplished with a rack consisting of shoes, harness, belay device, chalk bag, a streamline rack, a daypack with water, and a few eatables—and nothing else at all. How little or how much gear we take mostly concerns the rack, or how much protection we take along.

Sara Matisse with the minimum. Not!

SARA MATISSE

Topos and fellow climbers can recommend required gear for a given route, but only experience will tell you how much more or less to take of the standard rack. Erring slightly on the high side is not a bad tactic, but beware of believing that more gear means a safer ride. "Safety" is largely a matter of how we climb, something technology can never accomplish for us in and of itself.

Once we ease toward the speed climbing game, where light and fast are critical issues, security becomes increasingly compromised as we prune the rack to bare bones. Going ultra-light is a game of diminishing returns, and at some point is always a trade-off with security. But by the time you reach that level, advice from most any source is a moot point.

could never retreat off the thing with one rope and eight nuts, half of them wires, which added high voltage to the adventure.

In a couple of hours, nearing the top, we gained the spectacular Knobby Wall. I had grown up studying photos of Willi Unsoeld pulling up this steep dark face with the great sweep of the southwest buttress of El Cap towering behind him, and I was onto those knobs like all get-out. This wall was glory, and I thought it wrong and cowardly that, evidenced by a string of rusty ring-angle pitons, the route veered off when the knobs kept on straight above. I took the direct line, of course, feeling like Hermes clad in kletterschuhe, loving life and climbing and all of creation when just like that the knobs ran out, and there was no crack and no pro, and I was out maybe 50 feet off a fixed ring-angle peg from old Willi Unsoeld's very rack, and far below, Bullwinkle was belaying off a single antediluvian soft-iron peg that likely would rip should I ping for the big one.

Following this close call was a ghastly downclimb to slightly better holds, and a sketchy traverse to escape back onto the normal route. A short while later, we crawled over the top of the East Buttress, sunburned, dry as driftwood, hungry enough to eat the hind legs off the Lamb of God. With each weary stride toward the East Ledges descent route, I grew up a little more as a rock climber, till we finally staggered back down to the loop road and I dove into the Merced with my boots still on, and I swear that river dropped a foot by the time I slithered out onto solid ground. I would go on to climb El Capitan many times after that first jackass junket up the East Buttress, and I would never again underestimate the seriousness of a big traditional rock climb, hard or otherwise, or assume that if holds were there I could simply pull on through to glory.

Tony Sartin turning the 5.12 roof on Le Toit, Tahquitz Rock.

GREG EPPERSON

CHAPTER 29

First Ascent of Stoner's Highway

John Long

The first ascent of Stoner's Highway, on Middle Cathedral, Yosemite, came out of the hours we spent traversing at the base of the formation. One day I found an interesting-looking section and climbed up about 15 feet and said, "I think there's a route here." The others looked up at the wall shooting overhead for 2,000 feet and asked, "What makes you think so?" or something like that. I didn't have an answer, but was willing to find out.

Back then I was part of a small band of a few dozen Valley climbers who were spending their first of many summers up in the Valley. I'd already climbed a handful of the longer routes on Middle including the East Buttress, the Direct North Buttress (DNB), and the North Face. Several other of my friends were likewise keen on Middle and sometimes in late afternoon, after we'd climbed all day on other formations, we'd hike up through the pines and over the scree field to the base of Middle and boulder along the base of the wall on diamond-hard gray-orange granite. Peppered with holds and averaging 75 to 80 degrees, the wall was perfect for Megatron traverses down low. The exercise was exacting and dialed us into the nuances of climbing on Middle. We all knew there were great new worlds to explore on Middle Cathedral, but first

Partnerships

On projects, especially big intimidating ones, "safety in numbers" becomes a meaningful concept. It's a way to share the physical and psychological burden. On new routes, especially ones with bolting, speed is rarely a concern or even a possibility. The aim is to get up the route safely, or at all. Good friends are helpful in that regard. If you have three or four climbers along for the "FA" (first ascent)—a number entirely impractical for normal climbing—chances are that one of you will feel like jumping out there on the business end and having a serious go of it. And so you recruit the strongest climbers you can find to share a rope and you throw down a collective effort.

You'll generally climb two on a rope for routes of any length, but on the first ascent of many seminal climbs, from Norway's dreadful Troll Wall, to the ice-frosted monoliths in Baffin Island, three- and even four-man teams were common for the reasons stated. Going back to the early days of American wall climbing, the first ascent of Half Dome involved a three-man team; the Nose on El Cap featured a summit team of four; the Salathe Wall, three; the North American Wall, four. When the going gets tough, some make it a party.

off we had to fiddle in the shore break, so to speak, before swimming out into deep waters. And we were ready to swim far.

Each big rock formation is fashioned slightly different than the next stone over, and with enough time spent on a given cliff, you come to intuitively know how to move and what to expect. That is why you will probably do your hardest climbing on familiar ground. The rock at the base of Middle Cathedral was starting to feel like home. After a dozen or so forays spread out over a couple months, we started bouldering a little higher, to access new holds and fresh sequences, and that's when our eyes were drawn up instead of left or right.

One afternoon Kevin Worrall and I were puttering on the wide-open face between the Powel-Reed route and the Chouinard-Pratt route when I spotted that series of discontinuous flakes that, beginning about 100 feet up, appeared to stretch upward for several rope lengths. The only native features were small corners and overlaps, widely spaced. Few looked to go for more than a couple body lengths. We'd have to link them with face climbing—exactly what we'd been doing along the base for weeks. But there would be long stretches with little to no protection. Plus we could only see holds for the immediate 50 feet or so. Anything beyond that was guessing. The entire wall was a kind of super slab that didn't vary in angle for many hundreds of feet, so we hoped that since the bottom was climbable, the upper part would go as well. Jumping up on a huge, mostly bald, Yosemite face was almost unheard of on anything but much lower-angled Glacier Point Apron, which most of us considered a screw off area for rest days.

Anyhow, Kevin and I decided to get some gear and have a go on our imaginary route.

We had no experience establishing long routes, so we rounded up all the guys we could find in camp who especially enjoyed face climbing—Mark Chapman, Ed Berry, Kevin, and me. Perhaps we collectively could work things out. I was the

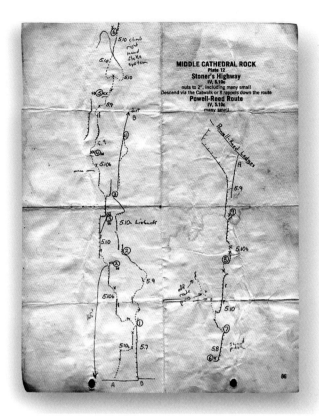

Steve Grossman's Old Stoner's Highway topo from the George Meyers 1978 Yosemite topo guide.

JOHN LONG

designated leader since I had already established some open face climbs down at Tahquitz and Suicide. Unfortunately, those routes were only a few hundred feet long, and Middle reared up like a granite tsunami. I decided to set my sights on the first 50 feet, found the likely start, racked up the bolt kit, a few thin pitons for seams in the back of those corners, tied in, and started up.

The first move off the ground was 5.9 and it got slightly harder from there. There wasn't a flake or crack system at the start so I ran the rope about twenty and sunk a bolt on a small hold. We'd have to use bolts on this route, probably a lot of them,

Drawing the pump on the Gunsmoke Traverse, Joshua Tree.

BEN HORTON

but we hoped to hold the "hole count" to a minimum. I was basically climbing hold to hold and
was almost surprised that the next stretch was only
5.10a. I sunk a second bolt and came down.

Kevin climbed up to the high point, traversed
right at stiff 5.10, and ran the line to a third bolt
and a short traverse right to a belay stance. As so
often happens on new face routes, the other three
of us freely offered advice on where to go and what
holds to use and how Kevin was the man and what
was taking so long—we wanted to go climbing.
Quite naturally the view from out on the business

end was different from the ground, where the risks
can only be imagined.

This first pitch looked the blankest and we'd
done it fairly easily with only three bolts. But when
we followed we decided to add another bolt to
prohibit the huge pendulum fall potential after the
crux traverse. We had a hunch this route might be a
classic and figured no one would repeat it if ghastly
falls were part of the bargain. That was very opti-
mistic, thinking we would climb the entire route
having climbed only the first 100 feet. But we were
young and could do anything. As they say, only a

fool does the impossible, because he's the only one rash enough to try.

I had jumped up on that wall thinking we'd divine the best route by dead reckoning, following the likely holds and connecting the obvious features, sinking knifeblades and small wired nuts when we could and hopefully limiting protection bolts to a couple per pitch. But a few days later, when Peter Barton moved up and left onto bald rock on the second lead, we faced questions we'd never before considered—the same ones everybody meets on a big new face route, then and now.

The climbing was too spooky and ill-defined to draw a breath and start pulling down. It's always a much different game once a route is established. You know that the climb is doable, and each section is rated as well.

Here, the terror was the real chance of committing to moves you could never downclimb, and after a long run-out, finding rock you could not climb. There was a mammoth whipper waiting for everyone out there on the sharp end, and no leader in his right mind did not take that prospect seriously. So the leader moved slowly and cautiously for fear of climbing himself into a dead end. The wall was mostly smooth with little to hit during a huge fall, but no one was keen to take one.

Every effort was made to preserve the traditional mode of bottom-up, on-sight climbing. Nobody went up on aid to check things out, first, because there weren't sufficient cracks to aid, and second, because the idea was to try and climb the route on-sight, with no dicking around or shenanigans. On a route of any size, most teams will have to approach trad routes in this way because any other method takes too long. While upper-end free climbs often are sieged, and take weeks, even years of attempts to succeed, these efforts are so specialized and rare that they have no part of this book. Ninety-nine percent of the time, present-day trad climbers will approach a route attempting to on-sight it, not to hang around till they can boulder

out the moves and then return for the redpoint. Few climbers have that kind of time, or desire.

I vividly recall standing out there on the lower leads of Stoner's, sometimes for 15 minutes, often a ways out from funky knifeblades, like a kid teetering on the end of the high diving board, trying to muster the courage to cast off, trying to divine sequences from visible holds, wondering if it was possible, peering down into the abyss—and finally launching off and hoping for the best. Such moments-of-no-return were encountered three or four times on every pitch, and it was always sac-tightening when the leader glanced down and said, "Okay, I'm going for it." These moments were not soon forgotten by anyone out there on the lead.

Flakes and corners, few more than 4 or 5 inches wide, often had cracks in the back, but in some cases the usable holds and the little corners did not line up and we had to scale a blank wall looking at cracks, and protection, to either side. That felt weird and totally wrong. The protection opportunities and the line of least resistance were not necessarily in the same spots and that was a realization—having to bypass protection options in order to carry on.

In fact the moment we pulled off the deck, our only concerns were to arrange pro and find a climbable line, in that order. This holds true on any big face climb, so understand the principle. Back then, pitons were on the outs and used on free climbs but in rare instances, where nothing else would do. And with these thin corners, often too incipient for even the thinnest wired Stoppers, only a knifeblade or Bugaboo would work. Modern camming devices have not solved this problem. In seams, it's often a pin, or nothing. Question was, did we hammer the pegs home and leave them fixed— we were so broke back then we had no extra tackle—or clean them and risk the route getting pin-scarred to hell after a few dozen ascents?

Also, because the route followed no specific "line," and was little more than a succession of face

The Run-out Calculus

Running the rope out above the protection is likely the most electrifying facet of climbing. Each inch we creep above pro is an extra 2 inches to fall if we pitch off. Falling will always feel sketchy because most every leader fall would be catastrophic if it weren't for the rope. We know this at a visceral level and we feel it all over once we get out there on the lead and range above the pro. What, then, do we need to understand about run-outs? It's called the "Run-out Calculus," and if you memorize anything, memorize this.

First is to try and make conscious all the relevant factors to help separate out natural concern from irrational fear. Evaluate the protection. How good is the last nut, cam, or piton? The security of modern bolts should not be a concern since the instances of them failing in good rock are so few. But we need to realistically evaluate how big a fall a given piece is likely to hold, then extrapolate out the length of the largest possible fall we might take. Second, where is the next likely protection point, and what might we get in there? Then we survey the rock below the run-out and determine what, if anything, we might hit—a concern on any wall below about 95 degrees. Lastly, how hard is the climbing likely to be on the run-out?

That gives us five basic considerations: 1) How good is the pro before the run-out; 2) how far to the next pro, and what might it be; 3) what is the longest fall I might take on the run-out; 4) what might I hit if I fall off; and 5) how hard is the climbing.

Once we guesstimate some answer to these five questions, we start correlating the data and make a decision based on the facts as we see them. Of course the above assumes we are talking about running out the rope directly above a nut or cam or whatever. If we must climb laterally as well, sweeping up left or right, vectors and swing must be figured into the "calculus" as well.

If the pro is sound and there's nothing to hit, we likely have little to fear, though no fall is without risk. People trip up on the rope, flip upside down, and smack their melon. Or get limbs entangled in the line. Or skid on hands and knees. Remember to try not to climb with the rope between your legs. Have it over the outside of the foot—left leg if you're moving right, right leg if you're moving left.

If the pro is questionable, and the rock below is featured with ledges and corners to impact during a fall, the crucial factor is difficulty. You might choose to risk a long fall on chunky terrain if the going is easy. But think hard about challenging yourself in more than one of the five categories at the same time. For example, if a long fall is possible, make certain the pro is good, there's nothing to hit, and the climbing is not too hard for you. If the climbing is hard, the run-out should be manageable, the pro good, and the rock free of obstacles. The calculus says: The more categories you challenge at one time, the risks increase exponentially.

As a rule of thumb, for big run-outs on hard terrain—which you will inevitably encounter—you must have solid pro, and the fall zone must be free of obstacles. Include rope stretch (up to 30 percent) when calculating the max fall potential. And remember, a few measly feet can make the difference between a harmless skidder and a compound fracture.

While the Run-out Calculus might sound confusing and hard to wrangle, it becomes routine and usually easy to implement with a little experience. It's mostly common sense and a little bonehead math.

holds, there were few ledges or features to head for, so the strategy was to keep climbing and not sink a belay till the rope nearly or totally ran out. But what if the leader wanted to return to the belay, and he was more than halfway out (more than half a rope from the belay)? He'd need two ropes to get down. And because we normally climbed on 11-millimeter ropes, that meant dragging 22 millimeters worth of cordage behind you, which felt like pulling a fire hose up the wall. And if this wasn't enough, the old climbing shoe rubber was poor for smearing and friction, which is the majority of what is found on Middle Cathedral.

Like I said, the challenges we faced are the ones every party will face on any climb that ascends a wide-open face in which you are assaulting onsight, ground-up. Where is the line? The challenge is to find it because it is not imposed by a corner or crack system or, say, a prominent dike or intrusion. Often the exact route is unknowable from below and you only know the line when you're on it. Where is the protection?

Without at least some natural features, it's going to be bolts all the way and that's a massive ordeal on a ground-up climb of any magnitude, where every hole is hand drilled. A difficult climb—beyond a cruiser route like Snake Dike (5.7) on Half Dome, which ascends a huge and featured intrusion—will usually require at least six bolts per pitch on less than vertical terrain, and many more if the rock steepens to vert or beyond. And a pitch is demonstrably more difficult to climb when you're first reckoning the line and hand-drilling all the bolts, as opposed to the coolio who sashays along later and floats the lead with a rack of quickdraws, wondering what the fuss was all about.

Anyhow, as we worked out the upper pitches over a period of days, we learned to climb very cautiously and to only commit to a no-reverse sequence if we had decent pro nearby, and the fall was such that we wouldn't smack anything. Clearly, it was madness to at once challenge ourselves in

terms of both difficulty and protection, trying moves we might not manage, with little or no pro. For max difficulty, you had to have pro, and you could only sanely run the rope on manageable climbing. Anyone who seeks their technical limit with no protection is not long for the sport of rock climbing.

We wandered off the eventual route many times, but avoided logging the truly giant ripper. Our trick for keeping the bolt count down was to place protection bolts at the end of any easy section. There wasn't much easy climbing on Stoner's, but the idea was to hold off with the bolts till the end of the obvious holds, which is hard to do if you've just dicked a good run-out and finally got onto easier ground. You want a bolt like a thirsty man wants a drink. But as we have seen, time and energy need to be managed on long climbs, and sinking bolts prematurely means even more drilling before the next hard bit. So it's often best to suck it up and go to the end of any well-featured section before drilling. Not once did anyone fall off an easier, but unprotected stretch, so this is basically one of the calculated risks you take on such an adventure if you ever hope to succeed. And because dragging two ropes was unrealistic on hard face climbing, a leader largely resigned himself to finishing a lead once started. The business of fixed pins had no handy solution and we ended up leaving a few blades in key spots. Ideally, all pitons should be sunk to the hilt and left en situ, or fixed.

For us, on our initial big first ascent, the real adventure was the improbability of the climb and the fact that such a route was largely unprecedented in world rock climbing, things we were not aware of at the time. All the way up we kept saying, "If we only can get this next bit, the route is ours." That's a whacky thing to say when 200 feet up a 1,200 foot climb, but we said it dozens of times, bottom to top. And as the days passed and we kept pushing the route higher over various attempts, the progress remained painfully slow for fear of making a big mistake.

There were few routes anywhere that featured more than a few 5.10 pitches, and virtually every lead on Stoner's was 5.10a or harder. Perhaps the biggest lesson was that difficult and potentially dangerous on-sight climbing is intense and slow going. Climbing up to a high point was accomplished in a fraction of the time taken during the first ascent of that same terrain. Once you knew how the climb went and that the pro was there, if only barely, the entire dynamic shifted in your favor. No longer was the route a game of survival, but of efficient motoring.

After we'd climbed the first four or five pitches, I

Route Engineering on First Ascents

Most climbers will never bother with, nor are they interested in, making first ascents. For those who do, consider the following.

For routes following features such as cracks and chimneys, where all the protection is passive (nuts and cams), we don't engineer a route, we merely climb it. Route engineering begins with installing bolts and permanent belay anchors, which force future parties to climb the route as we've designed it.

Darrell Hensel drilling the last bolt on Picante (5.12) at Suicide Rock, BITD.

KEVIN POWELL

Strive to keep all new routes on tolerably good rock. Forcing a line up a junk cliff to tick another FA is asking for trouble because someone is bound to get hurt. Next, run-outs are fine, but consider drilling when obvious stances present themselves. It is considered bad form to engineer a route to a standard above its natural difficulty. For example, 5.9 routes should feature climbing attainable for a typical 5.9 leader. Engineering a 5.9 with such meager pro that only a 5.12 climber would dare try it is vain and cowardly. Save the 5.12 run-out for 5.12 routes, where the clientele can handle the action. Scaring the novice is amateurish.

Always engineer the climb so some protection is possible near the belay to reduce the chance of a leader logging a Factor 2 fall (just about the worst lead-climbing fall) directly onto the anchors. Go easy on the bolts, but never started relaxing into the rhythm of the route, trusted my instincts, and managed to lead one of the hardest leads, pitch 6, in about a half an hour, pounding two bolts in the process. The lesson here is that once you can capture the feeling that you belong up there, that you're up to the task, the game changes to your favor. Many years later I went back with Bill Price and later with a girlfriend and repeated the pitches; I was almost proud of what we'd done when we didn't know shit from shineola. Those were the great times, the Golden Fleece of the trad game, making stuff up as you go, "building the ship as you sail it."

Alex Honnold during the first free ascent of Giraffe (5.13), El Gran Trono Blanco, Baja, Mexico.

ANDREW BURR

with belay anchors if needed. It's best to have done a host of bolted routes before you start making your own. Perhaps the most telling advice per new routes comes from the following anecdote.

A young kid from Wisconsin strode up to a famous hardman's table at the Yosemite Lodge cafeteria and asked him how he might get started doing new routes. "Go to a little crag and practice doing routes that don't matter and where your errors won't be noticed. Move on to bigger stuff carefully." The kid looked insulted. "What the hell? The Chosen One never bothered fiddling with any small crag. He just jumped up on the big stuff and gassed it." "That's true," he said. "But I never had to ask anyone how to do it."

If you have to ask how, it's probably too early to start on the new lines.

*Zac Robinson on
After the Fall (5.9),
Little Cottonwood
Canyon, Utah.*

ANDREW BURR

CHAPTER 30

Thrust to the Edge on The Crucifix

Peter Croft

Once I had a taste of climbing new routes, I knew it was the most powerful medicine one can take in mountaineering. Standing at the base of virgin territory is the singular point where anything is possible—success or failure, fun or horror—and it rarely goes completely as planned. I had done dozens of first ascents in Canada, but when I finally tried my hand in Yosemite, the task changed from home fix-it chores to remodeling the east wing of Notre Dame.

The Crucifix on Higher Cathedral Rock is one of the Valley's classic long routes and my part in its history is one of a carpenter hired to finish the trim on a cathedral. Kevin Worral and Jim Bridwell, using a touch of aid, first climbed the route in 1973 with hexes and stoppers, a fuzzy, 150-foot, 9-millimeter rope, one quart of water, and no falls—bad ass! Six years later, Max Jones and Mark Hudon freed all but five or six aid moves and the following year, Bill Price added Mary's Tears, a brilliant four-pitch independent start. The original Crucifix began on the popular Northeast Buttress (5.9) and traversed in after four pitches. Bill's direct start brought the lower part in line with the upper burliness and into radical free-route maturity—almost. There were still a handful of aid moves, and I latched onto this final challenge like a tick.

First free ascents (FFAs) have their own altar in the trad climbing pantheon. Although not the same as establishing a new route, FFAs carry much of the same cachet. In some minds a single point of aid on a 1,000-foot route can soil the purity of the ascent, labeling them as a "failure." Extreme? Well, anyone swinging around by their fingertips half a mile up a rock wall is probably extreme by design.

The crucial aid section on The Crucifix lay at half height, where a thin corner arches over left, then abruptly back up and right. I made an initial probe with Rob, a fellow Canuck, to clean out the mud and give the section a go. I feared something futuristic and was delighted when I got it first try at moderate 5.12. We rapped off from the top of that pitch and immediately made plans for a full sweep of the route—bottom to top, all free.

I had climbed the route with the few points of aid several years before and knew the basic architecture, including a long fist crack at two-thirds height. And because some of the belays required wide gear as well, I knew I'd have to be frugal with the wide cams. The next day, following our recognizance, we hiked up and bivied with our heads flush against the first footholds.

Morning light comes early to east faces, especially when they start 1,500 feet up off the Valley floor. Swirls of yellow and orange rock lit up like a granite canvas and we scrambled to get started. The first pitch of Mary's Tears slowed us with techy 5.11 weirdness—tricky to climb and trickier to protect. Soon we were well on our way and by late morning at the base of the crux. Although June temps were hot and I was sweaty, I lurched through the 5.12 section straight away and quickly found myself at the next belay stance, eyeing the long fist crack. Rob jumared up, handed me the rack, and right off I noticed one of our larger cams was missing, left or maybe dropped somewhere below. With only

Herb Crimp on Hand Delivery (5.11+), Long Canyon, Moab, Utah.

Managing Danger

We already covered the "Run-out Calculus," which seeks to objectify the potential danger. Here's the rest.

Squaring off with a big run-out is one of climbing's most intense moments of truth.

Leaving that last piece of pro is a lonely feeling, akin to setting ourselves adrift, while knowing there is no one to save us if the situation goes south. Making the decision and committing to the journey is the closest many of us will come to free soloing. Some of the soloists' headspace, and plan of attack, is applicable here.

Whenever possible, rest up before going for an unprotected stretch. Do not simply launch out because of shot nerves—a common, reckless reflex. The suspense of hanging with the tension might be relieved by having at it, but it's always better to pause and gather yourself before casting off on perilous ground. Remember, the more intense and critical the work, the greater need for a calm and sober approach. A climber literally drunk on fear and adrenaline is in no shape to tackle a run-out requiring his full faculties. If the tension feels too much to handle, go down.

Once rested and settled, commit to the moment, to the next move—not to the end of the pitch. If anything we'll probably need to slow down and spend that crucial moment longer to hit that edge just so or to milk those jams. It's important to move smoothly and deliberately, to try to make every move one we can reverse so we can downclimb to that rest hold or good jam—we might have to.

Keep in mind the estimated length of the run-out. This gives us something tangible to shoot for—a crack, a ledge, or a bolt on which to anchor our concentration. We never stop halfway to gauge our fear. Once we cast off for real, it's unlikely we will feel better about the situation the farther we are above the protection. Being decisive is what it's all about. Decide. Commit. Go. Concentrate on the climbing and only the climbing.

two pieces of large pro on my rack, the next pitch would have been hair-raising—with one it would be terrifying.

I jammed as far as I dared, directly off the belay—maybe 30 feet, fearful of the dreaded factor-2 fall—before plugging our sole big cam into the crack. Then I shut my mind off, to gear, safety, and every last thing except the overhanging crack in front of me. I fist jammed for what seemed like a mile, crested a bulge, and kept going. Near the top of the never-ending pitch, I paused to chalk up and glanced below. The rope swept down clear of the rock as far as I could see before disappearing beneath the bulge. My muscles tensed and my mild pump became debilitating as a cascade of thoughts and terror thrust me to the edge. I was roughly 90 feet out from my last piece. Add rope stretch and I was looking at a 200-foot fall. The wall was steep and clean so presumably I could survive the big ride, but with that much air time, dying of fright seemed likely.

The crack above was totally uniform. I had nothing that would fit. With both hands cramping and sliding from the jams, I decided to at least fall trying, and somehow wobbled my way to a slight

Committing to an All-Free Ascent

There are no rules stating that we must free climb every inch of a route, whether on a first ascent or an established classic. All of us have reached thresholds we cannot cross and our experience is rarely spoiled because we yard through on a piton or hang on a crux like a sack of cement. For some, such compromises mean little or nothing. But for others they are measuring sticks along the way, as projects to possibly shoot for in the future. Tastes differ.

Initially, when technical levels were comparatively low, the advantages of free climbing were speed and the need for far less gear. Times change. Styles evolve. From the 1950s on, many came to consider it bad form to resort to aid because your heart is pounding and you're cracking a sweat. Luckily, though, free climbing has no random rules to follow like in hockey or bridge. No matter what, free climbing puts us more completely in touch with our environment.

Once we've committed to "all-free or bust" assault, we hold ourselves to a higher level of gamesmanship, a personal vow not to get lazy, not to thrash and dangle no matter what. Most climbers find that this decision automatically makes the adventure more exciting. The promise we make to ourselves, to rise to the occasion by whatever means possible, often takes us to another level.

Peter, pulling for another level, Red Rocks.

GREG EPPERSON

Dave Shultz and Peter Croft jamming the splitters on The Crucifix.

DAN MCDEVITT

recess, leaned in, and listened to the thundering of my heart. Right in front of my face was a constriction. I fumbled in an endwise Stopper—I was saved! Rob took forever to follow the pitch and it took all of that time for my composure, psyche, and adrenaline stores to return to normal levels. Climbing was once more fun, and after a couple of cruisey pitches I faced the last hurdle.

The ledgy crossbar of The Crucifix itself led directly into the final crack system. For a number of reasons it made sense to link the next two pitches into one. A difficult stemming problem quickly led through a technical 5.11d thin crack and when finally I latched a jug-handled flake I knew I was home free. One hand on the flake, one palmed out for balance and smug in my awesomeness, I yelled down to Rob, "That wasn't even that bad!" I casually reached my free hand into my chalk bag and in that moment my balance shifted. Fifteen feet out from my last piece, I slowly barndoored into space and launched into a backward swan dive, dizzily scanning a Ferris-wheel panorama of rock, the summit roofs, the blue heavens above, and as I curved back toward earth, the upside down Cathedral Spires, hanging like stalactites from the bottom of the world.

I failed at a no-falls ascent but the adventure was otherwise magnificent. The fall was the most scenic I have taken—and also the most unnecessary. Vanity coupled with clumsiness, 100 feet shy of the summit, gave me the spanking I richly deserved. I was lucky to escape with bruises and embarrassment.

Hubris

Most of us have made the mistake of taking success for granted. Blowing off homework, for instance, because we're sure we've got the material dialed. But whereas lousy grades at school result merely in a smacked-down ego and furious folks, smugness on the wall can ruin your longstanding dreams—and a whole lot more. There is a time for gloating, like on a summit—if we've got plenty of daylight left, or in the saloon, provided we have a driver. Spacing out or indulging in visions of grandeur while still in the thick of it is asking for trouble. Firing a crux and immediately getting loose out on the sharp end, before we've safely reached the top, is a surprisingly common way of blowing the on-sight or inviting an epic.

For some, the main challenge in doing long routes is in maintaining a level of mental and physical tautness. Loose rock, tricky routefinding, rotten fixed gear, and inobvious climbing all pose challenges. Even common sense and experience sometimes gets trumped by summit fever (the uncontainable desire to finish the climb now) and potential bragging rights. It's natural to feel proud about pulling off a dream—we just have to make sure we complete the climb before we start to brag about it.

Retreat off Washington Column.

ALEXANDRE BUISSE

CHAPTER 31

Central Pillar of Frenzy (CPF)

John Long

It was May, and Jim Bridwell (the "Bird") showed me a list of new routes he planned to attempt in Yosemite in the coming years. One took a bold, penciled line up a black-and-white photo of Middle Cathedral, which at that time was my favorite rock. The line followed striking features—splitter cracks, thin corners, a roof, some open face work, hanging belays for sure. The length, projected at twelve pitches, made the adventure seem especially dramatic. Since the Bird set most of the tempos and temperatures in the Valley back then, I knew this route was a done thing.

A few weeks later, in conventional military fashion, Bridwell commanded a platoon of Camp 4 draftees to a high point of 900 feet. Here, buckling knifeblades and holdless granite halted progress, though the Bird thought it possible for the squad to execute a "column left" and traverse off to easier rock on the flank. In the spring of the following year, the platoon did just that, and the route was completed: the Central Pillar of Frenzy (IV 5.10b).

No less than ten climbers had their hand in the final ascent. Angered at my exclusion, I chose the next best thing, an early repeat—folks were already queuing up for this one, a classic from start to finish. Over the following years, the initial five pitches would become one of the most traveled climbs on earth (though the lines did not reach all the way to Fresno as some claimed). When Jim Orey and I climbed up to the last pitch, we were amused that the route "finished" by traversing off at the first real difficulties, though not amused enough to brave

Unquestionably the busiest roof crack in America. Pitch 3, CPF.

KARL "BABA" BRALICH

the buckling blades and holdless granite above. So we traversed off like everyone else.

Enter Tobin Sorenson and Gib Lewis, the next team to attempt to straighten the Bird's line. Tobin's oeuvre could not yet rival the Bird's for

"Crimpgirl"—that's Dr. Rennison to you, buster—on pitch 2, CPF.

KARL "BABA" BRALICH

Checking Sources

Ask three people to talk about the woman walking out of the theater and you'll hear descriptions about a Peruvian, an Italian, and an Arab boy because no two people ever experience the same thing the same way. And no two descriptions, written or verbal, are quite the same. That's one reason the topo map came to replace the old route descriptions. A tree is hardly debatable, and it's easy to pencil onto a map with some accuracy. Nevertheless we try and cross reference our route information from several sources, and a few more if the route is long and serious. The route itself will likely be obvious once you start up—most popular climbs follow prominent features. However the approach and descent can be easy or epic, depending.

As a general practice, whenever considering a long route, particularly in wilderness areas, make it a casual study for a month or so, reading trip reports and so forth when you can remember. And maybe spend an evening boning up online before gearing up for the push. Things change year to year as anchors are replaced and natural features shift and slough off; but getting to and getting off a given cliff or formation usually remains the one constant, and whatever overall feel you can work up, drawn from random sources, is likely to give you useful but perhaps not perfect information. As with all trad climbs, the moment we cast out on the sharp end, we're on our own, and everything we read and committed to memory has gotten us right about there. Now we climb it.

No two mountains, nor two climbs, are ever the same.

JODY LANGFORD

ambitious construction, though he certainly had the elder's level of inspiration. Tobin would traverse off only at gunpoint. Gib, then the stronger face climber, thieved up the holdless pitch, which ended in slings beneath a thin crack chocked with grass. The final 300 feet, leading to the U-shaped bowl, looked climbable, but they'd need a rototiller to clean this next 40-foot stretch. Of course Tobin was never one to rap off, under any circumstances. Over the course of a climb his ideas generally gathered conviction. So naturally Tobin punched out the jungle pitch on aid and the two carried on, encountering a superb, 1-inch splitter (5.10c) on the next and final lead. The complete line was finished: V 5.10d, A1.

The Bird had been usurped on his very own route, and as the High Lama of American rock climbing, he resolved to immediately tidy up the Lewis/Sorenson direct finish. He dragged Billy Westbay and I down to El Cap meadow for a look-see with high-powered binoculars. Fresh off a lap up El Cap, Billy, the Bird, and I were on a roll. The Bird would never pause and allow his career to be summed up by one route, however august and historic. Jim was always about the next climb—and the next climb was the Central Pillar of Frenzy—all free.

By noon the next day we three were hanging in slings beneath the jungle pitch that Tobin had nailed. According to the Bird, I would try and free it, ungardened, and if that failed, Jim would clean it with a long-picked alpine hammer. Straight off the hanging belay, I clawed up and left over greasy acorns and gained the seam.

"Impossible," I said, frantically scratching about the dirt-filled crack for a lock, a hold—anything.

Steep jamming on the lower cracks of CPF.

KARL "BABA" BRALICH

Repeating Current Routes

We break in on the classics, just as the aspiring rocker spends ages in his garage, trying to play old Metallica covers on his brother's electric guitar. We'll never get totally past repeating the classics. Why would we? But once we develop some little mastery, we'll want to climb ourselves out of the garage and into the present moment. We'll want to "climb current." At any given time at every crag on earth, there are trendy routes, newish stuff that generates the buzz and gets climbers up on their hind legs. Such routes run the gamut from 5.9, and all the way up. It's sound practice and plain fun to bag which-ever of these trendy routes we can manage because it climbs us out of ourselves and into the conversation, breaking the isolation that some haul to the crags, determined to do things their own way. No harm in that, but why miss out on the break-ing wave? Get with the program and step up to the hot routes. Do them on the sly if you must stay incognito and separate, but never deprive yourself of the current shizzle. Even the most sociopathic climber will never regret repeating a current classic. He might hate the idea of following anyone else's foot-steps or chalk marks. But this is just a concept, a preference. The great routes are there to do. Do them. As mentioned, they run the full range of difficulty. If you're going to the considerable trouble to climb at all, climb the hot stuff. Climb current.

Matt Kuehl, climbing current, Icebox Canyon, Nevada.

MATT KUEHL

Jim Bridwell and John Long in Joshua, 2012.

DAVE VAUGHN

Sandbagging

Sandbagging is deliberately downgrading the difficulties or providing misleading information. You describe a pleasant mist, while knowing the team will confront Gorilla Monsoon. There is a long heritage of sandbagging in the climbing world. The original idea is to elevate one's apparent technical prowess by professing that climbs and circumstances are less difficult or serious than they are in the real world. It's a trivial business, he says with a sweep of his hand. After all, no more than a handful have died on the thing and that was with lug-soled boots and goldline ropes. A modern, gym-trained commando will dispatch the thing in . . . yada yada. Sandbagging and one-upping world-class friends is part of every sporting game. Doing so to unwitting, weekend warriors is craven and evil. But it happens, quite often, which is all the more reason to double- and triple-check your sources.

I slugged in a Bugaboo, which drifted to the eye with one blow.

"Sounds bunk," Billy warned. My feet greased off those acorns the moment I clipped into the Bugaboo, which straightaway shot out, lobbing me down the wall in a perilous arc and scribing a nasty groove in the back of Billy's legs as I wrenched straight onto the belay bolts.

After aiding up and hoeing that pitch with the ice axe, the Bird swung back to our hanging stance, smiling through a mask of topsoil.

"It's clean now!" said the Bird. "Great locks to the end, then one thin face move and we're up."

Those "great locks" were something less, with only sketchy wrinkles to boot, so at the end of the crack I found myself barely hanging on. Leaning off a soiled tip-lock, my right hand pawed the face for bump or crinkle.

"Grab the vine," shrieked the Bird.

Perhaps 8 feet separated me from the flawless 1-inch splitter, streaking up the wall to easier ground. The vine, several feet out of reach, dangled from a scrawny stump budding from the start of the crack. Pencil thin, furry, and shaped like a corkscrew, the vine seemed an unlikely target to lunge for, but with a nut at my feet, what the hell?

"Watch me!"

I sprung up and right, latched that crooked root which crackled and popped, elongated horribly, and uncoiled straight as a guitar string as I shock loaded onto the stump.

Holding my breath, I hand-walked a body length up the vine and grabbed the root, held fast by an inch of soot and a frozen cobweb. I started mantling up, but reconsidered, reached down and snapped off the vine. Once I'd seized the vine I stopped looking for face holds and had no idea how hard it would be to actually climb this section, or if one could at all. The 1-inch crack above was a marvel at 5.10c, likewise the upper wall, right to the U-shaped bowl. The Central Pillar was finally complete: IV 5.11.

A couple years later, I was kicked back in Yosemite Lodge and in walks Englishman Ron Fawcett (with whom I'd first climbed El Cap) with an antsy young upstart at his side. Hot on Middle Cathedral, the kid had hiked many of Middle's finest routes, and wanted the dope on Central Pillar, unrepeated in its entirety. The kid had the topo in his hand.

"A real plum," I said, pointing to the vine-climbing pitch. "The crux is just here. Following some 5.7 liebacking, there's a crafty friction step here, then a quick slap for a stump. The rest is casual. Great route, man. Have fun."

CHAPTER 32

El Capitan:
Pop Tarts, Sardines, and "Chew"

Peter Croft

Yosemite Valley overshadowed anything else I was inclined to do. It always felt like time and money well spent to drive the thousand miles to Paradise. Spring and fall, year after year, I bummed lifts or rode Greyhound buses to climbing's Holy Land. For almost any type of trad climbing, the Valley had the archetypical testpiece, recognized around the world. Butterballs was the most famous finger crack on the planet—ditto for Half Dome and The Nose of El Cap, the most renowned and coveted big walls in any land. But even Paradise loses its luster after a couple months, when all the pilgrims have gone home.

It was a late afternoon in mid-October and I was waiting for word on a ride north when I stopped by the deli in Yosemite Village and ran into Eric Ziesche, who was also marooned. Eric was from North Carolina, and at times his cat-howling accent made it nearly impossible to understand him, his volume so over-the-top that I had shied away from hitting the crags with him. Now his rowdiness was subdued from burnout. We both were cooked and eager to leave.

As talk turned to future seasons, we discovered that neither of us had done The Nose, the most sought-after rock climb on earth. Our psyche rekindled in a flash and a few hours later found us bivied at the base of El Capitan. We were begging for trouble: a hastily conceived plan to climb the biggest rock I had ever seen, with a partner with whom I had never shared a rope. Sometimes, though, an unexpected bit of wackiness, tossed in

The Big Stone.

ED BANNISTER

from left field, is the splash of cold water that wakes us up. So while logic said, "Hold on here," I instinctively felt this was the right time with the right partner.

We planned on a 2-day ascent, with the second jumaring and toting the bivi gear.

This way we avoided hauling the "pig" (which I knew nothing about). The plan made great sense. We hardly discussed going for it in a push, and leaving the pack behind. El Capitan was still too tall for any experimentation or heroics. In retrospect, given the hellish experience of jugging with a heavy pack, we would have been far better off going for a 1-day ascent.

At 3 a.m. we started up and I found out almost immediately that picture-book theories are cruelly deceptive. I had little experience and no knack for climbing a rope with ascenders (jumaring, named after the archetypal Swiss ascenders, or simply, jugging), with a full load besides, which made the slabs feel vertical and the vertical, atrociously overhanging. Only 300 feet up on a 3,000-foot wall and we already were bathed in sweat, a rude beat-down that could have sent us rapping for cover. Luckily, it was still dark.

Six hundred feet up and still inky black, Eric launched off on the pendulum into the "Stove Legs," the legendary, laser-cut hand cracks that shoot directly to Dolt Tower, 900 feet up the wall. The trick is to lower down some 40 feet off the top

Spontaneity

Spontaneity usually surfaces as a non-sensical blip in a sea of normalcy. Often, however, it is a response to stifling order and too much sameness. It is the subconscious's way to thwart boredom and burnout, providing a breath of fresh air we didn't know we needed till it's ours.

While a long-term plan is advisable, and we'll want to know (and like) our wall partner, it is also worth the risk, now and again, to take a flyer, to go with our gut or a sudden change of heart. Our feelings of control in the outdoors are usually overstated. Trad climbing, on any kind of scale, involves so many variables it is impossible to plot out an unfailing roadmap to success—and usually foolish to try. Unforeseen twists of fate might land us in a situation we would never have chosen, but also one we never, ever would trade when all is said and done.

B Sharp, Utah.
ANDREW BURR

How Fast?

To bivi or not to bivi—this is the question when looking up at a big wall and trying to reckon the logistics. Our answer will determine our plan: What time do we start; how much junk do we carry; how thrashed will we be at the end of it all. Whatever you choose will involve trade-offs: speed, or ease and comfort; a big rush, or depth of experience; an energy bar and a quart of Cytomax, or a case of King Cobra and pigs-in-a-blanket; a short story, or a novella.

A 1-day attempt features a chance of grabbing most of the fun of climbing a mega route, minus the labor of lugging and hauling the dreaded pig. Plus the rush of dusting off a big chunk of stone in one exhilarating go—and that's a blast in any language. On the other hand, planning for a multiday adventure gives a party the security of knowing any bivi should be a cushy one—providing the pig bears sufficient grub and libations—as well as the fun of vertical camping on the cliffside.

If experiencing a real live bivouac is high on our bucket list, we should have at it right off. In the middle of the night it is a wondrous thing to peer down 1,000 feet of moon and starlit granite to an inky forest below—and glorious to wake up to a sunrise on a crazy ledge or hanging tent.

If, on the other hand, we would like to make a 1-day ascent but are unsure if there's enough hours in the day or juice in the guns, then we need to work the arithmetic. If we can imagine ourselves cranking the route in 2 days, hauling or jugging with a pack (with all the extra time and toil that entails), then if we were to get a predawn start and go super light, we might very well get up the beast in a day. A gamble? Sure it is, and not the coin we toss before establishing our abilities and knowing well the local terrain. We never push the boat too far out into deep waters if conditions would make an unplanned bivi perilous or miserable. The ideal place to test our abilities is in a Yosemite or a Squamish—under ideal

weather. This way if we guess wrong it'll simply be a few hours of lost sleep and perhaps the benefits of getting to know our partner a whole lot better!

Battening down the hatches on Keeler Needle, High Sierras.

AMY NESS

bolt and start swinging back and forth, mad-dash right, timing a last-second leap over a wide, left-facing corner while keeping momentum enough till you can stab a jam into the foot of the Stove Legs. No easy task in the dark.

Eric timed it all wrong and smacked face-first into the dihedral—I looked up to see his headlamp spinning like a firefly as he spewed the most blasphemous, shocking, spectacular cursing I had ever heard. The sight of this all in the predawn gloom coupled with the Tourette's-like string of Southern dirty talk reduced me to pants-peeing convulsions. Given our lousy logistics and poor wall technique, it was only this running cartoon, played over and over, that carried us up the Big Stone. Exhausting jugging and gobied wall hands stood no chance against so much fun.

We flailed mightily but finally managed the double pendulums off Boot Flake (the notorious "King Swing"), got lost in the nebulous gray bands, and had our minds blown at the lip of the Great Roof—surely one of the most brilliant stances in the vertical world. Sleeping at Camp 5, a tiny atoll 2,200 feet up there with 800 feet to go, made the hideous pack toting seem trifling. We lay back and watched the stars come out, dining on Pop Tarts and sardines. Brilliant.

Next day in cool morning shade we raced up the corner cracks. With the pack weighing almost nothing, jugging was no longer clumsy torture. We arrived on top by lunch the next day. We were chuffed—Eric so much that he insisted on having a summit "chew," having packed a tin of Copenhagen (an especially robust brand of "snooze") as a kind of pauper's champagne. I'd never gone for the chewing tobacco myself, so I let him have at it, watching curiously as he packed his jowls, slipped into eyes-rolled-into-his-head bliss, and promptly collapsed onto all fours, barfing and dry-heaving like a dog. On one of the most celebrated summits in the world, this was our crowning moment.

Good Humor

It is worth repeating—nothing takes the edge off fear, suffering, and anger better than a good belly laugh. While it is tempting to pick a partner for their technical skills, these are small consolation for dealing with a jackass—no big thing on crag routes, but on longer climbs, suffering a fool can be the worst of times. We've seen that on mega routes there are countless things that can go wrong, piss us off, sap our strength, and be the beginning of the end if we let them. Pick someone who is a hoot to be with and the bushiest, ant-infested rubble pile becomes a treasured safari—maybe.

Friends on the wall, high up on El Cap.

SARA MATISSE

CHAPTER 33

El Cap Part 2: High and Dry

Peter Croft

Flush with success and sunburned horribly, I headed for the Mountain Room Bar for the Valley climber's equivalent of a victory lap. Coming straight from the rappels off the East Ledges on El Capitan (the standard descent after climbing the wall), anything in the shade sounded good. So I dove into the smelly shadows of the tavern, licked the froth off a Budweiser, and hoovered the baskets of free snacks.

In the crowded room of clinking glasses and competitive bragging, the hushed voice with the Scottish accent caught my attention. Word had leaked out that we had just summited The Captain, and this furtive stranger wondered if he might have a word. Pleased as I was with our ascent, we'd set no speed record or done any remarkable free climbing, so I could see no reason why anyone would care to interview me. It quickly became clear, however, that the stranger's interest lay not in my awesomeness but in up-to-date info about those sneaky rangers milling about the summit area of El Cap. The Scotsman was planning a predawn (and totally illegal) BASE jump off the abrupt summit lip just east of the Nose. At that time BASE jumpers were seldom-heard-of and rarely seen creatures. In a bar full of huge talkers, I took this unicorn at face value—good entertainment, but nothing more.

Next day was my last in the Valley, and I lounged about on a Merced River sandbank till late afternoon when a deluxe party was coming down at a beach downstream. I was next in line to squeeze into a station wagon bound for hot dogs,

ice cream, and girls who might be wearing bikinis, or God willing, making do without, when someone tapped me on the shoulder. The gist of the ensuing conversation was that Scottish-accent Guy from the night before had indeed hopped off The Captain, with the trio that now stood before me. Their flight had gone as planned, except Scotty took a wrong turn into the face, collapsing his chute as he accelerated down the cliff—nightmare stuff, and his survival depended on a miracle. And that's exactly what he got.

Halfway down the overhanging east face he tumbled onto a ledge—miraculously unhurt, but marooned on the wall. Astonishing! Ridiculous! This is where I was requested to step in. They couldn't hail the rescue team without alerting the rangers, which meant fines, gear confiscated, deportation—that sort of thing. All of which brought them to me. I freely offered a host of good reasons for them to find someone else, anyone else, but they quickly countered every one. Time was the issue. Scotty had already been trapped on the wall for a whole day, without water. And so I waved goodbye to the station wagon with the frankfurters and ice cream tubs—and to the girls who, I was now certain, would be bathing without bikinis.

I grabbed the necessary gear, wrangled up Rob, another Canadian, to belay and jug, and started up the Nose as a starry night fell over my valley. The weather had been blue sky for weeks, so we blew off checking the forecast and carried no rain gear. It hadn't rained all month, and I was supposed to leave the next morning anyhow. No way would a storm move in at this, the worst time of all.

Heavy weather, Castle Valley, Utah.

ANDREW BURR

We reached El Cap Tower, 1,500 feet up the wall, by early morning. We tied our three ropes together and lowered some jumars down to a ledge down and right from the Tower, having been briefed on Scotty's position. His friends assured me that Scotty was a climber competent in the use of ascenders, so he would know the drill. No problem.

After some yelling back and forth and a long wait, Scotty chugged into view. All was good—till he drew close and I saw he wasn't clipped into the jugs. At all! Three rope lengths of steep jugging, and now only connected by his badly pumped arms. I lunged for Scotty and clipped him in. Hoo Boy! Another couple feet and his arms would have blown out and Scotty would have pitched the distance—and they'd find so much haggis on the deck. Now all we had to do was go down.

The Scot introduced himself as Billy, and he was a tough bugger. Although not much of a climber, he claimed he was fine, just a wee bit thirsty. Then he downed two quarts like they were shot glasses.

Rob and I launched down the rappels, keeping a close watch on our charge. Now afternoon clouds that had been lurking out west were surging our way, conveyed by blasts of cool air. October days are short. Parties of three are slow. Darkness caught us in the Stove Legs, where the rappel route diverges from the Nose. It started pouring rain.

Weather Check—Don't Become a Victim

In fair weather locales, weeks or even months of solid sunshine can lead to a delusional laxness—"It hasn't rained in ages, I wouldn't worry about it." If it hasn't rained in ages, then it's overdue for a storm.

If you do find yourself heading up to help someone in trouble, it is especially key to check the forecast. Jacked up for all the right reasons, don't let adrenaline switch you into high speed in your haste to do good. If someone is in trouble, things have already turned bad. It's important you don't just run out the door and make it worse. Heading up into the first winter storm of the season dressed for summer could turn rescuers into more victims. The first rule in all rescue work is to never imperil the rescue team, which would require yet another team to bail them out.

I hadn't checked the guidebook but I knew the rappels headed straight down over blank rock, and we slowly battled down through the first big storm of the season. I didn't know that one of the anchors was way out of line with the others, making it tricky enough to find in daylight and nigh impossible to spot at night. I swung back and forth in huge arcing pendulums, wiping out and spinning across the sluicing rock like a cut-loose haul bag—but no luck finding the next anchor. Eventually I jugged back up to the station and broke the bad news. Billy popped his emergency chute as a kind of bivi shelter, which helped against the gale. Without a trace of a ledge, hanging off three bolts, we lay against the rock, ice water gushing over us as the first and second stages of hypothermia seeped through us.

At this darkest moment, when survival seemed unlikely, Billy told us, in his thick brogue, to leave him hanging there in the rain and to run for our lives. He'd gotten himself into it, and we should get ourselves out.

Then we heard voices below. A group of friends had hiked up to the base. It was four rope lengths to the ground, and we only had three ropes. We tied our three lines together and Rob rapped down as one of the ground crew hiked up the talus with a rope. After an interminable time of toss and catch,

Rob finally snagged the cord and a gateway back to the living opened up.

Never had the ground felt so delicious, although the spectacle held some last surprises. On the second to last rappel, Scotty could no longer control the rope with his shivering hands and ziplined in a free fall the entire length of the line, all the way to the next knot, his rappel device sending sparks into the night when he bounced a few times on the way down. When he stopped he simply muttered, "Oh, I'm here already," switched over to the last rope and rapped to the ground. Immediately his friends swept him up and started hustling him down to the blasting heater of their waiting car.

In the comforting chaos of sopping gear, slippery talus, and warm friends, I turned to see Scotty had hiked back up to meet me at the base of the wall. Wrapped in a blanket, he shivered out that he wanted to pay me. When I refused he said, "Well then, at least let me shake your hand." When I reached a mitt he slapped a wad of cash into my palm, bolted for the car, and roared off.

The rest of us got back to Camp 4 at around dawn on Sunday morning. I counted the bills that Scotty had palmed off and realized it was just enough to take all my wet friends to the breakfast buffet at the Ahwahnee hotel. I may have missed out on the picnic, but I made it to the brunch.

Do the Right Thing

No matter how much we learn, we will always get some things wrong, and no matter how careful we conduct business, we will still screw up on occasion. We usually survive the smaller mistakes. But we need to appreciate that our bumbles could turn out badly indeed, that we just got lucky; otherwise we are a car wreck looking for a place to happen. When we encounter someone else in an epic or an accident, we are obliged to help so far as our capacity allows.

Climbing is essentially an individual adventure, but we are intimately connected to our actions, to the people we know and places we visit and experience. It is often a weird community, but it is important we look out for each other. It could be as simple as waiting on top with our headlamps for those who forgot theirs, or sharing food and water with the parched and starving. On the other hand it could be a dire emergency where someone's life hangs in the balance.

Usually any climbers in peril will be strangers, but that lack of familiarity should never be a reason to avoid involvement. It will also likely be happening at a lousy time—late in the day or in bad weather. One thing we can count on is that it will, at best, be inconvenient. But the more we help the less likely land managers will step in and close their gates, or that parks will impose additional rules and fines. Think of it—by being lazy, selfish, and scared we could eventually become outlaws when we head to the rock. But put that aside for a moment. Before we are climbers we are just people. What we do when we encounter those in trouble is not a test as a climber but a final exam about who we are.

Off-width gorilla, stand-up dude.

MATT KUEHL

Epilogue

Twenty years later I was living in California. One day, while toasting another dreamy sunshiny day, the phone rang. The caller had a strong Scottish accent. He wanted to know if I was a climber, if I had been to Yosemite, if I had been involved in a stormy rescue, if . . . the thick accent choked up and rang off, quickly rasping out that he couldn't talk now but he would call later.

Next day he called again, and the story came out that he'd been trying to find me for years but with no last name or contact info, it wasn't until now that he'd finally tracked me down. He told me about the big and small in his life, about his family, about how things might have turned out very differently on a night 20 years before.

When Things Turn Epic—Check and Double-Check

Once a situation requires a rescue mission, double-check that you have sufficient hardware, clothing (including rain wear), water and food, and any relevant first-aid gear. Also find out whatever you can about the victims. Are they experienced? What are their skills? If you have any doubts, err on the side of safety.

For instance, with the BASE jumper on El Cap, I was told he knew how to jumar. He knew the bare basics—but not the lifesaving trick of clipping the jumars into his harness. As he pulled over onto our ledge, his hands and arms cramping, he was a whisker away from jumping the bottom half of The Nose. I still shudder thinking about that. In that situation (and with the same info) now, I would rap down and set him up—just an extra 10 minutes to make things bombproof.

Monitor the victim every inch of any descent, even if they're not injured. If it's a rappel, clip them into more than one piece at stations. Pre-rig their rappels and watch the ends as they descend in case they lose control. Never count on them to keep it safe. Offer them food and water. The more they take in the more strength they'll have—and the easier and safer it will be for everyone. The moment you throw in for a rescue, you become a guide, with all the attending responsibilities.

ANDREW BURR

CHAPTER 34

Avoiding the Red Zone

Peter Croft

The world at large bears countless tales of honest efforts gone awry, of well-planned experiments blowing up in people's faces. There also are those marvelous larks where the objective strived for becomes secondary in the course of events— a pharmacist tinkering with a cure for headaches invents Coca-Cola, say, or a sloppy scientist returns to find his unwashed petri dishes moldy—and "discovers" penicillin. In a universe tending toward chaos and entropy, screwy things happen.

In the haphazard course of hurling myself at rock walls, I tried out all kinds of ideas. Never taking a rest day was a bad idea. Never warming up—certainly a bad one. Eating a whole loaf of cheese bread before an afternoon of hard soloing—probably a bad one, but something I did for a whole summer, with nothing worse to show for it than an occasional stomachache. Eventually I got wise, though rarely from studied reasoning. Oftentimes the "Aha!" moment came unexpectedly, the epiphany blindsiding me while I searched for results somewhere else.

In between dusting the big routes, my friends and I hit the short crags, fine-tuning our jamming skills and falling off testpieces. By late afternoon, our attention often shifted to bean burritos or some version of cocktail hour. But if we felt especially motivated, with little time left to bag more pitches, many of us would throw toprope laps on a handy pumpfest—standard practice for a generation of climbers. For me, however, all that lowering off was time not spent climbing, so I took to downclimbing

On the Gangway, Whitney Portal.

BILL McCHESNEY

227

Terminal Pump

Averting the terminal pump is an ongoing and crucial goal. This often means exploiting rests, then climbing quickly and efficiently till we arrive at the next foothold or bomber jam. We camp at good rest stops until we feel ready to charge—then wait a few minutes longer.

Why? Because we often see fit climbers cruise the crux then pump out on easier climbing because they rushed their business. On marginal rests, learn to recognize the point where you've reached maximum benefit and will only tire further if you dally longer. Developing this skill takes seasons to master. The more mileage we have, the better we are able to read ourselves. And that's much of the game.

Once we commit to casting off, climb with purpose, generally placing and clipping gear at chest level to save strength. Although tempting, avoid triggering pro at full arms' reach: It's easier to pick the wrong size, it's more strenuous to place, and takes more time and effort to clip, usually requiring stuffing the rope in our mouths while we reel out slack. Especially on steep climbs where there's nothing to hit, there's no reason to place and clip at full extension. The strength saved by slotting gear directly in front of us means feeling fresher on that run-out over pumpy ground.

instead, tagging but not weighting the ground, then starting up once more for another burn. This was ideal endurance training—pure and simple—and I didn't look for much beyond that.

Soloing began to become a bigger and bigger part of my normal curriculum; guilt over how much belay time my friends had to endure was replaced by longer and longer solo sessions. In the process I discovered that hand jams are the king of all holds—better than perfect fingers or an all-time jug. In the midst of heart thumping effort and a choice of holds, the difference between good and great became vast. The trick—or more accurately, the guiding principle—was to keep the RPMs out of the red zone, and the best way to accomplish that was to hand jam as often and as efficiently as possible.

Thumbs-up on Boney Fingers, Whitney Portal.

BILL McCHESNEY

My basic technique was refined through repetition and country miles of downclimbing, which greatly improved my ability to reverse out of scary places. Such refinements were to be expected. What I wasn't looking for was an understanding of jamming seemingly lost on other climbers, an understanding that came mostly from climbing down, often with significant pumpage.

At Squamish, for example, there is an area called the Smoke Bluffs, featuring a particularly vicious overhanging finger and hand crack called Hot Cherry Bendover, first climbed by legendary Valley master Bill Price, during one of several visits. The route quickly became the testpiece for the trickiest size of all, the dreaded off-finger crack—too wide for fingers and too narrow for hands. Constantly changing in width, sprinkled with the odd thin finger jam and rounded at the lip to prevent an avid liebacker from thugging his way up it, Hot Cherry Bendover was the ideal pitch to lap out on. With an

Pumping Laps

This is a great way to score a stack of extra climbing with a small investment of time—maximum bang for the buck. Pumping laps is generally done late in the day when we're too bushed for another long approach but motivation for rock is still high. Lapping is obviously a fine way to squeeze out the mileage, but perhaps the greater benefits include increased fitness and the chance to fine-tune technique.

Often called "endurance training," mileage days more likely entail both power and endurance components. "Endurance" usually refers to aerobic endurance, our capacity to exercise without producing excessive lactic acid. Chucking laps on a steep hard route is about trying to manage that lactic burn. With the safety of the toprope, which eliminates the psychological game, we can go right to the brink of lactic overload. By training ourselves to function in this state, our bodies become better adapted and less apt to produce lactic overdose.

Picking the right route to lap out on is critical, but first we need to decide whether we are going to just climb up, or up and down. If we're only climbing up and then lowering down, the route can be more difficult. If there is a choice it often is helpful for a number of reasons to pick a slightly easier climb, then lap up and down. Eliminate lowering and the training is continuous, an obvious benefit if the pitch is short. This also is a perfect time to fine-tune our downclimbing skills—something underappreciated, until we really need it.

Mega mileage is a proven drill for smoothing out our technique, particularly if the route has sustained climbing of our weakest technique. That thin hand jam that once felt precarious begins to feel like an anchor after half a dozen runs on Energy Crisis. Along the way we experiment with our footwork, hand position, etc. and also find whatever tricks we can to "allocate the pump."

"And they cross'd themselves for fear"— a well-worn Camalot.

MATT KUEHL

assortment of tricky jams to try on for size, mile-age weeded out the inefficient and reinforced what methods worked best. More than anything, when the clock was ticking, making big moves with the least effort was key to keeping the RPMs out of the red zone. Downclimbing through the overhanging bulges, I found I could make longer reaches and often avoid the cruxiest bits simply by jamming thumbs up.

Though contrary to what I saw in books or magazines, or at the crags, sticking with thumbs-up jamming entirely changed the way I climbed. The more I experimented with this approach, the more it made sense. Once I understood the advan-tages, the more I focused on it—striving to climb a pitch in less moves, hence, less time and therefore less effort. I found that in crucial passages, where before my strength would circle the drain, I could now recover. Using the ruthlessly wired crack Hot Cherry Bendover as an educational hamster wheel was instructional, but what I needed to do was put it into practice on new terrain and on a grand scale.

Later that year I was avoiding another stint of grim Canadian weather by escaping once more to Leavenworth. A burly hour hike up the hill finds Midnight Rock, one of the area's proudest cliffs—fine-grained granite, around 400 feet tall with an assortment of fearsome fissures. Virtually all the climbing launches off a halfway ledge accessed by an airy creep-across from the left flank. In the cen-ter of the wall loomed an old mystery aid line, a narrow open book sporting a few ratty fixed pieces hinting at long-forgotten first ascensionists. As a free climb, this mystery line looked like a peach, and I set to it.

It took a number of efforts, snapped edges, and resultant wingers to make it into the finger crack. Both walls of the shallow dihedral overhung; as I pulled up into the first thin finger jam, the sun rounded the corner, turning up the heat. Just above, the crack flared out and pinched off, leaving a slightly rounded offset for liebacking. I fired in a few

thin pieces, alternately pasting my digits and slotting gear, and then punched it. My internal tachometer was spiking hard and my forearms felt twice their size when I realized I would come up short. Two feet out of reach was a hand jam, but so what? In the midday sun my toes were sliding off their smears as I pawed off the flared seam, postponing the inevi-table. The pitch went on for another 50 feet. There was no way I could recover from such a death pump no matter how big the holds got up higher.

Or was there? I distrusted the stoppers I'd hastily placed below; but in the off chance that a hand jam could be my savior, I decided that trying the move and falling was better than taking the jump. The near certainty that my strategy wouldn't work actually calmed me down. There was nothing creative about this—I was too far gone to even chalk up. Running my feet up high, I coiled up and launched off a left-hand, fingertip layback and watched in amazement as my right hand crunched deep in the slot.

Because of the angling nature of the corner, I could only manage a thumbs-down jam—plenty secure, but the lactic acid kept mounting. The lunge had only won me a couple feet and a short reprieve. Too far gone to consider placing pro, I last-ditch pimped off a near useless left edge, whipped the right out of the pod, and slammed it in thumbs up. Home free! Even with my feet skittering on the blank rock below, I could feel the freshly oxygen-ated blood washing out the pooled up lactic acid. Eventually I was able to swap out hands, fully shake out, and gun for glory.

A pitch this proud needed a stellar name, and as a visitor to Leavenworth, I felt it deserved a moni-ker with local flavor. On the drive home we passed a local landmark inn promising military games, XXX adult movies, and hourly rates, an experi-ence that for some, apparently, was the ultimate entertainment package. The Steven's Pass Motel on Highway 2 was later closed for indecent infractions, but the route that bears the Steve's name still stands proud on Midnight Rock.

Thumbs Up

Emphasizing thumbs-up jamming on finger and hand cracks is the single most important aspect to maximizing fitness and reach. Thumbs down will give us extra camming action/torque but in most circumstances that benefit pales beside the ability to reach 30 to 50 percent farther, and all while using less effort. While climbing next to others who are taller, I've routinely ticked cruxes with less moves or avoided the crux altogether, simply by milking the last good jam thumbs-up, then going for the massive reach.

**Soloing the finger crack
Tips at Yosemite Valley.**

GREG EPPERSON

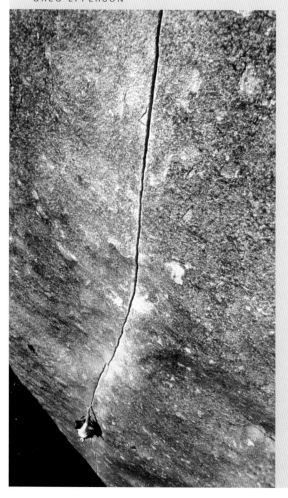

To develop a feel for this work, hold both arms in front of you, thumbs-up. Now go thumbs down. Notice how it immediately feels awkward. Now pantomime trying to go for big moves with the thumbs-down attitude. Note how it's hard to pull down past the chest. A key point to remember, which applies to all climbing, is that awkward positions always use excess energy. Now go back to thumbs up and try it again. This way we can sweep ("windmill") our arm down until the imaginary hand jam could be used as an undercling.

Once the technique is understood and the benefits appreciated, thumbs-up jamming is mastered like most every other basic technique: time on the rock. Don't expect this style to immediately feel great or even to always work. In some cases, owing to the way a crack angles, we may have to go with our hand thumbs-down. Perhaps we can change it out later—or not. The point is to do it as much as we can, till we clearly see that the slight but natural torque advantages of jamming thumbs-down are far outweighed by the ergonomic ease and vastly greater reach achieved when going thumbs-up. The more we practice this technique, the greater the rewards. Being more natural and less strenuous, the thumbs-up attitude is the least strenuous position in which to place gear, an especially important consideration on long burns.

CHAPTER 35

Green Arch

John Long

Tahquitz Rock was one of America's hot climbing spots, with a pageant of pivotal ascents reaching back to when technical climbing first came to the States. John Mendenhall, Chuck Wilts, Mark Powell, Jerry Galwas, Joe Fitschen, Royal Robbins, Tom Frost, T. M. Herbert, Yvon Chouinard, Bob Kamps, Tom Higgins, and many others had all learned the ropes there.

Our little informal band of "Stonemasters" arrived on the scene just as the previous generation of local hardcores were being overtaken by house payments and squealing brats. We were all young, vain, flat broke, and excited to do things our way. We'd grappled up many of the old classics not with grace, but with gumption and fire, and the limelight was panning our way. Not surprisingly, some of the

Tobin drew his inspiration from the unseen.

JODY LANGFORD

old guard saw themselves elbowed out of the opera house by kids who could merely scream. And none could scream louder than Tobin Sorenson, the most conspicuous madman ever to lace up Varappes.

Climbing had never seen the likes of Tobin, and probably never will again. He had the body of a welterweight, a lick of sandy brown hair, and the faraway gaze of the born maniac. Yet he lived with all the precocity and innocence of a child. He would never cuss or show the slightest hostility, and around girls he was so shy he'd flush and stammer. But out on the sharp end of the rope he was Igor unchained.

Approaching the overlap, Green Arch, Tahquitz.

GREG EPPERSON

The Limits of Boldness

Humans have always honored courage and self-sacrifice. The world's great religions, our creation myths, and timeless sagas are filled with do-or-die Jasons and Odysseuses who wrestle with gorgons and cyclopses and prevail by sword and moxie. On the cliffside, however, do-or-die is a good enough way to die. Still, there are rare cases where some of us might consider a large but calculated risk. Just know that as a standard strategy, overt boldness is eventually fatal. So where lies the line between courage and recklessness, between serious effort and desperation? Like most thorny questions, there is every reason to want a pat answer—but none exists in any language.

For many of us, the only "courage" that makes sense comes through challenging our own fears, respectful that we all have a line that when crossed, we rattle and roll and become swamped with rogue chemicals and wild thoughts—in a word, chaos. This power, this experience of climbing out past our comfort zone is dynamic, poten-

tially lethal, and intoxicating. It shrivels us, strikes us dumb. But it also makes ducks quack and makes the world go round and if we can hang on the edges of it, waist deep in the eddies, so to speak, we can ride resources we never knew existed and for a charmed moment, transcend ourselves. But one step too far and we're into the riptide. Then swept over our heads. Then gone. Too much seawater will kill us, but a drop adds flavor. All of trad climbing and all of adventure sports are about portioning out that drop. It is always self-administered. There are no instructions.

The right amount of exercise makes us stronger; the right amount of bookwork makes us smarter. Carefully ladling out the boldness, a teaspoon at a time, allows us to handle increasingly headier situations. Too much, too fast will overwhelm us and set us back, or worse. Start small.

Start small.

ROBERT MIRAMONTES

Over the previous summer he'd logged an unprecedented string of gigantic falls that should have ended his career, and his life, ten times over. Yet he shook each fall off and clawed straight back onto the route for another go, and usually got it. He became a world-class climber very quickly because anyone that well-formed and savagely motivated gains the top in no time—if he doesn't kill himself first. And yet when we started bagging new climbs and first free ascents, Tobin continued to defy the gods with his electrifying whippers. The exploits of his short life deserve a book. Two books.

One Saturday morning, five or six of us hunkered down in the little restaurant in Idyllwild—the same one Royal Robbins and the others met at over the previous 30 years. Tahquitz was our oyster. We'd pried it open with a piton and for months had gorged at will; but the fare was running thin. Since we had ticked off one after another of the remaining new routes, our options had dwindled to only the most grim or preposterous.

During the previous week, Ricky Accomazzo had scoped out the Green Arch, an elegant arc on Tahquitz's southern shoulder. When Ricky mentioned he thought there was an outside chance that this pearl of an aid climb might go free, Tobin looked like the Hound of the Baskervilles had just heard the word "bone," and we had to nearly lash him to the booth so we could finish our oatmeal.

Since the Green Arch was Ricky's idea, he got the first go at it. After 50 feet of dicey wall climbing, he gained the arch, which soared above for another 80 feet before curving right and disappearing in a field of big knobs and pockets. If we could only get to those knobs, the remaining 300 feet would go easily and the Green Arch would fall.

But the lower corner and the arch above looked bleak. The crack in the back of the arch was too thin to accept even fingertips, and both sides of the corner were blank and marble-smooth. But by pasting half his rump on one side of the puny corner, and splaying his feet out on the opposite side,

Ricky stuck to the rock—barely—both his ass and his boots steadily oozing off the steep, greasy wall. It was exhausting just staying put, and moving up was accomplished in a precarious sequence of $\frac{1}{4}$-inch moves. Amazingly, Ricky jackknifed about halfway up the arch before his calves pumped out. He lowered off a bunk piton and I took a shot.

After an hour of the hardest climbing I'd ever done (in the old high-top, red PAs, which had the friction coefficient of a shovel), I reached a rest hold just below the point where the arch swept out right and melted into that field of knobs. Ten feet to paydirt. But that 10 feet looked bleak. There were some sucker knobs just above the arch, but those ran out after about 25 feet and would leave a climber in the bleakest no man's land, with nowhere to go, no chance to climb back right onto the route, no chance to get any protection, and no chance to retreat. We'd have to stick to the arch.

Finally, I underclung up into the arch, whacked in a suspect knifeblade piton, clipped the rope in—and fell off. I lowered to the ground, slumped back, and didn't rise for 10 minutes. I had weeping strawberries on both ass cheeks and my ankles were rubbery and tweaked from splaying them out on the far wall.

Tobin tied into the lead rope and stormed up the corner like a man fleeing Satan on foot. He battled up to the rest hold, drew a few quick breaths, underclung out to that creaky, buckled, driven-straight-up-into-an-expanding-flake knifeblade, and immediately cranked himself over the arch and started heaving up the line of sucker knobs.

"No!" I screamed up. "Those knobs don't go anywhere!"

But it was too late.

Understand that Tobin was a born-again Christian, that he'd smuggled bibles into Bulgaria risking 25 years on a Balkan rock pile, that he'd studied God at a fundamentalist university and none of this altered the indisputable fact that he was perfectly mad. Out on the sharp end he not only ignored all

Kay Okamoto out on the wide-open face, where the bolts are often few and far between. A steady hand and cool head are prerequisites for keeping the activity sane and manageable.

GREG EPPERSON

consequences, but actually loathed them, doing all kinds of crazy, incomprehensible things to mock the fear and peril. (The following year, out at Joshua Tree, Tobin followed a difficult, overhanging crack with a rope noosed around his neck.)

Most horrifying was his disastrous capacity to simply charge at a climb pell-mell. On straightforward routes, no one was better. But when patience and cunning were required, few were worse. Climbing, as it were, with blinders on, Tobin would sometimes claw his way into the most grievous jams. When he'd dead-end, with nowhere to go and looking at a Homeric peeler, the full impact of his

folly would hit him like a wrecking ball. He would panic, wail, weep openly, and do the most ludicrous things. And sure enough, about 25 feet above the arch those sucker knobs ran out, and Tobin had nowhere to go. (Had he traversed right just over the arch—the now-standard free route—he would have gained tall cotton. But he just gunned it straight up for glory. And disaster.)

Because Tobin was 25 feet above the last piton, he was looking at a 50-foot fall, plus some for rope stretch. But the gravest news was that I knew the piton I'd bashed under the roof would not hold a 50-foot whipper. On really historic falls, the top

Going for It

We've reviewed the inexact calculus for estimating potential risks, and a general strategy of how to approach same. But how about when the risk calculus says forget it, but for whatever reason, we feel like taking a flyer. On this count I (JL) can only offer my own thinking during the few times that I intentionally rolled the dice. Early on I was climbing 300 days a year and was intent on pushing standards. It was easier to justify taking occasional risks than it might have been for a recreational climber. Through all of that climbing, I came to know myself, which probably is the most important factor for surviving dangerous situations. I was athletic and especially good at explosive moves, off-vertical face climbing, which I grew up doing, and wide cracks, which were made for my body type. My considerable weaknesses included being way too big (6 feet 1 inch, 205 pounds) for thin cracks, and overly static, overhanging faces that greatly favored a lighter article. When I occasionally gambled, I stayed on the off-vert faces and wide cracks, risking bad falls only on familiar feeling terrain, always convinced I could pull it off.

Most of all I knew that tempting fate, however calculated it felt, was a practice reserved for rare moments when I felt as though I had some little grace period to steal Thor's thunder. I knew the practice was not sustainable—not for me, anyway. I also knew I might be misreading the moment, the rock and my ability, and was staring at the next world, thinking it was Fat City. Beforehand, you can never determine the outcome per risky adventures. Many end poorly. This is our only guide, and knowing the stakes going in. If you can live with the results, perhaps a given risk is something to consider. But do-or-die climbing is never part of mainstream trad climbing, in any shape or form.

Calculated risk.

MATT STANICH

piece often rips out, but the fall is broken sufficiently for a lower nut or piton to stop you. In Tobin's case, the next lower piece was some dozen feet below the top one, at the rest hold; so in fact, Tobin was looking at close to an 80-footer. Tobin must have known as much because his knees were knocking like castanets and he was sobbing pitifully and looking to plunge off at any second.

There is always something you can do, even in the grimmest situation, if only you keep your nerve. But Tobin was gone, so mastered by terror that he seemed willing to die to be rid of it. He glanced down. His face was a study. Suddenly he screamed, "Watch me! I'm gonna jump."

We didn't immediately understand what he meant.

"Jump off?" Richard wanted to know.

"Yes!" Tobin wailed.

"NO!" we all screamed in unison.

Tobin reached out for those knobs so far to his right, now lunging, now hopelessly pawing the air as the falling man grabs for a cobweb. And then he was off. The top piton shot out and Tobin shot off into the grandest fall I've ever seen a climber take and walk away from—a spectacular, tumbling whistler. His arms flailed and his scream could have frozen brandy. Luckily, the lower piton held and he finally jolted onto the rope, hanging upside down and moaning softly. We slowly lowered him off and he lay motionless on the ground and nobody moved or spoke or even breathed. You could have heard a pine needle hit the deck. Tobin was peppered with abrasions and had a lump the size of a pot roast over one eye. He lay dead still for a moment longer, then wobbled to his feet and shuddered like an old cur crawling from a creek.

"I'll get it next time," he grumbled.

"There ain't gonna be no next time," said Richard, who had a knack for reining in Tobin's more adventurous work. The fall had taken the air out of the whole venture, and we were through for the day. The "next time" came 3 years later. In

Old EBs.

KEVIN POWELL

one of the greatest leads of that era, Ricky flashed the entire Green Arch on his first try. Tobin and I followed.

Tobin's singular gift was his scattershot exuberance. As the years passed and Tobin became a formidable alpinist, his fire never dimmed, though he brought it under a more scrupulous control. He would go on to solo the north face of the Matterhorn, the Walker Spur, and the Shroud on the Grandes Jorasses, would make the first alpine ascent of the Harlin Direct on the Eiger, the first ascent of the Super Couloir on the Dru—for years the hardest climb in the Alps—would repeat the hardest free climbs and big walls in Yosemite, and would sink his teeth into the Himalayas. Toward the end of his short career, he was widely considered the world's greatest all-around climber.

But nothing really changed: He always climbed as if time were too short for him, pumping all the disquietude, anxiety, and nervous waste of a normal year into each route.

Promised land.

JODY LANGFORD

I've seen a bit of the world since those early days at Tahquitz, have done my share of crazy things, and have seen humanity with all the bark on, primal and raw. But I've never since experienced the electricity of watching Tobin out there on the quick of the long plank, clawing for the promised land. He finally found it, attempting a solo winter ascent of Mount Alberta's north face. His death was a tragedy, of course, something that his close friends never really got past. Yet I sometimes wonder if God Himself could no longer bear the strain of watching Tobin wobbling and lunging way out there on the sharp end of the rope, and finally just drew him into the fold.

Knowing When to Quit

I had a football coach in college who always stopped practice when a drill was going poorly. "You guys are just practicing doing it wrong," he'd say. Pressing on with blind willpower was frustrating and fruitless and a sure way to keep doing things wrong, picking up bad habits in the bargain. You'd think because this was only "practice"—a turn of phrase made famous by all-star NBA guard Allen Iverson—it wouldn't matter. But every good coach knows that games are won or lost in practice. And for us trad climbers, unless a route is trivial, there are no practice climbs. All are the real deal. All technical climbs are sport only through the sage use of the roped safety system.

Sometimes when we go riding or climbing or skiing or surfing, we're all thumbs, our heads feel slow, and we can't get the lead out. We usually can muddle by, and if we drove all morning and gave up our weekend and paid a C note in gas and hiked in besides, we're going to get something out of the adventure no matter how off we feel. But just as we need to know when we're "on," and should try that hard project or early repeat, when our game feels compromised, we need to gracefully back down. Trying to press the action when everything feels impossible is asking for trouble—and Old Man Gravity is happy to oblige us in that regard. Better to coil the line and relax, or throttle down and go for mileage, aiming for quality or star value, instead of a high grade.

Nobody has their "A" game every time out. Knowing when to quit for the day is an advanced technique open to us all. Most of the longish falls I have taken were when I felt at half speed and tried to force the action. I was a slow learner. The crag isn't going anywhere.

KARL "BABA" BRALICH

CHAPTER 36

Learning to Climb Smart

Peter Croft

I always viewed climbing as a simian activity. Once I'd mastered the basics I figured the meat of it was animalistic, instinctual—fight or flight. To a certain extent this was true—just not yet. I still needed to rein in my excitement and strategize my routine. As it was my psyche for various milestones would build to a flashpoint and I'd hurl myself at the next big thing with little thought to strategy, route geometry, or common sense.

I needed to warm up before huge efforts, attempt hard routes at the ideal times (shade), and come to appreciate the benefits of good rope handling and do away with the near sobbing dreadfulness of rope drag, a problem I often encountered. In granite areas like Yosemite and Squamish, the climbs usually played out on flat walls where drag was hardly a factor. The blocky nature of some routes, however, laid bare my ignorance.

Common sense was always my weakest subject. I must have been the last person to put a standard warm-up into my routine. Why risk wasting valuable juice when I could get to work on the main course? I knew the argument, of course—that muscles perform much better after some moderate mileage, but I hadn't considered that there was more to it, that the mind-body connection and even the mind itself needs a warm-up phase before it can perform at max output. In fact, without

Low down on Sentry Box.

PAT MORROW

warming up I was weaker, less coordinated, and none too bright.

Sentry Box was the hardest free climb in Canada. It was first freed by local hotshot Eric Weinstein at 5.11 and first repeated years later by Californian Bill Price, who upped the grade to the mystical 5.12 standard. By the time I finally attempted the climb, Eric had been gone for some years and nobody after Bill had even pawed at the thin finger crux.

Then one morning I had the distinct feeling that it was meant to be—and "it" would be momentous. We drove to Squamish in Tami's brown Vega, trying hard to keep it close to the speed limit, stopping in the Klahanie Inn for my favorite breakfast—tall stack of pancakes with all the syrup they could soak up. I was ready!

First into the parking lot, I yarded the driver's door open, grabbed the edge of the roof with my left hand, swung in—and slammed the door shut with my right. Horrified, I looked up to see my fingers squashed between door and frame. I opened the door and gaped at my bent and bruised digits, swelling up like sausages. Remarkably they were unbroken, but hurt like the devil.

It took some weeks but my fingers healed, my psyche returned, and the planets lined up like before. Out to Squamish, wolf down the syrupy tall stack and race to the car—left hand on the roof, swing in, slam the door. Nooo! Not again!

Three weeks later I was back and managed to eat breakfast and get into a car without injuring myself. At the base of Sentry Box I was bubbling with excitement and launched up soon as I was

Crux first-joint finger jamming Sentry Box.

PAT MORROW

Warm Up

The saying, "If you don't have time to warm up then you don't have time to climb," should become every climber's mantra. We climb harder, have more fun, and suffer far fewer injuries when we slowly ramp up the section. Through the process our muscles and connective tissue become more elastic, hence, harder to rip or snap. Our circulation picks up nicely to dispose of that pesky lactic acid. Otherwise a stiff initial pitch can shock our system before it's ready, rendering a crippling flash pump. Throw in a few easier pitches and we cruise that first crux with a fraction of the pumpage. Even our mind-body coordination improves after a bit of mileage. It's all of a piece.

For an enjoyable warm-up drill, move with exaggerated precision. No matter how large the hold, place each foot slowly and exactly. Eliminate all arty flourishes and faux dancing and practice first-strike footwork—that is, don't skip and tap your foot around or pause with pointed toes ("Euro Fluffer"). Strive to make one direct and exact movement, and make it count the first time. We see people speed through a few easy pitches, perhaps climbing in dusty running shoes to save time and prove manliness. This only promotes clumsy footwork. Using precise technique on easy ground also provides better core warming (and strengthening). Slowly lift your foot to that high edge, rather than swinging or tossing it into place. Any sloppiness and we're always having to readjust our feet, even on moderate ground, so we can't suddenly expect to turn on the suave when a crack thins and the angle jacks up.

When fighting for our lives we revert back to our normal actions. If we normally use sloppy footwork—so we go in a pinch. Think of it like target practice. The more we aim for the sweet spot, the more likely we'll hit it when it really counts.

on belay. Halfway through I turned an arête and passed a roof. The rope slid into the crack at the lip; I kept going. Fifteen feet higher I screeched to a halt when the rope jammed tight. I hadn't placed any slings to extend the lead line so it now created a sharp angle right at the roof's edge. Nothing to be done except bobble my way down with an accumulating loop of slack. Flipping the cord out, I tried again—same thing. This time I placed a nut right in the notch—not for pro but to keep the rope from sliding back in. And this worked.

Finally I arrived at the crux where a vertical thin slash diagonaled up right into shallow tip locks. Jittery from adrenaline, nervousness, and maple syrup I whipped a stopper into the best slot and realized it also blocked the best (and only) finger-lock. Naturally the stopper got stuck as I fiddled madly off painful jams to remove it. Tantrums and cussing had no effect and finally I slumped back on tension. I got the nut out but had blown the onsight. I lowered down.

Next try it almost seemed straightforward as I pulled through the technical pinky jams to the anchors. A celebratory whoop froze in my throat. I had a wellspring of psyche but no caution and little common sense. I pictured the entire game as a matter of pulling moves, of physically climbing this crack or that face—which rarely was the problem. It was everything else that kept thwarting me, and I continued to come up short and injure myself in embarrassing ways.

Peter Croft pulling over the top of Sentry Box.

PAT MORROW

Critical Placements

Conveniently placed pro is often a slam-dunk—throw it in, clip, and go! Sometimes, though, things are not so simple. With thinner pro, for instance, we can't get in the habit of placing it too high over our heads, risking a greater chance of misjudging the size, getting the TCU or stopper poorly set, but stuck—then wasting more strength trying to remove it. Placing difficult pro in front of your face, you get to toggle the placement just so. And be mindful not to slot a piece into our best jam—difficult to avoid on finger cracks (or any time we're in a hurry). Believe it: approaching our limits, one bungled nut placement and we're out of there. So fluid execution, with no dicking about or do-overs, is essential.

ANDREW BURR

Always know just how the rope is running. Anytime we pull a lip, a bulge, or a roof we risk the rope jamming in the crack. When possible, place a preventative piece (or sling) to divert the cord out of the crack, whether we need the pro or not. Other far less obvious situations necessitate placing gear for reasons beyond the fall-factor. If the rope describes a sharp angle around a flake or arête, spelling possible rope drag or even rope damage, look for pro that might direct the cord into a better and safer passage. This is "rope management," a concept lost on me for years.

We also might have to place to let our second know which way to go, an especially key trick for wandering leads. What seems like simple routefinding to the leader becomes anything but when, say, an easy run-out allows the rope to dangle wherever gravity lets it. This direct line might be 5.11, when 10 feet to either side we're on 5.9 ground.

Remember to protect any traverses for the second, as well as for ourselves. Swinging pendulums while following are no joke and can be every bit as serious as a leader fall if a ledge or corner is in the fall line. Any traversing move that the leader needed to protect should also be protected as soon as possible afterward—we can easily see why. If you've ever followed someone across a hard traverse, unclipped from a bolt or bomber piece that protected Pedro wonderfully, whereas your looking at 20 feet to the next wire, and ledges and chickenheads below, then you can appreciate the need to shoot Pedro and get something solid the moment you can after hard traversing moves. Sometimes, however, if easy wandering immediately follows such a crux, it may be better to run it out until you can arc back over and arrange a virtual toprope over the pesky section. Bottom line, we should always be planning ahead and looking behind. That way there'll be no surprises, the gear will help rather than hinder, and our climbing partners will speak to us at the end of the day.

Instinct

As beginners we were guerillas in a threatening world and had to tread carefully. We needed to double-check before every step taken—three times before we leapt. But as our vertical mileage accrued, we started thinking less and reacting more, a natural enough process since our intuition can lead us much more effectively and safely than trying to methodically calculate our steps. On a steep and strenuous crack, for instance, we climb faster and more efficiently if we trust in our technique and move by instinct rather than painfully analyzing which hand to jam or whether we should go thumbs up or down. Particularly when our endurance is tested, success lies almost entirely with trusting our first instinct. A common sight at the crags is the climber who begins the correct sequence, is suddenly torn by doubts, climbs down a bit, and then tries something else. Then up and down some more before pitching off with a rude pump. Finally, they "unlock" the sequence—and it's almost always the one they tried the first time. If the clock is ticking then the window is closing and we need to go with our gut. It's our best chance.

When routefinding on a long climb, it's easy to get bewildered trying to match the chicken scratches on the topo with the intricacies of the cliff. The piece of paper says to head up the corner past a tree. We see three corners and bushes and a Sherwood Forest of trees. Best thing here is to stow the scrap and scope the rock. Again, the question we need to ask ourselves is: "Where would I go if I were doing the first ascent?" It's amazing how often this shows us the way.

Ask any super experienced trad climber about working out the line on new routes. Most agree that the dead reckoning they use amounts to little more than hunches based on the accumulated data from hundreds of routes climbed over many years. Perhaps we can't quantify why we feel this is the way to go. Much of what we take in floats around our subconscious, which weighs, contrasts, and calculates entirely on its own, below awareness—meaning these "feelings" are not mere voodoo. They are data to hear and consider.

The same instincts that help us with technical cruxes and routefinding can also help us divine the weather. We're likely out of cell phone range so weather updates are out. But if those weird wispy clouds moving in are giving us the creeps, a real and present threat might be half an hour off. Experiencing the willies, if nothing else, gets us to consider options if the weather craps out on us. And if a plunging barometer can lock the joints of old sea dogs, that gives us a jump on the weatherman every time.

CHAPTER 37

El Cap in a Day

John Long

It happened over a couple beers in the Yosemite Lodge reading room, when Jim Bridwell hatched the plan to try and make the first 1-day ascent of The Nose, on El Capitan. El Cap was a monument and an altar to many climbers worldwide, so Bridwell's plan felt like a big deal at the time. Whether it meant much beyond the climbing world is debatable, but we all knew this was a once-in-a-lifetime opportunity.

I was the designated (by Jim, of course) free climber and would lead the first leg to the top of Boot Flake, seventeen rope lengths up—comparatively straightforward crack pitches we presumed would go quickly. Billy Westbay, a Colorado climber superb at both aid and free climbing, would lead the more intricate middle section from the Boot to Camp Five, the twenty-fifth pitch (Billy, then slaving away on a Montana oil rig, was yet to be informed of his duties, but Jim assured me of his fealty to the "team"). Then Bridwell would take it on home with the last nine pitches. In my mind the plan quickly took on fantastic importance, the kind only a 19-year-old could attach to it. When Jim, Billy, and I stalked toward the base of El Capitan on

Turning the roof.

ALEXANDRE BUISSE

249

Majesty in granite.

KARL "BABA" BRALICH

Memorial Day, the following year, I felt like a leath-erneck going to hoist the flag over Iwo Jima.

Since this ascent, decades ago, speed climbing has become a popular and vital part of modern rock climbing. Understand that speed climbing is a spectrum, ranging from those attempting to set records for quickest elapsed time, to teams trying to climb efficiently in order to maintain a schedule. Climbing a big wall involves so many aspects that the more processes you can simplify and eliminate,

the better your chances at completing the route in manageable style while avoiding epics. Time is a commodity that requires managing on a big climb, just as it is in business, war, and love. Managing time on a wall is the result of having a realistic plan, and organizing your effort around that plan. The plan will vector largely off your projected speed, which determines the amount of gear (water, at 8.3 pounds per gallon, is the single biggest concern and commodity) you will haul along. Get up on a wall with too little or too much gear and your chances decrease dramatically.

Most plans change up on the Big Stone; but revising a plan is much easier than creating one on the spot. Not surprisingly, most teams tend to perform up to the level of their plans. A common maxim, already mentioned, is that if you bring a haul bag you are almost certain to bivouac. A lack of sleeping gear is strong incentive to finish a route in a day. But the business of planning a big climb is nuanced and full of intangibles, preserving the adventure of the climb. (See the sidebars for more.)

As mentioned, our plan for the 1-day ascent was for me to lead from the ground to the top of Boot Flake, a prominent feature at the 1,200-foot mark. We started about 90 minutes before sunrise. The first 400 feet went under headlamps, and smoothly. That put us onto Sickle Ledge and the Nose proper, where the southeast and southwest faces converge to form the great sweeping prow the route is named after. Beyond 50 feet of easy terrain off Sickle Ledge, I started fumbling with some stemming, made dicey by darkness. Now 40 feet above my last piton, my headlamp flickered on and off and dawn light was slow in coming. I finally pawed up to a bolt and yelled down I was going to wait a few moments before trying the pendulum, so I could see what the hell I was doing. "You're gonna what?!" Bridwell barked.

I blindly swung right and found the 5.8 hand crack. In a minute I hung in slings as Jim and Billy raced up behind—Jim "jugging" (on ascenders) the lead rope, Billy on the trail rope, both funky, 9-millimeter lines. (One of the cords, an exhausted old yellow one, had several holes in the sheath and a long oil stain on one end.)

The plan was all worked out in advance: The man jugging the free rope would wind sprint up to the leader with a third rope and a spare rack, and start belaying him before the man cleaning the previous pitch had arrived. That was the concept, anyway, and was meant to save time. But since I

hadn't set any nuts or pitons in the crack, they both arrived simultaneously, in mere moments.

And off I went. At the 600-foot mark we gained the first big pendulum—a wild running swing right to the Stoveleg Crack (so named because on the first ascent, Harding nailed it using four crude pitons forged from the legs of an old stove scavenged from the Berkeley city dump). From the top of a long bolt ladder, I lowered down about 60 feet and started swinging back and forth, kicked hard right, and hurtled around a corner. As momentum ebbed, I dove, plopping a hand into a perfect jam just as my legs started swinging back. I kicked a boot in and was on line. A laser-cut gash shot up the prow for 350 feet of primarily perfect hand-jamming, the wall flush as a mirror and not a ledge in sight, each lead ending in stark, hanging belays.

I had hoped for a wealth of fixed pitons, but found few that were usable. We'd only brought a couple of big nuts, none of which I had on the first difficult pitch, thinking the fixed pins I saw above were good, soon to discover that the eyes had been blasted off by greedy hammers leaving useless wedges of aluminum in the crack. I didn't get a single nut in that pitch.

We were so new to speed climbing that we didn't yet realize that for several reasons, the favored technique was husbanding strength, climbing efficiently, and maintaining a manageable pace. I was still thinking I had to break off these pitches like quick reps. So I kept climbing recklessly fast and Jim and Billy kept gassing up the lines so quickly that they gained the belays sucking wind. Then one would hand me the rack and Bridwell would ask what I was waiting for.

I took our few big chocks on the next lead, but only got one in. Two hundred feet higher, I chugged out an oily off-size slot and mantled onto Dolt Tower—and was face to face with Peter Metcalf who would later run Black Diamond, and his young partner, both just slithering from their sleeping bags. It was 6:30 (*not* 7) a.m. and the two begged to know what we were up to. When Billy arrived he explained that we'd forgotten the haul bag and had to make time or suffer a rough bivouac, without gear or food.

"Jesus," one asked, "How far do you hope to get?"

"Back to the car before dark," said the Bird. The partner looked as though Jim had asked him why the chicken had crossed the road. We pressed on.

Dolt Tower is flat and spacious, and is the first place to pause and take stock of things. Our brief rest, ordained by Jim, consisted of taking time

Inspiration

We've talked about landmark routes, classics, "climbing current," and so on. We've mentioned how trad climbing is largely unregulated, leaving us the freedom to do things our own way. Adventurous spirits have always put a premium on self-direction. Nevertheless, like charisma, God-given talent is a responsibility and a gift that transcends the individual. All but the most self-absorbed of us are inspired by the great achievements of our peers. Not that these men and women climb for our benefit, or that we are made whole by their efforts. But we live off inspiration, and when great things occur, we are roused back to life and into action.

Anyone gifted has an unstated obligation to try and live up to their potential, and it's a blow to mankind when the person can't be bothered and begs off, retreats into money grubbing, hard drink, etc. We might believe it doesn't matter. What's another difficult climb really mean? What many people have told me, that's what—that the only reason they got through Desert Storm, say, or a horrific childbirth, was thinking about Lynn Hill free climbing The Nose in a day, or Herzog slogging up Annapurna. We all have our epics, and if the thought of Alex Honnold soloing Half Dome lightens our load by a single pound, we are grateful to the mountain climber.

I was fortunate to be party to some historic climbs and know the thrill belonged to everyone and meant little till shared. But we cannot live off old heroes. Inspiration has a shelf life and each generation must replenish the pantry—or starve. If you have the mojo, and it's yours for a decade, or for one immortal pitch, "bring the bacon" and the rest of us will thank you, through starlight and storm, in our own silent way.

Climbing to failure.

AMY NESS

enough for a sip of water. Then Billy put me on belay and I tensioned right, into a steep laybacking corner, and ran two pitches together. Aside from the pendulum points and the bolt ladder above Dolt Hole, I'd managed only a couple nuts in the last eight pitches—a needlessly sketchy performance that would soon almost get me.

An easy bend and we were on El Cap Towers, a perfectly flat, granite patio. Now above the comparatively low-angle Stovelegs (80 degrees), the upper wall rifles up into cut-melon dihedrals. Out right looms the fearsome sweep of the Southeast Face, which during meridian light draws fabulous hues into its keeping. There lie the world's most notorious aid climbs, and a few futuristic free routes. Since climbers first scaled the face in 1963, what human wonders this great wall must have seen! All the tense leaders, their terrors and doubts and battered hands, hooking and bashing their way up its overhanging immensity, where a dropped piton strikes nothing but the ground, meters from the wall. A few specialists thrive on this kind of work, but I've rarely been one of them.

Jim bestowed us another short break. We were about halfway up the wall and it wasn't much after 7 a.m. We peeled off our sweaters, cinched them into a knot, and pitched them off. Down below, the meadow started to fill with our friends, with an occasional car horn urging us to even greater speed. We'd made no secret about our plan, and over the previous few days dozens of climbers approached us to wish us luck. Did we need any gear? Did we need a ride to the base? Did we want someone to meet us on top? Mike White summed it up when he told me to "Do us proud." We had a meadow full of friends to account to if we failed.

Just above El Cap Towers an unprotected chimney gained the top of Texas Flake, a thick, exfoliating block whose shape suggests the Lone Star State. Just off it, a 50-foot bolt ladder finds Boot Flake detached, and resounding to the thump, and recently free climbed at a top grade. I clipped up

the bolts, reached the crack on the right side of the Boot and immediately cranked into a layback, anxious to power it off and be done with leading. Foolishly, I chose the jackass tactic of trying to run out the entire Boot without bothering to place a single nut for protection.

All went swimmingly till perhaps 30 feet above the bolt ladder, when a cramp suddenly paralyzed my right forearm. My fingers curled into a fist. The fall looked like a large and unpleasant one, directly onto about where Abilene would be on Texas Flake. I dangled off an ever-creeping left jam and desperately tried to shake the cement out of my right arm. No good. Somehow I managed to downclimb a few moves, slot in a borderline nut, and hang on it long enough to jiggle the cramp out. Partially recovered, I jammed up to the top of the Boot, clipped off the bolt anchor, and kissed the rock. My part was done. It was 7:40 a.m. Everything was happening exactly to plan—even better, since we had climbed the initial pitches much faster than expected. Now we switched to phase 2 of our plan.

Jim had the lead switch all worked out. I clipped the rack of gear onto the haul line and slid it down to Billy, then put him on belay—on the haul line. He drew a breath and shot off across the King Swing, an enormous pendulum left. He latched the first fixed piton, lowered, then swung left again and fired up into a steep groove.

The course now passed through a 300-foot gray diorite band involving the only nebulous climbing on the route. In a magnificent bit of anything goes, Billy would yank up on a bashie, crank off bleak laybacking, edge up onto a fixed pin, go unprotected over loose face climbing, pendulum this way and tension that way. He never made anything look too difficult, either for himself or his partners, traversing the Captain so sweetly that for all its small holds and big air, the climb never felt intimidating. That takes talent to pull off, and Billy had it.

In no time we were on Camp Four, several small shelves below the Great Roof. Billy dashed

Heroes

We never presume to know how high or how low others should set their sights. Inherently we are no better off climbing 5.15 than we are slogging across a sand dune. But we can only coast going downhill. We work up the incline at our own pace, or we circle the drain because we are fated to keep expanding, growing, challenging ourselves and each other. As we've seen, we can use a mental telescope to dial into view the pioneers who have taken one step beyond, and we can draw power from being party to their efforts. And yet this power is rarely gleaned from the hardest or greatest climbs.

For instance, when I first learned that a blind person had climbed El Capitan and had led some of the pitches, I could not fathom how such a thing was possible. I still can't. Who was this man who had not merely overcome his handicaps, but lost track of them altogether? His name was Eric Weihenmayer and I discovered he went on to climb the Naked Edge, one of the storied free routes in America. In fact he'd climbed all "Seven Summits," the highest peaks on each continent, including Everest, pushing aside any thought that he might deserve sympathy. He couldn't see it if it was offered, anyhow.

We might review Eric's feats to ride an avalanche of enthusiasm in any direction we choose. But great moments are more than calls to action, and they are the exact opposite of a pep talk or sentimental overture. They are about human being—who we are, and might become. Most of us need occasional reminders of this, lost as we become in human doing, forgetting what life is, and who we are. The Eric Weihenmayers of the world are good in that regard. They are a privilege and a resource at no cost.

Walking the line. Lost Arrow Spire.

DAVE N. CAMPBELL

over some tricky face business and started clipping up a string of antique ring angles.

When Tom Frost, Chuck Pratt, Royal Robbins, and Joe Fitschen made the first continuous ascent in 1960, they all agreed the Great Roof was "easily the most spectacular pitch in Yosemite." Not for challenge, but for the splendor of this colossal arc of creamy granite, which ends at an edge-of-the-world sling belay. Billy got us there by eleven o'clock.

A pitch up the Pancake Flake, thin as a flapjack in spots, a decent jamming pitch, and we were on Camp Five—another terrace in the sky. It was barely noon, and we knew we only had to keep plugging away at an easy pace. Or Jim did, since he now had the lead. And Jim needed a breather. While Billy and I had spent the previous months doing long routes and rounding into peak form, Bridwell had "honed up for The Nose in a day," as he said it, by playing billiards and bouldering down in San Diego. At that time, there probably wasn't another climber alive that could have gotten away with this. By Camp Six, the last big ledge two pitches higher, I cursed myself for not having worn a harness, as my swami belt—two wraps of 2-inch webbing—chafed right down to my spleen. We'd all worn free climbing boots that were murdering our toes. The water ran out. Jim smacked his thumb with the hammer. When the trail line snagged a pitch higher, instead of rappelling down to free it, I simply yanked as hard as I could, eventually pulling off a granite block the size of a Shetland pony.

"You imbecile!" Bridwell yelled. "You might have cut the rope and then what would we do?!"

"Take our goddamn shoes off," said Billy.

Fatigue was catching up, an open invitation for a mishap. We briefly discussed, regrouped, and Bridwell led on.

We were over 2,500 feet up the wall now, into the really prime stuff. Here the exposure is so vast, and your perspective so distorted, that the horizontal world becomes unintelligible. You're a granite astronaut, dangling in a kind of space/time warp.

And if there is any place where you will understand why men and women climb mountains, it is here in these breezy dihedrals, high in the sky.

Pitch after pitch fell beneath us. By the time we gained the bolt ladder leading up the summit headwall, our feet were so sore we just wanted off. Other routes are steeper, more exposed than The Nose. But no route has a more dramatic climax. The headwall is barely 50 feet long, and once climbed, everything ends abruptly after a few friction steps. But since Harding's day, some madman has reengineered the last belay so that it hangs at the brink of the headwall, where all thirty-four pitches spill beneath your boots. It's a master stroke, that hanging belay, for it gives climbers a moment of pause at one of the most extravagant sites in all of American climbing. Cars creep along the loop road three-quarters of a mile below, broad forests appear as brushed green carpets and, for one immortal moment, you feel a giant in a world of ants.

From the start, all the way up to this last hanging belay, I found myself torn between confidence and the fear of climbing recklessly fast. But now I had gotten above all measuring, and my mind had taken a back seat to relish our effort. Men talk of dreaming gardens of Eden and cities of gold, though nothing could touch being pasted way up in the sky like that. But it wasn't over. Jim had scrambled to the top and was yelling for me to hustle up so we could get on with our lives.

But I couldn't move. I kicked back in my stirrups and looked around. I didn't know why. I had never lingered before, always pressing on with gritted teeth, surging, fighting both myself and the climb to gain the top. Suddenly I was free of all the incessant rushing; so I just hung there and took it in, and for the first time in my climbing career I seemed to fully appreciate the fantastic nature of what I was doing.

Finally I stepped from the anchor and stumbled to the top. On the summit there was no celebration, no elation at all. We didn't so much as shake hands. Topping out on El Capitan after the first 1-day ascent should have been one of those few momentous events in our lives. But, typically, those first few minutes on horizontal ground brought on a transitional spin where little registered but our exhaustion and throbbing feet. I only remember coiling ropes and slogging for the East Ledges descent route, everyone cussing at having not brought a pair of sneakers. We got down to the loop road just as darkness fell.

Drained by the nervous depression that always follows a wall, we stumbled around a bend and El Capitan burst into view, shimmering under a full moon. If there is anything whose magnitude can blow a person off his feet, it's that first ground-level view of a wall they've just climbed. The second we saw it, we three stumbled out into the middle of the road and gaped up with our mouths open. El Cap looked 10 miles high. And how long ago it seemed we'd been up there, and how strange, as though we'd seen it in a movie, or in a dream, and had suddenly woken up, only vaguely remembering what we had dreamed. My feet suddenly felt fine, and the majesty of the cliff, and what it meant to us to have climbed it in 1 day, finally struck home.

Lea Lynn Leopoldo chilling high on The Nose, El Capitan.

VICKY SU

CHAPTER 38

Astroman

John Long

"Watch me close," I said to Ron Kauk, remembering my first time on this pitch, several years before. "This might get funky."

I felt anxious, amazed, primed—everything all at once. El Capitan in a day was a done thing. In traditional-style rock climbing, free climbing a genuine big wall remained the last and greatest prize. We wanted to be first and here was our chance to close the deal, eleven pitches up the overhanging East Face of Washington Column. From the start I warned the boys this last pitch might shut us down, so we were bursting at the seams from the suspense of battling all the way up here and still not knowing.

"Get us off this thing," said Ron.

His eyes couldn't decide if they should slam shut from fatigue or bug from excitement. He was only a kid. Seventeen, I think. I outweighed him by sixty pounds, but Ron had caught me many times so I didn't question his hip belay. Reaching an arm from a patch of shade, John Bachar passed me a couple slings and said, "You're the man."

That helped. All the way up we'd cheered and prodded one another as aid pitch after aid pitch fell to our free climbing efforts, pitches that soon became classics: The Boulder Problem Pitch, with its fingertip laybacking and scrabbling feet; the Enduro Corner, a soaring dihedral that goes from thin hands to big fingers, right to the belay bolts; the ghastly Harding Slot, a bottomless flare that in coming decades would dash the hopes of so many Europeans; and the flawless Changing Corners, a

John Long (left) and the late, great John Bachar beneath the Enduro Corner during the First Free Ascent of Astroman.

JOHN LONG

vertical shrine of shifting rock planes with a continent of air below. For over a thousand feet now, the blond orange cracks kept connecting in remarkable ways, and we kept busting out every technique we knew. Never before had we experienced a route so continuously difficult. To our knowledge, no climbers ever had.

Fifty feet to go.

Stepping back for a second, the question is: How do you go about making the first free ascent

257

of a big wall? First, the final product, the all free ascent, is often accomplished in increments, where successive parties keep whittling down the aid till it becomes obvious that an all-out attempt is worth the time and effort. Per the East Face, when I first climbed the route as my first big wall, we managed to free climb at least half of it, maybe more. The spectacular hand and fist crack off Overnight Ledge had just been freed by Mead Hargis, and the two long crack leads below the final headwall always went free at easy 5.10. Steve Wunsch and others went on to free climb all the way up to the Enduro Corner. Ron went up later and led this pitch free, and so by the time John, Ron, and I had at it, perhaps 70 percent of the face had been free climbed. Same with the Salathe Wall and West Face on El Cap (the first free routes up the face), the Regular Route on Half Dome, the Chouinard/Herbert, and the West Face of Sentinel (which still has a couple points of aid), and many others of the Yosemite walls that eventually went free. When you hear about climbers going to an area and on-sight free climbing a big route, it is almost always something well within their abilities. Anything more most often takes various pilot ascents to get the whole shebang dialed before it finally falls, all free.

This is an important point to appreciate if and when you are either attempting a first free ascent of an existing big wall, or are venturing to a wilderness area with designs on big routes. Especially in backcountry areas, weather is often a factor, often an obstacle, and simply getting up a formation is probably more important than free climbing same. "Working" a pitch in Patagonia, say, when the clouds are gathering and you have another thirty-five pitches towering overhead, is rarely an effective strategy. A real-world calculus about this would generally indicate that time and weather determine how hard you're going to free climb. More on this later.

Returning to the last pitch during our ascent of Astroman: My toes were curled painfully inside my EBs but I reached down and cranked the laces anyhow. Sweat dripped off my face onto the rock. We passed around the last of our water as I racked a few small pitons and several Stoppers and Hexcentrics on the sling around my shoulder. I slowly chalked up, glanced over at John, and said, "I'll take some tunes if you please."

John reached into his daypack and punched the button on our little cassette deck. Jimi Hendrix's "Astro Man," our theme song for the route, blared through the top flap. John flashed that insolent grin of his and said, "Rock and roll, hombre."

John Bachar. Just then, smirking on that ledge, he was 18 years old, and looked about 12.

I took a last sip of water and shuffled out on the stoppering ledge, around a corner and over to moderate laybacking up the left side of short pillar, ending at a 25-foot headwall. All the way up the rock was diamond hard, but here it turned to choss. Three summers before, I'd nailed this last bit via rickety pins bashed into a rotten seam. All through the previous night I wondered how we might free climb this seam; one glance confirmed we never would. However, just right of the seam and straight up off the pillar, the vertical face bristled with sandy dimples and thin, scabby side pulls. I'd have to toe off pure grain and yank straight out on these scabs, praying they didn't bust off. The only protection was several tied-off baby angles slugged into that seam. While organizing our gear I'd talked big about not bringing a bolt kit, going on and on about high adventure, cha cha cha. What an ass. I couldn't hang my hat on those pins. The only nut was in the layback crack, 10 feet below. It was one of those surreal fixes where I was plainly screwed yet had to somehow make do.

I reached up and grabbed the first sidepulls. It felt hard just to hoist my feet off the pinnacle and I stood sulking for several minutes. Here was the chance of a lifetime and I was too gripped to commit. Maybe Ron should have a go? He would just race up this, I thought. Ron was the most gifted climber we had ever seen. He'd hiked the Endurance Corner in nothing flat. Same with the Harding Slot.

Continued on page 262

Free Climbing Big Walls

"Free big wall" generally refers to routes that are hauled and aided by the masses but are freed by very skilled climbers, including the short list of pros leading the charge. But the definition is fluid. Take a route like the West Face of El Capitan, first done as a multiday climb and largely aided. Once the route went entirely free, it slowly lost its appeal as an aid climb, most subsequent ascents happening in a long day, all free. Not so the Salathe Wall, around the corner to the right. Though first free climbed in 1988, successful free bids rarely number more than a few each year, the other dozens of ascents still accomplished the old-fashioned way—with aid slings and a portable dinner, artesian well, and hotel jammed into a haul bag.

It follows that a big wall first aid climbed and later freed is not necessarily a true "wall" any longer if by wall we mean a route "typically hauled and aided by the masses." So for our purposes, "mega route" is probably a less ambiguous term, still referring to routes usually first climbed by direct aid in a multiday effort. What's more, since many of the harder mega routes require 2 or more days, free climbing these beasts tends to involve some big wall tactics by most climbers—i.e., haul bags, bivouacking, often a second who follows on ascenders, etc.

That much said, free climbing mega routes is too broad a topic to cover in blanket statements. The determining issues are scope (size of the route) and difficulty. Both factors determine how long you will spend on a given route, which radically affects your approach. For instance, the first big walls free climbed in Yosemite Valley, such as Chouinard/Herbert on Sentinel, Astroman on Washington Column, The Rostrum, the free version of the Gold Wall, Ribbon Falls, and the aforementioned West Face of El Cap, are all quite doable (none harder than 5.11c), and none take more than a day, usually far less, to complete. Moving up to the Regular Route on Half Dome, say, or the Freerider on El Capitan, we are basically doubling the footage, though not necessarily the difficulty. But neither route is routinely on-sighted free in a day. The logistics alone are prohibitive. Crank up the difficulty and the climb is no longer a true adventure route, where the on-sight is a reasonable or even a desired goal. Here, the rhumba becomes more of an aerial bouldering fest requiring, in some instances, multiple attempts spread out over several years, the redpoint only possible after dialing in the entire route, down to the last hand jam—an exhausting process broadly known as "projecting." So runs the gamut in general terms.

Free climbing a mega route is not the same as cranking a crag route at the Gunks or in Estes Park. Nor is it a totally different animal. A true mega keeps coming at you, but fundamentally you're not doing things any differently than you are on one- or two-pitch climbs. Only this time it's a dozen pitches—or more. Sometimes many more. The biggest shift most climbers experience when breaking into the rarified realm of mega

Continued on next page

Continued from previous page

free climbs is that their endurance base becomes an equal or greater determining factor than their explosive power. Any veteran will tell you that maintaining both max strength and max endurance is nearly impossible. Spending a summer blitzing free walls in Zion or Yosemite will transform you into an endurance animal, but your sport climbing and bouldering are bound to tank owing to the difficulty of practicing, so to speak, both long-distance (endurance) and sprinting (explosive) disciplines at the same time.

Who has energy to go bouldering or work the campus board after climbing twenty pitches? You will learn how to maintain a balance of power and endurance over your career, but forget about starting out on free walls that require crazy hard technical climbing and mega power-endurance as well. Tic a couple of the shorter, easier free walls, then clamber your way up. During the winter months leading to the longer summer days, ideal for mega routes, shift your focus to "massive footage," trying to log as many meaningful miles on the rock as you can.

Climb straight through good rests and bang out laps with less and less down time. Gym time is spent ticking as many routes as possible, mixing in traverses every few days while keeping a heads-up for injuries. Injuries from footage climbing are far less likely than from max difficulty routes and bouldering. But overuse injuries are common, so ample rest days, good hydration, and nutrition remain key factors. All of this will force you to climb ever more efficiently, which is half of the game for mega routes.

Checklist for Mega Routes

- Where is the approach, exactly, how long is it, what is involved in terms of terrain, and how much time might it take to reach the base of the route? Get a topo map if needed (essential if there's no trail).

- What is the route? How many pitches? Where are the crux bits? What is the beta/topo?

- What is the recommended rack? Is any special gear needed, such as Big Bros, huge cams, etc.?

- One rope (60m? 70m? 80m?) or two?

- How will the pitches be divided? Who wants to lead what—even or odd pitches, or block leading?

- How long will it take to complete the route including the descent, factoring in an extra 30 percent for unforeseeables? What is the estimated time for the entire adventure, including the drive?

- How much food and water will be needed, and what pack/bag will be needed to carry the rations?

- Where, exactly, is the descent, what is involved in terms of terrain, and how long should it take? Review various descriptions and draw topo if necessary.

- What clothing will be needed? Any bivy and haul gear?

- Set a departure date and time.

- Purchase rations and organize/pack gear.

- Check weather report and pack at least a light rain jacket.

- Inform a loved one or associate about your plans, writing down all the details to avoid mistakes. Specify the route, and be realistic about your estimated return time.

- If you'll be in an area that has coverage, power up your cell phone for emergency calls. Make sure your climbing partner brings a phone as well—your service chances improve if you have different service providers.

- Most trad climbers have a very hard time with this last one, but experts agree it is wise: Establish a cutoff time. If you're not back by a certain time, initiate a rescue.

Your first free wall should be the shortest one you can find that best fits your abilities. That is, the climber who feasts on hard face climbs, but little else, will probably starve on the Salathe Wall and Astroman, which feature sections of "the wide" with names like "The Monster Off-Width Crack," and "The Harding Slot." Better to chase routes that sport short, thin cruxes. The idea is to keep those initial efforts manageable, and the surest way is to limit the size and the difficulty. If you can only limit one aspect, do the

shorter route. At the outset, difficulty is easier to manage than magnitude. And you better believe it— the size of the mega routes, the sheer effort required to climb them, and the continents of air below your feet are things that take some getting used to.

Rare is the climber who waltzes into the Baltoro or Patagonia, say, and straightaway bags the biggest climbs without breaking stride. Most of us need a few seasons kicking around the feet of the giants to stop cowering in their presence. The Chinese have a saying: You can't eat an elephant in one bite. Or is it the Indians who say that? Either way, the elephant, and the walls are both bigger than we can imagine. So knock off the small ones first. Usually it only takes a couple mega routes to make the walls our own. As the fear recedes—never vanishing completely—the focus shifts to magnitude.

Heading out.

ANDREW BURR

Continued from page 258

Nothing could stop him. But I couldn't give him this one.

When Ron first turned up in Yosemite when he was 14 years old, it was like Sitting Bull returning to Standing Rock. The chief had finally come home. The Valley seemed fashioned just for him. In some nameless way, fundamental as wind and chain lightning, Ron Kauk was father to us all. Not long after that afternoon on the Column, Ron spread his wampum across Europe, hurled it at the Karakorum and beyond, closing the circle on the traditional era of rock climbing. But I couldn't call him now. Too anxious to sleep, turning this last pitch over in my mind like a pig on a spit, I'd fairly dragged Ron and John out of their sleeping bags, had burgled the two

"Projecting" a Mega Free Climb

Projecting a climb is a strategy that has been around for 50 or more years. It started on the boulders at places like Stoney Point in the San Fernando Valley, in Southern California, where the Yosemite pioneers used to practice after school and work. As free climbing took hold of the climbing scene, leading folk began tackling routes requiring multiple efforts to achieve. Sport climbing took the concept of "aerial bouldering" and made it de rigueur. If you were doing the route first or second try you were dogging it and needed to jump on something harder. In music, you do another take, and keep at it till you get the desired result. In climbing, you take another burn. In sport climbing, projecting became a generic approach to a climb that initially was over your head. Projecting a mega free climb was the obvious next step, and while the actual climbing process and routine, the working out of a given pitch, naturally stays the same on Fitzroy in Patagonia as it does in the City of Rocks, Idaho, the logistics of playing on the grand stage changes the opera in telling ways.

The various strategies, ranging from reconnaissance probes to working a route from the top—rappelling down to practice certain key pitches—to the often involved freight hauling during the final ground-up push for glory, are parts of a complicated and exacting protocol that we all learn in stages, through direct experience and from many people and varied sources. By the time you reach the level where you're projecting mega free climbs, you will have gleaned enough knowledge to fashion your own curriculum. But as you work toward the sky, keep an eye open for accounts of how people went about their work. No need to reinvent the wheel here. Most every challenge has been met and addressed by someone. Read, learn, execute.

Owing to their great length, many mega routes connect vastly different crack systems via varied techniques. That's to say on a free wall of any length, expect to encounter most every style in the standard opus, plus a few you've never seen or heard of. Just as a single vocalist is never so skilled on pop tunes as she is on ballads or Motown covers, there is no such climber without gaps in her technique. We each have an Achilles heel or two, and we generally despise and duck that style that gives us fits.

leads up to this crumbly face, and now I couldn't muster the sac to pull a single move.

I hated this situation. I loved it too. Not a soul, not even God stood between me and the decision I faced. Do or fly, the moment my feet left that pillar, my life would change forever. Gritting my teeth and fingering those useless pitons, I peered up at the flaky holds, shifting foot to foot on my tiny stance. It felt like the route was taunting me, playing my ego off itself so I'd lose patience, crank into something stupid and plummet terribly as the whole Valley howled.

But there were holds, and I only had 25 feet to go. Maybe less. I glanced left and growled, "Here goes." Then I blanked my mind and pulled off the pinnacle.

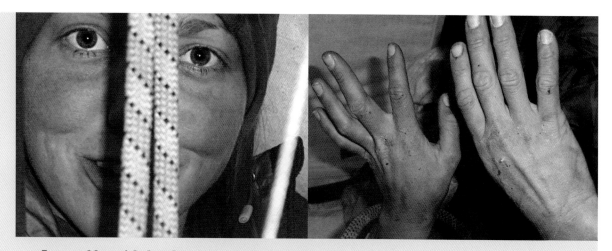

Amy and her girly hands.

AMY NESS

Free walls are Old Man Gravity's way of making us bone up on the hateful "wide," or explosive moves that favor the boulderer, not the granite astronaut. Point is, and with maddening frequency, whatever we run from will be featured prominently on the very wall of our dreams. Case in point, one of the great free wall climbs on earth, Salathe Wall, on El Cap, requires difficult boulder-type moves up high, exactly the kind of movement largely avoided by the celebrated Steph Davis, resolute as Job, and suave on the cracks to be sure. The solution is to make a special study of, and to literally "project," your weakness. In our example, Ms. Davis coiled her cord for an entire winter and did power yoga and bouldering in preparation for the Salathe Wall.

We all have our weaknesses, so be prepared to shore yours up once you take aim on a world-class mega free route. It often is the process of expanding our capacity, rather than ticking another legendary climb, that is the lasting reward of the adventure.

Peaking for a Project

Peaking for a project, a big meet, or competition remains a key aspect of athletics. The need to peak or stopper tells us we maintain peak fitness only briefly—nothing can run at redline for long. How we go about peaking is a science beyond the scope of this book, but understanding the concept is enough to put you on the path to discovering how it all works. Everyone responds differently to training and resting, so you likely will pass through the peaking cycle several times to get the process dialed. For super active climbers, peaking might merely involve shifting to a specific type of climbing for a few weeks, perhaps ramping up the footage, and working in enough rest days to feel fresh before the onslaught.

The rest of us must follow a more systematic routine, raising our level of activity and hitting the chosen route at the top of our trajectory before work and life limit our practice time once again. Basically it's a matter of climbing ourselves into top shape, as time and motivation allow, knowing the time window will soon close. By and large, the closer your project is to your technical limit, the more you will benefit from modern training methods and strategies found in countless books, magazine articles, and blogs. "Hit it when you're hot" is standard in every field.

AMY NESS

The aim here is to consciously schedule when you are "hot," and to bring up the flame slowly enough that you don't burn out in the process. As one approaches a big climb, always err on the side of extra rest and a full tank, rather than extra training or climbing. Following a disappointing performance, you'll hear boxers talk about "leaving the fight in the gym," another word for overtraining. Knowing when to ease off is as crucial as pushing through the pain, lest you "leave your climb on the ground."

After a body length I knew I could never reverse a single move, so I accepted that I was basically soloing. Strangely, I relaxed. If this is what the route demanded, I'd just go with it. The climbing felt like 5.11, scared as I was of snapping an edge, doing screwball twisty moves to keep some weight over the granular footholds.

After about 10 feet I stretched high off a flexing carbuncle and pinched the bottom of a big grimy tongue drooping down, clasping both sides in turn, anxiously wiggling a few sketchy wired nuts into the flaring grain. The only pins that would fit behind the tongue were bashed into that seam below. But hey, if the route was going to pull a fast one like this, so be it. I'd press on out of spite. I was hard like that.

Fifteen feet to go.

Bear-hugging up at mid-5.10, I gunned for the roof, feet bicycling the choss as grain rained down. The tongue flexed and groaned. My eyes zeroed in on the short hand crack extending down from the roof, but after a few more bear hugs I reached a sloping sandbar. Unfortunately, I'd have to straight mantle to stretch a hand into the crack.

This was bullshit. The Valley was laughing now. If I blew off here I was going for a monster whipper and probably hitting the ledge. I hated this route with all my heart. Piece of shit goddamn garbage wall from hell!

"What's going on over there?" Ron yelled from around the corner.

"Just watch me," I yelled back.

"We can't even see you," said Bachar.

"Just watch the damn rope," I said.

I splayed my feet, soles flush on the crud, one hand pawing the tongue as I raked the sandy berm, trying to get down to solid rock. Cocking into a mantle at last, I pressed it out like molasses, gingerly placing a foot on the crunchy veneer and stepping up with my teeth chattering and no hand holds. Finally I could stretch up to the crack, sink a hand jam, and slot a bomber hex, the first decent pro in a mile.

Home free at last, I leaned back off the jam and gazed down at the pitiful wires festooned from the tongue and the loose face, patted with chalk marks, plunging to the tied-off pegs. This was like the best pitch I'd ever done. Perfect, really. And beneath the pinnacle, diving 1,200 undercut feet straight into the talus—a face of wonders. I felt like the Valley's favorite son. Reaching out over the roof, I could just clasp a good, flat-top hold. I pulled up and realized my hands were on the top of Washington Column.

We called it Astroman. Following an early ascent, British ace Pete Lively called it, "The world's greatest free climb," a title that stuck for the next 15 years. During that time the last pitch, "the sting in the tail," cleaned up nicely following a thorough brushing and hundreds of ascents. Several long thin pitons were welded behind the tongue, as well as some big copperheads to provide somewhat adequate protection. But the caveat for the last pitch remains the same as it did in July 1975: Don't fall.

ALEXANDRE BUISSE

CHAPTER 39

Anything I Could Imagine . . . Usually Came into Play

Peter Croft

In the black months of Canadian winter, the only bright moments were my daily hand traverse workouts in my dungeon of a basement, and the wide world of high places I gleaned from books. Any fitness I took from the cellar sessions was usually offset by my calluses ripping open right down to the red meat. But the epic climbing tales both nourished and freaked my psyche like a raw liver smoothie. Through the decades a pantheon of square-jawed dirtbags had shown such gutsiness and impossible cool that I wasn't sure whether to emulate them or dive under the covers and hide. No matter what, I gained a visceral appreciation for history I had never felt before.

Yosemite and other hotspots around North America held historical significance, but it was in the Hobbit-scape of England that modern rock climbing was born. It seemed a joke at first, considering the UK's shrimpy cliffs. But while Americans were Daniel Boone-ing around trying to conquer the wilderness the Brits, because of their pastoral setting, smaller rocks, and sense of fair play, had embraced the truism that it wasn't what you did but how you did it—emphasizing free climbing, clean climbing, and trad climbing before those terms were ever heard "across the pond." At a time when alpine summits, bolt ladder directissimas, and national pride dominated the European press offerings, scruffy English plumbers and laborers quietly reinvented the game of rock climbing. Books could only take me so far. I saved up enough for five

Valley trips and steamed for rainy Britain to see where it all began.

The cliffs were small and it rained—a lot. On the other hand the climbing scene was fantastic. From tiny tots to grizzled granddads, rock climbing was entrenched in the landscape of Great Britain. And in a country often known for a stuffy upper class, it was refreshing to see that the best climbers were often scruffier than me.

Few things furnish a fuller understanding or a sounder bitch slapping than a trip back to the beginning. Britain is where the first nuts (quite literally, threaded machine nuts recovered along the railroad tracks) were used for protection and where double-rope technique was developed for wandering pitches to avoid hateful rope drag. The locals were quite artful in the use of slings—girth hitching tiny spikes, jamming knots into funky constrictions, and threading a single strand through mini tunnels and tying them off, often one-handed, for a key point of pro.

Style was developed and refined: The limestone cliffs were first used as practice aid climbs, then for hard free routes, and Gritstone crags remained bolt free from the beginning. Unlike the spoiled brats of sunnier areas, these poms climbed in all conditions, sometimes pulling wool socks over their climbing shoes, hoping for some extra stick in the rain. Coming from Canada, crummy weather was hardly news and neither was wet rock. But regularly going out in full conditions, often climbing in a drizzle, was a new experience.

One of the biggest benefits of this trip was the chance to sample a wide variety of rock types.

267

Kevin McLane climbing at Gogarth.

PETER CROFT

Every visit to a new area slapped me back down. Each place crag had a different and unique character. The Lake District resembles the nicest neighborhood in Hobbiton; Llanberis Pass area feels like the mountains (even though it's just a few thousand feet above sea level); and the sea cliffs of Gogarth, when the high seas are rolling in, are the biggest small cliffs in the world.

A common experience on many of these crags was the hollow spookiness I felt when launching out with no gear in sight—no pins or bolts to clip, and no obvious cracks ahead. When nervousness turned to fear and was heading for panic, a small seam or flake would usually appear and I would fiddle, whimper, and finally sketch together a couple of Stoppers, kept in place, say, with a tensioned sling round a down-pointing flake, or maybe an up-slotted nut. I grew better and better at climbing up and down to sort out a situation, slowly developing the under-appreciated art of fiddling.

Any crag-aineering scenario I could have envisioned usually came into play. Most common was the classic big gulp as I left good gear far below and committed to a series of hard moves, just as the first raindrops fell—that happened a lot. Other incidents I never could have foreseen, like the curious business with the sheep. I better explain that.

Climbing in the Rain

Sooner or later we all climb on wet rock. We might find ourselves halfway up the route when an afternoon thundershower hits like a punch. Maybe we were moving slowly, or the forecast was whacked, but we're suddenly faced with a different medium. A few rules of thumb prove helpful.

Even without falling rain, early season seepage can surprise us with wide wet streaks running down open faces or crack systems streaming like rain gutters. But wet rock does not always mean retreat and defeat. Glassy slabs are much trickier; but given positive holds and solid cracks, wet rock simply increases the difficulty and slows our pace. Place more gear and yard on pro as needed, especially on long routes with limited daylight. Mostly it boils down to time spent on wet rock and getting used to the novelty. Our first experience will likely be a nail biter. Once we get some mileage, though, we find that it's rarely as bad as it looks. Indeed, on well-featured (but wet) rock, we'll have significantly better purchase than some of the dry glacier polish in Tuolomne Meadows. And the modern sticky rubber shoes still adhere well on wet rock—not perfectly. But good enough in many cases.

Always look for square cut edges and use only the roughest, crystal-laden slopers for footholds. If the rock is soaking wet and it's raining as well, we cinch our chalk bags closed. As they're seldom waterproof, I take the added precaution of stuffing it up in my shirt or down in my pants. Remember that wet rock has far better friction than slime. Doesn't really matter whether the ooze is green or black—stay clear. It has far less stick-um than Teflon.

Naturally we hurry as bad weather approaches, more so when we start getting wet. Good thing about getting soaked, though, is that we can't get any wetter. That's the time to slow down and play it safe. Panicked rushing is dangerous in any conditions, especially when the rock is sluicing rain.

Mystery moves and funky gear. Peter Croft using double rope technique in North Wales.

PETER CROFT

Something in Reserve

Anytime we head up into unknown territory, we must always hold something in reserve. That's standard procedure in all fields. We can gain a modicum of beta from people and observation, but if things don't unfold the way we hoped and planned for, we need an exit strategy. First is confidence in our ability to downclimb out of trouble. This may also amount to climbing up and down a number of times to get used to the moves before we commit. There are technique subtleties in downclimbing that are somewhat different than going up. If we never practice downclimbing, we will likely feel awkward, clutch up—and ping. Till we set that first good piece, the rope is so much ballast. Put differently, we're basically soloing till the rope gets clipped.

We also need confidence in our endurance. In a run-out situation, we're in trouble if we have no go-for-it left, and only that sinking, "I'm too pumped to downclimb" feeling. Thankfully, most "heady" or poorly protected routes are well advertised as such in guidebooks and online so we can know the score before heading up. For most of us, the best prep work for potentially dangerous leads is doing lap work—including plenty of downclimbing, reversing the ascent, not just climbing to the anchors and lowering off. This skill is underappreciated—till you need it. And some day you will.

Sunrise on the shoulder of
Half Dome.

ANDREW BURR

My girlfriend Tami and I had just climbed a route on Clogwyn Dur Arddu ("Cloggy"), the dark high mountain crag above Llanberis Pass, Snowdonia, Wales. Fast forward past the pitches of climbing, spectacular and exposed, past the summit belay anchor, consisting of my crotch straddling a very sharp arête, and to the beginning of the descent, where we heard the nasal bleating of sheep. Nothing too strange about that. The shepherds let their flock cruise all over the hills there. Soon, though, we came across a mother and lamb 30 feet down on an exposed ledge. The lure of a little oasis of lush grass had lured the two down there. By the time we arrived, though, they'd eaten it to the roots and

were now too starved and too weak to get out. Any attempt to climb down and the mother threatened to launch off into the abyss.

Trad climbing inevitably presents you with situations that are not in any manual. This was one such moment. Inevitably you will find your own. You can shrug, do an about face and say, "Oh well,"— and your girlfriend hates you. Or you can Mac-Gyver up some sort of a rescue.

I flaked out the cord and tried to figure how to make a limp kernmantle into a lasso that would stay open in mid-flight. After several tosses I found it was only one part the knot and two parts the toss itself. I latched the mother first but the knot

ANDREW BURR

Fiddling

From Phoenix to Patagonia to Pakistan, many classic routes feature well-rehearsed or easily protected endurance pitches, sections where we amp up the momentum and climb at full speed. Here, "motoring" may be our only hope of success. On the other hand a speed approach can prove disastrous on routes with hard to find pro, maddeningly difficult to wiggle in and often awkward and strenuous to place—that is, "fiddling." Patience, endurance, and plenty of calm are required as we piece together the protection and the moves.

We want some notion, some tentative plan before we cast off on the lead. So we glean what we can from the guidebook, then eye out the pitch for obvious features and anything else that might betray protection opportunities. Once on the rock and confronted with challenging protection, we get as comfortable as possible before we commence fiddling—or we quickly flame out from dangling in awkward attitudes. Hang straight-armed whenever rode up around her neck and almost hanged her, but I eventually hauled her up to safety. The baby was cagier, darting to and fro, and I had to scramble down a ways before I successfully threw a loop round his belly. Once I'd roped the lamb, I tied off some slack and went to climb back up. I'd made a bad guess on the distance, though, and the rope came tight 15 feet shy of the top. Afraid the lariat might come loose if I backed down, I continued climbing, dragging the lamb, bouncing about and baa-ing like a baby.

Close calls happen all the time—in climbing, driving, even operating a barbecue (lost my eyebrows on that one). But near death moments are something else, and they stay with you afterward, the hope being that something will be learned.

One day in North Wales, Tami and I hiked up to a remote cliff called Cyrn Las. Scrambling up the steep talus to the overhanging wall, I took time to spot the route we hoped to climb but didn't bother scoping for protection possibilities. Jacked for action, I tied into the double ropes and swung out and up on sharp angular holds. Progress slowed as I entered into the don't-fall zone with no pro in sight. Surely something would show up. I passed into the can't-fall zone—and still no gear. I looked down at the elephant traps of jagged boulders lining the base, and felt the rising panic inflate my

possible—we'll use far less strength when our bones instead of our big muscles bear the bulk of our weight. If we're going off finger or hand jams, go thumbs up whenever we can—again, less strenuous and generally less awkward. Switch off from arm to arm and foot to foot to avoid flaming out one appendage.

Fiddly placements require that we choose the right piece as well as the correct orientation, or setting. Stoppers (aka tapers) designed with offsets or a curved profile may be junk one way, but spun 180 degrees, suddenly become bomber. Smaller pieces often require subtle handling. Camming units can also require some fiddling when plugged into funky slots and hollows. Expect to see cams on one side that are closer together than the cams on the other—particularly important for shallow and otherwise tricky protection options. Again, we place a unit one way and it might not hold

body weight. We pull it out and try the same piece the other way and it might anchor our truck. For camming units, much depends on the relative flare and shallowness of the crack and if the cams can be set deep enough for adequate purchase.

If one piece doesn't inspire confidence we'll build a cluster of pro, possibly including another piece that does no more than hold the others in the correct orientation, especially if we have to traverse. If the pro is an unknown, toss in one more piece before launching.

If our strength is fading fast and we must choose between two different-sized units, opt for smaller over large. Too small and the piece will still go in and usually provide some security, even if additional pieces are required. If it's too big we're hosed, and will likely spend extra time and effort struggling to make things right.

*Descending in a storm on
The Nose of El Capitan*

ALEXANDRE BUISSE

forearms. It was too late to try to go down, but
I saw some bigger holds a body length higher. I
surged up with hands turning to clubs and latched
a couple of big sloping pockets. Above the climbing
turned much harder so I had no chance of continuing. Forty feet up, looking down on potential
gravesites, I caught the scared rabbit look in Tami's
eyes. I'd felt fear before, but never impending doom.

I pitifully tried to shake out and as my arms
grew progressively more and more cooked I stuffed
my hands deeper and deeper into the holes. It

would come soon now—the falling, the scream,
and the silence. I crammed my left hand in up
past my elbow in the dark hole and felt something
wriggling in the back—it was the fingers of my
other hand! A rat hole of a tunnel connected the
two pockets! A surge of hope gave me the strength
to quickly thread some slings through the back
and clip my ropes in. With safety assured, strength
flooded back into my arms and, with what felt like
a coffee mug of adrenaline, the thirst for life was
shifted into momentum that swept me to the top.

274 THE TRAD CLIMBER'S BIBLE

CHAPTER 40

Cooking on the West Face, El Capitan

John Long

Shortly after Jim, Billy, and I made the first 1-day ascent of El Capitan, I wondered how I might squeeze more adventure out of the speed climbing game. It was never my understanding that I was inventing something new. But there was plenty of room to refine what was a pretty open game back then.

Nevertheless, the usual suspects had done some amazing speed climbing given the comparatively crude gear of the 1960s and the sheer novelty of big wall climbing. There couldn't have been more than a few dozen people climbing Valley big walls back then, so by most any definition, speed climbing was an esoteric pursuit.

Starting with John Salathe and Alan Steck's first ascent of the North Face of Sentinel, questionably the first route up a Yosemite big wall (circa 1950), subsequent ascents kept whittling down the time until Royal Robbins and Tom Frost went all out in June 1963 and climbed the route in 3 hours and 14 minutes. This was likely the first climb that established speed climbing as a genre unto itself, existing for its own reasons. Three years later, Steve Roper and Jeff Foot climbed Half Dome in a day, and the next year, Frank Sacherer and Eric Beck repeated the difficult West Face of Sentinel in a 12-hour push. Meanwhile the Leaning Tower became a day outing for leading climbers, as others shaved days and hours off ascents on El Capitan, Washington Column, The Rostrum, and all the rest.

In this context, NIAD (Nose in a Day) was merely the logical refinement of a dozen-year-old Valley tradition.

While these particular speed climbs deal with records, the activity, in its broadest interpretation, is the practice of trying to climb as efficiently as possible. For this reason speed climbing deserves study by anyone practicing trad climbing. Said differently, few people are going to race a stock car at Daytona or a Formula One car at Silverstone. But the innovations learned from these venues trickle down and are incorporated in our street cars. Same concept holds with speed climbing. Time is a crucial commodity in trad climbing, requiring judicious management, especially in wilderness settings where foul weather can ruin your day—and your life. In short, at least some of the time, you'll need to move fast to have any chance at success, so we briefly study those moving at top speed to see what we might learn for our own purposes. As with all the material in this book—take what you like, and leave the rest.

Anyway, following the NIAD, what was the next logical speed climb challenge? Without question, the most exciting aspect of the entire game of ascent was on-sight climbing—encountering a given route for the first time, when every inch and every challenge was fresh and unknown. For the NIAD, we all had done the route once before and had enough combined knowledge to work out a plan nearly down to the pitch. Later, when the Nose became the equivalent of a track race, people

The West Face roughly follows the prominent black-water streak shortly below the left-hand skyline.

DAVID SENESAC

vying for the record had climbed the route upwards of twenty times and had worked things out down to individual cam placements in attempts to shave off another 30 seconds of elapsed time. Conversely, climbing on-sight would be a totally different adventure, and I was itching to see how it might play out. Most of all I wanted to try and make a few bold pronouncements before the art began to stratify. This always happens quickly in the climbing world, where one might pick up on a development when the innovative work has already been done. This always feels more like opportunism—or more of the same—than creative curiosity. And just then I wanted to get back up on El Cap and try to on-sight a second 1-day ascent.

The problem was that only two other routes— the Salathe and the Triple Direct, which combined the lower reaches of the Salathe with the upper two-thirds of the Nose—seemed possible in a day, but I had been on both routes many times by then. The only remaining possibility was the seldom-climbed West Face, which was 2,200 feet long but wasn't on the main wall of the Captain. Nevertheless it seemed like an interesting challenge. The route had first been climbed 8 years before by Royal Robbins and T. M. Herbert in 4½ days. At that time, my So Cal buddy, Robs Muir, was the only person I knew who had climbed the West Face, and I think he made the fourth or fifth ascent.

There was almost no information available on the West Face aside from Roper's spare verbal description in the old Yosemite guidebook. Normally, with any big climb, you ferret out all the "beta" you can, from the approach march, bivi sites, availability of water near or at the base, all the route logistics, and detailed info per the descent. We knew where the route started, but had nothing much beyond that.

Dale Bard and I hiked up late one afternoon and bivouacked at the base. The march up to the West Face is hours long and one of our friends, Peter Barton, had been killed where the trail works over some steep slabs and hummocks a short ways from the base.

Peter's pack had apparently pulled him over backwards into a tumbling and fatal fall. A helicopter was summoned for the body recovery and just as it was setting down to snag Peter, the transmission jammed and the bird slammed into the deck. The crew scattered just before the copter exploded into flames. Now the gutted, rusting remains were a reminder that a man had died here and others had nearly joined him.

It's worth noting that even a cursory review of climbing accidents reveals that many of the world's greatest climbers have perished on seemingly moderate terrain, often from avoidable accidents. This underscores the fact that it is not so much the terrain but lapses in concentration—or simply bad luck—that factors into many fatal incidents.

At a big flat area beneath the West Face, Dale and I spent the little remaining daylight craning upwards, trying to get some idea where the route went. It began in a prominent arch that melded into a shallow corner 150 feet above. The start was clear. But beyond that we couldn't see much of a line. The wall was certainly lower angle than the routes ascending the sweeping South and Southeast faces. But this wall was several thousand feet high, was entirely devoid of big corners or chimneys or salient features, so we'd just have to get up there and start dead-reckoning.

We rose at dawn and brewed up some coffee, powered down some fruit, gorged ourselves on water, and blasted off. Guzzling water before a big 1-day push is standard procedure, the thinking being that if you can get enough liquid on board, you'll have to haul less on the wall. I'm not entirely sure this ever works out as advertised. It seems like every time I chug big water I piss most of it away over the following hour or so.

Robbins and Herbert had placed only a single bolt on the first ascent. And this being an early ascent as well, fixed gear and pin scars—dead giveaways of the route—were entirely absent. Once we climbed past the first arch and got into the corner above, we never again looked at the route description I had jammed in my pocket. The face was spectacularly featured with orange and black knobs and edges, and at 80 degrees we could climb most anywhere.

Having learned valuable lessons from previous epics, we devised a game plan built for speed and safety. The route, then rated Grade VI, 5.10, A4 (during the third ascent, Peter Hahn had free climbed some of the cracks up to the 5.10 standard), was largely a mixed free and aid route, but Dale and I intended to climb most of it free. We had a leader's rack of sixteen assorted nuts, from big hexes to small wires, in addition to half a dozen small pitons. This rack seemed almost foolishly thin, though probably was enough. We brought one 11-millimeter rope. We'd swing leads. Thinking it would be faster, the second would follow each pitch on ascenders. We had one daypack—with two quarts of water and a bag of gorp—which the second carried on his back, thus doing away with hauling. I loved climbing with Dale. He was one of the few guys back then that would never back down or freak out, pander excuses, or beg off the hard bits. Whenever we got on a route together, we just charged till it was done. Dale was one of the best all-around rock climbers on earth back then who brought to the game a rare amalgam of physical and intellectual strength. He would go on to climb El Cap over fifty times.

After the first few leads, we starting stringing pitches together and stretching the leads out to maximum distance, often straying off the standard line and following a more direct path as holds allowed, rarely looking for an anchor till at least 120 feet out from the last belay. Normally this was not a very sage tactic but here, the rock was well featured and diamond hard. And so far, good anchors were plentiful and quickly arranged. And so we took to stringing pitches together, which when convenient, is usually a big time saver. We were having a blast. There was nothing rote or formulaic or even familiar about speed climbing because we had done so little of it on any kind of scale. And here we were, throwing down.

There was a lot of open face climbing up shallow corners and bottoming cracks which nonetheless readily accepted nuts. So far the line had gone 99 percent free and very fast owing to the moderate angle, plenty of big face holds, and us running out the leads to maximum distance. Our strategy worked so well that I almost climbed us into disaster. It seemed to happen once on every big route.

About mid-height, Dale free climbed an entire pitch at moderate 5.10 and set a belay from good nuts on a big horizontal dike. The West Face had

some unique features in the form of giant black gargoyles and intrusions and huge glittering crystal beds. Anyhow, we were motoring so well that the momentum from one pitch carried over to the next, and once more I climbed myself into trouble by following a line of holds that eventually just ran out. But unlike my prior epic on the East Buttress, where I carried on blindly, almost to those Pearly Gates, I stopped up short, maybe 40 feet out from my last pro, traversed to a crack where I set a couple bombproof nuts, and carefully clawed my way back onto the established route. In fact with such giant face holds spangling the wall, a skilled or reckless climber could scale much of this route a dozen different ways. My "red dot" variation—as it thence appeared in topos—actually bypassed what later was the crux, 5.11c crack pitch (when the route went totally free).

From the start we climbed quickly and efficiently, stopping briefly at obvious rests and protection opportunities, ever migrating upwards after shaking out a limb or drawing a few easy breaths. Nothing reckless or breakneck about it. Just quick and steady. Aside from the aid on the lower arch, we reached Thanksgiving Ledge, just a few hundred feet below the top, never having broken out the aid slings and only grabbing half a dozen placements, rather than pausing to study a move. An easy 5.10 corner and we reached a ledge and a big chimney system where we coiled the rope and soloed to the top before the sun ever touched the wall.

By stringing together the pitches, we climbed the normal twenty pitches in sixteen, and were sitting on top of El Cap 4 hours and 50 minutes after leaving the base. Knowing the descent well, we jogged off and were back down on the valley floor in 90 minutes, where we wolfed down some food and had to immediately march back up to the West Face because we'd left all our sleeping gear at the bottom of the route.

Speed climbing

Speed climbing covers a spectrum of techniques. The methods are exacting and take practice and considerable skill in risk management. Yet most active climbers will find basic speed climbing tactics well within their abilities. The citizen version of speed climbing, commonly practiced by thousands worldwide, is not so much physically climbing faster as it is decreasing the time team members are not moving. The more radical methods involve reconfiguring our standard belay methods, through either short fixing or simul-climbing, techniques beyond the scope of this book. While short fixing and simul-climbing are reserved for the very cutting edge, generic speed climbing techniques are part of most active climbers' arsenal.

Paradoxically, speed climbing, which is generally riskier than plodding, can be used to skirt the greater dangers often found in alpine settings, where the less time spent exposed to objective dangers like avalanches, storms, and rockfall spawned the common maxim, "speed is safety." Move fast and you'll also have more time to deal with the unexpected: a snagged rope, routefinding challenges, or those slow Californians up ahead.

Even for the many who love meandering on high and have no inner need to hasten the process, external needs such as fading light and no water have occasionally forced every trad climber to pick up speed or suffer like a dog. Surprisingly, many have found that when stripping down and going light and fast, climbing becomes fantastically new and wild.

Basic Approach

The leader doesn't rush, but seeks to move quickly and efficiently up the pitch, generally placing protection only to safeguard hard sections, though avoiding needlessly long run-outs when slotting pro is fast and easy.

During every belay, one or more of the team is not moving, so the aim is to reduce the number of belays by running pitches together, stretching out the lead to its practical end. This does not mean that the leader should blindly gas it, enduring hideous rope drag, or rigging a belay off crap anchors in the middle of nowhere. Rigging makeshift belays swallows more time than if we'd stopped 30 feet below on the ledge. The idea is to stretch the lead till we gain the next "good enough" belay. We don't need perfect. We won't be there long so "good enough" will do.

If the leader is heading for an established belay station at the end of the rope length, the process is straightforward. But when stringing pitches together, we sometimes will belay off provisional stances; so all along the belayer should bark out how much rope is paid out, starting at the halfway point. And make sure your rope has a *clearly marked halfway point.* Without the belayer alerting the leader how much line is out, the leader has little to gauge his location on a given pitch. Once he knows he has so many feet left, he can judiciously use his remaining rack while staying on the lookout for the next belay station. Always briefly review your rope commands at the start of every route to help eliminate guesswork and yelling.

As the leader gets to the belay, she yells down to the belayer, "Safe!" or "Off Belay!" as soon as they get to a station but before they've set up the whole belay. Very often the second can see the leader approaching the belay or can see there's only 20 feet or so left and can start breaking down the belay. However, the second should always remain clipped to at least one bombproof piece—lacing shoes, taking a last sip, shouldering the pack, and generally getting set for liftoff. If the second is jumaring the moment the leader yells down that the rope is fixed, the follower releases the tag or haul line (if there is one) and is off. Remember, when the leader hits the next anchor and the follower is still anchored below, upward progress has stalled out. Get through this transition quickly. More on following/cleaning in a moment.

DAVE N. CAMPBELL

Once at the belay site, the leader quickly builds a bombproof anchor. Remember, the key to speed climbing is to cut down on the time that one or both climbers are stationary. So it's important for the leader to get the anchor rigged and yell down that the lead line is fixed. Only then can the belayer get off his belay device, break down the last anchor point(s), shoulder the pack and/or release the haul line—and hit the rope running.

If the second is climbing the pitch, the leader should pull up all the slack before attaching her belay device. Such fine points might seem negligible, but when you add them all up, over the course of a twenty-pitch route, 30 seconds saved here and there accrues to a half hour overall. And that's big.

If the second is following on ascenders—standard for difficult terrain—and the leader is hauling a bag or a crag pack, the leader should rig the hauling device or, at any rate, get the bag or pack off the lower anchor as soon as possible. This way the second can clean the lower anchor and get a move on. If you're hauling through a pulley, just as you do when belaying a second, pull up all the slack before attaching whatever auto-locking device you are using to haul.

Experienced speed climbers routinely haul and belay at the same time. Modern auto-locking devices like the GriGri and the Trango Cinch make this somewhat secure with practice. Once the leader has the bag or packs at hand, tie it off and get the rope stacked so it's ready for the next lead.

Meanwhile the leader is sorting and perhaps lapcoiling the other line, getting the rack arranged, placing the first gear (the "Jesus nut") on the forthcoming lead, and generally getting everything squared away so the moment the second gains the belay, time spent at the "changeover" is minimal. During the last few minutes before the second arrives, the leader eats, drinks, scans the topo, and decelerates as much as she can before it's game-on once more. Take your rest when you can get it. A few consciously relaxing breaths can rejuvenate you wonderfully.

The biggest time suck is usually the changeover, that interval where the second on the rope gains the belay and changes over to leader, a phase when neither climber is moving. Once again, strive to cut the changeover time. One proven way to hasten the entire process is to lead in blocks, which directly affects how we perform the crucial changeovers.

Leading in Blocks

Swinging leads is arguably the least efficient way to speed climb on difficult climbs. Once the leader enters the "sharp end" mindset, staying there is easier than getting there. So let one climber lead a consecutive block of pitches. This preserves the leader "head," as well as her momentum, while allowing the fresher climber to move first. Naturally, the smart money sends the fresher climber out on the sharp end. In a relay race, you hand the baton off once you've done your part—same thing here. And for a block, each climber has one part: leader or follower. On easier climbs where both climbers are cruising and there is minimal pump factor, swinging leads is often faster.

Blocks are described by pitches or time. If a climb sports a block of leads especially in one climber's wheelhouse—say a long stretch of wide cracks—let her lead the entire section so the team can cover some ground. If all things are equal, consider dividing the blocks by time, ending a given stint when the leader tires or when his psyche starts to ebb—or when you hit a handy place to swap leads, like a ledge. Once the team gets their protocols squared away and finds their rhythm, block leading is likely the single most effective speed climbing tactic short of simul-climbing and short fixing.

Changeovers

Changeovers while block leading can be swift and fluid. Many teams tie double figure-eight knots in each end of the lead rope and attach themselves ("tie in") with doubled, wide-mouthed, locking biners clipped through their harnesses. Because there are virtually no instances of failure per two biners with opposing gates, locking biners add little additional security. So consider going with simple screw sleeves

as opposed to those crabs with push-pins, magnets, spring-loaded sleeves, and whatnot, requiring secret-handshake type moves to even unlock the units. Best to just forget those.

Here is one of several ways to execute a changeover at a belay. The second jugs to the top belay anchor. Staying clipped to her ascenders, she clips herself to the anchor with slings. If the team is block leading and the follower is jugging (on ascenders), for the moment she hangs on her jugs. The goal is to get the leader moving as soon as possible. She quickly swaps ends of the rope with the leader, both momentarily unclipping from their double biner tie-in, then swapping knots. The second is now tied off directly to the anchor with the climbing rope, and the block leader (also secured to the anchor with a personal tether) is also clipped into the free, business end of the lead line. Personally I don't like to do this (I just stay tied in till the top). With more steps it just inserts one more thing to go wrong (in a big way). On the longer routes, which is what we're talking about here, recognize the inherent danger in this system—when climbers get tired and/or darkness falls it is safer to keep it simple.

The second stands up straight as the leader unclips just-cleaned gear from the second's gear loops. The second does likewise, clipping gear straight onto the leader's harness, according to how she likes it racked or onto the leader's rope between his harness and the anchor tie-in. Little things such as leaving gear behind that is not needed for the following lead and doubling up on any appropriate size, are done as a matter of course.

DAVE N. CAMPBELL

Then the leader is put on belay, unclips his tether—and off he goes. Repeat till exhausted or you reach the top, whichever comes first.

FalconGuides author and climber Sarah Garlick has likened belay changeovers to NASCAR pit stops, where the team is perfectly synced and works together to get the car—or leader—on the move ASAP. Sarah listed a handful of tricks and options, paraphrased below, for "ramping up a lightning-fast, full-pro pit crew for your next multipitch, lead-swinging adventure." Note that these tactics are not for block leading, but when two climbers are swinging leads. Nevertheless, the basic points mostly apply to block leading as well. As with all advice, take what you like—and leave the rest.

Sling: On big wall aid climbs each climber carries her own gear sling, the follower re-racking as she cleans, keeping things ordered. On long mostly free routes, harness clipping is the norm. During the changeover, you only re-rack whatever gear the leader has left—then you're off. If you're following at your max, forget the sling. It's likely easier to harness-clip the pro and sort it later.

Swap and Topo: Agree on a procedure to swap gear. Some hand over all the gear on a sling; others clip it off piecemeal, clipping it into the leader's rope between the leader's figure eight and the anchor. Pick a method and stick with it. Also know who will deal with the topo—it's often best if both climbers have a copy. Do you switch it back and forth, or does one partner keep it for the duration?

Swap it: Belay your second off the anchor's master point with a self-locking belay device (GriGri,

Reverso, ATC Guide, Madlock, etc.). When the second reaches the belay, tie off the rope's brake side and clip it off to an anchor point. While you re-rack, nab the partner's belay device and put him on lead belay. De-rig the original device on the anchor, and give it to your partner before he heads out on the lead.

Blabbermouth: Never stop just shy of the belay to rave about the awesome pitch—that's a common time suck. Save essential chitchat for when both of you can be busy re-racking, stacking the rope, etc. It's tempting to talk smack at belays, burning precious minutes spraying about that off-size crack you just dicked. Better to zip it and get moving. Save the chin-music for the pup tent.

Stack it: Stack the rope as you belay. If you drape coils off your harness, a sling, or a foot, make them long. One trick is to make a loop by grabbing the rope on the far side of your tie-in, making a sling-sized loop, tying an overhand, and clipping it back in. Now stack the rope back and forth through this. This allows for a customized "sling" size and

Alex Honnold pulling through the final bolt ladder while establishing the current speed record on The Nose, El Capitan.

DAVE N. CAMPBELL

saves the actual slings for the pitch ahead. Fewer coils mean less potential tangles. Shorten coils as you go (by 6 to 8 inches, long enough that each loop is obvious at a glance) and avoid snagging loops when paying out line during the next lead. This takes some practice.

Tag Line: Need two ropes for the descent? Sixty and 70-meter lead ropes have nearly eliminated the need to ever take two ropes—but not entirely. One option is to trail a 7.5 to 8mm tagline. Once at the belay, the leader pulls up the remaining tagline before spooling in the lead line. If the tagline snags, the second can free it. If the leader needs gear or the crag pack, the second clips it to the tagline—and hauls away.

Five-Minute Rule: A trick from wall climbing, when on long aid pitches, the leader will yell "Five minutes!", this the estimated time to the belay. This alerts the belayer to be ready for seconding mode—breaking down the anchor, lacing shoes, etc. On shorter free pitches when the leader's in sight,

the belayer should (as discussed) button everything up before the leader reaches the next station.

Conclusion

Again, the practices of simul-climbing and short fixing are vital strategies for the ambitious speed climber, but are so potentially dangerous that explaining as much in books is a crap shoot we've chosen to avoid. Know that there are many sources online that break these strategies down in great detail.

While speed climbing seems like a simple enough term, referring to a team racing up the cliffside, we've seen that the practice runs the gamut, from attacking mega routes with a scaled-down rack, one rope, a light pack and moving like chain lightning, to simul-aid climbing multiday walls. Understand that as a general rule, the potential danger increases the faster you go. Time- saving tactics actually promote efficiency and security; but once the physical climbing takes on the aspect of a race, safety is usually compromised. Be careful out there.

CHAPTER 41

Link-Ups
(aka Enchainments)

Peter Croft

Over time, road trips became the defining feature of my year. Weeks and months appeared as contrivances drummed up by bored office workers—the seasons alone determined my place in the world. After Christmas I'd go to Joshua Tree; early spring to Smith Rocks and Leavenworth; late spring to early summer I'd make Yosemite my home. Summers were mostly spent in Squamish before shortening days and grim weather forced a reversal of the schedule.

Due to my fascination with long routes, Yosemite remained king in my world. Even when visiting a face-climbing mecca like Smith, I'd focus on the crack routes in order to be ready for the next mega burner in the homeland.

Over an 8- to 10-year period I worked my way into the harder and lengthier Valley testpieces. The Rostrum North Face, one of the most iconic Valley climbs, came slowly because I kept ducking the terrible off-widths on the final leads. Many times we'd climb the first five or six pitches, chuffed at our ability to cruise the 5.11 thin cracks, only to rap off before inserting so much as a single chicken wing into the final flare. I so hated off-width climbing I refused the toprope sessions on things like Generator Crack on which my friends wore themselves silly and bragged about endlessly. This aversion retarded my progress. As mentioned, Yosemite delights in exposing our weakness, rubbing our nose in our fear, and dancing on our exhausted remains.

It is a cruel feature of the place that wide cracks lurk on most celebrated routes; the law of averages meant that, like it or not, I found my share of the "wide." By the time I finished off the Rostrum, my terror was largely gone but so, too, was a lot of skin as I wedged and shimmied to the summit.

Astroman was the next step, and it was a big one. The aura was tremendous. Speaking conservatively, often in hushed tones, people called it the most famous mega free climb in the world. Its pedigree was bound up in the über-sustained climbing, outer space exposure, and first-rate orange granite. As well, its renown was enhanced by the free ascensionists John Bachar, John Long, and Ron Kauk. For these three to merely descend on the deli for sandwiches would have set Camp 4 buzzing, but for them to have made this historic climb together stamped the route with greatness. As a final touch they renamed the futuristic route Astroman—and a rock climb became a legend.

Years later I made my own pilgrimage to the route. The night before I hadn't napped. My eyelids were spring-loaded shutters and they wouldn't stay closed. My climbing partner, Peter Mayfield, had done the climb before and so showed up relaxed and well rested. Once on route my psyche bordered on psychosis, and I laced up my climbing shoes so tight that by halfway up blood oozed from between my toes. Long story short, we topped out, but it wasn't pretty. The summit was a gritty mix of chalk, blood, and dried sweat—telltale signs of the whooping I had received. But instead of mere punishment, the torn cuticles, gobied hands, and bone-deep exhaustion served as a clear directive for the next step in my curriculum. It no longer was sufficient to simply manage a given grade, or link

Peter Croft on the
Excellent Adventure,
Rostrum, Yosemite.

GREG EPPERSON

together an equivalent number of pitches at a small crag.

On a legitimate big wall, magnitude is something I needed to experience to appreciate. Up high we find strength sapping hanging belays, must haul the daypack with a chunk of residual pump, and push on with the inevitable dry-throated thirst, draining our resolve with every successive lead. Even without the lead weights of awe and fear, the mega route package is a great deal more than a sum of its parts.

I needed more mileage.

The next year I was back; following my own advice, I had come up with an ambitious plan. To further my scheme for added mileage, I started doing link-ups of multiple long climbs, often on my own, sometimes with a partner. My latest concoction was sure to be a doozie: Astroman in the morning and the Rostrum after lunch. No climber was interested in joining in for both hot links, so I scavenged two friends, Greg and Terry, to split the load. Canadian Greg Foweraker was my best friend and would join me for Astroman and in the afternoon, if I was still standing, Terry Lien from Washington would accompany me on the Rostrum.

There was just one problem—and it was a big one. That April and May the weather included biblical rains and massive flooding. Tent cabins in Curry Village were washed off their foundations. The river overflowed like the Ganges and the only campers who stayed dry slept in their cars. The walls were sodden and routes that sometimes sported

Stacking the Odds

As we pull toward the outer reaches and world-class terrain, the demands on the climber increase exponentially, a fact reflected in these sidebars. Many are not bothered or motivated to push so hard, but for those who are—here goes:

Bad weather and lousy fortunes can cause us to lose the focus on the bigger picture and our deeper aims. When frustrated with soggy conditions or a partner gone AWOL, look at the positive what-ifs and prepare for the best. Some write gratitude lists. There are a thousand methods. The aim is keeping the psyche revved, knowing that the rain has to stop sometime and good things can happen—but only if we're ready. If we've let external conditions determine our mood, when the clouds part we first have to crawl out of a dark hole. If we work to stay positive we're good to go the moment we can. Though simplistic sounding, few among us are able to stay highly motivated, because it takes work and desire and the courage to face discomfort.

To stay sharp for the long routes, get out and get wet. In most areas we can find something dry to climb on: perhaps only half a pitch, but if it's suitable for laps we can stay fit and keep our hands tough. If not, while the storm rages and the stone is soused, trail running or hiking is a low-risk way to maintain endurance. No matter the weather we can take ourselves toward the red line between gasping and collapse. For this the steeper trails are money in the bank. Such training increases our lung capacity while improving our capacity to process lactic acid—especially handy when we once again hit the crag and start huffing up that endless off-size crack. Work things out your own way so when the sun comes out and we cast off our strength, endurance and skin haven't all gone soft.

Dividends

There is always a point where improvement stalls out. It is a mistake to assume that this is our natural limit. We'd love to see improvements tracing a smooth, never-ending upward trajectory. This often is not the case. The process is more likely a game of consolidation (plateau) with occasional jumps in progress. We read all about things like "Seven Minute Abs," but the serious trad climber must invest in the long term and prepare for the long haul, because that's the basic nature of the work.

Eventually, time spent on the various techniques becomes second nature and we move by instinct rather than thought—a much more efficient mind-body adventure. Couple this with steadily improved fitness, and that's when we really leap forward. The process often follows its own schedule, which can be maddeningly hard to track and impossible to totally manage. But providing we throw down a consistent effort, we will improve.

Moving on instinct.

MATT KUEHL

damp sections now ran with waterfalls. And no one climbed—no one, that is, except for an absurd Canadian who was both cursed and blessed to grow up in a rain forest.

Each morning I'd make the rounds, bumming for a belayer. I knew two pitches in the Valley that always stayed dry—what I was careful not to mention is that they were at opposite ends of that Valley. Eventually someone would take the bait, and we'd load up on climbing gear and ziplocked bags of dry clothes and head off into the rain. I was acclimated to foul weather and had loads of raw enthusiasm, but mostly I was looking ahead to a day of sunshine. I was determined to be ready.

In such a torrential season all the bad weather stand-bys were soused. The only two that remained useable were the Kaukulator on the west flank of the Rostrum, and 1096 in the Royal Arches area. Kaukulator is a fantastic finger hand crack, marred by a final 5.11 OW—short but stout. 1096, while a beautiful orange flake, is fundamentally a spooky 5.10+ chimney. My aversion to wide cracks was finally overcome by my compulsion to climb.

The soggy drudgery of the approaches meant that both pitches were lapped to exhaustion. Repetition made the tricky sizes of thin hands and rattly fingers feel much more secure—and off-widths and chimneys lost their fear factor, allowing techniques

Peter Croft on the
Excellent Adventure,
Rostrum, Yosemite.

The Excellent Adventure.

GREG EPPERSON

Jumaring or Following

On moderate multipitch climbs, it makes sense and is generally much more fun for the second to follow (climb) rather than jumar. Even on difficult routes, the favored scenario sees both climbers experiencing the route entirely, both climbing every inch, bottom to top. Even if the second requires a bit of tension here and there, the experience remains basically the same for both climbers.

On difficult climbs, though, it is now commonplace for the leader to enlist a "subby" (sub man/ woman) to jumar, usually with a pack. The advantages for the leader are substantial. After all, anyone who can climb can belay and haul a pack. It is the pitch after pitch repetitiveness of the rope-handling, however, that takes a big chunk of extra juice from the forearms. Basically, when the leader has only to lead, and doesn't waste energy having to belay or haul or schlepp water and food on his back, all of his energy goes toward climbing the route, and he or she also gets a break to recover as the subby jugs up cleaning the lead. Conserving the leader's energy in this way becomes increasingly key as the route approaches our physical limit, where every bit counts.

A dedicated leader (one leader for the entire route) is basically looking at two options for her system. One, she has one rope for leading and a trail line for hauling the pack. She finishes the lead, hand hauls the pack, and immediately belays the second up while stacking the rope for good measure. Or two, she leads (without the trail line) to the anchor and ties off. While the subby jugs and cleans the pitch (on the lead line), the leader takes a nap, perhaps asking the second, when he arrives, for a neck rub. The difference is night and day—we can easily see why.

Using a subby is the favored method for cutting-edge climbers worldwide. Over the course of a long day, when the leader is freed up from belaying and hauling, the extra rest time amounts to hours. The use of sub men—though dating back to early free ascents of Astroman in the 1970s, and possibly before—didn't become widely popular till the 1990s, and is rarely mentioned in the climbing media. But using a sub-man is a much-used technique and is probably critical to those gunning for top-shelf mega free routes.

Heather Hayes assists with the haul on the third pitch of the Lowe Route, Angel's Landing, Zion.

LARRY COATS

like heel-toeing and basic inchworming to become second nature. As much of the mileage was hand size, the hand jam became my ace in the hole. All other holds and jams were to some extent an attempt to hold on to the cliff. Hanging off a hand jam, I was plugged in.

By the time high pressure hit the Valley I had mere days left. The sun was out but wet streaks lined the walls. I waited till my last full day. The night before, Greg and I bivied beneath Washington Column, all pins and needles under a full moon. The sleep that finally came was shattered by a roar around midnight—over on Half Dome an avalanche of snow and ice leapt off the visor. The face itself was deep in shade but the debris cascaded out and caught the moonlight like a silver waterfall.

Too amped to sleep, we started in the dark by headlamp. I linked the first two difficult sections: the boulder pitch into the enduro corner. Halfway up the corner the lamp went out and suddenly I was on a 5.11c lieback in total blackness, the moon having already set. Climbing blind I shuffled my hands up the crack till I'd bump into a fixed pin and I'd clip and go. Placing pro while liebacking

is always challenging—in the blackness it was all braille. Greg followed on jumars as the first hint of dawn crawled down Tenaya Canyon and onto the wall.

Four pitches up we reached the Harding Slot— so feared and so flared. A scary enough feature in prime conditions, it now was running water. I plunged right in. In any previous year I would have slipped like a minnow in a monster's fist. But my time spent on the flared and gimpy 1096 was not wasted and I squirmed my way to the belay.

The rest of the route was dry and we raced to the top. On the summit Greg said to scram while he coiled the rope. After Astroman the smaller and much drier Rostrum felt like a formality—even the 5.10 off-widths felt facile. Later I ate dinner at the Four Seasons with my friends, fingers and feet drumming to a metabolism I couldn't crank down. Lost in thought I realized how much those days in the rain had added up to success. In a mini universe with countless variables, unexpected events like wet rock and broken headlamps are bound to happen—sooner or later. It also dawned on me how much I now felt I had in reserve, which is exactly what I needed.

*The mother
of all roof cracks*

ANDREW BURR

CHAPTER 42

Bouldering Junket

John Long

We were rolling along in John Bachar's red VW van, heading from Boulder to Pueblo, Colorado. Steering with his feet, John began torturing his alto sax—the same one I had wanted to toss into the Rio Grande for going on a month. Of course that never stopped him, and the dire honking served as a running soundtrack for our bouldering expedition. His goal, he always said, was to play one perfect note—but I never heard it.

Following a summer climbing long routes in Yosemite, we had carpooled east to Colorado, armed with a copy of Pat Ament's *Master of Rock*—a picture book to most, but to us a magical treasure map charting the adventures of bouldering pioneer John Gill. The plan was to find and climb every problem in the book, a venture that had taken us to Eldorado and Boulder Canyons, Fort Collins, Split Rocks, Estes Park, and the Needles of South Dakota. Along the way we barbecued buffalo burgers with Lakota Indians and swam the Yampa River in flood—and many other things that should have landed us in jail—having a blast in the process. But it went beyond fun in every direction. We both had a fierce inner drive to be great at something; ticking the Gill problems was confirmation that we mattered. Now we were motoring down to meet the Master himself, and Bachar was ecstatic.

There are several points illustrated by this trip of which we were only vaguely aware at the time, and which are worth noting by all trad climbers of all abilities. First is that variety is the spice of climbing. Back then, Yosemite was the center of the rock climbing world. It had the best weather, the best rock, and by far the most magnitude. You could go to plenty of other areas and find huge walls but the chance of getting stormed off were, and remain, high. The Valley was ground zero, and we never strayed far. But here and there we had to venture into the wild places to help keep the game fresh and exciting.

Many trad climbers get swallowed whole by life commitments and hang up their boots for good. But almost as many burn out over a period of years, especially if a few road trips are not interspersed with yet another foray to your home crags. Staying psyched is most easily accomplished through a varied diet of short and long, hard and otherwise, towers and walls, slabs and pinnacles, splitters, and jug hauls, from desert to mountain to jungle to that urban scrap heap that will always be home. Vary the fare and you'll keep your appetite. Hole up in one place, even a wonderland like Yosemite Valley, and your days are numbered.

Next, to review a running theme, regardless if you are a weekend warrior or a sponsored athlete, we all are sustained by projects and dreams. It simply is not enough to go to the crags year after year and just do whatever you feel like, deciding on the spot. You can't live your life like that nor can you sustain a climbing career in such undisciplined fashion. You have to draft occasional plans. And when you pull them off, you have the landmarks, big and small, that fashion a deliberate career.

Returning to Bachar and my bouldering expedition: From our first day in Eldorado, Bachar insisted we skip the rope since Gill so rarely wore one in the

Lisa Rands on
the business.

ROBERT MIRAMONTES

book. With crash pads still a dozen years off, we had to sack it way up to tackle problems like the over-hanging Gill Crack in Boulder Canyon, the dynamic Mental Block and Eliminator problems at Fort Collins, and the sky-high slabs and traverses at Split Rocks. In most cases we had to on-sight these problems, doing them first try, or risk bad falls and injuries. In this sense our bouldering junket felt much the same as trad climbing on high, and that's how we approached the work. Bachar was the ideal partner for this crusade, and it's worth a few pages to understand how such a champion came into being.

Back in high school, half a dozen years earlier, I'd get midnight calls from John about his new climbs or boulder problems, meaning I had to immediately beg a car or even hitchhike to wherever so I could bag these routes as well. Then I was calling John and bragging about some crack out at Rubidoux or overhang up at Mount Baldy that he simply had to do, and in this way we prodded each other to levels unattainable on our own.

The Stonemasters were originally an informal group of about six or eight teenagers that teamed up in high school. About the only thing we had in common with the prevailing climbing scene was each other. Back then, most climbers were wilderness buffs. Bachar and I both grew up in the city and didn't know, or care, about any wilderness. We were hardcore athletes who lived to play baseball (me) and pole vault (Bachar). Then I saw the National Geographic special about Kor, Ingalls, and Hurley scaling the Titan, and Bachar found a copy of Rébuffat's *Starlight and Storm* at K-Mart, and we became climbers.

Staying Consistent

Given the reality of most climbers' lives, how far we might go is usually determined by how consistent we stay with our climbing and training. Many factors can haul us off the rocks, half of them unavoidable. Our activity level will invariably wax and wane depending on energy, motivation, and time. The trick is to try to best manage the few things we can control. Most of us take a few months off every year to let their batteries recharge and any nagging injuries to heal. So long as you remain active, climbing back onto the cliffside is usually a fluid affair. Perhaps the most important factor to manage, one that stalls out more careers than any other, is injury prevention. Again, there is a regular mountain of information on this topic, available from many sources. But remember these general principles. Always warm up before pushing limits.

This must be your mantra if you desire longevity in climbing. Warming up and adequate rest are the best preventative medicine for all athletes and the least adhered to by climbers. No matter how strong or technically proficient you are, if you get injured, it all stops.

Whenever something starts hurting, stop. Seek professional attention for any lingering conditions. There is little to hasten recovery from tendon injuries but it's best to know if you have one. Only resume climbing when the pain has gone. Limit strength training to three sessions a week (campus board, et al). Work the antagonistic muscles, not just the pulling muscles, or risk an injury prone, out-of-balance physique. Always drink more water than you think is necessary. Take rest days. Have fun.

Peter Croft, left, bouldering with John Gill in the Happy Boulders, Bishop, California.

JODY LANGFORD

Our partnership lifted off out at Joshua Tree, when the campgrounds were vacant and the desert felt like Mars. We'd climb till early afternoon, then boulder ourselves to smithereens, often using headlights or Coleman lanterns to squeeze in a couple final moves past sundown. I could never wear Bachar out, which surprised and annoyed me. He looked more like a math geek than an athlete, standing 5'11", a buck forty, with a stringy blond mop, two silver buck teeth, and a pain threshold so high that he'd keep pulling after his tips had turned to ground round.

From very early on John displayed the baleful economy of movement he would later bring to bear on the greatest free climbs of the era. He had a trashed old Suzuki 175 motorcycle and every day after school he'd blast from his home near the LA International Airport out to the Stoney Point boulders, a round trip of over 80 miles. With his drive and athleticism he became world-class in just 6 months. By the end of our first season out at Josh, we'd repeated most of the existing routes and had started free climbing a few old aid lines around the main Hidden Valley campground as well.

One afternoon in early 1973, I persuaded Bachar to join me soloing Double Cross, a popular, 100-foot 5.8 crack that we had climbed many times. It was like releasing a shark into the ocean.

Even on that first solo I can recall John's sphinxlike bearing, the hips-in, shoulders-back posture and the liquid sequencing of moves that distinguished his climbing, unroped or otherwise, for the next 35 years. Within a month, John was regularly soloing fifteen or twenty routes in succession. Twenty routes soon became fifty, and toward the end of our second winter at Josh, I joined John for a "century," soloing one hundred routes in a day. We usually soloed up to mid-5.10, generally sticking to routes we had done ten or more times. But John was at heart a jazz player dedicated to the romantic idea of spontaneous, unfettered art, so I knew that sooner

rather than later, John's soloing would extend into on-sight efforts.

The following season, Bachar began free soloing at a difficulty never before seen or imagined in the rock climbing world. By 1976 he'd soloed scores of routes that only a handful of climbers had managed with a rope. While these efforts were often do or die, Bachar made it all look as casual as hiking a flight of stairs, bringing to the party his unique blend of artisanship and focused valor that is the sovereign state of any free soloing session. To see him soloing in person, so high above the boulders—it felt like some exalted game, like someone

Cross Training for Trad

For the active trad climber, bouldering and gym climbing remain convenient modes of cross training for mega routes. Many prized mega routes require difficult face climbing and it is unrealistic to expect success without putting in your time in the gym or on the boulders. There's little profit here in glossing over the ways to increase performance in either venue, but it's instructive to remember how it's a different thing to train for that fifty-pitch free route on Great Trango Tower, say, than it is for that 40-foot 5.14E at Abner's Quarry. Err on the side of strength endurance and you just might own the future—though nothing is a given in the trad world.

Bouldering remains a favored training tool for routes of all lengths.

ROBERT MIRAMONTES

fulfilling a dream. No doubt he set a style above and beyond the danger quotient, though no one was quite sure what it was because such wild expression didn't fit anyone's experience or imagination. Bachar's art seemed mostly his own as it required a degree of commitment and connoisseurship that dismayed and shocked most climbers.

People had actually been free soloing for years; but John's was a palatial investigation of the theme with such unalloyed strength and newness it seemed

Like father, like daughter. Tia Stark, whose father Woody was a leading climber at Joshua Tree in the 1960s.

to exist almost in a parallel world. The practice seemed so sketchy, and the experience so ungraspable, that many dubbed him a daredevil or psycho. Some folks got ill by watching. Most could only wonder what he was truly about, his movement less resembling athletics and more like mythic streams pouring out of his hands and feet. But his brand of climbing felt deadly and some people were made anxious and awkward by his presence.

When Bachar offered $10,000 to anyone who could follow him for a day, many figured that he was all about man versus man—a primitive but dramatic ego game. When it later became known that most of his solos were conducted in private, with no one watching, his quest was viewed as man against Nature. Only those close to him understood that behind the bluster and physical genius played the greatest show on earth: man against himself. John Bachar was all about self-mastery, and up on the steep he faced, in the sharpest possible relief, the peaks and vales and shadows of his mind. His soloing was no vocation, but a calling, and like all callings, it was personal.

And so John and I had set out to do all the John Gill problems we could find, with Ament's Master of Stone as a guidebook. Finally, we were heading down to meet the man himself. Just past mile-high Colorado Springs, the sage, junipers, and piñon pines thin to jade grasslands rolling into Pueblo, with the Sangre de Cristo Mountains rising 30 miles south. The last time I'd been in Pueblo (with Michael Kennedy, then editor of *Climbing Magazine*), Gill had led us to one area after another till my hands were bloody claws. This time, Bachar and I arrived a day early to jump on problems I was too gassed to dick the first time around.

At the Ripper Traverse area, Bachar soloed up and down the Little Overhang, then darted across the Ripper like he was hanging on a rain gutter. If a panther could climb, it would move like Bachar moved that afternoon in Pueblo. Just then he was almost certainly the finest free climber on earth.

Next day we met up with Gill and drove to the Lost Canyon, with its dark arroyos and quicksand, cow pie landings and scores of Dakota sandstone boulders that local vaqueros sometimes used for target practice. Black clouds boiled up high and distant thunder clapped down rocky gulch walls. The wind, thrust forward by the edge of the storm, seemed to drive gravity from Lost Canyon. Perhaps inspired by Gill's quiet presence, Bachar put on a magic show, glimmering from hold to hold, weightless, flashing nearly every problem he tried, including the gymnastic Juggernaut.

As the first drops began to fall, Gill and I sat back and watched the quiet brio of this remarkable individual. He somehow had reconciled the heart, mind, body, and soul of adventuring with an unmitigated strength that, even during its highest expression, had the intriguing aura of something rare working its way out and forward. We must have known someday others would come along and put John's best efforts in the shade. But it wasn't so much his feats on the rock, marvelous as they were, as his progression, which seemed limitless, no ceiling or horizon in sight, that was a miracle to witness firsthand.

All bouldering—which at bottom is soloing—is quixotic as a drum solo, and like all drum solos, it means everything and nothing. One of the paradoxes of soloing in general is that for all its dependence on spontaneity and real-time creativity, its most resonant influence has been through the medium of still and silent rocks, where a climber's truest statements, in the mineral lexicon of ascent, are literally fixed in stone.

Gill smiled slightly before remarking, "He doesn't fall much, does he?"

"Not so much," I said.

From that charmed afternoon in Lost Canyon, Bachar never stopped soloing till the day he finally broke through to the next world. Scattered behind him, written in chalk on a thousand faces, lies his audacious legacy, slowly fading, like a last and perfect note from a saxophone.

Free Soloing: Part 2

Because a few adventurous climbers solo with a rope, a method full of tricky rope shenanigans, the term "free soloing" was coined for those soloing free of all the roped safety devices. That is, climbing without a rope. With no backup in case they

Peter Croft on Thin Ice, Needles.

GREG EPPERSON

should fall. No safety net. No nothing. There are few subjects in climbing that have sparked more controversy and fist waving, evoked more judgments and vitriol than free soloing. The public knows about the discipline because the era's great soloers, including John Bachar (1970s), Peter Croft (1980s), Dean Potter (1990s), and Alex Honnold (2000s), to mention a few, have appeared widely in popular media. But the practice remains an emotional powder keg for many. When looked at soberly, however, free soloing is fairly cut and dry.

Soloing has always been a part of trad climbing, and it always will. Of course, not all soloing is equal. Scrambling unroped up 3rd-class slabs to gain the bottom of a big wall is qualitatively different than scaling a 5.11 crack on Devil's Tower, sans cord. Fact is, in the trad galaxy, roping up for every inch of technical terrain is impractical, especially in wilderness areas, where time is a commodity that needs prudent managing and where oftentimes, when the storm clouds rumble, "speed is safety." Soloing discussions typically lose their way, or devolve into circular arguments, the moment we assume that all climbers are made the same, or should be.

Of course there is no such thing as a "typical climber." The climbing world is diverse enough to embrace all corners, regardless of orientations or ability. In a real sense, we're all tied into the same rope. Of course what we want or expect from climbing varies person to person, and no group or orientation has an exclusive on what is right or proper or true. A highly skilled climber is no "better" than a hacker and a conservative old duffer is no safer than the young woman free soloing that polished slab in North Conway.

Once we start drawing a demarcation line in the sand about how much risk is justified, beyond which it is reckless and so forth, there is no countering these arguments on rational grounds because logically, we shouldn't be climbing at all. Some have taken a militant stance against free soloing. Ironically, ranting about anything betrays a lack of emotional containment, a prerequisite for any free soloing at any grade—meaning those screaming loudest are themselves least qualified for the work. So as long as they heed their own words, that soloing is just plain bad, they are unlikely to go out and get hurt. Insisting that the entire climbing world conform to their criteria per safety and commitment is misguided—we can easily see why. What's more, expressing outrage that others don't see things as they do, is selfish in the extreme, which ironically, is often the charge leveled against those out there climbing without a rope. We can understand how such discussions quickly go circular and spin into a hole.

But the real crime here has little to do with soloing. Rather, rock climbing has always been a peerless vehicle for self-expression. No one needs play off the next guy, adopt his values, or follow her lead. We're free to make our own mistakes. Insisting that all climbers adhere to any kind of code or have their behavior regulated is fighting the current and is contrary to the spirit of climbing itself. What Joe or Shelly

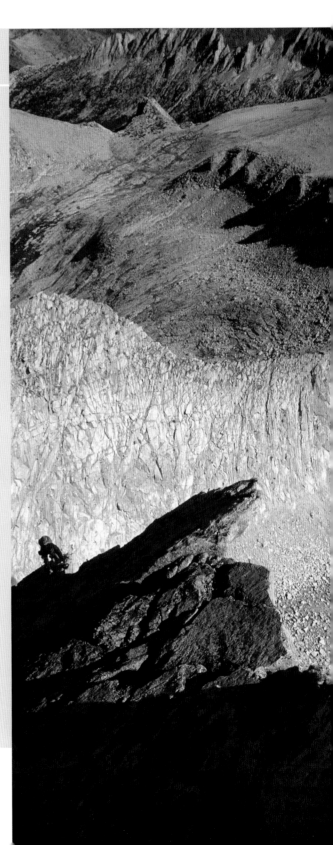

Soloing on the North Ridge, Mount Conness.

CHRIS FALKENSTEIN

*Might as well
be soloing . . .*

ANDREW BURR

do on the cliffside is their business. I'm reminded of the old Hank Williams song: "If you mind your own business, then you won't be mindin' mine!"

Of course the free soloing expert has no right to cajole someone up on the steeps without a rope. This is the Devil's work and it very rarely happens. Likewise, any request for handy or appropriate routes to solo is clear evidence of a lack of experience. Beyond that, the choice to free solo, or not, lies entirely with the individual. No one can or should make such a choice for anyone else. As mentioned, climbing unroped over easy to moderate approaches and descents has always been part of trad climbing and there's no way around this if you aspire toward bigger routes. That much said, for those who choose to free solo at a higher level, a few rules of thumb are worth mentioning—not so much for the expert, who will figure things out for herself, but for the weekend warrior who for untoward reasons, is forced to go unroped over technical terrain, or who finds himself on rock so entirely unprotected that his climbing basically amounts to free soloing. Someday you'll probably find yourself right there.

The most critical point, from a stay-alive point of view, is to understand the risk.

Regardless of whether one is actually tied in or entirely cordless, the scenario must be regularly evaluated to assess if one is entering free solo territory. Even in sport areas and certainly on gear routes it is not unusual to go for the second or third piece of pro and then clutch up at the realization that a botched clip would plant you at the base of the cliff. A cool spatial awareness from the get-go would prevent the surprise and resultant barely get-it-clipped puckering that destroys all poise for the rest of the lead. Even well into the meat of a moderate climb, well-spaced pro could mean entertaining a virtual ground fall if there are ledges or ramps in the line of fire.

Approaches to long routes are the most likely places for novice soloers to blow off the rope. Just because the topo doesn't identify this as real climbing, the risks are real enough with a heavy pack, gravel under your tennies, and 100 feet of vertical scruff between you and the plunging mouth of the gully below. This is not the time to gape up at the perfect hand crack on the fourth pitch.

For most purposes soloing requires a sober, unhurried demeanor. Some years ago I was climbing Basin Mountain (near Bishop) with my dog, PeeWee. Halfway up the final headwall, right where a 3rd-class ledge cuts left, she freaks, bolts up a 5.7 crack, and gets the doggie version of Elvis leg—all shook up—with 500 feet of mountain air below. I sprinted up and dyno-ed for the collar, tackling her, and dragging her to easier terrain. I had nightmares for years after that one. Careful appraisal of the terrain is the first step (unless, of course, you're a border collie).

On approaches, all hardware, shoes, and ropes should be securely stowed in the pack or clipped to

Easy soloing on a summit ridge, standard practice on many mega trad routes.

LARRY COATS

the harness. What's more, none of it should be allowed to obscure the holds or get in the way of the climbing itself—no dangly rock shoes or loopy daisies and no hastily coiled ropes coming uncoiled at the worst possible moment. If the climbing looks remotely tricky, put on your rock shoes. Slow down and make sure the soles of your shoes haven't picked up any grit. Treat the approach like real climbing—because it is. If it gets any more real, stop and flake out the rope.

Anyone who delves into multipitch trad will encounter that decision point on whether to rope up or keep soloing—or, up high, whether to keep the rope on or untie and 3rd class off. Much will be determined by one's personal brand of pragmatism, the rest by circumstance and on-the-fly calculations. A little more risk on cruiser terrain might well mean more daylight and a lot less gambling on that complicated descent. A bit more speed here to avoid run-out slabs in the rainstorm that's headed your way.

Free soloing, without any intention of using gear, could become necessary if an emergency arises and one climber needs to 3rd class out for help. It could also become irresistibly appealing if some circumstance finds you alone, staring up at a potential climb of a lifetime. Just keep in mind that a lifetime is supposed to be a very long time.

If, however, the move is made to solo, the first step is clean shoes. Sounds prissy, but clean rubber is required for precise footwork and footwork is the bedrock of all technique. Exacting

attention to technique on easier ground transfers to the tricky bits higher up. Imagine the jarring grinding of gears if, after hundreds of feet of adrenalized herky-jerky movement, a crux was encountered requiring velvety smooth precision.

In climbing, as well as in the world at large, much revolves around risk management. This, however, is an unwieldy and sometimes counterproductive concept as we struggle with our own ideas of actual risk versus perceived risk. A distracted belay from a partner more concerned with checking his Facebook page can be more deadly than the quiet focus of the free solo. If you embrace a gamble, your one trump card is understanding the gamble—and that means understanding yourself. That might sound simplistic, but that facile motto is the entire key to free soloing at any level. This is crucial to understand for all potential soloists. We all want enlightened advice on the "secret" that makes soloing routine, but no such advice exists. But if we know and respect our strengths, our weaknesses, how we function under stress—in short, if we know our real capacity, this alone is what can shift a reckless game of dare-devilry into a sober and calculated exercise in self-mastery.

In any arena with the potential for risk—and this is especially true for the soloist, the dictum "Do it for the right reasons" must be the Prime Directive. Yes, just like in *Star Trek*. Of course no one can tell you what the "right reasons" are, and if you don't know yourself—rope up.

CHAPTER 43

Charakusa

Peter Croft

Who knows what first drew us to climbing? For many of us, spectacular mountains had a great aesthetic appeal. And what they required of those who would venture there—the effort, the athleticism, and even gymnastics necessary for difficult routes. And feelings of discovery: There was always more to learn. But if I had to boil it down to one thing, it was the ability, better yet, the necessity, to choose—what, where, when, and with whom. After years of arcane rules, Cub Scouts, and school sports, climbing gave me free will. At first I felt this suited my temperament. Later I discovered this freedom requires great discipline and courage, and this is what elevates the climb and the climber.

Entering the panorama.
GALEN ROWELL

Sponsar Brakk—The Ridge, roughly 8,000 feet long!

GALEN ROWELL

I got a chance to join an expedition to the Karakorum with Galen Rowell and Conrad Anker. Galen was an adventure photographer famous for his worldwide mountain adventures. While not a brilliant technical climber, his endurance was mythical and his climbing resume near endless. Conrad was a yellow-haired Viking and perhaps the best all-arounder I'd ever seen. The fact that I could out free climb him was a negligible factor when measured against his big walling, ice climbing, and skiing. And that look: tall, blonde, and square-jawed—a kinder, gentler (and slightly stoned) version of Clint Eastwood. Girls loved him. Queuing up next to such star power while passing through Pakistani customs was demoralizing. I was just another scruffy Canadian with a bad haircut.

Our plan was to visit a secret part of India that Galen had spied on an epic ski traverse some years before. Mile-high granite walls lining a never climbed-in valley sounded too good to be true—which in a way, it was. Mere days before departure, the long-standing border dispute between India and Pakistan erupted. Whether triggered by big guns or bad manners, we never found out. Our permit was suddenly revoked and we were given the sole option of exploring a different obscure valley called

Charakusa. With no photos or any info at all, we went for it. We spent days getting to Pakistan, only to wait days more in Third World triple-digit heat for lost bags to finally arrive, and then days more of sketchy jeep junkets through terrifying river gorges just to get to the beginning of the fun part.

Finally back on foot, we trekked into the valley with fingers crossed that there would be something worth climbing. We passed a couple of biggish walls on the second day, turned a corner, and were blown away. In the same way that Yosemite left me with weak-kneed awe, the Charakusa did the same, but more so, planting huge alpine faces on top of Half Dome and El Cap–size walls. Virtually every peak ended in a minaret summit, tiny pinpoints that drew the eye from miles away.

One feature forced all else into peripheral vision: a bronzed, granite knife-edge soaring off the glacier in a single, 8,000-foot-long blade. I took off ahead of the others to scope the arête and prostrate myself before such perfection.

The following morning I came down with an evil lung plague. It was a terrible tease—I had arrived in heaven, but had to stay inside with the flu. Our trip was short—we only had a few weeks. While the others climbed some smaller routes, I spent my wretched days hacking vile green jellies out the tent door. Finally, with just a couple days left, I was finally able to look up.

An 8,000-foot route coupled with the mysteries of an unclimbed summit and unknown descent meant speed was critical. A team of two was the only logical way to go, and it came down to Conrad and me.

Conrad Anker on the route.

PETER CROFT

On the edge.

CONRAD ANKER

We set the alarm for 2 a.m., but it didn't stop raining till 5. Surely this was too late. We had one more day before we were due to leave. Maybe then? It was at this point that our coffee stash came into play. National Geographic had funded our expedition, but it was Peet's Coffee that had sponsored our caffeine addiction—to the tune of twenty pounds of Arabica. Cup followed cup till we were gibbering like spider monkeys. When a peep of blue materialized, we shot out of camp. With such a late start we'd be racing the sun. We had one 60-meter rope, a light rack of cams and stoppers, and no bivi gear. Once again I felt the tremulous, giddy sensation of getting

out there that I felt on my first big adventures.

We led in blocks, simu-climbing till the leader ran out of gear and we'd bring up the second.

The leader, now rested and with a replenished rack, immediately forged on. Routefinding was mostly straightforward. The farther we strayed from the crest of the arête, the scabbier the granite became. Staying religiously on the very fin of the beast produced some of the wildest and most picturesque climbing I had ever done. Long finger and hand cracks soared skyward till rudely pinching off, forcing us onto vastly run-out face climbing. Moving together, the leader had to work to keep the rope running straight to avoid rope drag. On short pitches a few zigs or zags wouldn't have mattered much, but with the full 60 meters out, even gentle angles will quickly compound the drag.

Roughly halfway up the knife, the edge narrowed even more and went horizontal—honed by the elements into geological craziness, like the frozen lip of a wave that couldn't decide which way to break. For long stretches we straddled the cockscomb till the eeriness and mind-crippling exposure forced us to swing down and hand traverse. We kept on till our arms ached, forcing us to throw a heel hook up and over and hump our way back into a straddle once again.

We'd sling horns whenever they appeared, slot cams and Stoppers when cracks showed up, and when pickings were slim, we wound back and forth on the ridge searching spikes and notches. Always, though, our concerns for adequate pro had to be balanced against our increasing need for speed. We still had a couple thousand feet of technical ground to cover as the sun accelerated toward the horizon.

I hit the top right as the sun went down, coughing from the thin dry air and residual lung funk. The summit itself was the merest blade, something to do a pull-up on so as to peer down the other side. Joining Conrad on a small ledge, we discussed our limited options. The temperature, pleasant all day long, now plummeted, the higher altitude atmosphere unable to hold any warmth. A bivi seemed apropos given the remaining few minutes of light, but we decided that continuing the descent through the night was the safer option.

Conrad, longtime wall master, led the rappels down the far side of the peak. He would disappear into the blackness, swing back and forth searching for the next place to set anchors, kicking off refrigerator-sized blocks that sprayed sparks and roared hundreds of feet to the gully below. Each anchor was a truck stop—no crappy single-skinny-Stopper stations for us. Nothing was rushed, no

Growing Complacent

As we start to dial in the various disciplines required in trad climbing, it's easy to grow complacent, sometimes staying too long in our comfort zone. As we tick off climbs that once seemed untouchable, we start to believe that we've got it figured out. But in adventure climbing, there is some danger in believing this.

With so many real-world variables, there is always more to learn. Those who reach the next level are regularly made aware of their weaknesses. One danger is losing the quest for adventure—or the unknown, which is the same thing—that was so appealing in the first place. Real adventure has a component of not knowing—a mystery waiting to be experienced and unraveled. Stretching ourselves toward the unknown remains the essence of exploration and the key to deeper understanding of what we do and who we are as people.

As we push farther out there and the unknowns stack up high, it is natural to dwell on the possible downsides—all the things that can go wrong. If we're careful and prudent, we'll have our setbacks. Life happens, but little usually trips us up for long. More often, countless things go entirely right and in ways we never expected. Again, if we're watchful, we'll find more than we looked for.

Alpine Starts

Early starts prevent more epics than anything else in climbing. Getting up predawn gives you that greater time cushion that will help you to avoid getting stuck behind other parties, caught in lousy weather, trapped by darkness, pitches from the top or on a nasty descent, etc. Alpine starts are also a magical part of the day where cliffs loom twice their size and strange animals are afoot. The empty hours of the night and the crack of dawn is when we all speak in hushed voices because the whole damn thing is just that awesome.

Alpine starts take some getting used to, particularly for late risers. We often need more time than we think we need. Neophytes regularly assume 15 minutes to half an hour is plenty of time between waking and stumbling onto the trail. With experience we find that an hour is minimum, particularly if caffeine is any part of the program. In pitch dark, an hour easily stretches to 90 minutes. We never want a frantic exit from camp. We'll invariably forget a climbing shoe or the rope. We've all done both. We need time to check and double check, both of which are impossible when we get up late and are playing catch-up for the duration—and we never do catch up.

Karine Croft on the High Sierra classic Third Pillar.

CHRIS FALKENSTEIN

short cuts, as this was when we were most vulnerable. Exhausted from the biggest rock climb of our lives and hungry for sleep on a moonless night, the thrill and adrenalin faded into the dull tunnel vision of our headlamps and the desire to get down.

After dozens of rappels we reached what we hoped was the relative security of a snow gully. Instead we found ice. I rappelled first. Conrad, sans crampons, but armed with a single crag hammer and makeshift pick we'd scavenged off a trekking pole, proceeded to downclimb—or rather, he down campused, lowering himself as if on a rope ladder, his sneakers pedaling in place while I belayed nervously from a bergshrund. The descent continued like this and would have been entertaining but for the seriousness. Whereas we had those truck stops

Just another 3,500 feet to the summit.

PETER CROFT

above, now his rappel anchors were usually just
his butt cheeks planted on a ledge while my belay
anchors were me wedging myself like a chuckwalla
in a crevasse.

We finally descended to low-angle terrain as the
half moon popped over the skyline, etching a saber-
tooth panorama of spires. The descent was every bit
as intense as the climb, and all the way down we

plumbed the unknowns between the superpow-
ers of inspiration and the kryptonite of fear. There
also was the dumb luck to be tied in with a Viking
like Conrad. Such an exploration always takes the
measure of the person on the other end of the rope.
There is no one word or thing that encapsulates
a true adventure better than the people we meet
there who become friends for life.

Bivi or Descend

Once we push into the dawn to dusk climbs (or longer), it is unlikely we will accomplish every climb in a day. Everything from jammed ropes to freak showers can maroon us high on the cliffside. That means occasionally we must decide whether to bail off a climb or suffer an unplanned bivi. If we are flush with down jackets, snacks, and fire-making materials, and the descent is nasty and harrowing, the decision is easy—we have a pleasant campout. On the other hand if we've gone extra light and a bivi would be a battle against hypothermia, it's probably best to push on—even if we're moving to simply stay warm.

If we decide to spend the night, we do whatever possible to find some shelter—beneath or in the lee of boulders, trees, or bushes. At this point a tiny lighter or pack of matches can be the difference between a teeth-chattering suffer-fest and a smoky and smiling night laughing over stupid jokes. Assuming we're still pals at this point, spooning is also a valuable survival tool. (Depending on our respective machismo, we may need to be sworn to silence.)

If we descend in darkness we need to slow down and take extra care. The time to rush is over. We are not naturally nocturnal. Even with headlamps we need to take the time to avoid pitfalls that could send us off a cliff, or over a root or small rock that sprains or snaps an ankle. Once it's gone dark, it can't get any darker. That burst of adrenaline to avoid a bivi now needs to be suppressed. Believe it: This is the most common time for fatal mistakes. If rappels are in order, we back up anything questionable. In poor light it is nearly impossible to properly check all slings and rap anchors. But we must try.

As long as we make logical decisions, we usually can get through these memorable moments with another good story to tell. This is not about getting to the bar on time—it's about getting back to friends and family every Thanksgiving and Christmas. Sadly, not everyone does, and the vast majority are lost to human error. It is impossible to mention even a hundredth of the things that can go wrong. But every expert agrees that extreme vigilance is our best safeguard.

CHAPTER 44

High Sierra Link-Ups

Peter Croft

Alpine rock climbing lies at the outer edge of traditional rock climbing, right on the cusp of chop-and-stomp mountaineering. It is an arena often claimed by both the chalk-dusted crag rat and the thick-waisted snow plodder. Here lies the most varied rock climbing voyage one can take. Long approaches, alpine starts, and unpredictable weather help fashion the setting. Out here the actual stone found on a single peak can be as changeable as the skies, with the flawless granite of the buffed wall morphing into the frost-fractured summit ridge and finally the sluiced kitty litter found in the descent gully. With so many variables, everyone's skills get stretched. Elegance might be achieved, but groveling will definitely be involved.

I had dabbled in the alpine game but mostly felt time spent on the roadside vertical was superior to huffing huge pack loads hour upon hour only to wait for good weather. My perspective began to change when Yosemite locals hinted at what lay in store just outside the Valley—in the other 95 percent of the Sierra Nevada. Longtime guide Randy Grandstaff told me about a seventy-pitch link-up/traverse in the Palisades. That got my attention. Stories of even bigger traverses, according to Tuolomne aces Vern Clevenger and Claude Fiddler, swept me to soaring, exposed sawtooths no longer measured in feet, but in miles.

GALEN ROWELL

Most of the big enchainments were, by necessity, of a lower order of difficulty. With many thousands of feet of climbing ahead, the idea of projecting or even getting pumped on a given section was ridiculous. By the very nature of our planet, such mega traverses will always remain the longest rock routes possible. Whacky as it sounds I became hell-bent on finding a climb so long I would be stretched to a point where one more step was impossible.

Following countless predawn to post-dusk link-ups in Yosemite, the Bugaboos and elsewhere, mega link-ups felt like the next level. The ultimate aesthetic of these routes is to follow the skyline, reveling in the summit experience not from a single point, but for miles. That's the idea, anyway, though it rarely works out exactly like that.

For several years I ticked off the classics, content to experience the masterpieces. I marveled especially at Claude and Vern's vision of traversing the Minarets, a crooked row of black fangs gnashing at the sky. Because these ridges are so long, offering shifting panoramas into neighboring horizons, they inevitably lead to other possibilities.

The 7-mile-long Evolution Traverse is the finest I've done (so far), the Mother of All Ridge Traverses. Not the Granddaddy—that would likely be the slightly longer, scrappier, and surlier Palisades Traverse. The Evolution, however, is the hot Mama:

Groveling

Of all the skills involved in long climbs, groveling is the least appreciated. It is usually a messy mix of scrambling, wriggling, and skidding. Sometimes it is about knowing how to wipe out correctly—at other times, to use momentum and high-speed boulder hopping to avoid the crash. Often the loose gully we are following is preceded by or ends near impenetrable bushwhacking, where progress is possible only through masochistic gymnastics. It is an arena where brilliant climbers are often brought to tears, the contrast with their earlier grace on the stone too much to bear.

The problem for typical rock climbers is that most of the thrashing usually occurs after finishing a long strenuous route, a time when desire and focus pans to the fleshpots of civilization. Cooked from the effort on high, it is a nasty surprise to suffer a shin-scraping, face-scratching bushwhack and endless talus. But, like anything else it gets easier with experience. Many train for these adventures through crag climbing and mileage on groomed trails; the best preparation is cross-country travel. Scrambling up and down easy peaks provides the real-life experience that teaches us how to deal with ragged terrain.

ALEXANDRE BUISSE

Working down the talus blocks.

ANDREW BURR

Though mundane and necessarily clumsy compared to technical climbing, groveling is a studied practice with a fair amount to learn. Loose rock and talus figure prominently and we must recognize which kind of talus is loose and which is likely solid. We often experiment, zigzagging to find the best or only route through. Usually this line will follow the larger blocks, though if the smaller ones are solid, this often provides easier passage.

Rock texture and friction determines how solid the slope is, so similar-looking slopes can differ with different rock types. Grow aware of which footholds or boulders are likely to be loose and always be ready to react if something shifts suddenly or gives way. Usually we move with our legs slightly bent to quickly react when a block shifts.

No matter if the groveling involves bushwhacking, gully scrambling, or talus hopping, whatever load we carry must be packed properly. The rope, if not stowed away, needs to be tightly coiled with no chance of it coming undone at inopportune moments. No slings, daisies, etc. should hang down off our harnesses.

Always look ahead to avoid routefinding mistakes. We are not on a trail and need to be constantly on the lookout to spot crucial landmarks and clearings distant and close by. It is easy to put our heads down and march, but we need to stay watchful. If the nastiness is likely to occur on a descent, we should scope out possible lines from up on the climb, spying out the best path.

all clean lines and primo composition, a curving arm of granite cradling a lake and meadow-filled basin.

My first trip in was again with legendary Galen Rowell, pro photog and endurance freak. At base camp Galen couldn't hold back and charged off to find a new route on one of the peaks while I, eyeing the enormous skyline, lounged by the lake, filled up on snacks, and let myself acclimatize to the thinner air. I knew I'd need this break-in time. It was one thing to bomb up and down a single mountain, where a tiny fraction of the time is spent at the highest elevation; but I knew we'd be spending most of the next day above 13,000 feet.

The next morning we rose way before daylight and aimed for an inky black cutout of night sky. Right away Galen insisted we miss out the first peak as it didn't have a name. My argument to start at the beginning and run the whole ridge fell on deaf ears, so we missed out on the first mile—a mile that would haunt me, a big "but" I would have to qualify for future small-talking about this Grand

Acclimatizing

Apart from foul weather, insufficient, poor acclimatization is usually the main reason people fail on mountain routes. Climbers blame failures on exhaustion but time and again the real culprit is a failure to take the time to acclimatize. Most people live in cities at low elevations, so the bulk of those approaching higher peaks need time for their bodies to adjust.

Arriving as early as possible and sleeping at a high trailhead or ski town can be a helpful first step. A better step is to show up a day earlier and spend a couple of nights (and the extra day) hanging out with only light exercise.

Given that altitude is such a large factor, keep other stresses to a minimum. Staying up late and partying hard because we're finally off work is a poor aid to acclimatizing. So are radical changes in diet. Going from balanced meals at home to handfuls of gorp all day sounds tasty but spells a stomachache for many. The communal gorp bags are not without risk. People seldom wash their hands properly after pit stops—so those stinky fingers are sifting through your snacks. Not good.

It is tempting to camp close to the peak, but if a lot of elevation gain is involved we're far better off sleeping lower down. "Climb high and sleep low" is the maxim to follow. Far better to get a good night's sleep than to risk headaches and nausea in order to shorten the approach in the morning.

Especially at altitude it is vital that we drink plenty of water. In longer endurance activities, hydration becomes even more important. Start the climb as well hydrated as possible. That means tanking up in the days leading up to the climb, and taking lots of sips all day long—far better than holding off till the halfway ledge or the top. Hydration packs are far handier than water bottles in a pack. Both climbers often have a small hydration system so both can drink whenever they want, with both sharing the load.

Big days out are exhausting, and sometimes it is impossible to haul enough water. Here, we are particularly prone to cramps. High-quality sports drinks like Cytomax contain electrolytes and are

Course. However, the day was brilliant and after the first few peaks I knew we had struck Sierra gold. The best rock and finest climbing was on the very crest, virtually the entire time, and we jammed, hand-traversed, and straddled this striking knife-edge for miles. As the spine of bedrock swerved south and then west, new gems of turquoise lakes came into view.

Just over halfway Galen, his hands rubbed raw from the coarse granite, opted out and headed for camp. I damned his persistence the day before, climbing some forgettable route just prior to this whale of an adventure—but such restless energy was also what I admired about him. Almost 20 years older and he still couldn't resist the call. I continued on in a daze, loving the solitude but wishing I could share it.

On the last few peaks I needed to ration the water as well as my strength. On ridge crests, all water drains away so there was no opportunity to get more. To conserve strength I had to avoid any routefinding errors, any loose talus, and any clumsiness. As one becomes increasingly dehydrated

Water: Sometimes at altitude, you have to make it.

AMY NESS

excellent endurance aids. I initially thought such supplements were bogus but soon changed my mind when I tested them out on big climbing days. The cheaper versions are little more than sugar water though and accomplish little. Some taste like ass; others are indistinguishable from powdered fruit juice, and these we are far more likely to drink—and thus stay better hydrated.

coordination short-circuits and the smooth gliding athlete turns into a lurching, faltering robot with crossed wires. With my thirst gone bone deep, I summited the last mountain with the grace of Frankenstein. But I'd heard the violin.

Late in the day I could finally let my guard down and stumble onto a meadow-lined trail leading back to camp. As the dream deepened my buzz hitched on that skirted mountain.

I would be back.

Perseverance

GREG EPPERSON

The longer an activity stretches on and the more variables involved, the greater our success might hinge on the will to gut it out. It might rarely come to this—but in the trad world it eventually will, sure as day follows night. In bouldering and sport climbing, a route is a kind of pop quiz—we either pass or we fail. It may take numerous, exhaustive tries, but if the fitness and talent is there, we will likely succeed. In trad climbing the countless factors that can, by themselves, complicate the process may in concert turn a casual romp into flat out chaos. On the tenth pitch of an eleven-pitch route, a gust whips a loop of rope around a distant flake, jamming it tight. While we nervously try to swing over and free the line we realize, as the first raindrops fall, that the wind was the harbinger of a thundershower. By the time we unjam the cord and regain the belay, it's pounding rain. We wriggle into our rain parka but we've forgotten the headlamps and now it's dark—and the next pitch is the crux. You get the picture.

For many—understandably so—the rewards of mega trad are not worth the risk nor the effort. Many say, "No way!" to the epic, while some among us say, "Bring it on!" Bottom line is, unless we love the weird and whacky of the whole adventure, the fullness of the trad experience is probably for the other guy. To thrive up on the steep, we need to be enamored of the walls and the struggles. Otherwise the utter failures we all experience will become a permanent condition, rather than a call to action. As we hose off the mud, yank out the thorns, and exhaust our stores of tape and Band-Aids, we can't wait to get back at it as we reckon how things might play out next time.

There are many times when the outcome has little to do with ability, when our strength and technique won't be enough. The earth and the sky have plenty to send us packing. But while the elements change their mood, so long as our intent stays the course, good things can happen even as our minds are blown. Where many flail and retreat, a few learn to thrive, not by controlling the uncontrollable, but by learning to surf, so to speak, the riptides and tsunamis of the steep. This is where protocols and techniques are of little value.

This is the threshold of the great trad milieu.

CHAPTER 45

Flint Hard and Flawless

John Long

Anyone reading this manual probably has a taste for the fantastic history of trad climbing. It is from these stories that we learn where we came from and maybe pick up a little lightning in the bargain. One of the greatest stories of them all concerns the first "ascent" of the Lost Arrow Spire. While hardly instructive to the 21st-century climber, it tells us in dramatic terms how avid and flat-out crazy our forefathers were about bagging their summits. We applaud their courage—and

Lost Arrow Spire is the freestanding pinnacle on the right-hand wall flanking Yosemite Falls, second-highest waterfall in the world.

ED BANNISTER

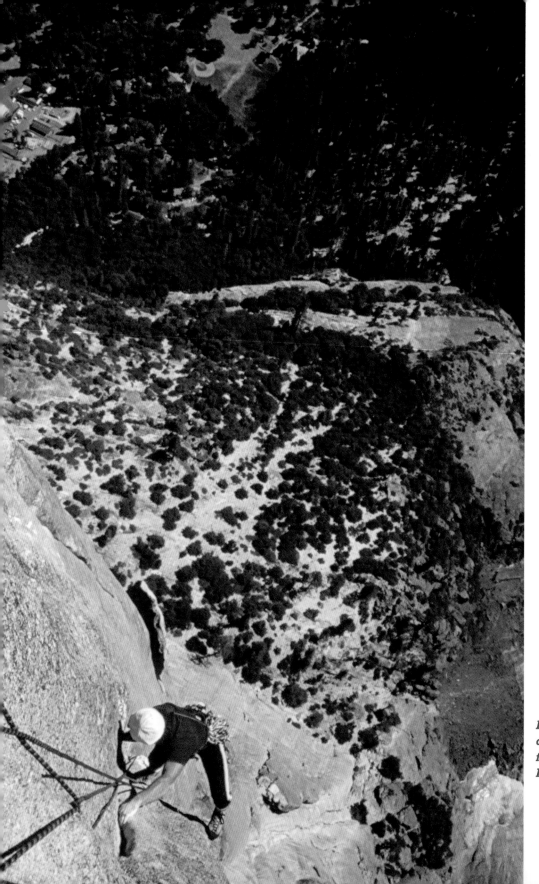

Bob Gaines during an early free ascent on Lost Arrow Tip.

forget their methods. You be the judge, but I don't know a single modern trad climber who would consider repeating what follows.

For those who don't know, the Lost Arrow Spire is a 250-foot bullet of tangerine granite sprouting half a mile up the steep north in Yosemite Valley. It is one of the most classic and novel summits in American climbing. Bold, freestanding. Mere yards to the left plummets Yosemite Falls, topped only by Angel Falls in its vertical plunge. Wind whipped, sun blasted, yet often misty, the Lost Arrow Spire at once terrified and enchanted Yosemite's first climbers, a bold group out to bag the most exhilarating summit: And to be sure, Lost Arrow Spire seemed the summit to bag. But how?

The Spire posed a logistical quandary for the raw techniques of 1935, when people first started looking at the formation and wondering how to climb it. While the Spire's summit and the North Rim roughly coincide, they are separated by a 100-by 200-foot cleft of mountain air. Someone could rappel into the notch between the Spire and the main wall, but then what? The Spire's inside wall looked both dead blank and fearsomely overhung. They couldn't just stitch the Spire with countless bolts. When glassed from below the Spire's face admitted only the faintest crack, and this vanished some 50 feet shy of the top. And this was 1935, when the requisite thin pitons were soft iron and bent like taffy when slugged into the rock.

And what about the ghastly exposure, hundreds and thousands of feet of air below their feet? Alternatives were discussed. The Spire's girth is slim, but an 80-foot lasso seemed preposterous, a parachute landing too dicey, a catapult ridiculous, a cantilevered telephone pole all the more absurd.

Finally, in August 1947 Yosemite big wall pioneer John Salathe managed to nail to within 50 feet of the summit before blank rock turned him away. The very next weekend, Anton Nelson sneaked up to the North Rim with Jack Arnold, Fritz Lippman, and Robin Hanson. Hanson's forte wasn't climbing, but baseball, and Nelson figured that if Hanson could hurl a line over the Spire's rounded summit, a lunatic could ascend that line to the top. Again—and get this—the idea was that Hanson would chuck from the rim's edge, winging a tethered weight the 80 or so feet out and over the Spire. The line would then snake down the Spire's exposed face—they hoped. Climbers in the notch could edge out over the void, climb up to Salathe's high point, nab the free line, and ascend it to the summit.

The plan sounded basic, but countless attempts saw the line slide off the domed summit and whizz through the defile. The four climbers were not laughing at the cord's furious retreat, or the smack of the weight to granite, 80 feet below. But Hanson kept at it. Finally, in late afternoon, he threw the perfect strike. Now weighted with marlin sinkers, the thin line slithered down to Salathe Ledge, just as planned.

Nelson and Arnold rappeled into the notch the next morning. Because the line didn't reach all the way down to the ledge, even with the notch, they had to aid climb up to the first ledge to get the end of the tossed line. Salathe had fashioned custom pitons from stout, Model T axle stock. Nelson and Arnold only had old soft iron pins, and they were making very little progress. Frustrated and embarrassed, Nelson and Arnold retreated up to the rim, leaving a line fixed from the first ledge. They still had another 30 feet to line's end on Salathe Ledge, the same reached by Salathe 3 weeks prior—during his solo reconnaissance.

The following day Nelson and Arnold quickly regained the first ledge, but after several miserable pitons, the crack pinched so that no amount of blasting could set their soft iron. They could all but touch Salathe Ledge, yet were stumped. Desperate, Nelson lassoed a tiny horn, then ordered the slender Arnold to hand-walk it 20 feet to the ledge and the pitched line, 40 hours after the successful toss. Stout lines were pulled 150 feet up the sheer wall, then 100 feet over the gap to anchors on the rim.

In Our Heads

All the way up the Tip we believed we were making the first free ascent and therefore deserved special dispensation from the world and everyone in it for feats of strength and glory. I even wrote a sprawling history of the entire Lost Arrow saga, for a leading British magazine, with color photographs of our ascent, captured from various dramatic angles, including a nice angle of myself cranking the unctuous mantle, and Bob dangling in midair about the breathtaking defile. Then I learned that my history was all wrong because Dave Schultz and friends had made the first free ascent a month or so before. I had to eat my words about our heroics on the "Flint hard and Flawless" tip but the fact is, I enjoyed the experience of believing we were making the first free ascent because I didn't know any better. It certainly felt like we were the first, and in retrospect I hardly cared.

Even though it wasn't an FFA, we had a great experience based on what we believed. Point being that our ideas profoundly affect our experience, good and otherwise. For example, many bouldering areas have been "discovered and developed" by successive generations knowing nothing of the Mohicans who enjoyed the place 10 or 30 years before. In many ways, the whole climbing experience is "in our heads."

Now, would they draw straws? No, for according to Nelson, "the stern code of the climber decrees that the lightest man shall lead doubtful pitches." Of course there was no such code or decree. This was just impromptu jive, invented to preclude the corn-fed Nelson from going first. These codes and decrees were news to Jack (who spent several years in a German POW camp during World War II, often fantasizing about the Arrow), now pacing, chain smoking, and stealing sad glances at the free rope, dangling in the breeze. The view below appeared equally sobering. Arnold frantically huffed three cigarettes, then according to one author, "placed his weight on the rope and began his lonely odyssey to the summit."

While the saga of the tossed cord is common knowledge, few realize the spire's top is not so much minuscule as it is rounded, with only the slightest crease to check a free line held in place only by weight on the business end. Imagine a kite string draped over a bowling ball and you've got it. And when Arnold began his ascent, he enjoyed not the handy ascenders of today. Rather, he used prusik knots—little slipknots pushed slowly and strenuously up the free line. This 150-foot prusik would provide him with ample time to mull his fate should the rope twang off the top and send him swinging, once and for all, roughly 60 feet straight into the north wall.

Amazingly, the rope didn't move, and at twilight, Jack Arnold became the first man to stand on the most radical summit of the day. After drilling an atomic-bomb-proof bolt anchor, Nelson prusiked up and the real fun began: a fearsome aerial traverse—a "Tyrolean"—that would become a hallmark of Yosemite climbing.

After long hours of rope exchanges, reanchoring, etc., a taut line spanned the 100-foot gap from tip to rim. Nelson checked his knots for the thousandth time, heaved a sigh, then in total darkness, he sent Jack Arnold across. Village lights twinkled a half mile below, but Jack's eyes were welded to the rim. The following year, over 5 grueling days, John Salathe, starting at the base of the wall, ascended the fearsome Lost Arrow Chimney and finished up on the "flint hard and flawless" Arrow Tip, which over the following decades became one of the most sought after summits in America.

Thirty-seven years after Arnold and Nelson first stood on the summit of the Lost Arrow Spire, Dwight Brooks (D.B.), Bob Gaines, and I were panting about the notch's shattered blocks, tortured by overhead sun, scrambling to find a decent anchor. It was Bob's idea for us to go up there and try to free climb the whole thing. No one to our knowledge had claimed an all-free ascent, and we were excited by the prospect of nabbing the FFA of such a spectacular summit. There are only a few climbs like the Lost Arrow anywhere on earth. We were all in top form and we wanted this one badly.

Brad Wilson hanging from slings on the super-exposed Salathe Ledge.

BEN HORTON

Courage

With our improved nutrition, training methods, space age gear and Xtreme mindset, we naturally think we have the kind of "minerals" never found in climbers of yore. This is to wildly underestimate our fellows, and to potentially climb ourselves into dire jams if we take the wrong action on these assumptions. For instance I know several climbers who were well aware that the Lost Arrow Chimney (a 1,000-foot dark gash leading to the notch and the Tip) was one of the Valley's notorious free climbs, first led free way back in the early 1960s. So they set off to free solo the route, believing anything completed so long ago was duck soup.

Both parties ended so very high in that ghastly flare, clinging desperately to crumbly rock, begging God's forgiveness if only He let them off alive. The routes were easier in years past for various reasons, but lack of courage was never one of them. For example, imagine rappelling off El Capitan in a Dulphersitz, as they did in the 1950s, where you weren't even attached to the rope. Or prusiking a free-hanging goldline, which stretched like a rubber band and took an hour per rope length. Or heading up a 5.10 flare with no protection over 4 inches. We rarely hear about people removing bolts from routes done 30 or even 40 years ago. It's always a matter of adding more to make an old route "safer."

Slab master Darrell Hensel, running the rope on 5.12 face climbing.

KEVIN POWELL

Dwight Brooks on poorly protected 5.11 before the final bolt ladder.

BOB GAINES

Dave Schultz on the exciting 5.12 finish to Lost Arrow Tip.

WALTER FLINT

We'd hiked to the rim the previous afternoon and rose at dawn, yet a Slavic team had somehow slipped in before us and the threesome were currently on the first lead, leaving us to pace around the notch in the heat. I could barely contain my desire to get out there and sink my teeth into the tip. I'd never been on it before; the climbing looked hard and the location, poised 2,000 feet off the ground, spectacular.

Half an hour later, Bob tiptoed out a brief ledge, his heels a half mile above the Valley floor, and worked up a short thin corner to a 5.10 wide crack and Salathe Ledge, distended like a ship's prow over a vertical sea of granite. Dwight and I followed; the wall dropped off like the edge of the world. Lashed tight to the anchors, we talked about how Salathe Ledge is where Jack Arnold prusiked the tossed cord. I looked up at the summit, 150 feet above, then 80 feet across thin air to the main wall, and then down to the Valley floor, two counties below, and knew Jack Arnold had a bucket of balls to have ever made it up that tossed line draped over the top of that spire.

Tradition

Traditions give meaning and resonance to our experience. But some traditions deserve the dustbin. No one is anxious to repeat the rope trick that first delivered Jack Arnold and Anton Nelson onto the Lost Arrow Tip. And note that for decades, an airy Tyrolean traverse—essentially a horizontal zipline—remained the method of choice to escape the Tip and regain the adjacent rim. Teams would rappel into the notch and climb the Tip while trailing the rope still attached to the big pine tree 60 feet across the defile. Once on top, they'd winch the rope tight as a kite string, then one by one, shimmy across the line, re-creating the classic Tyrolean traverse used to exciting effect by virtually every party since Salathea. They'd double the line for the last fellow across, then pull it through once he hit the pine.

Problem is that cranking a dynamic rope so very tight and buzzing hoards across is a sure way to trash a rope. A much easier and equally exciting escape was to pull the trail/rim line tight, attach one's ascenders, and rappel off the tip with another line, gently and slowly angling across the void, soft as church music, till you contacted the opposite wall and could ascend the fixed line up to the Jeffrey pine. People still enjoyed the air-ride across the defile, without hammering the rope. And this method was much quicker as well. Remember that completing a climb the traditional way is not always the best option. Always reserve the right to do things your own way. Standard methods, usually arrived at through trial and error, are generally sound. But on rare occasion we all practice the wrong thing till someone says, "Hey, wait a sec . . ."

Lost Arrow Tyrolean, a tradition for over 50 years in Yosemite Valley.

GREG EPPERSON

D.B. cast off and the blue rope hung free off the sheer wall. The only protection was fixed mank bashed into pin holes, but D.B. just clipped the faded slings and started madcap laybacking—hinging out, then back, then out again. The rope inched out. Down below, Memorial Day traffic honked along at a clogged but steady clip, each car with exclusive moves, yet all part of one continuous flow. Meanwhile D.B., one leg dangling, the other hooked above his head, was yanking on poor holds, sweat flying, his hands now crossed, neck craned, feet pawing on nothing. Still, he moved up as we screamed encouragement. Then he was pumping up a good crack and set up a hanging stance beneath the last lead: a ladder of bolts streaking up the flawless headwall. D.B. hung free from the anchor and his silhouette on the vertical plug was spectacular.

Soon we were cloistered around one bolt, hanging on the convex spire, that puts one not so much on, as out there like gnats on a flagpole. We felt every inch of the wall below. The air was dead, suffocating, but I wasn't budging till calm and settled. Plus the Slavs were still wrestling with the Tyrolean, and I somehow managed to free climb the 30-foot headwall. I wanted to gain a vacant summit.

Finally I nodded to Bob who said, "Get it done." Twenty feet passed moderately on sharp holds. I clipped an ancient bolt and several thin moves gained a thick, down-hanging flake where I could undercling out and survey the bulging crux. It's flint hard, but there's a flaw—a shallow, bottomless V slot, above which looks to loom a good lip. A body length of grim tip locks and I could just reach up and match hands on a greasy beach ball of a mantleshelf. I shuffled my feet up on unlikely smears. Above, the Spire angled off 20 feet to the top, but mantling over the bulge felt horrific.

"You've got it," Bob yelled up.

"The hell I do. Watch me!"

I cocked my elbow and started pressing out the mantle, my hand greasing off in the cruel heat, now high-stepping the beach ball as my foot started sliding so I slapped a hand up, hit a bucket, and frictioned up the last 15 feet to the rounded summit, 38 years after Jack Arnold. My whole body was running sweat, my clothes and even my boots soaked through. Later, while securing ropes to the rim, Bob said that the whole venture seemed like a hallucination: hiking up to the rim and scouting the striking granite bottle; the wild climbing and sci-fi-like summit.

"It ain't over yet," D.B. laughed, clipping into the taut line and zipping out over the defile.

KARL "BABA" BRALICH

CHAPTER 46

Bridalveil Falls
on Our Heads

Peter Croft

Not all epics occur on the cutting edge. Sometimes when you're cruising along monsters lunge out of deep cover to tear out a chunk or go for the jugular. All active climbers go through seasons where, through too much time on the stone, their eyes become a little jaded, the guard drops slightly, and they don't see it coming.

For roughly half a dozen years I was a guide in Yosemite, climbing on my days off as well as my days on. One day in early May I met a client and decided to climb a notorious but obscure route called Bridalveil East, one of Yosemite's initial upper-end 5.10 routes first climbed by Frank Sacherer, "the father of American free climbing." I can't remember whose idea this was so I've changed my partner's name—call him Dr. X—to protect his innocence. Of course it hardly matters whose brainwave it was. I should have asked around and gotten the beta. It might have helped.

Bridalveil East is of course close to Bridalveil Falls, a popular tourist attraction and picnic spot, memorialized in a billion postcards. Only later did I discover that the Miwok Indians knew the entire area was haunted by Pohono, The Evil One, who

Bridalveil Falls, 1897.

Vigilance

Experience can lead to complacency. We forget to give the rock and environs its due respect. This is especially true when approaching easy to moderate climbs that are easily within our grasp. Complacency carries with it a great risk. Old Man Gravity never sleeps. Nor do raging waterfalls.

Most of the potential hazards we face on world class climbs also exist on trade routes. Some, in fact, may involve greater risk. Easier climbing and classic status usually means far more climbers—and far more people dropping things. Carabiners, belay devices, rocks, etc. all fall just as fast and hit just as hard on trade routes as they do on hard ones. Extra traffic also means more polished stone. Often guidebook beta fails to show a climb's evolving status due to polishing, holds breaking, and vanishing fixed protection. Sometimes areas have horrific sandbags—and in our ignorant bliss we may be approaching the very worst.

The same awareness we bring to the harder climbs should be summoned on every climb we approach. Starting late and getting caught behind other parties is awkward and dangerous be the route 5.7 or 5.11. Failing to clean off the soles of our shoes before padding up an easy but run-out slab, say, is one of many ways to scamper into the danger zone. It's important to remember that most accidents happen on the easier terrain. Attention to technique, weather, and what's going on around us will never be wasted.

We might nod off here and there, but Old Man Gravity never sleeps.

ANDREW BURR

- Experience can lead to complacency, especially on climbs well within our grasp.

- Most accidents happen on moderate terrain—Old Man Gravity never sleeps.

- Attention to detail, the weather, and to what's happening around us is never wasted.

- Diligence, not strength or technical prowess, is what keeps us safe and sound.

inhabits the bridal veil of mist billowing off the falls. More to the point is the mercurial wind that lurks there.

So Dr. X and I were just heading up on a six-pitch 5.10c, as if numbers were all that mattered. Scurrying past the blast of spray, we quickly climbed past a short section of wet rock, gaining a series of dry ramps veering up left, away from the falls. Home free.

A couple pitches up, an unexpected gust hosed us down. It was spring so although the air was warm, the falls were essentially fresh snowmelt—icy cold. Luckily, the higher we ascended the angling ramps, the farther they took us from a threat that appeared from nowhere. We hurried on but another windblast, stronger than the first, swept the left-hand curtain of the falls onto our very heads, sousing our clothes with bone-numbing ice water.

Our pace slowed as the frequency and duration of the drenchings increased. In hindsight, we should have beat a retreat after the first dousing. Trouble was, the crack system we were following led directly back down into the cascade. We had climbed ourselves into a trap.

Higher, I huddled on a tiny stance, my clothes useless as wet salmon skin. This time I saw it coming, a dark wave that washed across the whole section of cliff that we were climbing. Through a brief lull I glimpsed the rope disappearing into solid water. Pulling as hard as I could produced no result. It was as if my line was stuck on the bottom, hitched off to a pine. The feeling drained out of my arms, then an ice cream headache started that quickly got worse till finally my head went numb. Looking down, I could see families picnicking on the boulders near the base, eating potato chips and asking for more ice in their lemonade, I'll bet.

I forced the rope into a directional higher up, inverted and pressed my feet against a small roof above me, cranking in opposition to hoist the Doctor—nothing. Had he drowned? I could feel the strength leaving me. Soon I wouldn't be able to help anyone or do anything. That's when a nightmare solution occurred to me—I could untie and solo out!

Knowing When to Retreat

We retreat when conditions dictate—when our partners get wiggy, when the weather craps out, when the rock gets chossy, etc. That's the theory, anyway. All too often, however, the logic of descending is battling one or more egos aching for the summit. At such times we often delude ourselves that those thunderheads will dissipate or that it's not nearly as late as it seems.

Only through dispassionate observation can we avoid needless epics. We establish a cutoff time for gaining a certain point—otherwise we bail. If the weather is forming into thunderclouds, we take heed. If our climbing partner seems nutty, we don't go climbing.

As the seconds dragged on the likelihood of his having drowned increased. The whole situation turned surreal. I had been in many tight spots before but I had never felt hunted till now. Pohono had stalked us from pitch one and now he meant to kill us.

I abandoned the idea of a solo escape, unable to make the jump from mountain guide to murderer. Then the tensioned rope slackened off and began to move. The ice water had abated for a moment and I could see X slowly picking his way up. I bellowed at him to leave the gear and just climb, but he stopped along the way to clean the pitch, using up a fair chunk of our brief reprieve.

When he arrived he explained how he had holed up beneath an overhang, using this meager shelter as a breathing space. That was why the rope wouldn't budge. I couldn't have yarded him up with a winch.

I cut out left away from our route and off into no man's land—anything to escape. Running the rope out, I emerged from an overhang onto a last slab, thankfully dry. Unable to even see my last pro, I stopped to make the mistake of chalking up—nothing but white glop. I wiped the paste off my hands

Climbing Near Water

In most climbing areas bodies of water, flowing or otherwise, are rarely an issue. But if we choose to climb in the vicinity of water we need to be aware of the potential risks.

Climbing on exposed coastlines, and even on lakes, can expose us to high seas. Sea cliff climbing in particular has been compared to a mix of mountaineering and roadside cragging. Sitting at a hanging belay above angry surf while our partner makes noises about retreating (when the only retreat is up) is a challenging place to be. Checking a marine forecast is always a good idea when starting at sea (or large lake) level.

Vital concerns are keeping the rope dry and the importance of not dropping anything. Items dropped above dry ground may or may not be destroyed but anything dropped into the water—it's just gone. Keeping the rope well stacked out of reach of the water is obviously important and so is safeguarding our cord while rapping down to start a pitch that begins just above the waves. For this we need to have the lower ends stacked in a pack or through a sling in such a way so they feed out as we descend. Rapping after finishing a route near water often presents opportunities to drop the rope in the drink. Penduluming off to one side and running one strand through a leaver-biner on a bolt or fixed pin allows pulling the cord and having the rope get stopped by the lower piece before entering the creek or lake. Then one more hard pull from the side and, with any luck, the rope neatly leaps to the side onto dry land.

Venturing onto routes in the proximity of waterfalls presents special hazards. On larger cliffs it is common for winds to be calm first thing in the morning. As the day heats up, the hot air rises and produces breezes that can become blustery by afternoon. On a hot day these winds are usually welcome. If we're near a waterfall, however, this can spell trouble. Inevitably these windswept cascades gravitate to the nearest climbers they can find. The East Buttress of El Cap in Yosemite is a classic example. Spied from the valley floor at breakfast time, it appears as though the nearby Horsetail Falls will simply be a pretty backdrop. But by mid-afternoon and halfway up, the waterfall is scoring a direct hit. It's always a good idea in these cases to ask around and also check out the routes the day before in morning and afternoon.

Seas can rise in a heartbeat and wash you away.

ANDREW BURR

and prepared for the last 50 feet to the top. We were as good as done. Out of a dead calm and a clear blue sky, a last whip of wind and waterfall made a mad lunge my way, soaking the friction slab and leaving me marooned on my little foothold. Nothing to do but wait for the rock to dry. That, and make another promise to God that I knew I'd never keep.

The Edge, one of the most exciting leads in Southern California.

KEVIN POWELL

CHAPTER 47

The Edge and Turbo Flange

John Long

Check the Webster's under *lunatic*: "A man whose actions are marked by extreme recklessness." That was Tobin Sorenson, a man whose exploits at Joshua Tree included following a difficult climb with a noose round his neck.

He did other vexers, but I think his ultimate moment of madness came on a route at Tahquitz, which for a decade was known simply as The Edge (this edge is formed by the left corner of the Open Book's 300-foot dihedral).

A route along this spectacular arête would yield some kind of milestone, or so thought veteran climber Mike Heath, who was first to climb up for a look. Mike discovered that if anything, the route was insane. After about 40 feet of 5.8, The Edge bulges and becomes doubly extreme, offering no place to stop and place a bolt for at least another 100 feet. This was verified by Paul Richardson, who inspected the entire arête on a 700-foot caving rope strung from the crag's southern shoulder. "Maybe it's climbable," said Richardson, "but it's lunacy on the lead." And since the ethic at Tahquitz discouraged placing protection on rappel, The Edge was immediately written off as a viable prospect.

Naturally, soon as Tobin heard about this, he was on it. There would be no inspection. Tobin was far too impatient to do anything but just go for it and see what happened. He was infamous for this tactic, which countless times led to colossal falls that should have killed him ten times over. How he stayed alive confounded us. Everyone knew his transcendental luck would someday run out. It had

to, and it did—but not on the day he started up The Edge.

After the 40 feet of 5.8, the arête bulged and Tobin found the rock unclimbable. Raw boldness would not help. Noting that the angle eased slightly 40 feet above, he moved left to Jensen's Jaunt (5.6), climbed 40 feet, and made a desperate traverse back right to The Edge. Trembling on a 5.10 foothold, he made an astonishing bolt placement and straight off told belayer Eric Ericksson, "Hold on, I'm going for it!"

"Going for what?" begged Ericksson. The Edge was as bald as a vase, the only visible feature a wee shelf roughly 90 feet above. Regardless, Tobin cast off, clawing up the very edge of the right-angled arête, one hand slapping around right, his feet scatting smears on the left side.

According to Ericksson, Tobin was absolutely maxed, out of control. He looked to hinge off at every move. Upwards of 45 feet out he started sliding down, and as the story's told, only checked this by paddling his feet like a duck before flight. Finally, gaining the merest whisker of a hold, he paused, but could not let go. Looking at an astronomical fall, he started sobbing. Ericksson said he felt like throwing up from the stress and fear and anguish. Somehow, Tobin began drilling, dropping the gear after every hammer blow to frantically reclasp The Edge and reset his quaking boots.

After an hour, the hole was almost deep enough. Then the bit broke and Tobin began pitiful wailing. Finally he lost it altogether and screamed to Ericksson that he was going to go for the shelf above (50 feet of 5.10), or jump. Ericksson begged him to

Josh Higgins deep in the business of The Edge, Tahquitz Rock.

BEN HORTON

Philosophy of Risk

We might read 1,000 illuminating quotes about risk, how you have to lose sight of the shore to ever find new oceans, cha cha cha. The entire game is really about discovering potential, and that to discover just how far we might go, we have to risk going too far. The sticking point is generally our fear of failure. To this the great Paul Tillich once said, in so many words, that if we risk and fail we can be forgiven. But should we never risk and never fail, we end up a failure in our whole being. This is true because risk answers a fundamental need we can meet through no other means. The poison is the medicine, but a drop too much and we're done for. Simply put, risk taking in trad climbing is a serious business. But everyone has their own Turbo Flange, and it's been looking for you all along. Who do you want to be? That is the question.

The belay.

KEVIN POWELL

do neither. Following another hour's grief, Tobin secured the bolt, and ran out the 50-foot section to the shelf, where he slapped in a two-bolt belay. Terrified, Ericksson refused to follow, unwilling to repeat the epic on the next pitch.

The following weekend, Tobin returned with Gib Lewis, regained the hanging stance and, sure enough, ran the rope all the way to the junction of The Edge and the classic Traitor Horn. The most exciting climb at Tahquitz was completed.

While The Edge produced a landmark route, Tobin broke virtually every standard trad climbing rule in establishing the first ascent. I have never even heard of a climber who would dream of casting off on a bald arête in the hopes of finding a drilling stance "up there," while from below, none was visible. Remember this is balancy and insecure climbing that one is unlikely to ever reverse, so if that stance had not appeared, what does Tobin do? Push on, till he finally runs out of rope and he's totally high and dry? I still find it hard to get my head around a climber throwing himself at such a route with no visible options per protection and on rock that was so clearly extreme.

The Edge and Turbo Flange   **337**

Darrell Hensel nearing the first hanging belay on The Edge.

KEVIN POWELL

It goes without saying that a sane and sober leader must have some notion about where his immediate moves will take him, what protection he might find in the process, and what the difficulties are apt to be along the way. Except on The Edge there was no visible indication that there was a way, or any protection, or that the climb was even possible with a toprope. Rather, Tobin apparently just put up a prayer and cast off, hoping for the best.

Anyhow, sticky boots have reduced the difficulties and a handful of thrill seekers had a memorable experience repeating The Edge. Yet, the entire edge had not been climbed; there was still that 35-foot lower bulge that Tobin had traversed around. Every local knew the completed climb would be the lead of a lifetime, but no one was willing to carve into their lifetime to accomplish this. As the last Tahquitz plums were getting plucked, there was talk of placing a bolt on rappel. When a young local presented that to me, I said he might as well spit on Tobin's grave.

Tobin had been shot down early. Despite his amazing accomplishments, the climbing world, which rarely looks back, had forgotten him. I felt I had to do this one for Tobin before someone botched the adventure with extra bolts. Granted, this was a calculated risk, but I wasn't going off half-cocked. My thinking ran like this:

I had repeated the original Edge route with Matt Cox and knew I could do that bit with some degree of safety. I was bouldering and climbing a lot just then and was in top form. The bottom part of the Flange was only 5.8, leading to the bolt, and the remaining unclimbed section was only the next 30 to 35 feet, at which point the Turbo Flange melded into Tobin's original Edge. We replaced the protection bolt with a new one, there was nothing whatsoever to hit on the wall below the bolt, and because the actual edge at that point was just a fraction steeper than the upper bit, I didn't figure to encounter climbing of another magnitude of difficulty. All told, I liked my chances, and figured the route was worth a solid try.

I had been climbing regularly for going on 15 years and knew there were very few routes that would be as iconic as the Turbo Flange, which made me want it even more. The point of all this is that there are times in a trad climber's career when extending yourself feels like the logical thing to do. The practice is not sustainable—climbing that far out of your comfort zone—but is something to seriously consider on rare occasions. Unfortunately there are no hard and fast ways of knowing when you are taking a justified risk and when you are climbing toward those Pearly Gates. That, simply put, is adventure. It's not for everyone.

I went up with my longtime partner, Dwight Brooks. When I clipped the bolt below the bulge, I promised myself one, and only one, all-out effort. The rock below was smooth—no bulges. At a solid 215 pounds, Dwight could hold any fall I should take. Like the upper section, you clasp the arête and paste your feet up at chin level, left hand pawing for anything to check the barndoor effect. My feet stuck nicely on the glassy wall but a hasty move meant hinging off into oblivion. The last move involved a teetering no-hands high step to clip Tobin's first bolt—not too severe, about 5.11a, but the slightest tremor and I would have gone for a 70-footer. Thank God I didn't rip.

Now I had to polish off the traditional Edge,

and I took off before I could reconsider. The climbing was much easier up here, lower end 5.10, but there are few routes that deliver such a visceral thrill as the Turbo Flange, with that first pitch featuring 155 feet of continuously difficult liebacking along an exposed arête, with only three bolts for protection. The second pitch was every bit as exciting. From the sling belay, you continue up the edge to an obvious dark, lower-angle spot. Tobin's original Edge goes left at this spot, while Turbo Flange continues straight up. The only protection are dubious Stoppers in a shallow gash by the dish, off of which you crank a mambo run-out on solid 5.11 terrain. As master face climber Darrell Hensel wrote, "If the gear pulls, it's one f'ing hell of a monster ride right onto the belay. Hence, I personally think the second of Turbo Flange is a scarier proposition than the first."

I'll remember that climb always, but I've never gone back. The Turbo Flange and I were "one and done." I hope Tobin would have been proud of us.

Whatever the route, it's always one hold at a time.

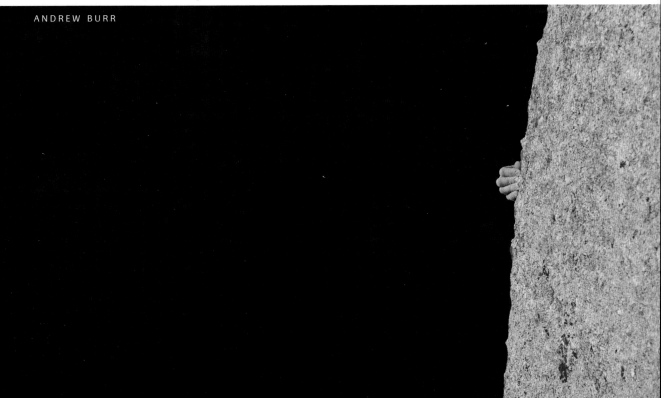

*Steep crack climbing
on The Fox, Red Rocks.*

MATT KUEHL

CHAPTER 48

Mount Wilson, and the Epic in My Mind

John Long

B ack before the urban sprawl reached the fringe of Red Rock Canyon, the 10-mile drive out from Las Vegas followed an arrow-straight, two-lane road cutting through barren, wide-open plains. Richard Harrison and I made that drive many

times, and as the gray, white, and red rocks crouching on the western horizon slowly swelled to giants, our eyes were always drawn toward the hulking Northeast Face of Mount Wilson, shouldering 7,068 feet into the sky. Much more a mountain than a rock face, Wilson had a standalone, sphinx-like majesty. I couldn't look on the face of that

The 3,500-foot-long North Face of Mount Wilson towers in the background.

JOHN HEGYES

giant and not consider its great age, and wonder how many eons had it brooded over the lonely sands spread out below. Blazing in summer, frosted in winter, Old Man Wilson had his experiences, but he kept them to himself. Aside from a mixed route along the left hairline, as it were, of the central wall (established 8 years before by Red Rocks pioneers Joe Herbst and Larry Hamilton, and never repeated to our knowledge), the Old Man was a mystery. Richard Harrison, bold and tireless pioneer of Red Rock classics, was caught on the summit in a sudden snowstorm after he and I made the second ascent of Jubilant Song, one of the first long free climbs at this seminal American crag.

One evening in Randy Grandstaff's ghetto hacienda just south of the gaudy Vegas strip, Richard and I decided to finally go up and see what the Old Man had to say for himself. Early the next morning we tossed together a small rack of nuts and a few thin pins, three bolts (shorty, ¼-inch Rawls, known as "coffin nails," nearly worthless in soft Red Rock sandstone, but all we had and better than nothing) and one rope, a natty, 150-foot, 9mm haul line, our last functional cord after 4 months in the Valley. We stuffed two quart water bottles and a few candy bars into a daypack, push started my VW van, and motored for the Red Rocks.

A rutted old wagon road, now closed, ran close to the mouth of the canyon. Ten minutes along a dry streambed and we veered left up a brushy slope toward the 65-degree lower wall, a chossy 1,500-foot-long washboard bristling with trees and shrubs. After an hour's easy soloing, we roped up for a 5.9 corner that deposited us on a big flat ledge 50 feet deep and running across the entire face, with a colossal pine tree that cast a shadow like a thundercloud. We kicked back, smoked a few Camels, and studied the 200-foot, high-angled slab sweeping skyward—the start of the upper wall. We needed to get into a big, U-shaped bowl just above the slab, where we hoped to follow crack systems climbing up and left. With only three bolts, I knew straight

off that we'd never tick this lower slab, which from below looked casual enough but up close looked bald and hard.

Since climbing Wilson was my idea, I started begging Richard's pardon for us having to go down. He said that since we were already there, and had the three bolts, there was no harm in going up to "Have a look." Then he tied in and ran the rope nearly 100 feet on rickety warts and desperate carbuncles before sinking a single bolt. Twenty feet higher, he found a foot-long crack and banged home a baby angle, then sunk the second bolt and brought me up. The U-shaped bowl was still quite a ways above us, but I did have the one bolt left, and since we were already there, I decided to climb up a ways and "Have a look." I had used this look-see strategy reaching back to my first time up Valhalla, at Suicide.

The wall above steepened and I quickly found myself on sketchy terrain, and drove our last coffin nail. The rock above was smooth as a bottle and the bottom of the bowl hadn't gotten a hell of a lot closer.

The recon was over and we now had to honestly appraise what the hell we were getting ourselves into here. I could climb back to the belay and we could rap off on a single line. We'd have to leave the rope and down-solo that 5.9 corner below, a stunt I wasn't particularly high on but figured we could do if we had to. But once I cast off from here, retreat was impossible with one rope, and the only way off would be up. From the ground, a continuous crack system looked to form the left margin of the bowl, running all the way to the summit. But clinging to that slab, we couldn't see any of it. We decided to throw the dice.

It's impossible to know what is involved in making such a decision, which on the face of it seems irrational, even reckless. If the situation does seem that way you simply must go down. But it didn't feel that way up on Mount Wilson, not at that moment, and I'm rather sure we weren't delusional

Belay stance at Cloud Tower, Red Rocks.

MATT KUEHL

or trying to fool ourselves into bagging another big FA. We'd both been climbing nearly continuously for a decade, much of it together, and in the whole swirling Gestalt of the thing we believed that somehow, between us, we could push on and figure something out, that we weren't climbing ourselves into oblivion. Maybe it was fortune questioning how much commitment we could muster, what

magnitude of adventure we could mentally handle. We'd put in a lot of mileage on the rock leading to that moment, and the decision to press on seemed right. Either way, most trad climbers who stick with the game long enough will face their own version of this decision. Some have decided wrong and are no longer with us. We have every reason to want a protocol, some criteria to help us decide correctly.

But once you reach this level and encounter such challenges, for better or worse, you're entirely on your own.

Like most first ascents on open faces, route-finding was crucial. We'd basically free soloed from the start, but I couldn't go running the rope here without extreme diligence because that coffin nail, nor yet the belay anchor, could sustain a king-size whipper. So I juked around trying various lines and downclimbing back to the bolt before discovering an unlikely traversing line along a pliable black scab, followed by easier but run-out dog-paddling to a big ledge at the bottom of the bowl. We were all-in now, and the following hours were some of the

No Exit

Nowadays, 70- and 80-meter ropes have almost eliminated the need to take two lines to effect an escape off a big trad climb. But not always. Mount Wilson was such a case that when doubled for a rappel rope, an 80-meter line would still have left us stranded. There are other common modern scenarios where a long single rope will leave you high and dry. Speed climbers often only take one rope. Same for alpine climbing. Going up on a mega route with just the one line, with no possible retreat, is as committed as you can get. Most experienced trad climbers face this challenge on occasion, but few make it a habit. It is a "bold" practice when all goes well, and downright "reckless" when the tables turn. Either way, and for better or worse, one or two ropes is a decision we face on most every mega route, and any decision made will usually involve a trade-off.

The biggest trade-off is likely the time-consuming hassles of managing a second cord, versus the unencumbered speed of going with the one rope. One thing is for sure—if you cannot get off a climb with one rope, and you go with one rope anyway, you better feel the odds are overwhelming in your favor of completing the routes as planned. Even if you make it unscathed, this is a dangerous practice.

Keeping two full-length ropes sorted is the climbing equivalent of herding cats.

LARRY COATS

Heather Hayes nears the belay on Moe Route (5.11a), Buckhorn Wash, San Rafael Swell, Utah.

LARRY COATS

most exciting Richard and I ever experienced on a rock climb—not for what we found, but for what we might find. Or not find.

We worked up and left, following a fold inside the bowl. The higher we climbed, the less I liked the looks of the off-size roof crack jutting into space at the end of the fold. I cringed to think of punching out that thing with only our one big hex, though it looked as though one of us would soon have to try. Following a suave lieback and stemming pitch,

Richard started bridging up toward the overhang and to our vast relief, found a crack that skirted around left. Then he vanished from view, a trend that continued on the many pitches that followed.

Anxiety runs high on a big first ascent, especially when retreat is physically impossible, and especially so here, where the leader would typically move up 20 or 30 feet and disappear round a corner. When you can't see much of where you're going, if what you're up against can only be

*Larry Coats rappels
from the Crying
Dinosaur, Superstition
Mountains, Arizona.*

LARRY COATS

imagined, it's a sure bet that in time, your mind will start seeing vultures circling overhead. Lucky for us the cracks kept connecting, though we understood that the higher we climbed, so rose the odds that somewhere, perhaps soon, the crack would blank out or pinch to nothing or run into a holdless roof, leaving us high and dry. The only diversion was to jump out on the lead and get lost in the function, leaving the belayer to count the vultures.

The massive outback tracks of the Red Rocks are a miraculous, visceral place, especially in late afternoon, when long shadows slither into canyons and up the great walls. An eerie solitude exerts itself, and a penetrating silence that reaches back to the birth of Old Man Wilson. And for the belayer perched high on a rock face, as the shadows play over him and his partner mounts out of sight, it is sure he will come to experience what it means to be alone. It can condense the mind wonderfully, or shrivel a person up, or do both in turn. Such are the mighty Red Rocks I will always remember with awe and gratitude.

We climbed for hours, on everything from hand cracks to flares, then suddenly the wall leaned back

New Routes: Follow the Features

The basic protocol for new routes was established years ago when climbers saw a formation, often an impressive-shaped summit, or maybe a spire, and wanted to climb it. Over the decades as equipment and climbers improved, and new route options became fewer, focus shifted to climbing great and salient features, usually soaring corners and chimney or crack systems that described a natural "line" up the cliffside. Once a majority of these lines had been climbed, the folks started looking for anything that was new, from linking discontinuous crack systems to dikes, intrusions, and lines of face holds.

If there's anything to remember from this progression, it's that blank rock, even slabs, requires bolting and routefinding not generally encountered on crack systems. So if you're in a wilderness area and ever want to get up something, the wise choice is to stick with the prominent lines. Even a mere 200 feet of blank face can, as we have seen with Mount Wilson, throw a monkey wrench into the works.

Shingo Ohkawa drilling on a new route, Little Cottonwood Canyon, Utah.

ANDREW BURR

Mount Wilson, ancient sentinel, rising in solitude.

JOHN HEGYES

and a little scrambling found a cairn on the summit. The panoramic view was spectacular, as was our relief that we didn't get marooned on the wall. But the fun was just beginning.

The cairn indicated that ambitious hikers had worked out a descent route somewhere on the Byzantine backside of the mountain, but even if we could have found it we'd have ended up miles from my van. So we scrambled down the right shoulder and dove into the most promising-looking gully, and 10 minutes later were performing the first of many half-rope-length rappels off saplings and horns. This went on for ages, and the farther we descended, the steeper it got. Nearing the bottom, out of water and food and almost out of gear, the shadows overtook us.

The second to last rap was partially free hanging and ended on a small ramp. Our entire rack, placed as anchors, lay on the gully above us—except for one last knifeblade. We scratched around and managed to slug the blade home in a thin

crack where the ramp met the main wall. The rising ring told us the pin was bomber—for a blade. Then we chucked the doubled rope into space and peered over. The ends looked to reach the ground, and fortunately they did, with a few feet to spare. We stumbled out to the dry streambed and it was pitch dark by the time we gained the van. And darkness in those canyons is true darkness.

High above, Mount Wilson stood out from the night sky like a giant black sentry. The route we climbed, though hazardous down low, was not nearly the climb I kept imagining in my mind, the one, thank God, we never found. Only Old Man Wilson can say why the cracks never ran out or got impossibly hard, and the Old Man never said. Instead, he took all of our gear, water, food, and for committing our lives to him for a blustery fall day, he gave us an experience to remember. When I look at the guidebook now and see "Woodrow, Grade IV, 5.10b," it sounds almost casual.

CHAPTER 49

El Cap and Half Dome in a Day

Peter Croft

A few hundred yards from the basalt bluff where I started climbing, I found a geological anomaly: a dark gray and white granite globe, weighing perhaps a hundred pounds, nestled amidst a jumbled black scree field. Even then the magnetic mythology of Yosemite granite compelled me to act rashly, and I spent hours stumbling and wrestling the precious piebald stone to the base of my practice bluff.

To the outsider it must seem odd that meadows, trees, and magical rocks, fitted into a mile-wide ditch with a river running through it, could focus the energies of feral boys and girls and charm them into the Valley and onto dangerous ascents. From the inside, of course, the long drive down from a cold Canada was a crusade. When we'd stop in Manteca for gas and Doritos, we all accepted the shimmering heat as coming from the center of the universe.

The idea of link-ups, or "enchainments," was not entirely new, but in my case was mostly limited to solo adventures on the smaller walls like Sentinel, the Cathedrals, North Dome, and so forth, the challenge being how many of these formations I could tuck into a day. But year after year as I topped out on the various points along the rim, it became impossible to ignore the bald-faced enormities of El Cap and Half Dome.

I clearly remember that early summer's day when I met John Bachar. Fresh out of the Canadian winter and stale from the 24 hours of beelining it to Yosemite, my friends and I postponed setting up camp and instead stopped at the first crag we came to: Reed's Pinnacle.

I'd come there single minded. For 2 years I'd obsessed over the idea of linking El Cap and Half Dome. Friends considered me deranged. What I needed was the perfect partner—namely John—but the awe he inspired held me back. Too shy to approach him, I needed some lucky confluence of events to throw us together. I needed a miracle. As it happened, I was digging for a chalk bag and shoes when John's black Toyota 4Runner swept into the turnout.

John jumped onto the pavement and my head dropped deferentially—I couldn't help it. Here was climbing royalty. He strode up and asked if I wanted to go soloing. I stammered "Y-y-y-yes."

In a minute we were scrambling up through bay trees and boulders toward the base of the cliff. As soon as we were out of earshot of the others he fired the question: "You wanna do El Cap and Half Dome?" At that point the walls could have fallen to the Valley floor and I wouldn't have heard a thing. It is the closest I've ever felt to the divine taking a personal interest in my grubby little world.

Today it's unfashionable to use terms like "hero." I'm not sure why. Maybe because when we draw in close, we see all the rust on the shield. Even Alexander wasn't Great all the time, it is true, and off the rock, John stumbled through the same mine fields we all face. But at the fusion of vision and action, John Bachar's best moments were revolutionary.

John's legend was richer and more exotic than sound bytes and anecdotes in magazines. His aura swelled with the frightening stories about his solos that got whispered in the dusty Camp 4 parking lot, or when someone pointed out Midnight Lightning,

El Cap and Half Dome.

CHRIS FALKENSTEIN

that world-famous nugget of overhanging rock, where Bachar had been running laps for seasons on end. We all can still picture John cranking one-arms for 100 feet to the summit of the absurdly tall Bachar ladder hanging off the lip of Cyclops Rock in Joshua Tree. Under the weight of all that lore I heeded his advice. "Two full rest days," he said sternly. I nodded but inwardly I flinched, sure I would fall out of shape. "Eat as much as you can," seemed to compound the problem, as now I'd be getting weak and fat.

When we stood in the dark at the base of El Cap, however, it was as he had foretold—the fuse had been lit! Pitches glided out of our headlamp beams and we tiptoed past snoring climbers, clutching gear against our legs so we wouldn't wake them.

It got light around Boot Flake, and I had just followed the King Swing when John asked about the tag line. A horrified look down confirmed the worst. I had no idea how—but the line was gone. John was unperturbed. "Okay, this'll still work. Don't worry about it." With a word or a look he could easily have twisted the knife, but he was already flashing upwards as he joked about people still eating breakfast at the cafeteria.

We were not swinging leads, rather leading in blocks. Each man would lead half a dozen pitches in a row before we'd switch over. As I swung into the lead a couple pitches above Camp 6, I jumped up and grabbed a man-size block. The block teetered on its perch and my world spun nightmarishly backwards.

Several things happened spontaneously. I released the block and leapt, aiming at a tiny landing while freaking about a chunk of granite busting into pieces and ricocheting down the upper dihedrals below. Just an hour earlier we had passed five climbers.

Mid-jump, I caught a blur of color in my peripheral vision. It was John, lunging forward to shove the block back into place, a Superman moment but in real life. Once again, he would hear

Overhanging Rock at Glacier Point, northeast of Half Dome and Cloud's Rest, Yosemite, 1897.

H. C. WHITE CO.

none of my apologies, muttering something like, "That flake was so ready to go."

We pressed on, up the perfect finger and hand cracks to the overhanging last pitch, which extends like a brow over the very bridge of The Nose. Coiling the rope on top, the spark we began with had ignited a firestorm of momentum and we blazed to the East Ledges and down the rappels, hitting the ground at a jog.

By the time we got to Half Dome, storm clouds were already mushrooming over the high country, but the dark threat merely added fuel to our fire. The route follows several thousand feet of corner cracks—the result of the dome scaling away like an exfoliating onion—and right off we started simul-climbing. There were lots of climbers on the face, and in three separate places I wasn't allowed past until John showed up. Without a trace of arrogance,

El Cap and Half Dome in a Day   **351**

Enchainments

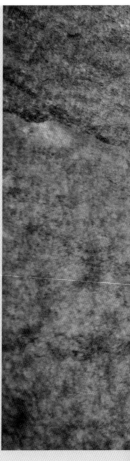

Enchainments, or link-ups, now provide some of the more exciting headlines in climbing. Yet they are things most of us have done to some degree—linking a half dozen single-pitch routes in Joshua Tree, say, a few three-pitch routes in Eldorado Canyon, or a couple of five-pitch climbs in Tuolomne Meadows. Enchainments are excellent ways for the motivated to accomplish the equivalent of a single long route, with a scenic tour thrown in besides. As gear has gotten lighter and climbers have gained endurance, knowledge, and efficiency, linking longer routes has naturally become a branch of the trad climbing experience.

A large part of successfully stacking routes is understanding how the ingredients in our enchainment will add up to more than the sum of their parts. The more variables we add, the greater our need to recognize potential pitfalls. With big link-ups we'll need to rise, approach, and probably climb in the dark. Dealing with darkness is where we'll likely leave key gear, get lost on the approach, and climb torturously slow. Preparation is key. We pack the packs, put new batteries in the headlamp, and check the approach the day before. Climbing by headlamp is doable but takes some practice—allow extra time for the slower pace. And what route(s) to do first? If one has a heinously slippery face crux we probably don't want to do that one in the sun; if one is very popular we'll likely crank that one first. In general it's best to jump on the biggest and baddest one straight off—psychologically you're cruising after that.

As we link bigger and bigger chunks of climbing, it becomes increasingly important to fine-tune our operation, removing all needless steps that suck minutes at the time but hours all told. We blow off things like the cordelette—much quicker to throw a figure eight straight into the belay. If equalization seems important we equalize with a double figure eight. Quickdraws are only used when necessary—less gear to carry when we clip single biners into fixed nuts and slings. If the pitch is straight we usually can get by with single biners on pins and bolts. Remaining watchful is key. The question from start to finish is: What can I be doing right now?

While at the belay, does the rope need stacking and gear organized? When using a tag line we stack it and clip the leaders end onto the belay so she can't fail to see it. We pop a biner onto the uppermost part of the belay so the leader can clip that as his first piece. If the leader is busy the moment he arrives, we clip the tag line onto his harness as well as clipping his lead line into that top biner. Both climbers need to get synched up per the strategies—like yelling "Safe!" or "Off belay!" as soon as we're secure and can be taken off belay. Then we fine-tune our belay while the second

Sky high on Free Rider,
El Capitan.

prepares to climb. The second makes sure he yells "That's me!" when the rope comes tight. All basic stuff, but the leader needs to know when to stop tugging and put us on belay.

Rope handling is the most repetitive physical action we make so we need to cut the labor to a minimum. When the leader reels up slack prior to belaying the second, he does not let tangles draw upwards and he doesn't extrude the line through his hands to force the kinks out. The leader must pull the weight of the rope through intervening biners with any and all rope drag. Adding our hands to that drag only compounds the effort.

Of course there are times when we simply have nothing to do—when we take a sip of water or a bite of food. If we need to we loosen off our shoes a bit and try to make ourselves comfortable. Taking care of ourselves is a priority, more so when pushing the physical envelope. The better we stay hydrated, fed, and comfy, the longer we can go.

Thank God Ledge.

PHIL BARD

Dropping Gear

Everyone does it—meaning when and how much are the questions—but lest we limit the gear we drop we'll never make the summit, we'll go broke, or both. We try to never drop a thing—and take extra precautions to secure certain crucial items. In the midst of multiple rappels, say, dropping the rope is a disaster. So we tie off an end so we can't lose it. A dropped shoe is also a nightmare, so they stay clipped in the moment they're removed. When speed climbing, the rack is pared down to a minimum, and we need to be particularly careful when handling the gear. Drop a cam or two and we'll face dire run-outs with a "suicide rack" that was thin to begin with. Climbing fast is not meant to be a sketchy, balls-out terror. It is about climbing as quickly as we comfortably can—without dropping the very gear we need to keep us safe and gain the top.

his face conjured deference from the slack jawed and, thanks to the rope, allowed both of us to blast on.

Once, though, at a hanging stance, the belayer more or less bowed to John, but when the rope ran out and I tried to pass, he leaned out mightily to block my path. Unable to jam the crack, I turned to wild stemming on the outer reaches of the corner. Then, as planets aligned, he leaned out even farther as I made a blind foot dyno, the stiffness of my board-lasted shoe making a loud thwack as it contacted his skull. I apologized, but felt as though I'd just kicked a goal for John.

Three-quarters of the way up the wall, I pulled onto the Big Sandy ledges and three big Germans eating lunch. On hearing that John Bachar was coming up right behind, they dropped their knackwurst, rushed out to the edge, and strained off their leashes, their greasy fingers clawing the air to get a better view.

The storm finally hit. Coiled static did squirrely things with our hair and jabbed our neck and hands with pins and needles. The cliff glistened and rivulets ran. But even the rain and crackling buzz of lightning couldn't douse the flame and slow our trajectory. Late that afternoon, we crested the summit to a double rainbow.

Peter Croft near the end of Half Dome.

Peter Croft and John Bachar enjoy the view atop Half Dome.

PHIL BARD

Loose Blocks

On new routes we commonly encounter detached flakes and loose rock. Clearly we need to take special care that we don't send these down onto our belayer or onto the rope. We'll also find these hazards on established classics climbed thousands of times. Just because they haven't come off yet does not mean they never will. In fact, most anything that looks detached will eventually slough off. Particularly in areas with harsh heat and freezing cycles, flakes or blocks that allow buildup or seep moisture are subject to "frost wedging"—which is just like it sounds. As the water freezes it expands, prying chunks of rock off the wall. Add the repetitive tugging of thousands of chalked hands and even the greatest block starts working free like a loose tooth.

Be the route brand new or a trade route, we treat all flakes and blocks as potential risks, stepping around them when possible and treading gingerly when clasping directly, making certain our line doesn't snag, if need be by placing gear specifically to hold the rope away. If the second can be absolutely certain there is no one below, a dangerously perched missile is much better launched than left to endanger subsequent parties. If, because of climbers below, we cannot jettison the hazard, sacrificing a sling and perhaps a nut to hold it in place is sometimes an interim solution—as well as a possible lifesaver to the next guy.

CHAPTER 50

Levitation 29

John Long

Lynn Hill and I spent the winter in Las Vegas, climbing daily at Red Rocks and plowing through nights at dead-end jobs. After roughly ten seasons of climbing 300 days a year, my learning curve had flattened, and I found myself singing the same old song. To outrun this, I kept switching venues rather than instruments. Although I didn't yet know it, everything would change later that summer, during a filming gig at Venezuela's Angel Falls, a jungle gusher sufficient to deliver me into television production and book writing (and where, after setting the world's record for the longest continuous rappel, Jim Bridwell and I almost perished in a helicopter accident in a driving monsoon). Several years later, Lynn joined the international competitive circuit and went on to become a many-time world sport climbing champion. We all know the rest. But that winter in Vegas found us in flux, searching for direction. Soon we'd find our separate ways, but before leaving Vegas for good, we'd also find, rather by accident, the archetype of the budding sport climbing revolution. Put differently, we pretty much stumbled into the first, large-scale sport route in the world.

If ever an area lent itself to sport climbing, it's Red Rocks. But back then, the idea of gym-bolting the now-popular sport areas never crossed our minds. We still followed a traditional approach. Bigger and bolder always meant better, so partly from a sense of duty, but more from force of habit, we focused on the many unclimbed, thousand-foot crack systems that slashed a half dozen canyon walls.

Only later would we realize that the classical "trad" days were all but over at the Red Rocks.

Since arriving in Vegas a few months before, we'd established a handful of long free climbs, often scaring ourselves stiff. Trying to limit bolts and pitons, or avoid them altogether—a perilous tactic on the sheer, friable sandstone—we'd sometimes find ourselves belayed to cosmetic nuts and running out the rope on steep, iffy rock. On the steeper lines, busting out onto the face often felt suicidal. The red sandstone offered ample holds, but usually ran too steep for lead bolting.

On one route, Negro Blanco by name, Lynn traversed from a bombay chimney onto the terrible face, busted a hold, and logged an airball screamer for the ages. Only a small hex in the guts of a grainy flare stopped her from smashing into the boulders from 60 feet. We had enough other frightful episodes that the most startling lines—well-featured, surging faces upward of 1,000 feet—remained futuristic projects to gaze up at in wonder. We could surely have climbed these walls with a giant toprope, but there was simply no way to protect them on the lead without initially climbing and setting bolts, or rapping the wall and pre-fixing the pro that way. It sounds prosaic now, but in those days, both methods were considered cheating, so we held off.

Then we met local climbers Jorge and Joanne Urioste, who comprised roughly a third of the hardcore Red Rocks climbing fraternity. Jorge knew a great line when he saw one, and he saw plenty. He also understood that the old trad rules could dash a free climber into a porcelain urn

Windgate sandstone. Ocher vistas. Red Rocks.

GREG EPPERSON

should he try to lead those tempting unclimbed faces. So Jorge began leading would-be face climbs on aid, installing bolts at convenient places—hardly a new tactic, though usually applied only to brief holdless sections of short testpieces, and, to my knowledge, never before the MO on what essentially were small wall climbs.

Jorge would dress the pitch, then Joanne would work the moves on a toprope till she could free climb the whole enchilada in one go. The bolting went slowly and the climbing more slowly yet. An anthropology professor at UNLV, Jorge enjoyed limited free time, so his ascents entailed miles of fixed ropes—meaning Jorge would siege each climb till the bolts were placed, with Joanne

free-following every move. Joanne would often need multiple days to free a single pitch, some of which were upper-end 5.11. Once the climb was "done," Joanne would return with another free climber and tick the redpoint.

Not surprisingly, the few Red Rocks locals were put off by the Uriostes' disregard for traditional style, a style that kept adrenaline levels high but also kept us in the cracks. I've wasted half my life on jackass pursuits, but I've never bothered to tell others how to climb, or live, or die. Nevertheless, Jorge's tactics privately confounded me.

As I scratched my head in the scree fields, Jorge quickly bagged a slew of outstanding lines, now widely considered classics. Though a few of Jorge's routes looked as if he'd loaded a Gatling gun with ¼-inch bolts and stitched a 1,000-foot vertical face from bottom to top, Jorge did all his drilling by hand. And more often than not, the climbing on his creations rocked.

In fact, the few times Lynn and I repeated a Urioste composition, the climbing was surreal. So accustomed were we to shouldering a bulky rack and placing gear that casting off with nothing but quickdraws and clipping bolts every 8 feet felt downright illegal. The experience immediately cast me onto the indefinite ground between two worlds: one known and established, the other a strange but alluring universe where fun meant everything and fear was the enemy.

No question, Jorge had queered the very rules I'd slavishly followed since first roping up. Other climbers with more natural courage or recklessness embodied the old trad ethic with native ease. In uncanny, elusive moments, I could get after it like a Bengal tiger; generally, however, whenever I started redlining, only devotion to the classical verities kept me in line. I fudged those rules, certainly, but trying to maintain an idealized level of boldness had set my experience on fire. So to see Jorge engineering the jeopardy out of the game was both perplexing and enticing. After hanging on for dear life for all of these years, I was starting to hear Jorge's tune.

That year, Jorge and Joanne were working on their biggest, steepest, most outlandish climb yet, a varicolored, 1,100-foot convex plaque towering over the tumble of Oak Creek Canyon, 4 twisting miles into the Red Rocks' backcountry. They'd pushed the route about 500 feet. On much of the climb, Joanne hadn't yet attempted to free-follow, though Jorge thought it possible to free most, if not all, of the climbing up to their high point. Possibly because Lynn and I were two of the few active climbers in the area, more likely because we lived a few blocks from the Uriostes, Jorge invited us to explore the free climbing prospects.

The expedition felt odd from the start. I wasn't used to someone so thoroughly setting my table, and during the 2-hour slog into the cliff, I felt unsure of the whole adventure. And one of the unique aspects of this route is that for a big sport

Pitch 1, Levitation 29.

JOHN HEGYES

Husbanding Strength on Mega Routes

Many people are confused to learn that most so-called speed climbing is not breakneck racing, rather brisk but not rushed climbing with the accent on efficiency. Notice how on a steep trail, we can push it to a certain pace, beyond which it seems to take twice the effort to go only slightly faster. Scaling mega routes is in part an exercise in finding that maximum maintainable speed and trying to exert the least possible effort to stay there. Cruxes require us to recruit our fast-twitch muscles for short bursts of max effort, and we'll have no such reserves if we've needlessly been revving our system all the way up. Husbanding strength is like reserving gas and requires a conscious effort to keep our mind and body in an alert state of calm. There are countless methods to teach us the fine points in this regard. Getting up on high, staying keyed up, and climbing on nervous energy is exhilarating, but we crash off an adrenaline high just as hard as if we'd breakfasted on pecan pie and ice cream. Keep the water and the calories coming; go with a steady pace; shield yourself from direct sunlight; when not moving, relax entirely and slow your breathing. Yippykaiya.

The notorious "bat hang" is an excellent way to get the weight off your arms—till you turn back upright and the blood drains from your melon. Then you faint and fall off.

MATT KUEHL

route, it was set well out in true wilderness. Trekking deep in those Red Rock canyons is like hiking back to the Pliocene.

The strange angles of both Oak Creek Canyon and the surrounding bluffs made everything appear askew, and we couldn't get a coherent fix on the wall until nearly reaching the base: It looked similar, in length and angle, to the business section of the Prow on Washington Column. Looking up and studying the wall, I sighed, figuring we'd get stopped cold at a jutting roof, 100 feet above. Maybe sooner.

Lynn led the first pitch, a steepening ramp/corner flush with that glassy, black desert varnish that earmarks the slickest stone on earth. She quickly pawed to the belay and yelled down, "Easy 5.10." Joanne and I followed. Above the first belay, the wall jacked up to dead V, and I cautiously worked over blocks and eyebrow roofs that looked grim from below but amazingly, passed at 5.9. Hanging off a jug, I gazed at the ladder of ¼-inch bolts cutting around the roof to the headwall above. A bomber Friend to supplement the bolts, a big stretch, one heaving layback, then incuts to a hanging belay. Minimal 5.11, but exciting with those ¼-inchers. The next lead looked like 5.10 yet provided the only easy (5.8) pitch on the lower wall, following generous rails and passing a cavalcade of those ¼-inch bolts.

Somewhere during that pitch I realized we were onto something rare. The cliff was as steep as the upper reaches of The Diamond or the Rostrum, both legitimate big walls. Because the route began halfway up a high canyon rampart, resting above a long approach slab spilling into shade, it felt like we were climbing on a wall triple the size. Dangling from those initial sling belays, right out there on the bold face, we'd peer up, doubting we could climb 10 more feet, only to find hold after bomber hold, with ready bolts to clip. After a few leads I found myself charging with more momentum than I'd felt in several years.

I had learned the hard way that only if I was looking at a climb in terms of free climbing could

Pitch 4, Levitation 29.

GREG EPPERSON

my mind get around the true possibilities. During my high school days at Tahquitz and Suicide Rock, we learned to aid climb on a handful of soaring cracks. When I was tapping up these routes, standing in slings, I never thought they would have gone free, even though at that time we already were doing extreme bouldering at Rubidoux and Stoney Point. Later, I made quick ascents of the Regular Route on Half Dome and the West Face of El Cap, which were both free climbed shortly thereafter. In both cases I didn't see the possibilities.

The West Face should have been an obvious candidate since my partner Dale Bard and I hadn't even brought aid slings for our ascent and used no more than a dozen or so aid placements during a speed ascent. But I never thought the 30 or 40 feet of aid we used would have gone free because I wasn't looking at the route in terms of a total free ascent, so I didn't "see" it.

We often find what we're looking for. Probably our best results come from trying our hardest to free climb a route and, providing we can muster a big effort with good enough security, keeping things sane, we let our performance determine if we can or cannot tick it. It sounds simplistic, but you'll never know till you try, and in the process, you might surprise yourself. I look at the Regular Route on Half Dome and the West Face of El Cap as routes that "got away," because with the right partner I could have gotten the first free ascent of both routes, rather than early repeats. Kudos to Jim Erickson, Art Higby, and Leonard Coyne, who saw what I did not. Anyway, this Vegas article was a route that would have looked improbable standing

in aid slings. But busting out there on hands and feet, the way opened up splendidly.

Following our unlikely success on the lower pitches, I'd achieved that suave flow where you can motor for miles, and I cast off on the next lead at speed. The route had, so far, traced intermittent cracks, which abruptly thinned to a shadow; for unknown reasons Jorge had skimped on the bolts. Though only 5.10, I found myself a good ways out on a ¼-inch "coffin nail," pulling on vertical rock that would require fifty ascents to totally clean up. Then an easy crack led to another sling belay beneath a headwall.

I lashed off, leaned back, and started laughing. I'd never climbed anything remotely like this. After the first pitch, the nut and cam placements had dried up. If Jorge hadn't pre-rigged the bolts, we wouldn't have made it past 200 feet. It amazed me that Jorge had beaten himself raw with all that drilling, and then for us to waltz in and pull down—it felt like grand larceny.

Far below, arid, brown plains—today a solid grid of prefab homes and soulless office plazas—swept

Shelly Pressman on the difficult and sustained Pitch 5 on Levitation 29.

GREG EPPERSON

Judging Routes

The view from above is often more telling. Amy Ness, High Sierras.

AMY NESS

Whenever I judged routes on how they looked, I was wrong, sometimes way wrong, more times than I can count. I've already mentioned doing mixed aid ascents of various routes, and that the process of grabbing and pulling up on gear blinded me to the possibilities of an all-free ascent. I remember doing aid climbs at Suicide Rock, keeping an eye open for the free climbing possibilities, and thinking there were none—this on the very routes I would go back and free climb a month or a year later. Here, seeing is not believing—a frequent occurrence. For example, few climbers hiking back into the Byzantine reaches of the Red Rock canyons will look up at the towering Eagle Wall and say, "Thar she blows. A great face climb, right up the middle of that bald, vertical wall. And I'll call it Levitation 29."

We were amazed by the plethora of holds on what from just a few hundred feet away looked sparse for relief and features, especially on the upper ramparts. In fact here was a unique sandstone canvass on which to paint four or five routes. But you have to get up there to discover the possibilities, and judge the route on how it climbs, not how it looks. Put differently, the shoe might fit, but you'll never know till you try that bad boy on.

gently into the gaudy Las Vegas Strip, 25 miles and a world away. Just above, a thin, bottoming gash snaked up a piebald wall averaging 95 degrees, occasional bolts festooning both sides. This looked hard and sustained. It was Lynn's lead, and I was glad.

Flexible people are rarely strong and strong people are rarely flexible, but Lynn has a wealth of both qualities, and I always had to lump it. As she steadily bridged, gastoned, crimped, and jammed up the pitch, the rope hanging free between bolts, Joanne

and I sighed, wondering how we'd manage. Every so often, between bolts, Lynn would slot a wire or plug in a small Friend. Then the rock bulged slightly, and she started cranking for keeps. She stemmed her left leg out at about chin level, toeing off something I couldn't have seen with the Hubble Telescope. I would never walk again if I tried that move. I was finished.

"You bring the jugs?" I asked Joanne.

"Nope."

"What the hell were you thinking?"

Caution in Wilderness Areas

Many historic trad climbs are located in wilderness areas (whether officially designated or not) such as the Apuis in Venezuela; the Hand of Fatima in Mali, East Africa; the Petit Drus in Chamonix; and domestically, the Black Canyon of the Gunnison and Long's Peak, both in Colorado—to mention a few. The farther back the route, the farther you have to retreat during a medical emergency. Cell phones help but coverage is not always available, nor are Medivacs in places like Mali. If you busted up way out in the sticks, with only your own devices to effect an escape, all the technology in the world cannot help—until it can, and that might be days. I've had the misfortune of sustaining considerable injuries miles from the car, and it's no fun making your way to civilization on one leg. So the simple calculus is that the farther off the map you are, the fewer risks you take—as a general rule.

This does not mean you start climbing so conservatively that you forget to manage time, say, and dawdle your way into trouble. This is the climbing version of "preserving the lead," also known as playing-not-to-lose. Because we tend to go passive in this mode, we paradoxically set ourselves up for failure. We still need to climb-to-win, bringing to bear our courage and resolve, while tempering it with an increased alertness for dangerous situations.

Injured climber hauled off the face of El Capitan.

KARL "BABA" BRALICH

"I think she's got it now," said Joanne, craning to see Lynn 100 feet above. "It eases there."

Fortunately, I have a 2-foot reach advantage on Lynn Hill and could stretch past the Chinese acrobat moves, thieving by on sidepulls and shallow jams. The pitch felt about 5.11c and perfectly replicated a modern sport climbing pitch, save that it hung halfway up a big wall. We had never seen or experienced anything like this.

The fixed ropes ended here, with 300 vertical feet looming above. Much as we wanted to press on and bag the whole climb, without Jorge's first installing another stack of bolts, we had no chance. It crossed my mind to grab our little rack, cast off, and hope for the best, but the next few hundred feet looked bulging, bald, and periodically loose. And even if I had a bolt kit, the steepness shot down any chance of lead bolting without aid slings. Yet, with luck, and a few more days of toil, the whole mother might go free, a concept so wonderful that, down at the base, I suggested Jorge immediately get back to work. A short, stout man with the perseverance of an Andean mountaineer—which he'd been in the Bolivia of his youth—Jorge finished bolting a month or so later. The next weekend Lynn, Joanne, and I were back at the high point.

I remember encountering some reachy 5.10 face work on the sixth pitch, and how the rope dangled in space as I belayed the girls up. Pitch 7 looked unlikely, wandering a bit and working through several projecting white ribs. Lynn got that one and then she got another dandy one—and a scary one as well. Most every long Red Rocks route passes through a vein of choss, with a few gong-like flakes. The wall kicked back for good maybe 50 feet above. If Lynn could smuggle past this last bulge, we were home free.

Lynn Hill. We called her "Little Lynny." She was a prodigy and everyone knew it. She carried her gift with quiet ease rather than chest-pounding or faux, awe-shucks humility. No female had ever

Pulling for sunlight in the Red Rocks.

GREG EPPERSON

climbed remotely as well as the best guys, so when Lynn began dusting us off—which she did with maddening frequency—folks offered up all kinds of fatuous explanations. Some diehards refused to believe a woman, and a 5-foot 2-inch article at that, could possibly be so good.

At Josh, Lynn excelled due to the quartz monzonite's superior friction, which catered to her bantam weight. In Yosemite, her success hinged on midget hands, which fit wonderfully into the infernal thin cracks. On limestone, she could plug three fingers into pockets where the rest of us could manage only two. In the desert Southwest, she enjoyed an alliance with shape-shifters in

A young Lynn Hill dead-pointing at the Manx Boulders.

KEVIN POWELL

general, and coyotes in particular. Even after a heap of World Cup victories, it still took the climbing world an age to accept Lynn as the Chosen One, and perhaps her legacy was never established, once and for all, till she free climbed the Nose.

From the early days in Red Rocks, it would take her several years to become "the" Lynn Hill. Nevertheless, she was always a supernova, especially on that funky pitch way up what would become the seminal Levitation 29.

This was one of those situations where you have to appreciate where you are—and we were in the middle of nowhere. This was far, far removed from most modern sport climbing areas, which typically are on the fringes of urban areas or at any rate don't require hours of hiking and nearly 1,000 feet of hard face climbing to attain. An injury accident here, or any place in true wilderness, will always be an epic, even if you are skilled in self-rescue techniques. Rescue, if needed, requires recruitment of a team and sometimes a helicopter, and that takes hours. So for this and other reasons, risks must be carefully appraised lest you invite an epic, or worse.

The problems with the pitch overhead were that the white sandstone was notoriously suspect and the ¼-inch bolts Jorge had placed, long since abandoned as protection in sandstone, were probably not good enough to catch a huge ripper. So Lynn had to climb the next bit with extreme vigilance and be prepared to back off rather than jeopardize the whole team.

"Watch me!" Lynn yelled as she liebacked up a sandbar, her feet pasted at shoulder height. Ten more feet and Lynn pulled onto easier ground. Modern topos call this pitch 5.10+, but it's basically unratable, what with the band of loose, white rock and the bizarre, sideways moves. An easy crack led a few hundred feet to the top. We rapped the route, stripping the fixed lines.

All the way back to the car and for several days afterward, I felt that electric glow that follows a royal adventure. I'd climbed stacks of walls that long and that steep, but never face climbing out on the bold wall, something unique to my experience. I can't remember if it was Joanne's twenty-ninth birthday, or if that came shortly afterward, but it factored into naming the climb Levitation 29. I hear the route's seen a thousand ascents, and that it's cleaned up nicely.

Over the radio today I heard Sarah Vaughn singing a classic Hammerstein lyric, which ran, "When I grow too old to dream, I'll have you to remember." The majestic hike in, the soaring wall, and the radiance of scaling that great stone wave are going the way of all memories. But a faint, visceral thrill of roving the open face lingers still.

CHAPTER 51

Coatimundi Whiteout

John Long

Our little group of Stonemasters was making a mass assault on a popular climbing area named Granite Mountain, half a day's drive away, in Prescott, Arizona. Unfortunately I had finals and couldn't shake loose. So the gang went without me and returned with stories about terrific crack climbs with names like Magnolia Thunderpussy and Hassawampa, and a near-successful free attempt on what they swore was the most spectacular route on the 600-foot-high formation: Coatimundi Whiteout, a soaring crack system topped by a "Great Roof," itself split by a 3-inch crack. I couldn't quite picture the thing, but it sounded wild.

I never found out exactly what stopped the free attempt. Something about poor protection on the traverse, and doubts about turning the roof crack out beyond. As I heard it told, Tobin Sorenson and John Bachar had a try at the roof, and both retreated to the belay stance. Tobin, for one, was convinced the route would go free and would be the seminal climb at Granite Mountain if not all of Arizona and the western United States—an exaggeration, of course, but the route was a surely a beaut. A couple years later, during spring break, I drove out to Prescott with Lynn Hill and Keith Cunning—with designs on Coatimundi.

A coatimundi (I looked it up) is a tiny mammal of the raccoon family, generally found in central and South American climes not known for snowstorms to say nothing of whiteouts, so I can add nothing relevant to the route name.

Pitch 1, Coatimundi Whiteout.

LARRY COATS

Perfect, Enemy of Good Enough

Let's say it again: Perfect is the enemy of good enough. These are inexact terms, impossible to quantify, which is simply part of the adventure. But the idea is that we can never expect—nor waste time always trying to arrange—hand-placed protection that is remotely comparable to the grid bolts found on sport climbs. The issue is not to go off half-cocked; rather, faultless protection is simply not to be found on many trad climbs. That much said, it is the rare established route in which the pro is not "good enough" for an experienced leader to proceed with a modicum of security.

Protection naturally varies, route to route, but we can never expect the trad milieu to be risk free. The virtues of courage, commitment, embracing the unknown, and managing fear have always been central concerns for all of trad climbing. Shall it never change.

The question every trad climber asks themselves twenty times on every route: Is that really good enough?

LARRY COATS

Anyhow, we got a late start and it was dark by the time we gained Prescott. Next morning we rose early and marched straight to the base of the route, where a vertical three-pitch corner shot up about 350 feet to the Great Roof, cutting across the top of the wall, jutting well out into space. Along the narrower left edge, a crack ran through the roof. That was Coatimundi Whiteout right there—up the corners, out left under the roof, then hopefully, up and over the roof via the hand crack, all free. It looked airy and strenuous. And totally classic.

The first two pitches ran full rope lengths, and both felt like 5.10. Nothing serious, but steep, strenuous jamming of various widths, from thin to a little off-width for good measure. Then a short lead up to a belay right below the Great Roof, where we could look out at the yawning traverse shooting left along a horizontal crack, where the roof met the main wall. The initial pro consisted of several sketchy fixed angles that I tied off and hoped for the best. I knew these pins were crap and would never hold a sideways ripper, but I figured they were good enough to maybe lower off if I found the climbing impossible and could maybe traverse back and gingerly weight the pegs. If I peeled off out of control, things were not going to end well. (Wisely, a local later installed a big bolt at the start of the traverse.)

I started hand traversing straight left, heading for the crack bisecting the roof, some 40 feet away. The wall was steep and the footholds were merely smears and wrinkles. The protection was never great and presented the special concerns caused by the hazardous vectors of traversing dead sideways. The juncture of the Great Roof and the main wall described a standard hand traverse as well as an undercling crack, Stoppering up into the ceiling, the two fractures offered eccentric options for horizontal travel. Cams and slotted nuts are not multidirectional. Cams can and will pivot when loaded across an arc; but they are known to rip out, especially when placed in horizontal cracks and subjected to lateral forces—exactly the case on this traverse. Stoppers are slotted with a particular direction of pull in mind, and unless keyed into a pod or bottleneck, horizontal loading will often cause such placements to fail. So what to do?

When using cams to protect a traverse, get the lobes back in the crack a ways to compensate for the axle shifting direction during a fall. During an arcing fall, as the unit is loaded it will normally shift with the arc, and hopefully stay put. Cams placed near the lip of the crack are especially prone to rip, given oblique and sudden forces. Pitons are usually good for any direction of pull, but with marginal placements, where only half of the pin is sunk, or is beat into a bottoming or wavy crack, as was the case on Coatimundi, it is nigh impossible to accurately gauge the security of the peg. I've had pins driven to the eye rip right out, and others that were tied off hold repeated whippers. There are several options for such a traverse as this one, most working off the "more is better" strategy.

For me, loading up the crack with marginal gear is less productive than working to get a few solid pieces—or as good as I can manage. On Coatimundi, where the traverse involved a dash of 5.11 climbing, hanging off my arms with scant footholds, I went for a couple of pins at the start and three decent cams as I moved across. The quickest way to bungle such

Heather Hayes turns the lip of the Coatimundi Whiteout roof, Granite Mountain.

LARRY COATS

a climb is to hang in the middle of the hard bits and try to arrange protection. Much better to get something "good enough," and gas it for a good stance or hold where you can work for another good enough placement. The climber fiddling about and unwilling to go a ways off decent pro will rarely succeed on a route like Coatimundi Whiteout. By the same token, you don't just keep traversing with nothing, hoping to eventually sink a Thank God cam or nut. If you can't get anything—forget it. Lucky for me I found sufficient good enough placements to keep pulling for that roof crack.

Forty feet out, a thin hand crack shot out from the horizontal crack, while to the right, perhaps

Fixed Protection

Old bolts, aka "coffin nails."

ROBERT MIRAMONTES

Various European manufacturers still market pitons, but in the United States, Black Diamond is the only company marketing them on any kind of scale. They come in four basic shapes: RURPS, blades (knifeblades and the bigger Bugaboos), horizontals (Lost Arrows), and angles (channel-shaped). Each model is either stamped or forged of alloy steel, and for better or worse, all are far more enduring than the hardest granite or limestone. Camming units and small Stoppers have replaced pitons in most instances.

The one exception is climbers making first ascents. It is rare even for them to use pegs, but in the case of a hole or a thin, parallel-sided crack often found behind flakes, sometimes only a piton can secure the desired protection, although in most cases nowadays, leading climbers just place bolts where they can't get in good chocks (dreadfully, sometimes even where they can). To preserve the rock and avoid future climbers having to place the pin, it is always left fixed. Never remove a piton from an established free climb. It's there because no passive protection can be arranged. To adequately judge the security of a fixed piton, however, you must have experience in placing them, and a hammer.

halfway out the roof, a wide crack joined the party from the side. I slotted two good cams in the roof, pulled out, kicked a leg straight up into the wide slot, then, milking both cracks, crabbed over the lip, where the exposure was staggering and the rope drag considerable. I set a belay up a few feet higher, as advised in the guidebook. A little easy scrambling and we were at the top.

On the hike back to the base, we spotted a sensational unclimbed arch on the lower wall, and we spent the rest of the day and part of the following trying to wiggle loose hexes into the sweeping undercling crack. The position was stunning, the climbing arm busting, and the final product was a 5.12 for the ages: Gunsmoke.

Traversing Lines

We have avoided delving into leading and ropework basics, but it's worth noting that difficult traversing lines require special vigilance owing to two basic factors. First, whenever possible, the leader will quite naturally place protection before any crux section, because otherwise she will have to do the moves well out from the pro. The problem for the follower is they don't benefit from the leader's pro; they must unclip and clean the unit before the hard climbing. Picture it: If you are second on the rope, and if you fall, you'll keep falling till caught by the next piece along the traverse. It's like being out on the lead and having to pull out a bunch of slack before each hard part.

The solution is for the leader to appreciate the dangers and consciously place pro as soon as they can after a crux section ("protecting the second"), lest the climber following will take the "ride" if he whips. And long, sideways falls can be trouble. The second concern is that any fall on a traverse loads the protection with screwy angles of pull that can cause pro to rip out. Camming units are designed to withstand lateral loading, but only if the rock is solid, the unit is deep enough not to pivot out, and the cam lobes are retracted to an optimum attitude—and SLCDs vary in this regard. Stoppers lodged in horizontal cracks must be keyed into a bottleneck constriction to withstand loading across the axis of an arc, as described when falling off a traverse. Since bottleneck placements are unlikely to be found at just the right spot, right before a hard traversing bit, camming units are normally our first choice for protecting traverses.

I Can't Believe It's a Girdle, a Joshua Tree classic.

KEVIN POWELL

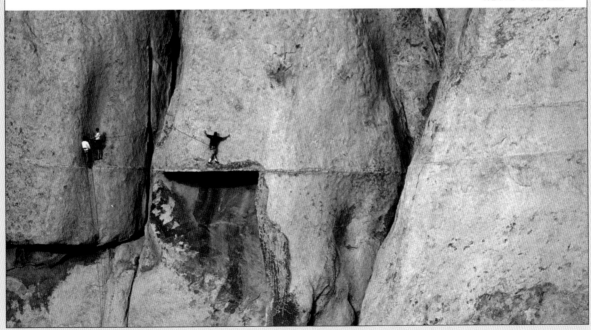

CHAPTER 52

Valkyrie

Peter Croft

There are few places that evoke emotion like the high peaks, with their push-me, pull-me medley of fear and inspiration. The sheer size and wildness steals our breath and our words, and attempts to quantify what we see and feel fall flat as a dime store brochure. Here are rock walls of grand complexity; unlocking their mysterious doors (i.e., logistics) is often just as adventurous as the climbing. In fact they are all part of a piece.

The Sierra Nevada runs roughly north–south for 400 miles, tracking eastern California. Its sky-slicing spine is formed by fanged and busted stump peaks. Scattered throughout this crest and its many offshoot sub-ranges are hundreds of walls. Many are better than a thousand feet high and would draw perpetual lines were it not for the lengthy approaches. Some Sierra cliffs rival those in Zion, the Black Canyon, and even Yosemite Valley. The tallest and boldest is Angel Wings, in Sequoia National Park. This hulking tan monolith lies in Valhalla, a high hanging valley girded by plunging walls and spiked summits. In Norse mythology, Valhalla was the awesome hall of Odin. For those fortunate enough to be slain in battle, Valhalla was the place you went, or rather, were carried to—by Valkyries! These were bikini-clad Viking goddesses,

Angel Wings, High Sierra.

GREG EPPERSON

bearing great steins of mead, who flew you to every Scandinavians' idea of heaven.

Dave Nettle was a 12-year-old Boy Scout when he first trudged the 16 miles into Valhalla and tied into a rope. The hook set deep, and today Dave has probably logged more vertical mileage in the Valhalla area than anyone else. When Dave asked if I wanted to have a go at trying to free climb a route up the tallest cliff in the High Sierra, I was up on my feet before he finished his question.

Angel Wings was already host to a handful of big wall routes—Grade Vs and VIs, each featuring long sections of aid climbing. We wanted nothing to do with any nailing. What's more, as buff as it looks, Angel Wings was infamous for large sections of crumbly rock. We wanted none of that either.

Dave had tried to free climb the wall before— and failed. Then he, backcountry freak Brandon Thau, and I marched in to finish what Dave started—and failed. We had suffered the extremes of weather. The wall was south facing, and the summer heat broiled us alive. We encountered hateful kitty-litter granite—and I, for one, came face to face with real fear. A thousand feet up the wall and 40 feet out from a sling draped over a scabby flake, I committed to a flaring off-width, finally reaching a blind seam where the hoped-for protection failed to appear. Just then the crack of thunder alerted me to the black thunderstorm headed our way. Another year the first winter storm forced the others to abandon everything in a mad dash for survival.

In 2012 Dave, Brandon, and I were joined by climbing photographer Greg Epperson, and we marched in once more, having no reason to believe

Grappling with the Angel.

GREG EPPERSON

Dealing with the cluster.

GREG EPPERSON

we should fare better than last time—but we had a feeling. We knew that midsummer was too hot and had too many thunderstorms, and that autumn days were too short. And October storms could be hellacious. But after so many beat-downs and narrow escapes, plus well over a hundred miles of tromping in and out, and days spent thrutching about the face, we were beginning to read the rock a little better.

Unlike most other granite areas, where classic routes typically follow big, obvious crack systems, the prominent wide fissures on Angel Wings were mostly shallow and flaring, bottoming out into loose crustiness. Success, we felt, lay in subtle features and shades of gray—meaning the big features were poor guides, so we had to play it on little more than a hunch.

We picked early September as our start date, banking on better temps and less likelihood of summer thunderstorms or winter nastiness. To save strength and avoid humping the crushing loads of a big-wall kit—plus the base camp luxuries so crucial to a middle-aged team—we hired a couple of cowgirls to wrangle a string of loaded mules right into Valhalla. This time we were doing everything right—almost. We forgot binoculars and I spaced the jumars, so I couldn't follow on ascenders and would have to climb everything.

After several days probing ever deeper into the upper headwall, we had 1,500 feet of rope strung for photog Greg Epperson and a decent idea of where we wanted to go next. We spent the rest day at base camp pacing back and forth along a lakeshore and peering up at those final pitches, giving ourselves headaches trying to decipher what lay ahead.

Next morning we head-lamped the approach and the first couple of pitches. Greg and Dave jugged up ahead while Brandon and I dug into the meat of the wall. The discontinuous line we had struggled to find in the beginning now flowed naturally together. At half-height our momentum stuttered when Brandon, on lead, launched a granite tombstone into the air just above me. I ducked—it whistled past and we shook it off.

The route swept up to skyscraper steepness, and as our luck played out, a string of sling belays was now broken by a series of perfect ledges. True wall exposure set in and we drank it in from the comfort of our virtual easy-boy chairs. I had spent the previous days bouldering out dead ends and sorting strenuous cruxes and was still feeling all of it, so while I belayed I took full sit-down advantage of the granite recliners.

Over the first dozen pitches, we encountered everything from slabs to overhangs and thin cracks to yawning back-and-foot chimneys. The thirteenth pitch was the crux, with a cross-matched fingertip edge and a dyno out right to a fat pinch. I stuck it first try, but was so spanned out I couldn't see my feet and had to go by feel. By early afternoon we reached our high point and Dave swung into the lead, stringing together a couple of rope lengths to a ledge at the base of the sixteenth—and final—pitch.

Over the last couple hundred feet the buttress narrowed to a blunt arête offering several options. The coolest-looking line, by far, tracked up the very

Brandon Thau forging into the upper headwall.

crest—and I followed it. Occasional short fractures accepted gear followed by long runouts on perfect rock with 2,000 feet of air spilling below, all perched on the quick of that arête.

After all of our previous epic failures spread over many days and thousands of feet, we had battled to reckon the complexities and true nature of the wall, all along butting heads with the cliff. Once we achieved a level of understanding, we finally were able to navigate by instinct. Here, at last, was Valhalla.

CHAPTER 53

Someday

John Long

Early winter—not unlike the day I drove out to Josh when I was 16 years old and joined Jack Schnurr for my first rock climb. This time, Peter Croft and I were part of a climbing seminar hosted by a popular Los Angeles CrossFit gym. We seemed to have Indian Cove entirely to ourselves. A little lower altitude and therefore warmer than the central, more populated venue a dozen or so miles across at Joshua Tree National Park, "The Cove" is mostly smallish (50- to 120-foot-high) domes and short walls with a density of fun routes at scattered locations.

When we first visited The Cove in high school, there were barely a dozen established routes. We immediately laid siege to the place and put up scores of new lines over the following few winters, mostly on chossy cracks and loose faces. These were great days, when we were first dialing in our technique, and new routes were everywhere for the climbing.

On the afternoon of the second day of our seminar, Peter and I strung a toprope on a terrific thin crack and watched several dozen Olympic-caliber CrossFit athletes entertain themselves thrutching up the coarse gash. The climb felt vaguely familiar. I took a second burn up the route and was pretty sure we'd made the first ascent of this gemstone about 175 years before, when my partner Richard Harrison would borrow his mom's snot-green AMC Gremlin wagon and we'd blast out to Josh after classes on Friday and scratch and paw at the grainy rock, lit up by the Gremlin's headlights, till the battery died in the wee hours. Yosemite loomed

Sue McDevitt, topping out on the Direct North Face, Half Dome.

DAN McDEVITT

huge on the horizon, and at this rate we were sure to get there—someday.

We never took any notes about the "new" routes we scored at The Cove, since it was all practice for the Valley and beyond. Later came all the fancy Josh guidebooks with glossy photos and neat route lines and the history officially typed out—except much of it was wrong. There in print stood scores of interlopers taking credit for and assigning the most precious, far-fangled names to routes we'd done a dozen or more years before. Not that we cared. The Cove had done us proud as a training ground for mega routes, and if others reaped desert glory they could have it. But it was never theirs alone—and it probably was never ours as well.

While researching *Iron Age: Yosemite Climbing* in the 1950s, I learned from Yosemite pioneer Jerry Gallwas (first ascent of the Northwest Face of Half Dome, etc.) that he, Chuck Wilts, Royal Robbins, and other original members of the vaunted RCS—the Rock Climbing Section of the Sierra Club—began climbing out at Josh in the early 1950s, putting up all kind of routes, and that John Mendenhall and others had been out there long before Jerry and the boys ever showed up. Several RCS members shared contemporary climbing pictures as well. All of this shed a lot of light on Josh's rather murky beginnings—including a 1936 RCS scouting trip and the first recorded climb in November 1949. No one fashioned a proper guidebook per what they had climbed, though there were some terse trip reports in the *Mooglenoos,* a Sierra Club publication from the Bronze Age (thanks to RCS historian Bib Cates). So for all I knew, Norman Clyde—or even Edmund Whymper, during an American junket he never wrote about—might have cranked the first ascent of the very crack Peter and I and that CrossFit ensemble were toproping at The Cove.

I hadn't been doing many cracks lately, so I threw down another burn, and another after that. There was no telling when the urge might strike and I'd have to make my way back to Yosemite Valley for another mega route. Josh could always invoke, in all of us, the inveterate nomad driven by dangerous curiosity, always dreaming of an exotic elsewhere, chasing the sparkle of distant stars, paddling across seas to reach distant shores and titanic stone walls. We might have fled things we couldn't understand, but always in order to define ourselves, seeking our place up high, in the larger scheme, even at the risk of self-destruction.

Now I had to be ready, with all those mega routes dangling on the horizon. I liked my chances and the way the crack was starting to feel, how the jams were flowing one into the next as I logged Massive Footage on Whymper's testpiece. At this rate I was sure to get my jamming dialed. Someday.

Crimson Chrysalis at Red Rock.

JOHN HEGYES

The Big Wide-Open Face

A new face climb is much more of a discovery than a creation because you're working with what is given, with what is already there—and so it goes with all trad climbing. Sculptures talk about a bust or a figure already existing in a chunk of stone. Their work is to eliminate everything that covers the embedded shape. In this sense, someone leading up a big open face seeks out the natural line by imagining the possibilities. That's what a trad climber is born to do. Once the rock gets smooth and steep and the run-outs start stretching out there, big, scary falls become possible, and life catches fire. You have to be curious about the unknown to thrive in such circumstances. If you can keep moving with some little grace and balance, you come to realize that the face goes on forever, and that the game is to see how high you can get before the shadows fall.

ANDREW BURR

Index

Note: Page numbers in *italics* indicate photo captions.

About the Authors

ROBERT MIRAMONTES

John Long is the author of twenty-five books, with over one million copies in print. He is the principal author of the How to Rock Climb series. His short-form literary stories have been widely anthologized and translated into many languages. John won the 2006 Literary Award for excellence in alpine literature from the American Alpine Club.

Peter Croft is a Canadian-born rock climber and mountaineer. He has climbed around the world concentrating much of his climbing career on long routes, enchainments, and alpine traverses. He has received the Underhill Award for rock climbing achievement from the American Alpine Club and was the first to hold both the Wingnut and Pacifier Awards from the Canadian Army. He lives in Bishop, California, with his wife, Karine.